Political Parties in Conflict-Prone Societies

Political Parties in Conflict-Prone Societies: Regulation, Engineering and Democratic Development

Edited by Benjamin Reilly and Per Nordlund

United Nations
University Press

TOKYO · NEW YORK · PARIS

United Nations University Press
United Nations University, 53-70, Jingumae 5-chome,
Shibuya-ku, Tokyo 150-8925, Japan
Tel: +81-3-3499-2811   Fax: +81-3-3406-7345
E-mail: sales@hq.unu.edu   general enquiries: press@hq.unu.edu
http://www.unu.edu

United Nations University Office at the United Nations, New York
2 United Nations Plaza, Room DC2-2062, New York, NY 10017, USA
Tel: +1-212-963-6387   Fax: +1-212-371-9454
E-mail: unuona@ony.unu.edu

United Nations University Press is the publishing division of the United Nations University.

Cover design by Mea Rhee
Cover photograph by Jocelyn Carlin/Panos Pictures

Printed in Hong Kong

ISBN 978-92-808-1157-5

Library of Congress Cataloging-in-Publication Data

Political parties in conflict-prone societies : regulation, engineering and democratic development / edited by Benjamin Reilly and Per Nordlund.
    p. cm.
 Includes bibliographical references and index.
 ISBN 978-9280811575 (pbk.)
 1. Political parties—Developing countries. I. Reilly, Ben. II. Nordlund, Per.
JF60.P6425   2008
324.209172′4—dc22   2008023990

Contents

Figures and tables

Contributors

Benjamin Reilly is Director of the Centre for Democratic Institutions and Professor of Political Science in the Crawford School of Economics and Government at the Australian National University. He is the author of six books and over 60 journal articles and book chapters on issues of democratization, constitutional reform, party politics, electoral system design and conflict management, and he has advised many governments and international organizations on these subjects. His latest book is a study of democratization and political reform in the Asia-Pacific region, *Democracy and Diversity: Political Engineering in the Asia-Pacific* (Oxford University Press, 2006).

Per Nordlund holds a PhD in political science from Uppsala University in Sweden. His previous work has been on democratization and local democracy in Africa and he is a co-author of International IDEA's 2007 report *Political Parties in Africa: Challenges for Sustained Multiparty Democracy*. He is currently the Senior Programme Manager for International IDEA's initiative on Research and Dialogue with Political Parties.

Florian Bieber is a Lecturer in East European Politics at the University of Kent, UK, specializing in inter-ethnic relations, institutional design and former Yugoslavia.

Ingrid van Biezen is Reader in Comparative Politics at the University of Birmingham, UK, and is the author of *Political Parties in New Democracies* (Palgrave Macmillan, 2003) as well as various articles on political finance, party organization and party membership in journals including *Party Politics*, the *European Journal of Political*

Research and *West European Politics*.

Jóhanna Kristín Birnir is an Assistant Professor at the University of Maryland, USA. Her work on ethnicity, electoral institutions and conflict is published by Cambridge University Press and in a number of academic journals including the *American Journal of Political Science*, *Comparative Political Studies*, and *Latin American Research Review*. Her work is currently funded by the National Science Foundation and the Department of Homeland Security.

Matthijs Bogaards is Associate Professor of Political Science at Jacobs University Bremen, Germany. His research interests include democratization, electoral systems, party systems and democracy in divided societies. His latest work is on measuring democracy.

Matthias Catón is a Programme Officer at International IDEA. Before joining IDEA, Catón worked as a research associate and assistant professor at the University of Heidelberg, focusing mainly on electoral systems, party systems and democratization.

Allen Hicken is an Assistant Professor of Political Science and Faculty Associate at the Center for Southeast Asian Studies and Center for Political Studies at the University of Michigan, USA. He studies political institutions and policy-making in developing countries, with a focus on Southeast Asia.

Denis K. Kadima is the Executive Director of EISA (formerly Electoral Institute of Southern Africa). Since joining EISA in 2002, Kadima has expanded the organization's programmatic scope, which now encompasses not only elections but also selected areas in the democracy and governance fields, including political party strengthening. His chapter is based on his doctoral research on political party coalitions in Africa, which is being completed at the University of the Witwatersrand, Johannesburg, in South Africa.

Krishna Kumar is a senior social scientist in the Office of the Director of Foreign Assistance at the US Department of State.

Iain McMenamin is a lecturer in the School of Law and Government, Dublin City University, Ireland.

Henry Okole is a lecturer in international relations and political and development studies at the University of Papua New Guinea. He is presently seconded to the Secretariat of the African, Caribbean and Pacific Group of States in Brussels, Belgium.

Vicky Randall is a Professor in the Department of Government, University of Essex, UK. Her primary current research interest is political parties in developing countries.

Fernando Tuesta Soldevilla is a Professor at the Pontificia Universidad Católica in Peru and Director of the Instituto de Opinión Pública. He has been the Head of the National Office for Electoral

Processes (Oficina Nacional de Procesos Electorales).

Jeroen de Zeeuw is a Research Associate in the Conflict Research Unit of the Netherlands Institute of International Relations "Clingendael", and a doctoral candidate in the Department of Politics and International Studies at the University of Warwick, UK.

Acknowledgements

The genesis of this book lies in two separate projects of the Centre for Democratic Institutions and the International Institute for Democracy and Electoral Assistance on political party development in divided societies and party regulation in new democracies, respectively. The fact that we were able to bring these two separate projects together owes much to the foresight and support of our respective organizations, as well as the United Nations University (UNU), which also supported this project from the outset.

This generous support for our work enabled us to identify a group of outstanding scholars from around the world working on parties, party systems and democratic development, and to bring them together in working meetings in Stockholm, The Hague and Sydney. Whereas the Stockholm and Sydney meetings were organized by the project principals, The Hague event was hosted by the Netherlands Institute of International Relations, Clingendael, whose support we also gratefully acknowledge.

A number of people's support has been essential at various points along the way, most notably that of Ted Newman from UNU. We would also like to thank Kenneth Janda, Peter Burnell and Pippa Norris for their very useful comments on earlier versions of the project proposal. Nuffield College, Oxford, provided a wonderfully congenial venue for the final editing of the manuscript. We would also like to thank all the authors for their enthusiasm and dedication to the task, not least in attending authors' meetings at opposite ends of the earth.

Finally, we would like to express our gratitude to our wives – Andrea and Malin – and our children – Madison, Phoebe, Ellen, Tove and Viggo – who put up with our sometimes lengthy travels in the name of this book. Thank you for your support!

Benjamin Reilly
Per Nordlund

Part I
Introduction

1

Introduction

Benjamin Reilly

Political parties have long been recognized as essential components of representative democracy. Indeed, it is difficult to imagine how the governance of modern states could be accomplished without meaningful political parties. By organizing voters, aggregating and articulating interests, crafting policy alternatives and providing the basis for coordinated electoral and legislative activity, well-functioning political parties are central not just to representative government but also to the process of democratic development in transitional democracies.[1]

Parties perform a number of essential functions that make democracy in modern states possible. Ideally, they represent political constituencies and interests, recruit and socialize new candidates for office, set policy-making agendas, integrate disparate groups and individuals into the democratic process, and form the basis of stable political coalitions and hence governments. Collectively, this means that political parties are one of the primary channels for building accountable and responsive government.

Beyond these functional activities, parties also provide a number of deeper, systemic supports that help make democracy work effectively. For instance:

- They mediate between the demands of the citizenry on the one hand and the actions of the government on the other, aggregating the diverse demands of the electorate into coherent public policy.
- They make effective collective action possible within legislatures. Without the predictable voting coalitions that parties provide, there would

Political parties in conflict-prone societies: Regulation, engineering and democratic development, Reilly and Nordlund (eds),
United Nations University Press, 2008, ISBN 978-92-808-1157-5

be chaos as legislative majorities shifted from issue to issue and vote to vote.

- By providing a link between ordinary citizens and their political representatives, parties are also the primary channel in democratic systems for holding governments accountable for their performance.

Yet in many countries, particularly in transitional democracies, parties struggle to play these roles. Instead, parties exhibit a range of pathologies that undercut their ability to deliver the kind of systemic benefits on which representative politics depends. For instance:

- they are frequently poorly institutionalized, with limited membership, weak policy capacity and shifting bases of support;
- they are often based around narrow personal, regional or ethnic ties, rather than reflecting society as a whole;
- they are typically organizationally thin, coming to life only at election time;
- they may have little in the way of a coherent ideology;
- they often fail to stand for any particular policy agenda;
- they are frequently unable to ensure disciplined collective action in parliament, with members shifting between parties;
- as a result, parties often struggle to manage social conflicts and fail to deliver public goods and thus to promote development.

These deficiencies in party development are so widespread that they have become a central concern in many emerging democracies, to the extent that they are increasingly seen as a threat to stable democracy itself. The recognition of such impediments to democratic development has spurred growing attention, both domestically and internationally, to how stronger, more capable political parties can be sustained and developed in fragile environments.

Internationally, the response by Western governments to this problem has been a plethora of party assistance programmes that seek to help political parties in new democracies become stronger, more coherent and more inclusive organizations – that is, more like the idealized view of how parties are supposed to operate. These programmes have received considerable funding from donor agencies and generated a considerable number of new training programmes and other initiatives. But these have had limited impact, rarely if ever transforming the fundamental organizational and operational characteristics of recipient parties.[2]

Domestically, a rather different response has been evident, with political elites in transitional states often seeking to influence their party systems by reforming the rules of the game regarding how parties form, organize and compete. These forms of party regulation and engineering represent an increasingly widespread and ambitious attempt to shape the nature of emerging party systems. For instance, a number of emerging democracies have placed restrictions on ethnic or other sectorally based parties, up to and including banning them from competing at elections. Others have introduced positive incentives for cross-national party formation, by introducing regional branch or membership requirements for parties to compete in elections. Some have introduced cross-national support thresholds or other kinds of spatial rules. Many emerging democracies use electoral systems to try to shape the development of their party systems, and a small but increasing number have also introduced rules governing voting in parliament as well, in an attempt to ensure greater party discipline. Finally, international organizations have become increasingly active in this field, intervening directly in party systems in post-conflict states such as Mozambique, Kosovo and Afghanistan.

This book is an examination of these various efforts in emerging democracies to influence party system development. It analyses the different regulatory and engineering strategies and innovations that have been applied in fragile new democracies. The individual chapters range across both thematic enquiries and regional case studies, and cover issues of concern to both scholarly research and public policy. What binds them together is a common focus on the trends towards overt and often highly ambitious forms of party regulation and political engineering in developing democracies. Although a worldwide phenomenon, these attempts to shape the path of political party development have been particularly prevalent in new democracies that contain ethnic, religious, linguistic, regional or other significant social cleavages – in other words, what we call "conflict-prone societies".

The story of this new enthusiasm for party system reform begins, like so many other recent developments, in the dramatic changes to the world since the end of the Cold War. The "third wave" of democratization and the collapse of communism resulted in a threefold increase in the number of competitive democracies around the world.[3] As these new and emerging democracies introduced competitive elections, drafted new constitutions and forged new political systems, there was a tremendous upsurge of interest in new institutional designs for democracy. Spurred by the liberalization of previously autocratic states in Africa, Asia, Eastern Europe and Latin America, the international community began to invest heavily in concepts of democracy promotion, electoral support and "good governance" as essential elements of economic development and the creation of stable and peaceful states.

The 1990s thus saw an explosion of interest in the possibility of party regulation and political engineering, as institutions were borrowed, adapted or created afresh for fragile and complex new democracies. Developments that took decades, and in some cases centuries, in Western countries – such as the evolution of an institutionalized political party system – were expected to be achieved in the space of a few short years. Concluding that the "solutions to the problem of democratization consist of institutions", an increasing number of political scientists argued that careful and purposive institutional design was not only possible but *necessary* to consolidate fragile new democracies.[4] This message was echoed by numerous other studies, reflecting a growing consensus on the importance of political institutions and constitutional design.[5]

As Ingrid van Biezen shows in Chapter 2 in this volume, this process entailed an ideational shift, with parties increasingly seen as a kind of public utility that needed to be regulated by the state, rather than the private associations of the past. This move into the public realm was accompanied by a new consensus on parties as essential components of well-functioning democracy, with "political engineering" a feature of the third wave experience.[6] But, despite being widely conflated in political science discussions, there is an important analytical distinction between "regulating" and "engineering", particularly in relation to political parties. Kenneth Janda argues that attempts to engineer party politics typically take place at founding moments, whereas subsequent reforms are more often a case of regulation. "Regulating" is thus an essentially reactive process, a response to empirical observation, whereas "engineering" is a proactive process, using theoretical knowledge to design a particular outcome. When it comes to political parties, both processes are observable, although, as Janda notes, the language of engineering is usually applied to political party formation, whereas regulation more often refers to changes in existing party systems.[7]

The distinction between engineering and regulating has important real-world implications. In those emerging democracies with relatively settled and stable party systems, the potential for political engineering is likely to be relatively limited, as parties already represent relatively clear constituencies and interests. Even in deeply divided emerging democracies such as Cyprus or South Africa, there may be limited potential for reshaping the party system, and political strategies need to focus more on encouraging bargaining and cooperation between the players. By contrast, in more fluid systems such as Afghanistan or the Democratic Republic of Congo (in which hundreds of nascent "parties" emerged from scratch at transitional elections), the potential to engineer emerging structures is much higher.[8] Both engineering and regulation strategies are examined in this book.

The chapters assembled here represent the first comparative examination of this subject of which we are aware. They include regional studies covering most of the main regions of the world, including Southeast Asia, Southern and East Africa, Eastern and Central Europe, Latin America and Oceania.[9] Surprisingly, despite the potential importance of this subject to the pre-eminent policy challenge of building and sustaining new democracies, the impact of party regulation on political party development has received limited attention from either policy makers or scholars. Although political scientists have paid a great deal of attention to the utility of electoral systems in democratic development, there has been little discussion of political party regulation in the scholarly literature on democratization. The nature and workings of these institutional reforms, their impact upon party systems over time and their congruence (or lack thereof) with broader social realities all require investigation. This book therefore marks an initial attempt to survey the growing phenomenon of party regulation and assess its implications for broader issues of democratic development and conflict management.

The crucial role of political parties

The central role of political parties in building consolidated democracies is now widely accepted. Policy makers and democracy promotion organizations often display a strong normative bias in favour of cohesive, organizationally developed political parties. According to the US National Democratic Institute, for instance, "political parties form the cornerstone of a democratic society and serve a function unlike any other institution in a democracy. Parties aggregate and represent social interests and provide a structure for political participation. They train political leaders who will assume a role in governing society. In addition, parties contest and win elections to seek a measure of control of government institutions".[10] Similarly, the United Nations Development Programme maintains that "[p]olitical parties are a keystone of democratic governance. They provide a structure for political participation; serve as a training ground for political leadership; and transform social interests into public policy."[11]

Scholars are similarly effusive. Some of the world's foremost political scientists have placed parties at the centre of the modern democratic experience, arguing that strong parties are a *sine qua non* of successful democratization. In his classic work on political change, for example, Samuel Huntington argued that strong parties are "the prerequisite for political stability in modernizing countries".[12] Three leading scholars of democracy, Juan Linz, Larry Diamond and Seymour Martin Lipset, have bluntly stated that, "without effective parties that command at least somewhat stable bases of support, democracies cannot have effective governance".[13] More recently, in one of his final publications, Lipset extolled the "indispensability of political parties" for the survival of both transitional and established democracies.[14]

Both political practitioners and political scientists agree on the virtues of stable and programmatic political parties for emerging and consolidated democracies alike, but they offer surprisingly little advice as to how such party systems may be encouraged or promoted. There are several reasons for this. Perhaps most importantly, political parties have typically been viewed as social phenomena beyond the scope of deliberate institutional design. Because political parties in theory represent the political expression of underlying societal cleavages, parties and party systems have usually not been thought amenable to overt political engineering.[15] Although some authoritarian states have attempted to control the development of their party system (for example, the mandated "two-party" or "three-party" systems that existed under military rule in Nigeria and Indonesia, or the "no-party" system now abandoned in Uganda), most democracies allow parties to develop relatively freely. Because of this, parties have until recently remained beyond the reach of formal political engineering in most circumstances.

The role of international actors and development aid agencies is also important. Although it is today widely accepted that stable democracy requires the development of a stable party system, there had in the past been resistance to the idea of direct international assistance to parties. Until recently, broader democracy and governance initiatives funded by the United Nations and development aid agencies often steered clear of working with political parties, in part because of the overtly "political" nature of such work, and also because aid agencies were often more comfortable dealing with civil society than with parties. There has been a considerable shift in international opinion in this field over the past decade, with more and more governments and international organizations choosing to include political party strengthening in their development assistance programmes.[16]

A final reason for the shift has been the clear lack of any meaningful party development in most new democracies, highlighting not only the dearth of effective parties but also the weakness of many international democracy promotion efforts. With few if any cohesive, programmatic parties emerging naturally in "third wave" democracies, attention has turned towards the possibility of engineering particular kinds of parties instead.[17] Such exercises typically focus on the operational rather than ideological aspects of party behaviour, but most contain an implied policy impact too. As noted earlier, a common pathology of parties in new democracies is their lack of ideological coherence. Parties that campaign on the basis of policy issues and developmental challenges such as health, education and economic growth are in short supply – in sharp contrast to the common situation in emerging democracies where most parties present the same generic policy positions (for example, more development, anti-corruption, national unity) or alternatively are based around identity (such as ethnic or regional ties) rather than policy differences. Many of the institutional reforms examined in this book contain the expectation that changing the party system will, over time, make more meaningful policy alternatives available to the electorate.

Party systems in conflict-prone societies

The importance of political parties in transitional societies is magnified in conflict-prone societies. As key agents of political articulation, aggregation and representation, political parties are the institutions that most directly affect the extent to which social cleavages are translated into national politics. For example, some parties adopt "catch-all" strategies, designed to elicit support from across different segments of the electorate and regions of the country in order to win elections. Others seek to represent ethnic cleavages explicitly, and appeal for votes predominantly along communal lines. Matthijs Bogaards notes in Chapter 3 in this volume that parties in such situations can perform one of three functions: aggregation, articulation and blocking. That is, they can aggregate socio-cultural divisions, articulate ethnic differences or organize on other bases, thereby blocking the political organization of socio-cultural cleavages. These strategies are associated with different kinds of party systems, characterized by multi-ethnic, mono-ethnic and non-ethnic parties respectively.

There is significant debate in the scholarly literature about the merits of these different kinds of parties. On the one hand, scholars argue that the appearance of mono-ethnic parties based on distinct social cleavages can presage an "ethnification" of the party system that ultimately leads to a spiral of instability and conflict based on the politics of "outbidding" in ethnically polarized elections.[18] They contend that, because ethnic parties make their political appeals specifically on ethnicity, their emergence often has a centrifugal effect on politics, requiring ameliorative "centripetal" institutions to combat this tendency.[19] Others dispute this negative assessment of ethnic parties, and maintain that communally based parties provide opportunities for interest articulation from groups that might otherwise be shut out of the political system. A longstanding argument of the consociational school, for instance, is that ethnic parties help dampen conflict by channelling demands through legal channels, particularly if all significant groups can be represented proportionately in government and state institutions.[20]

Although scholars disagree on such issues, there is widespread consensus on the core role of political parties in conflict management, and that different kinds of party system are likely to influence political outcomes and government performance. There is also increasing empirical evidence that variations in governance outcomes depend, at least in part, on the nature of the party system. Comparative studies have found that socially diverse states tend to have less cohesive parties, more fragmented party systems and higher turnover of elected politicians than their more homogeneous counterparts.[21] Other cross-national studies have found that an increase in the number of parties represented in the legislature leads to higher government spending on subsidies and transfers but lower spending on public goods.[22] In India, states with multiple parties in government spent more on personnel expenditures and less on developmental expenditures, and had poorer provision of public goods, than those with two-party systems.[23] Such findings suggest that variations in party systems do have a direct impact upon public welfare, and specifically that systems composed of a small number of large, cohesive parties are more likely to provide collective goods to the median voter than either one-party-dominant or fragmented multi-party systems.

Other studies of democratic transitions have also identified party systems as the key institutional determinant affecting the distributive impacts of economic reform. Thus, various works co-authored by Stephan Haggard have consistently argued that a system of two large parties or coalitions is the most propitious arrangement for democratic durability during periods of economic adjustment, and that fragmented or polarized party systems represent a major barrier to achieving economic reform.[24] Similarly, in his exegesis of the optimum conditions for a "democratic developmental state", Gordon White stressed the importance of party systems that are "relatively well developed, concentrated rather than fragmented, broadly based, and organized along programmatic rather than personalistic or narrowly sectional lines".[25] Such recommendations suggest a convergence of opinion on the benefits of aggregative and centripetal institutions for political development and stability. However, they also appear to ignore some other problems, such as minority exclusion.

Finally, a number of comparative studies have emphasized the benefits of such "moderate multi-partism" for the survival of new democracies. G. Bingham Powell's work on democratic durability, for instance, suggests that the most favourable party system comprises a limited number of cohesive and broad-based parties, rather than many small, fragmented, personalized or ethnically-based parties.[26] Diamond, Linz and Lipset's multi-volume comparison of democracy in developing countries concluded that "a system of two or a few parties, with broad social and ideological bases, may be conducive to stable democracy".[27] In the same vein, Myron Weiner and Ergun Özbudun found that the one common factor amongst the small number of stable democracies in the developing world was the presence of a broad-based party system, prompting the conclusion that "the success of democratic politics in developing societies is strongly associated with the presence of broadly-based, heterogeneous, catch-all parties with no strong links to the cleavage structure of society".[28]

If we accept that such cohesive and aggregative parties and party systems are desirable, the next question must surely be how they can be encouraged to develop. In the remainder of this chapter, I look at the main approaches to strengthening parties and remodelling party systems through the use of institutional incentives and constraints. The first approach attempts to constrain the development of ethnic parties by cross-national party formation rules that require parties to demonstrate a broad organizational base. The second attempts to use the design of electoral rules to reshape the party system. The third tries to strengthen parties from the top down, via measures to build greater internal party capacity and discipline in parliament. The final approach involves international interventions to assist parties in post-conflict democracies. A brief description of these four approaches follows.[29]

Building national parties

The most common means of influencing party system development in conflict-prone societies is to introduce regulations that govern their formation, registration and behaviour. Such regulations may require parties to demonstrate a cross-regional or nationwide composition as a precondition for competing in elections. Some of the world's most important transitional states have introduced such measures in recent years. In Turkey, for example, parties must establish regional branches, hold regular conventions and field candidates in at least half of all provinces to be eligible to contest national elections. In Russia, one of President Putin's first reforms required political parties to register regional branches in a majority of Russia's 89 regions. Nigeria continues to require parties to display a "federal character" by including members from two-thirds of all states on their executive council and ensuring that the name, motto or emblem of the party not have ethnic or regional connotations. In Indonesia, the world's most populous emerging democracy and largest Muslim country, parties must establish an organizational network in two-thirds of all provinces across the archipelago, and in two-thirds of the municipalities within those provinces, before they can compete in elections.

Attempts to build more nationally oriented parties have also been common in particular regions, especially Latin America and East Asia.

In Latin America, states including Colombia, Ecuador, Guatemala, Nicaragua, Honduras, Mexico and Peru have all introduced spatial registration requirements for political parties. In Mexico, for example, parties must have at least 3,000 affiliates in 10 out of the 32 states, or one-third of federal districts; in Ecuador and Peru, parties require officially inscribed membership levels in at least half of all provinces. In East Asia, in addition to Indonesia, states such as the Philippines, Korea and Thailand also place cross-regional thresholds on party formation. An example is Thailand's ambitious 1997 reforms to restructure its political system and reduce party fragmentation by requiring new parties to establish a branch structure in each of four designated regions and to gain 5,000 members drawn from each region within six months of being registered.

What is the impact of such schemes? The evidence to date is somewhat ambiguous, pointing to the utility of such mechanisms in achieving some goals – such as a more consolidated party system – but also to their propensity for unintended consequences. In Russia, for instance, studies indicate that the new party registration law did, to a certain degree, spur the development of nationally-organized parties in Russia's regions, even as other reforms undermined regional leaders and subverted democratic norms.[30] Jóhanna Birnir's analysis of Latin America's cross-regional party registration rules in Chapter 7 of this volume finds that nationally oriented parties often prosper at the expense of those representing geographically-concentrated indigenous groups, suggesting that the exclusionary effects of such rules may outweigh any gains that result from a reduction in party fragmentation. In Southeast Asia, as Allen Hicken shows in Chapter 4 in this volume, party formation rules have helped consolidate party systems, but in doing so appear to have assisted larger incumbent parties at the expense of minority interests.

So too, encouraging multi-ethnic party formation is easier said than done. Many countries in Africa, Asia and elsewhere have constitutional or legislative requirements that explicitly ban "ethnic" parties from competing in elections or require parties to be "nationally focused", or similar. As Bogaards notes in Chapter 3 of this volume, at least 22 African countries have bans on particularistic parties. Another manifestation was Uganda's now-abandoned "no-party" system, imposed by President Yoweri Museveni in 1986 on the basis that political parties inflamed racial and ethnic conflict. Even in Europe, which has tended to be more accommodative of minority interests, bans on ethnic parties have been attempted in Albania, Bulgaria and Bosnia, as Florian Bieber shows in Chapter 5 in this volume. However, in most cases these are essentially aspirational provisions that are not capable of being enforced effectively. What ultimately makes a party "ethnic" is not the nature of its composition or even its voter base, but the fact that it makes no attempt to appeal to members of other groups.[31] Especially given the apparent tendency of such arrangements to degenerate into de facto one-party rule, it is clear that, in democratic settings, party systems cannot be fashioned by government fiat alone.

Electoral systems and party systems

A second approach to political party engineering has been to use the electoral system to try to refashion the party system. There are several ways of doing this. One of the most common is to dictate the ethnic composition of party lists. In some countries, this has enabled a more deliberate strategy of multi-ethnicity than would have been possible otherwise. In Singapore, for example, most parliamentarians are elected from multi-member districts known as Group Representative Constituencies, which each return between three and six members from a single list of candidates. Of the candidates on each party or group list, at least one must be a member of the Malay, Indian or some other minority community, thus ensuring a degree of multi-ethnicity on party slates. A related approach has been used for some time in Lebanon, although there the ultimate composition of the party lists rests with the voters. Similarly, in Latin America, laws in Nicaragua and Peru oblige parties to open up space on their lists for indigenous candidates at local elections.[32]

Another approach has been to use technical electoral barriers such as vote thresholds, which prevent the election of many small parties to parliament. Probably the most extreme application of this is in Turkey, where parties must attain at least 10 per cent of the national vote (and constituency-level thresholds also apply) before they can be represented in parliament, thus discriminating strongly against smaller parties, especially those with a geographically concentrated support base.[33] This has led to some extreme vote distortions: in the 2002 Turkish election, won by the Justice and Development Party, so many smaller parties failed to clear the 10 per cent threshold that 46 per cent of all votes were wasted.[34] In Latin America, all countries bar Argentina and Brazil require parties to win a minimum share of the vote in parliamentary elections, ranging from 500 votes in Uruguay to 5 per cent of all votes in Ecuador.[35]

Other electoral system innovations can be used to counter party fractionalization and encourage inter-party cooperation and coalition. One example is the use of vote-pooling electoral systems in which electors rank-order candidates and votes are transferred according to these rankings. These systems can encourage cross-party cooperation and aggregation by making politicians from different parties reciprocally dependent on transfer votes from their rivals. Examples of such systems in conflict-prone societies include the single transferable vote system in Northern Ireland and the alternative vote models adopted in both Fiji and Papua New Guinea in recent years. In each case, encouraging the development of a more aggregative party system was one of the primary goals of the electoral reforms. However, the presence of vote-pooling electoral systems has not been enough to stave off political crises in Northern Ireland or in Fiji.[36]

A final option for promoting cross-ethnic parties is to introduce distribution requirements that oblige parties or individual candidates to garner specified support levels across different regions of a country, rather than just their own home base, in order to be elected. First introduced in Nigeria in 1979, distribution requirements have so far been applied to presidential elections in large, ethnically diverse states in order to ensure that winning candidates receive a sufficiently broad spread of votes, rather than drawing their support from a few regions only. The original formulation in Nigeria's 1979 constitution required successful presidential candidates to gain a plurality of votes nationwide and at least a quarter of the votes in 13 of Nigeria's then 19 states. In 1989, this provision was made even more onerous, requiring a president to win a majority overall and at least one-third of the vote in at least two-thirds of all states, with similar rules applied for the first time to parliamentary elections as well, as Bogaards discusses in Chapter 3 in this volume. The Kenyan constitution provides a similar threshold, requiring successful candidates to win a plurality of the vote overall as well as one-quarter of valid votes cast in at least five of the eight provinces.

Indonesia's 2004 elections used a combination of all these devices. Only parties winning at least 5 per cent of the vote or 3 per cent of the seats in the parliamentary elections could nominate candidates for the presidency, sidelining smaller parties. The election was conducted over two rounds of voting, and first-round winners had to gain over 50 per cent of all votes as well as at least 20 per cent in half of all provinces to avoid a second-round runoff.[37] The combined aim of these provisions was to ensure that the winning candidate not only had a majority of votes overall but could command cross-regional support as well. In this respect, the presidential electoral law shares a centripetal logic with Indonesia's new party formation laws, which aim to promote parties with a cross-regional support base. In the event, the winning candidate, Susilo Bambang Yudhoyono, won a landslide first-round majority, so the distribution requirements were not directly tested.

As with spatial party registration laws, there is significant disagreement amongst scholars as to the utility of vote distribution requirements, with some interpreting them as impotent or even harmful interferences in the democratic process, while others see them as potentially important mechanisms for muting ethnic conflict and ensuring the election of broad, pan-ethnic presidents.[38] The empirical evidence to date reflects this divergence of opinion. In Kenya, for example, Daniel arap Moi consistently subverted requirements that he receive cross-country support by manipulating tribal politics to ensure the continuation of his presidency, even as his own popularity was falling. Yet his successor, Mwai Kibaki, won a landslide victory in 2002 under the same system. Similarly in Nigeria, despite serious problems with the workings of the system under military rule, the vote distribution requirements have remained a feature of national electoral politics.[39] In Indonesia, the new laws attracted relatively little interest at their first use in 2004, in part because it was widely (and correctly) assumed that no candidate would be able to win a first-round majority, obviating the vote distribution requirement.

Electoral systems can also be engineered to increase the proportion of women in parliament, via explicit gender quotas or more informal party quotas. Both approaches have become increasingly common in recent years. Legal quotas to mandate minimum levels of women's representation are widely perceived to be the quickest way to rectify the problem of under-representation. Countries as varied as Argentina, Bosnia, Costa Rica, Mozambique, Rwanda, South Africa and Uganda have all dramatically increased their proportion of women parliamentarians by use of gender quotas.[40] Other countries such as Indonesia have followed the voluntary party quota model used in the Nordic countries, in which parties agree to nominate a specified proportion of female candidates, but these appear to be more easily circumvented than more formal legal quotas.[41]

Parties in parliament: Top-down approaches

A third approach to political party development in conflict-prone societies is what I call the "top-down" approach, which carries the expectation that parties can be "built", to a certain extent, not from below (as is usually the case) but from above, by strengthening parties in parliament. This approach usually focuses on increasing party discipline and cohesion in the legislature as a means of stabilizing party politics, in the hope that more disciplined parliamentary parties will lead to a more structured party system overall. One way to do this is to restrict the capacity of members to change parties once elected. This practice, which was once widespread in many Asian countries, has been curtailed in recent years by the introduction of anti-switching provisions in states as diverse as Brazil, Fiji, India, Papua New Guinea and Thailand. These provisions have made it difficult or impossible for a politician elected under one party label to change allegiance to another party once in office. In South Africa, by contrast, legislation to *facilitate* such party swaps was introduced by the governing African National Congress, as Denis Kadima explains in Chapter 9 of this volume.

However, such restrictions have little sway over party defections that take place outside the parliamentary arena or between elections. They also do little to combat the related problem of multiple endorsement, where the same candidate may be nominated by several parties or where parties endorse multiple candidates running within the same electorate. In such cases, more searching institutional innovation is required. Probably the most ambitious attempt at top-down party engineering has been in Papua New Guinea, one of the world's most ethnically diverse (and under-researched) countries. With over 800 indigenous languages and thousands of competing tribal groups, stable government has proved extremely difficult since the country's independence in 1975. However, as Henry Okole discusses in Chapter 8 in this volume, in 2001 a package of constitutional, electoral and party reforms was introduced with the aim of stabilizing executive government and building a more coherent party system. The intention of these reforms was to move parties away from being purely vehicles for personal advancement and to encourage intending candidates to stand for election under a party banner rather than as independents. Parties must be registered and meet basic organizational requirements, and politicians elected with party endorsement must vote in accordance with their party position on key parliamentary decisions such as a vote of confidence in the prime minister, or face a possible by-election. These reforms represent a serious challenge to established political practice and, although problems remain, political stability has increased significantly following the introduction of the new laws.

Another example of top-down party regulation is Peru's ambitious Political Party Law, which introduced a host of regulations governing party registration, including signature requirements for new parties, the establishment of provincial party committees and new rules governing candidate nomination, party alliances and financing. However, the success of the Peruvian party law remains debatable. As Matthias Catón and Fernando Tuesta Soldevilla detail in Chapter 6 in this volume, the enforcement of many of these laws was weak and sometimes non-existent, and the new laws appear to have created as many problems as they have solved. For instance, although they aimed to strengthen and consolidate Peru's party system, party fragmentation actually increased after the new laws were introduced. Lack of a strong regulatory body to enforce the new laws appears to be one reason for this. As Iain McMenamin notes in Chapter 10 in this volume, large-scale attempts to re-engineer party politics require a strong regulator to work effectively – a measure that was present in Papua New Guinea but absent in Peru.

External interventions

A final approach to political party engineering has been for external actors to attempt to intervene directly in the development of party systems in new or transitional democracies. This often involves channelling technical or financial assistance from international donor agencies, non-governmental organizations or multilateral agencies to party organizations in states where the international community has taken a prominent role, such as countries emerging from a period of violent conflict. Building coherent party systems in such post-conflict societies is particularly difficult, because parties often form around the very same cleavages that provoked the original fighting, leading to the continuation of the former conflict through the electoral process. Increasing awareness of the problems of polarized or otherwise dysfunctional party systems created by this process has lately spurred multilateral bodies such as the United Nations – which have traditionally been wary of direct involvement in party politics, preferring more traditional kinds of development assistance – to take a more active role in assisting political party development in some post-conflict countries.[42]

The most ambitious actors in this field have been the international democracy promotion organizations, which have proliferated over the past decade.[43] Because they are not bound by the same strictures as multilateral agencies, some of these agencies have attempted to intervene directly in order to shape party systems in what are seen as desirable directions. In Bosnia, for example, Krishna Kumar and Jeroen de Zeeuw show in Chapter 12 in this volume how international agencies deliberately assisted putatively multi-ethnic parties in preference to nationalist parties – although with limited impact. A range of reforms related to the electoral system and other areas introduced in recent years by the Organization for Security and Co-operation in Europe (OSCE) attempted to undercut nationalist parties by changing voting procedures and, in some cases, barring individual candidates from election.[44] Kosovo too has seen overt attempts by the international community to mandate multi-ethnicity in the political system.[45] However, despite some inflated claims to the contrary, the success of such interventions so far has been modest, and ethnic parties continue to dominate the Balkans' political landscape.

The vexed problem of transforming former armies into parties after a protracted period of conflict continues to trouble international interventions in this field. As one survey of post-conflict elections concluded: "Democratic party building is proving to be a slow process. In all the [post-conflict] countries, political parties are organized around personalities, narrow political interests, and tribal and ethnic loyalties."[46] In Kosovo, the ongoing worry that previous ethnic conflicts between armed forces would be replicated by ethnically exclusive political parties prompted the OSCE to introduce a network of "political party service centres", intended to support the territory's nascent political groupings and help move them towards becoming more coherent, policy-oriented political parties.[47] Whether such an approach to external party-building is actually feasible, however, remains to be seen. Historically, the most successful example of such a transition is probably the armies-to-parties transformation wrought by the United Nations in Mozambique, where a special-purpose trust fund and some creative international leadership succeeded in bringing the previous fighting forces of FRELIMO and RENAMO into the political fold.[48]

As Krishna Kumar and Jeroen de Zeeuw show in Chapter 12 in this volume, although international assistance for post-conflict party-building has sought to consolidate nascent democratization processes in the aftermath of armed conflict, international agencies often fail to follow a coherent and comprehensive strategy of post-conflict party development. Instead, their approach has typically been ad hoc and opportunistic. Interested donor governments, democracy assistance agencies and non-governmental organizations have focused their efforts on constitutional and legal provisions for political party development in post-conflict cases such as Afghanistan, Bosnia and Congo and on the transformation of rebel movements into political parties in cases such as Mozambique and El Salvador. But the relative "success" of such cases has been the exception rather than the rule, and policy-relevant thinking on issues of party law and regulation remains underdeveloped and often contradictory.

Conclusion

The idea of changing the way parties behave by reforming the rules of the political game is not a new one. The political reforms carried out by established democracies such as Japan and Italy in the 1990s, as well as the earlier political restructuring of post-war Germany or post-1958 France, all had party system change as a primary objective. In recent years, however, attempts to reshape party systems and to regulate party behaviour have become more ambitious in scope, more complex in operation and increasingly commonplace, particularly amongst newer democracies. The growing prominence of such exercises today brings a consequent potential for large and often unintended consequences. Yet, despite the impressive body of scholarship on constitutional design that has appeared over the past decade, surprisingly little attention has been given to this issue.

The chapters assembled in this book represent an attempt to fill this gap. Collectively, they seek to shed new light on how the systemic functions of political parties for democratic development may be fostered. Among the most striking manifestations of this trend are the overt attempts by domestic and international actors alike to intervene directly in party politics in new democracies and to shape the way parties and party systems develop by applying institutional measures to regulate their formation, composition, organization and development. In recent years, such "political engineering" has become an increasingly common means of influencing party system development, particularly in ethnically plural societies. Innovations in this area have been applied as a means of managing potential and incipient conflicts in new and emerging democracies, making them of the utmost importance to the task of building functioning democratic systems in fragile states. Despite this, viewing parties as malleable entities that can be engineered in the same manner as other parts of the political system remains controversial. Parties have traditionally been assumed to develop organically, rather than being designed in the manner of other, formal, political institutions.

Clearly, the new enthusiasm for overt party engineering entails many costs as well as potential benefits, as Vicky Randall notes in Chapter 11 in this volume. In countries such as Russia and Indonesia, new party registration laws served to restrict the level of political competition, raising major barriers to new entrants into the political marketplace. In Turkey, vote thresholds and bans on ethnic parties have not been able to constrain a further fragmentation of the party system or hinder the rise of Islamist parties.[49] In East Asia, regulation has helped reduce party fragmentation but also appears to have contributed to one-party dominance in cases such as Thailand – solving some old problems but creating new ones in their place.[50] Restraints on ethnic parties also carry many risks. If ethnic groups are unable to mobilize and compete for political power by democratic means, they are likely to find other ways to achieve their ends. Balance is key: if attempts to foster nationally oriented parties by restricting regional parties end up encouraging extra-constitutional action by aggrieved minorities, they will have exacerbated the very problems they are designed to prevent.

Regional differences are also important. In Africa and Asia, many post-colonial democracies were destroyed by the politicization of ethnic identity, so that today there is widespread acceptance of the need to limit the role of ethnic factors in party politics. In much of Europe, by contrast, minority parties already existed at the time of political liberalization, and the focus has therefore been on accommodating existing minorities where they exist – except in post-conflict cases such as the former Yugoslavia, where determined efforts to build multi-ethnic parties continue. This helps explain the legal protection – indeed, encouragement – offered to minority parties in Europe compared with other regions. The OSCE, for example, enshrines the right of ethnic minorities to form their own parties and compete for office on a communal basis in official proclamations such as the 1990 Copenhagen Declaration, which specifies "the important role of ... political parties ... in the promotion of tolerance, cultural diversity and the resolution of questions relating to national minorities",[51] and the 1992 Helsinki Document, which commits participating states "to ensure the free exercise by persons belonging to national minorities, individually or in community with others, of their human rights and fundamental freedoms, including the right to participate fully ... through political parties and associations".[52]

The situation outside Europe, particularly in Africa and Asia, is very different. Instead of supporting communal parties, countries such as Indonesia and Nigeria have deliberately attempted to subvert their appearance through complex spatial registration rules, and many other countries, especially in Africa, ban ethnic parties altogether. Although such constraints would constitute a clear breach of the international treaties that bind the European and post-communist OSCE member states, they appear to be widely accepted in other regions. A similar conclusion applies to the use of electoral thresholds: a number of European countries specifically exempt parties representing ethnic minorities from application of the threshold. In Germany, Denmark and Poland, for example, exemptions from the threshold apply to parties representing specified "national minorities". No such exemptions apply in the developing democracies of Africa and Asia; indeed, as the preceding discussion makes clear, any such provision would run counter to the general logic that seeks to restrict, rather than assist, ethnic parties.

Given this diversity of experience, it is important not to overgeneralize about the impact of party regulation and engineering in developing democracies. However, on the basis of the evidence assembled in this volume, a number of broader conclusions suggest themselves. First, political engineering has clearly evolved from being focused upon formal constitutional rules to include less formal organizations such as political parties. Second, developing countries rather than the established democracies of the West are at the forefront of this movement and have been clearly the most influential innovators in this field. And third, because many new democracies are also ethnically plural societies, they face the twin challenge of opening up the space for political competition while restricting the politicization of ethnicity. Many states have turned to party regulation in an attempt simultaneously to manage communal divisions *and* consolidate democracy – an experiment in political engineering that is likely to have important lessons for other conflict-prone societies grappling with these same issues.

Notes

1. There is a large literature on the contribution of political parties to democratic functioning. Some of the most important works include Seymour Martin Lipset and Stein Rokkan (eds), *Party Systems and Voter Alignments: Cross-National Perspectives* (New York: The Free Press, 1967); Giovanni Sartori, *Parties and Party Systems: A Framework for Analysis* (New York: Cambridge University Press, 1976); John Aldrich, *Why Parties?* (Chicago: University of Chicago Press, 1995); Stephan Haggard and Robert Kaufman, *The Political Economy of Democratic Transitions* (Princeton, NJ: Princeton University Press, 1995); Peter Mair, *Party System Change: Approaches and Interpretations* (New York: Oxford University Press, 1997); Larry Diamond and Richard Gunther (eds), *Political Parties and Democracy* (Baltimore, MD, and London: Johns Hopkins University Press, 2001).
2. See Thomas Carothers, *Confronting the Weakest Link: Aiding Political Parties in New Democracies* (Washington DC: Carnegie Endowment for International Peace, 2006).
3. Samuel P. Huntington, *The Third Wave: Democratization in the Late Twentieth Century* (Norman, OK: University of Oklahoma Press, 1991); Larry Diamond, Juan Linz and Seymour Martin Lipset (eds), *Politics in Developing Countries: Comparing Experiences with Democracy* (Boulder, CO: Lynne Rienner Publishers, 1995); Larry Diamond and Mark F. Plattner (eds), *The Global Resurgence of Democracy* (Baltimore, MD: Johns Hopkins University Press, 1996); Larry Diamond, *Developing Democracy: Towards Consolidation* (Baltimore, MD: Johns Hopkins University Press, 1999); Laurence Whitehead, *Democratization: Theory and Experience* (Oxford: Oxford University Press, 2002); Robert Pinkney, *Democracy in the Third World*, 2nd edn (Boulder, CO, and London: Lynne Rienner, 2003).
4. Adam Przeworski, "Democracy as the Contingent Outcome of Conflicts", in Jon Elster and Rune Slagstad (eds), *Constitutionalism and Democracy* (Cambridge: Cambridge University Press, 1988), p. 304.
5. See, for example, Arend Lijphart and Bernard Grofman (eds), *Choosing an Electoral System: Issues and Alternatives* (New York: Praeger, 1984); Rein Taagepera and Matthew S. Shugart, *Seats and Votes: The Effects and Determinants of Electoral Systems* (New Haven, CT, and London: Yale University Press, 1989); Matthew S. Shugart and John M. Carey, *Presidents and Assemblies: Constitutional Design and Electoral Dynamics* (Cambridge: Cambridge University Press, 1992); Arend Lijphart, *Patterns of Democracy: Government Forms and Performance in Thirty-Six Countries* (New Haven, CT, and London: Yale University Press, 1999); Andrew Reynolds (ed.), *The Architecture of Democracy: Constitutional Design, Conflict Management and Democracy* (Oxford: Oxford University Press, 2002). For a policy-focused approach to these issues, see Peter Harris and Ben Reilly (eds), *Democracy and Deep-Rooted Conflict: Options for Negotiators* (Stockholm: International Institute for Democracy and Electoral Assistance, 1998).

6. For examples, see Giovanni Sartori, "Political Development and Political Engineering", *Public Policy*, 17, 1968: 261–298; Donald L. Horowitz, *A Democratic South Africa? Constitutional Engineering in a Divided Society* (Berkeley, CA: University of California Press, 1991); Giovanni Sartori, *Comparative Constitutional Engineering: An Inquiry into Structures, Incentives and Outcomes* (London: Macmillan, 1994); Pippa Norris, *Electoral Engineering: Voting Rules and Political Behavior* (Cambridge: Cambridge University Press, 2004); Benjamin Reilly, *Democracy and Diversity: Political Engineering in the Asia-Pacific* (Oxford: Oxford University Press, 2006).
7. Kenneth Janda, "Clarifying Concepts in Democracy Assistance: 'Engineering' v. 'Regulating'", unpublished paper, 2006.
8. Thanks to Tim Sisk for his observations on these subjects at the first authors' meeting on Political Party Development in Conflict-Prone Societies, Clingendael Institute, The Hague, 26–27 October 2006.
9. It is a source of regret to the editors that other planned chapters on North and West Africa and on South Asia were not able to be included in the final volume.
10. National Democratic Institute for International Affairs, "Political Party Development", at ⟨http://www.ndi.org/globalp/polparties/polparties.asp⟩ (accessed 27 March 2008).
11. United Nations Development Programme, blurb for "A Handbook on Working with Political Parties", ⟨http://www.undp.org/governance/publications.htm⟩ (accessed 27 March 2008).
12. Samuel P. Huntington, *Political Order in Changing Societies* (New Haven, CT: Yale University Press, 1968), p. 412.
13. Larry Diamond, Juan Linz and Seymour Martin Lipset, "Introduction: What Makes for Democracy?", in Diamond et al., *Politics in Developing Countries*, p. 34.
14. Seymour Martin Lipset, "The Indispensability of Political Parties", *Journal of Democracy*, 11(1), 2000: 48–55.
15. See Lipset and Rokkan, *Party Systems and Voter Alignments*.
16. See Ivan Doherty, "Democracy out of Balance: Civil Society Can't Replace Political Parties", *Policy Review*, April/May, 2001: 25–35.
17. Although this is less true of some *re*democratizing countries, for example in Latin America, where states such as Uruguay have a long history of party politics.
18. Alvin Rabushka and Kenneth Shepsle, *Politics in Plural Societies: A Theory of Democratic Instability* (Columbus, OH: Merrill, 1972).
19. See, for example, Donald L. Horowitz, *Ethnic Groups in Conflict* (Berkeley: University of California Press, 1985); Benjamin Reilly, *Democracy in Divided Societies: Electoral Engineering for Conflict Management* (Cambridge: Cambridge University Press, 2001).
20. Arend Lijphart, *Democracy in Plural Societies: A Comparative Exploration* (New Haven, CT: Yale University Press, 1977).
21. See G. Bingham Powell, *Contemporary Democracies: Participation, Stability, and Violence* (Cambridge, MA: Harvard University Press, 1982), p. 101.
22. Bumba Mukherjee, "Political Parties and the Size of Government in Multiparty Legislatures: Examining Cross-Country and Panel Data Evidence", *Comparative Political Studies*, 36(6), 2003: 699–728.
23. See Pradeep Chhibber and Irfan Nooruddin, "Do Party Systems Count? The Number of Parties and Government Performance in the Indian States", *Comparative Political Studies*, 37(2), 2004: 152–187.
24. See Stephan Haggard, "Democratic Institutions, Economic Policy, and Development", in Christopher Clague (ed.), *Institutions and Economic Development* (Baltimore, MD, and London: Johns Hopkins University Press, 1997); Stephan Haggard and Steven B. Webb, *Voting for Reform: Democracy, Political Liberalization and Economic Adjust-*

ment (New York: Oxford University Press, 1992); Haggard and Kaufman, *The Political Economy of Democratic Transitions.*

25. See Gordon White, "Constructing a Democratic Developmental State", in Mark Robinson and Gordon White (eds), *The Democratic Developmental State* (Oxford: Oxford University Press, 1998), p. 46.
26. Powell, *Contemporary Democracies*, pp. 99–108.
27. Diamond et al., "Introduction: What Makes for Democracy?", in *Politics in Developing Countries*, p. 35.
28. Ergun Özbudun, "Institutionalizing Competitive Elections in Developing Countries", in Myron Weiner and Ergun Özbudun (eds), *Competitive Elections in Developing Countries* (Durham, NC: Duke University Press, 1987), p. 405.
29. The following discussion draws on my article "Political Engineering and Party Politics in Conflict-Prone Societies", *Democratization* 13(5), 2006: 811–827.
30. Bryon Moraski, "Mandating Party Development in the Russian Federation: Effects of the 2001 Party Law", *Journal of Elections, Public Opinion and Parties*, 16(3), 2006: 199–219.
31. Horowitz, *Ethnic Groups in Conflict*, p. 293.
32. See Matthias Catón and Fernando Tuesta Soldevilla, Chapter 6 in this volume.
33. Ergun Özbudun, "The Institutional Decline of Parties in Turkey", in Diamond and Gunther (eds), *Political Parties and Democracy.*
34. Soli Özel, "Turkey at the Polls: After the Tsunami", *Journal of Democracy*, 14(3), 2003: 80–94.
35. See Matthias Catón and Fernando Tuesta Soldevilla, Chapter 6 in this volume.
36. Benjamin Reilly, "Electoral Systems for Divided Societies", *Journal of Democracy*, 13(2), 2002: 156–170.
37. The second round of voting entails a straight runoff between the two leading candidate teams, with no distribution requirements.
38. See Timothy D. Sisk, *Power Sharing and International Mediation in Ethnic Conflicts* (Washington DC: United States Institute of Peace Press, 1996), p. 55.
39. Peter Lewis, "Nigeria: Elections in a Fragile Regime", *Journal of Democracy*, 14(3), 2003: 131–144.
40. Drude Dahlerup, "Introduction", in Drude Dahlerup (ed.), *Women, Quotas and Politics* (London and New York: Routledge, 2006).
41. Wahidah Siregar, "Political Parties, Electoral System and Women's Representation in the 2004–2009 Indonesian Parliaments", CDI Policy Paper 2006/2 (Canberra: Centre for Democratic Institutions, 2006).
42. See Benjamin Reilly, "Post-Conflict Elections: Constraints and Dangers", *International Peacekeeping*, 9(2), 2002: 118–139.
43. Thomas Carothers, *Aiding Democracy Abroad: The Learning Curve* (Washington DC: Carnegie Endowment for International Peace, 1999).
44. See Roberto Belloni, "Peacebuilding and Consociational Electoral Engineering in Bosnia and Herzegovina", *International Peacekeeping*, 11(2), 2004: 334–353.
45. Sven Gunnar Simonsen, "Nationbuilding as Peacebuilding: Racing to Define the Kosovar", *International Peacekeeping*, 11(2), 2004: 289–311.
46. Krishna Kumar, "After the Elections: Consequences for Democratization", in Kumar (ed.), *Postconflict Elections, Democratization, and International Assistance* (Boulder, CO: Lynne Rienner Publishers, 1998), p. 218.
47. See OSCE Mission in Kosovo website at ⟨http://www.osce.org/kosovo⟩ (accessed 27 March 2008).
48. Richard Synge, *Mozambique: UN Peacekeeping in Action, 1992–94* (Washington DC: United States Institute of Peace Press, 1997).

49. Özbudun, "The Institutional Decline of Parties in Turkey".
50. See Reilly, *Democracy and Diversity*.
51. Conference on Security and Co-operation in Europe, *Document of the Copenhagen Meeting of the Conference on the Human Dimension of the CSCE* (1990), para. 30.
52. Conference on Security and Co-operation in Europe, *Helsinki Document 1992: The Challenges of Change*, Part VI, para. 24.

2

Party regulation and constitutionalization: A comparative overview

Ingrid van Biezen

Introduction

Political parties have traditionally been understood and analysed primarily in terms of their linkages with society, and the growing disengagement of citizens from conventional politics in recent years is well documented and explored theoretically and empirically.[1] However, we know comparatively little about the other side of the process of party organizational transformation, i.e. what Katz and Mair have argued consists of a strengthening of their links with the state.[2] Because this relationship traditionally consisted of a linkage between parties and government, rather than the state *tout court*, it has historically been temporal, contingent and loose.[3] Whereas traditionally the relationship with the state could be used by parties, but was not constitutive of party, in recent years it has assumed an increased importance in terms of both legitimacy and organizational resources.[4]

What little we know about this relationship, moreover, tends to focus on the increased relevance of public subsidies as indicative of the strengthening of the party–state linkage.[5] Yet the relationship between parties and the state should be seen as multi-faceted rather than one-dimensional: parties not only are more dependent on the state (especially in financial terms), but can also extract state resources through the practices of patronage and corruption; in addition, their internal organization and external activities are increasingly managed by the state through

Political parties in conflict-prone societies: Regulation, engineering and democratic development, Reilly and Nordlund (eds),
United Nations University Press, 2008, ISBN 978-92-808-1157-5

public law and the constitution.[6] Despite the increased amount of regulation of party activity, organization and behaviour, however, the subject of party law is still a neglected aspect of research on political parties and often lacks a comparative dimension.[7]

The literature on party regulation is somewhat more extensively developed where it concerns newly emerging democracies, as well as conflict-prone and divided societies. In this context, however, its main focus tends to be on the possibilities for institutional engineering or design rather than regulation,[8] with the specific focus often on the potential of measures such as party bans, registration conditions or membership requirements for the management of ethnic conflict and preventing the politicization of ethnicity. The phenomenon of party regulation more broadly has hitherto received relatively little systematic scholarly attention – from either political scientists or constitutional lawyers.[9]

This chapter will discuss the various components of the body of state-based party regulations, including a discussion of the relevance of the national constitution as a distinct source of party law that deserves special scholarly attention. It provides an overview of the different aspects of party that are regulated, discusses the different objectives that party regulation may seek to achieve and considers the practice of party regulation with reference to empirical examples from various sources of party law in contemporary democracies. As a general conceptual background, it first outlines the shift in the character of political parties from being private and voluntary associations to organizations enjoying a (quasi-)official status as part of the state. Although the notion that political parties might be conceived as public utilities, as will be argued in greater detail below, has its origins in the analysis of European party politics, including both the old and the new democracies, it may be acquiring an increased relevance also in newly developing democracies elsewhere in the world.

Political parties as public utilities

In the new democracies that have emerged across the globe since the beginning of what Huntington has called the "Third Wave" of democratization[10] – whether in Southern or East-Central Europe or elsewhere in the world[11] – parties often either did not exist or were heavily controlled prior to the regime changes and, therefore, effectively had to be built from scratch. Party membership in these countries remains relatively low and, with a few exceptions, the levels of electoral participation have been declining, especially in comparison with the early phases of democratization. In the context of a relatively weakly developed civil society, political parties tend to lack strong links with their constituencies. Even in cases where they had initially espoused strong grassroots mobilization as part of their liberation struggle, parties such as the ANC in South Africa, ZANU-PF in Zimbabwe, SWAPO in Namibia or FRELIMO in Mozambique eventually turned their attention elsewhere as they became absorbed in the life of the institutions.[12] The contest of elections is often based on appeals of individual leaders rather than on substantive ideological differences between competing political parties. In terms of internal party organizational structures, the party in public office and, crucially, a small group of party leaders (founders) dominate party life. Parties, in fact, often depend on the fortune of these leaders for their survival, especially if in opposition.

While the linkage between political parties has steadily been eroding, the relationship between parties and the state has assumed an increased importance. This can be seen, first, in the fact that parties in many contemporary democracies are now increasingly reliant for their corporate survival on funding they receive from the state.[13] Indeed, despite some variation between countries and regions, the overall pattern in most democracies is that, without the support of the state, many parties would find it difficult to survive. Second, parties in contemporary democracies are more and more managed by the state, in that their activities are to an increasing extent subject to regulations and state laws that govern their external activities or even determine the way in which their internal organization may function. Indeed, Katz has argued that party structures have now become "legitimate objects of state regulation to a degree far exceeding what would normally be acceptable for private associations in a liberal society",[14] alluding to a possible infringement of associational freedoms.

Many of these regulations and party laws were first introduced or were substantially extended in the wake of the introduction of public funding for parties, because the provision of state subventions inevitably demanded a more codified system of party registration and control. Controlling party access to the public broadcasting media has also required the introduction or extension of the system of regulation, which again acts to codify the status of parties and their range of activities. From having been largely "private" and voluntary associations that developed within society, parties have therefore increasingly become subject to a regulatory framework that has the effect of according them a (quasi-)official status as part of the state. In other words, as the internal life and the external activities of parties become regulated by public law, and as party rules become constitutional or administrative rules, the parties themselves become transformed into public service agencies, with a corresponding weakening of their own internal organizational autonomy.[15]

The increased involvement of the state in internal party affairs, whereby parties become subject to a regulatory framework that grants them an official status as part of the democratic state and its institutions, has contributed to the development of parties away from voluntary private associations performing public roles and occupying government positions to the party as a special type of public utility.[16] The idea that parties can be seen as public utilities was observed earlier in the US context by Epstein, who defined them as "an agency performing a service in which the public has a special interest sufficient to justify governmental regulatory control, along with the extension of legal privileges, but not governmental ownership or management of all the agency's activities".[17] Whereas parties once drew their legitimacy from their capacity to represent the key constituencies within civil society, they now justify themselves by appealing to a conception of democracy that sees parties as an essential public good. Similarly, whereas parties today are seen as both essential and valuable institutions for modern democracy, in their early days they were seen as possessing neither quality.[18]

The notion of parties as public utilities implies at least four aspects. First, parties perform important functions that are necessary and indispensable for democracy, and thus benefit the community as a whole. Second, the value of the services provided by parties justifies financial support from the state, in the form of indirect subventions and (sometimes generous) direct state subsidies. Third, because of the special role of political parties in representative democracy, their internal affairs and external activities should be regulated by the state, both to enforce the proper management of their finances and to ensure that they perform their unique services effectively. Fourth, therefore, relative to other types of organizations, political parties merit a privileged status in public law. The changing conception of parties and democracy, whereby parties are understood primarily as public rather than private associations, therefore, has enabled and legitimized the increased intervention of the state in defining and prescribing political parties' external activities and internal affairs, as a consequence of which they have been progressively incorporated into the public domain and are now legitimate objects of state regulation in most contemporary democracies.

In all contemporary democracies, a growing body of legislation regulates the internal affairs and external behaviour of parties – including party financing, organization or ideology – through public law and the constitution, although, as Reilly notes (in Chapter 1 in this volume), most of the innovations have come from new democracies rather than the established ones in the West. More generally, from the perspective of normative democratic theory, this legal regulation of political parties raises serious important questions and concerns. The presence of laws specifically targeted at political parties often implies that the law either imposes greater restrictions on political parties in comparison with other organizations or, conversely, confers special privileges upon them. As Katz notes, this raises the fundamental question of whether parties ought in fact to be regulated differently from other types of organizations, and whether the special regulation of parties can be reconciled with basic freedoms such as the freedom of speech and association, which are thought to be essential to democracy.[19] Other concerns that may arise are similar to those emerging from the diffusion of constitutional review and the secular expansion of opportunities for judicial activism: these processes arguably undermine fundamental principles of democracy by in effect transferring powers from representative to non-representative institutions.[20] The legal regulation of parties thus arouses anxieties not only about the state centralization and control of political participation and public life, but also about the democratic legitimacy of transferring the ultimate decision-making authority on their behaviour and organization from the responsible organs of the party to a non-elected body of judges.[21] The arguments here, however, might well be "permanent and irresolvable", as Shapiro and Stone have argued with reference to the case of US judicial review.[22]

Looking at contemporary political parties in Europe, one can see strong evidence that the links between political parties and society have gradually but persistently been eroded. This is exemplified by the weakening bonds of loyalty that exist between parties and their voters, and corresponding increases in the overall levels of electoral flux and volatility. It can also be seen from the sharply declining levels of party membership across European democracies and in the lower levels of party involvement within their traditional social environments. Finally, it is evident from the declining levels of electoral participation, a trend that is visible throughout the advanced industrial democracies.[23] What makes the present era stand out in particular is the combination of the sheer scale of the erosion in the parties' social anchoring, on the one hand, and the pervasiveness of the phenomenon, on the other.

Sources of party law

Party law – or the body of state-based regulations that determine the legal status of political parties and that specify how parties may operate, must organize or should be funded – may take a variety of forms. For any country, the body of party law generally is derived from a series of related bodies of law, including (where existing) a law on political parties, political finance law, electoral law, campaign law and the constitution, as

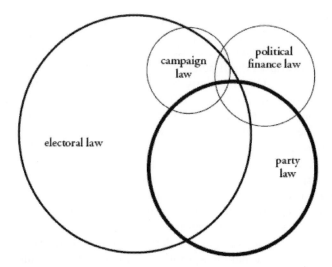

Figure 2.1 The body of party law.
Source: Kenneth Janda, "Adopting Party Law", working paper series on Political Parties and Democracy in Theoretical and Practical Perspectives, Washington DC: National Democratic Institute for International Affairs, 2005.

well as legislative statutes, administrative rulings and court decisions.[24] The possible relationship between these bodies of law is schematically represented in Figure 2.1, where "party law" comprises the total body of party law, regardless of its source, and the overlapping area between the circles indicates that part of the state regulation of political parties originates in the regulation of elections, campaigns and political finance.

Not included in Figure 2.1 as a source of party law is the constitution. Indeed, as Janda remarks, the constitution is usually not treated as a source of party law.[25] One of the main reasons for this is that constitutions, particularly those of the established liberal democracies, traditionally refrained from mentioning political parties or prescribing a role for them in the political system. As Bogdanor has observed of the British context, "it is perhaps because the law has been so late in recognizing political parties that constitutional lawyers and other writers on the constitution have taken insufficient note of the fact that parties are so central to our constitutional arrangements".[26] This reflects an earlier conception of democracy in which parties were not key institutions, let alone a positive condition for democracy. In the post-war period, however, their relevance for democracy has gradually become more widely acknowledged in constitutional terms too, to the point that pluralism, political participation and competition in many contemporary democratic constitutions have come to be defined increasingly, if not almost exclusively, in terms of party.

The constitutionalization of parties in Europe in effect began after World War II with the restoration of democracy in Italy and the Federal Republic of Germany, which were the first to dedicate a separate article to political parties in their constitutions. In Latin America, the democratic constitutionalization of parties commenced with the incorporation of political parties in the 1949 constitution of Costa Rica. In Germany, Article 21 of the Basic Law of 1949 regulates issues such as the freedom of political parties, their role in the formation of the political will, intraparty democracy and the duty of parties to account for their assets. Together with a similar, but less detailed, article on political parties that had previously appeared in the Italian constitution of 1947, the German Basic Law was one of the earliest constitutional regulations on political parties in Europe, investing parties with the status of institutions under constitutional law, and represented the most comprehensive set of constitutional rules on political parties in a European democracy.[27]

This practice has since been followed in constitutional revisions in many other polities, including the still dormant constitution of the European Union, which testifies to the currently predominant paradigm that political parties are important and valuable institutions for democracy by stipulating that "[p]arties at the European level are important as a factor for integration in the Union. They contribute to forming a European awareness and to expressing the political will of the citizens of the Union" (Art. 191).[28] In addition, in many of the more recently established democracies the very setting up of democratic procedures was often identified with the establishment of free competition between parties. It is in these newer democracies that parties were often ascribed a pivotal role and privileged position as the key instruments for the expression of political pluralism and political participation. Among the designers of the new democratic polities, a conception of democracy seemed to prevail in which political parties are the core foundation of the democratic political system.[29] The constitutionalization of political parties has gradually increased over the course of the twentieth century, both in scope, in that a growing number of countries incorporate political parties into their formal constitutions, and in intensity, in that constitutions tend to regulate a growing number of aspects of party activity and behaviour in increasingly greater detail.

In this chapter, the public regulation of political parties includes what could be called the constitutionalization of parties. In addition to the body of special laws (party laws, campaign laws, electoral laws, parliamentary standing orders), the public management of political parties now often includes quite detailed regulation of party structure, behaviour and activity through the constitution. In the following sections I will examine the different objectives and models of party regulation and discuss them in relation to specific sources of regulation.

Objectives and models of party regulation

Several types of state law concerning political parties can be distinguished, each of them seeking to achieve different objectives. In Janda's Database of Party Laws, for example, the 33 countries that are reported to have a special law on political parties[30] can be seen to regulate a wide variety of aspects related to party behaviour and activity. These range from the legal status and definition of parties to issues about their internal organization, mechanisms of candidate selection and party finances. Broadly speaking, as Katz has argued, party laws have essentially been enacted for three basic purposes.[31]

The first has been to resolve the broader question of definition and identity: who is entitled to be recognized as a political party? For this purpose, public law may determine the formal requirements for constituting a political party and establish who qualifies for ballot access, who benefits from public resources such as state subsidies or access to the broadcasting media, or who is entitled to share in the allocation of parliamentary committee assignments and government rapporteurships. The regulation of the legal status of the parties tends to concentrate on the conditions for the formation (or liquidation) of political parties, and usually involves requirements regarding signatures, deposits and formal accompanying documents that are needed to register a political party. The legal definition of a political party often involves the expectation that parties are voluntary associations, organized on the basis of common ideas or principles, aim to represent their members and/or voters, seek to exercise political power and participate in political life by means of electoral competition or the exercise of public office. In Indonesia, for example, a political party is defined as "any political organization voluntarily formed by a group of Indonesian citizens upon the basis of a common purpose and aspiration to struggle for the achievement of the interest of its members, the nation, and the state through general elections" (Art. 1).

A second important purpose of party laws is to regulate the types of behaviour and forms of activity in which parties may, or may not, engage. These may include permissible campaign activities, for example, or the raising and spending of (private and public) funds. By Finnish law, for example, parties are non-profit organizations. Similarly, in Israel, parties are not allowed to engage in entrepreneurial activities.

Thirdly, and probably most controversially, public law may prescribe the forms of internal party organization and political behaviour that are considered to be acceptable and prohibit those that are not. This may involve laying down conditions for the mechanisms by which the public office holders for the party are selected; for example, requirements that the electoral lists of the party are balanced in terms of gender or ethnic composition (by establishing quotas)[32] or constraints on the ideological content of the party programme or electoral manifesto. In Spain, for example, a recent law on political parties contains strict requirements with regard to the internal party structure (such as the need for parties to have a general assembly that represents the membership organization or that decisions of internal party organs are in principle adopted by simple majority) and the rights and duties of party members (such as the right to elect and to be elected to internal party offices or the duty to pay fees).

Different laws are aimed at regulating different aspects of the party. With regard to the regulation of parties, it is useful to think of parties not as monolithic organizations but as comprising several constituent parts. Generally speaking, for the regulation of parties as electoral organizations, the electoral and campaign laws tend to be the most important sources of law. For the regulation of the extra-parliamentary party – i.e. the party organization outside parliament, with its headquarters, permanent offices, paid staff, local branches and memberships – the most relevant source of regulation tends to be the law on political parties. Aspects of the regulation of parties in parliament and government can usually be found in the parliamentary standing orders. Finally, in an increasing number of contemporary democracies a special law on the financing of political parties (and election campaigns) now regulates the financial conduct of parties in some or all of these arenas. The different objectives of regulation of the various aspects of parties are usually scattered over several pieces of law, often acting as a barrier to the development of a coherent framework of legislation.

Laws on party financing

This section will concentrate on the relation between the increased importance of public funding for political parties and the growing quantity of party regulation. To be sure, the introduction of public funding is by no means the only motivation underlying the regulation of political parties. In divided societies, for example, party and party system regulation is often related to a desire to mediate potentially conflictual societal divisions and to cope with the effects of social diversity within the framework of a democratic system.[33] Furthermore, particularly in more recently established democracies, party regulation may be driven by the desire to compensate for weakly institutionalized party organizations and may consist of, for example, institutional incentives that discourage "fraction hopping", thereby enhancing parliamentary cohesion. The regulation of political parties may also be aimed at the pattern of public contestation and may be geared towards creating conditions that affect the fairness and equality of inter-party competition. One of the more universal driving forces behind the growing amount of party regulation, in both the older and the more recently established democracies, is the increased importance of state funding for parties. Indeed, the regulation of parties through the body of public law is strongly related to their increasingly strong financial relationship with the state, in particular their dependence on public funding, on the one hand, and their capacity to extract resources from the state through various illicit activities, on the other.

Parties in liberal democracies were traditionally funded privately rather than publicly, through individual or corporate donations, membership fees and trade union contributions, rather than the state. This mode of party funding reflects a conception of parties as private and voluntary associations. Today, however, political parties in the large majority of liberal democracies have access to public funding. In an earlier study, Kopecký and I found that, overall, in three-quarters of contemporary liberal democracies direct public funding is available to political parties.[34] The differences between the established and the newer democracies appear small. Parties receive direct subsidies from the state in 77 per cent of the older liberal democracies (India, Jamaica, New Zealand, Switzerland and the United States are the only exceptions), against 73 per cent of the more recently established democracies. Public funding is especially pervasive in the new democracies of Southern, Eastern and Central Europe, where state subventions are available in 91 per cent of countries. In Latin America and the Caribbean, 78 per cent of countries publicly subsidizes parties. Africa appears to be an exception to the general trend, as it is the only region where public funding of parties exists in just a minority (44 per cent) of democratic states.

There is of course considerable variation with regard to the relative importance of state subsidies. Large differences exist not only between regions but also between countries within a region, and even between parties within a country. Some countries provide parties only a small amount of state support in relation to their total income, whereas in other countries parties rely almost exclusively on the public purse. In Eastern Europe, for example, public funding in Bulgaria, Russia and Ukraine is merely symbolic in comparison with the resources parties obtain from private corporate donations, whereas in the Czech Republic, Slovenia, Hungary and Estonia the relative importance of state money is much larger.[35] In Latvia and Moldova, however, parties do not receive public funding. Among the established democracies, the United Kingdom provides only token amounts of financial aid to parties (earmarked for policy research), whereas parties in Germany, France and Israel benefit from significant subsidies.[36] Switzerland, by contrast, is one of the few established democracies where parties do not receive direct state funding. On the Latin American continent, countries such as Costa Rica provide generous subsidies to political parties; in Uruguay, the state has a longstanding record of providing parties with resources for their electoral activities, despite an otherwise relatively liberal system of political finance regulation.[37] Sub-Saharan Africa differs markedly from the general trend that is visible in other regions, in that public financing of political parties is rare and has so far been confined primarily to relatively modest experiments. These include the partial funding of presidential and parliamentary candidates in Tanzania or the direct funding of parties in South Africa, Benin and Mali.

Despite this variation, however, it is clear that it has become increasingly common for the state in contemporary democracies to provide direct financial support to political parties. The provision of direct state subsidies inevitably calls for a more codified system of party registration and control. Consequently, many of the regulations and party laws on political financing were first introduced, or were substantially extended, in the wake of the introduction of public funding for parties. Indeed, most countries that provide state support to parties also have a system of regulation of party finances; in only a few countries do regulations exist without a system of public funding for parties. Table 2.1 summarizes the presence of a system of regulation for party financing in liberal and electoral democracies, extending the findings of the earlier study by Kopecký

Table 2.1 Legal frameworks of party financing in liberal and electoral democracies

	Public regulation of party finances	
	Yes	No
'Free' countries	42 (68.9%)	19 (31.1%)
'Partly free' countries	25 (71.4%)	10 (28.6%)
All	67 (69.8%)	29 (30.2%)

Note: The data are from a comparative study on the financing of political parties and election campaigns by International IDEA, *Funding of Political Parties and Election Campaigns* (Stockholm: International Institute for Democracy and Electoral Assistance, 2003). The 96 countries included are drawn from the 144 countries that were classified as 'free' or 'partly free' in the 2002 Freedom House Index and have a population larger than 100,000.

and myself to include both "free" and "partly free" countries. It demonstrates that the large majority (nearly 70 per cent) have established a legal framework for party financing, with few significant differences between electoral and liberal democracies.

In addition to the growing relevance of public funding per se, a second important reason for the increased public regulation of party financing has to do with a broader concern with the functioning of democracy. That is, the regulation of political financing is often part of a concerted attempt to prevent or at least to minimize illicit financial practices and to enhance the accountability of political parties by increasing the transparency of party financing. This is done with a view to helping restore public trust in politics and parties and thus contributing to a healthier functioning of democracy. Indeed, political parties are among the least trusted institutions, enjoying far less public trust than any other private or public institution, less than big companies or trade unions and substantially less than institutions such as the army or police, or transnational organizations such as the United Nations and the European Union.[38] Moreover, nearly everywhere parties are now seen as the institution most susceptible to corruption, significantly more so than any other sector or institution, including the business sector, the civil service, the media or the police.[39] This is true not only in the regions where democracy has been established relatively recently, in many of which corruption is allegedly endemic, but increasingly also in the longer-established democracies.

As a consequence, a growing number of countries have introduced legal frameworks for the financing of political parties, introducing guidelines for the disclosure of income and expenditures, the reporting of party accounts to the relevant authorities and the monitoring of party finances by an independent body, and establishing the parameters of a system of enforcement that outlines sanctions to deter unlawful behaviour and imposes penalties for violations of the law. In this, they are supported by a host of international governmental institutions and non-governmental organizations, such as the European Parliament, the Council of Europe, the International Institute for Democracy and Electoral Assistance (IDEA) and Transparency International, all of which have advocated a greater role for the state in the financing of parties, in order both to facilitate fair and equal party competition through public subsidies and to improve the accountability of parties and the transparency of party financing through legislation and public control.

Parties and constitutions

The regulation of party finances gives us a first indication of the extent to which the activities and behaviour of parties are regulated by the state.

The constitutional regulation of political parties provides us with further evidence of the role of public law in defining their functions and responsibilities. National constitutions have become an important source of party law and an important source for investigations into the character of modern democracy and prevailing ideas about the place of political parties within it. Few, if any, institutional preferences and reforms are politically neutral, and choices and decisions about the desirability of party laws and constitutionalization, or the content of the regulations, can all have partisan implications. Therefore, the constitution, like laws and regulations in general, together with its establishment and modification, reflects a particular vision of what the distribution of power actually is, as well as what it should be, because decisions on the regulation of party activity, organization and behaviour follow from particular conceptions of party and the preferred internal power hierarchy of parties.[40] Different norms and conceptions of politics thus lead to divergent prescriptions about the appropriate legal regulation of parties.[41] The position of political parties as defined by the national constitution, therefore, sheds light on a number of what Issacharoff has called the "most vexing questions in the legal regulation of politics",[42] ranging from how parties should be understood in terms of normative democratic theory to how they are to be financed.

In principle, at least two types of party constitutionalization can be distinguished. The first defines political parties in opposition to the institutions of the state, identifies them as associations of the private sphere and outlines their position in terms of basic political freedoms and civil liberties vis-à-vis the state. The second, by contrast, is indicative of the formal identification of parties as public institutions and signals their incorporation into the public domain. Constitutions, for example, may define political parties as necessary for democracy, either in institutional terms (when the composition of one or more key democratic institutions or procedures, such as parliament, government or elections, is defined in terms of political parties) or in functional terms (when the constitution defines the democratic system itself, or one or more key democratic principles, such as electoral competition, political participation or the representation of the will of the people, in terms of political parties). Moreover, the constitution may regulate the activities and behaviour of political parties, their organization and ideology, as well as the finances of political parties and their access to the broadcasting media. In theory, the constitutional recognition of political parties can fall into either (or both) of these two domains. In practice, the incorporation of parties into the public domain and their identification as public rather than private entities seem to be increasingly predominant.

Elsewhere, Kopecký and I have provided an analysis of the extent to which political parties in contemporary polities are constitutionally

Table 2.2 The constitutional regulation of political parties in liberal democracies

	Constitutional regulation of political parties	
	Yes	No
Established democracies	9 (47.4%)	10 (52.6%)
New democracies	28 (96.6%)	1 (3.4%)
All liberal democracies	37 (77.1%)	11 (22.9%)

Source: Ingrid van Biezen and Petr Kopecký, "The State and the Parties: Public Funding, Public Regulation and Rent-Seeking in Contemporary Democracies", *Party Politics*, 13(2), 2007: 235–254.

recognized,[43] and we found that the large majority of contemporary liberal democracies across the globe presently regulate political parties in their national constitutions. Because constitutions contain very different types of references to political parties, we coded the constitutionalization of political parties as positive only if the reference to parties could be interpreted as an expression of their regulation by the state. Country constitutions that mention parties but only with reference to citizens' rights of expression or political association were assigned a negative score. Although this type of stipulation entails an important democratic entitlement of citizens to exercise their political rights through parties, it cannot be seen to regulate the behaviour, activities, organization, ideology or any other aspect of political parties and is thus not indicative of the public management of the role of parties in the political system.

The results of that analysis are summarized in Table 2.2, which shows that more than three-quarters of contemporary democratic polities regulate the identity, activities or behaviour of political parties in one way or another through the formal constitution. Importantly, there is a significant difference between old and new democracies: nearly all of the recently established democracies, whether in Latin America, Eastern Europe or Africa, have enshrined political parties in their constitutions. The one exception in Eastern Europe is Latvia, where the only constitutional reference to political parties states that "[e]veryone has the right to form and join associations, political parties and other public organizations", which is a reference to democratic rights and freedoms but not to the regulation of party activity or behaviour. In the established democracies, by contrast, the practice of party constitutionalization is much less common and can be found in only about half the countries with a written constitution. For example, in Belgium, Denmark, Ireland, the Netherlands, Canada and the United States, the constitution makes no reference at all to political parties. The lack of constitutional recognition for parties in these established democracies is clearly a legacy of a historical conception of political parties as private and voluntary associations. As such, there was no rationale for their inclusion in the constitution. Some of the newer democracies, in contrast, presumably prescribe the activities of political parties because of a legacy of the recent past where parties, especially the communist parties in Eastern Europe or ethnically based ones in Africa, were instrumental in the establishment and maintenance of authoritarian rule. Indeed, many of the post-communist constitutions follow what Janda calls a "prescription model" of party regulation,[44] banning parties from advocating totalitarian methods of political activity, for example, or dictating that they must be separate from the state.[45]

It is worth exploring the different dimensions of party constitutionalization in somewhat more detail. For the purpose of the analysis here, constitutional provisions that make reference to political parties are divided into four main categories: (1) democratic necessity; (2) activities/behaviour; (3) organization/ideology; and (4) finance/media. The differences between old and new democracies become more pronounced when we consider these specific dimensions of party constitutionalization. Instances where party constitutionalization involves defining parties as essential for democracy, or a democratic necessity, may entail one of two possibilities. The first is that the constitution defines the composition of one or more key democratic institutions (usually parliament or government) in terms of political parties. In Greece, for example, "The leader of the party with the absolute majority of seats in Parliament shall be appointed Prime Minister" (Art. 37.2); in Sweden, in elections for the Riksdag, the "votes shall be cast for parties, with an option for the voter to express a preference for a particular candidate" (Art. 1), "the seats shall be distributed between parties" and "only a party which receives at least four per cent of the vote ... is entitled to share in the distribution of seats" (Art. 7). References such as these can be found in constitutions of both old and new democracies. In Thailand, for instance, the 1997 constitution stipulates that the House of Representatives consists of 500 members, 100 of whom are elected on a party list basis (Art. 98).

Another possibility under the same heading of "democratic necessity" is that the constitution defines the democratic system itself or one or more key democratic principles – such as electoral competition, political participation or the representation of the will of the people – in terms of political parties. More specifically, these include constitutions that define democratic pluralism in terms of parties, define democracy in terms of a plurality of parties or competition between parties, state that parties contribute to the formation and/or expression of the political will of the citizens, or define political parties as a key instrument for political participation. The constitution of the Czech Republic, for example, states that "[the] political system is based on the free and voluntary formation of and free competition between political parties" (Art. 5). According to the constitution of Costa Rica, political parties express political pluralism, contribute to the formation and manifestation of the popular will and are the fundamental instruments of political participation (Art. 98). In Croatia, "a democratic multiparty system [is among] the highest values of the constitutional order" (Art. 3). The constitution of Argentina defines political parties as "fundamental institutions of the democratic system" (Art. 38). Interestingly, this type of reference seems to be much more common among the new democracies than the older ones. This underscores one of the contentions of this chapter, that the process of party regulation more broadly, and party constitutionalization in particular, reflects an ideational transformation of the perceived role and place of parties in a modern democracy.

There also appears to be a clear difference between old and new democracies in the extent to which they prescribe party activity and behaviour. In contrast to the older democracies, the recently democratized countries seem to regulate the activities and behaviour of political parties to a larger extent, with most of the constitutional stipulations either prescribing or proscribing what parties do. Of the old democracies, Norway for example includes in its constitution a more "permissive" provision stipulating that parties are entitled to nominate candidates for (parliamentary and/or presidential) elections. However, the most common provision among the new democracies is that parties should respect the principles of democracy, the democratic constitution and/or the rule of law, followed by the requirement that they respect national sovereignty and/or the integrity of the nation-state, and, finally, the prohibition of violent behaviour or activities. In fact, with only a few exceptions (e.g. Germany and France), most countries that prescribe party activity and behaviour are new democracies.

The same is true for the third category of constitutional provisions, i.e. the degree to which the constitution regulates the organization and ideology of the parties. One of the most common provisions in this context is that membership of a political party is incompatible with certain public offices, such as (constitutional) judges, members of the armed forces or the police, or the president of the republic. In Europe, Italy is the only older democracy to stipulate this incompatibility; all the other constitutions with this provision are in more recently established post-communist democracies.

Clearly, the intention here has been to keep parties separate from the institutions of the state. As such this reflects an important legacy of the past, in which the communist parties in Eastern Europe were instrumental in the establishment and maintenance of totalitarian rule and exercised more or less complete control of the institutions of the state.[46] The Slovakian constitution in fact explicitly states that "[p]olitical parties and political movements … shall be separate from the State" (Art. 29.4). In Slovenia, "[t]he State, the political parties, political and public organizations, and other institutions or persons, may not monopolize the means of the mass media" (Art. 44). A similar interpretation can be given to the banning of certain ideologies: in Poland, for example, parties are banned from advocating totalitarian methods and activities, and the Bulgarian constitution states that "no political party or ideology shall be proclaimed or affirmed as a party or ideology of the state" (Art. 11.3). These kinds of provisions are not the exclusive preserve of post-communist constitutions, however, and similar requirements can be found elsewhere. In Uruguay, for example, judicial magistrates, people in active military service and police officials, amongst others, may not be members of political parties (Art. 77).

Two new European democracies (Bulgaria and Portugal) have also established constitutional bans on the organization of parties along certain demographic lines ("ethnicity", "religion", "region"): Bulgaria bans parties organized on ethnic, racial or religious lines;[47] the Portuguese constitution does not allow political parties to use names that contain expressions directly connected with any religion or church or use emblems that may be mistaken for national or religious symbols, nor can parties exist with a name or stated aims that indicate a regional connection or field of action. This type of constitutional regulation is also very common in sub-Saharan Africa, on a scale that would be unrecognizable in either Western or Eastern Europe.[48] It is most vividly manifest in the ban on ethnic political parties or ethnically based mobilization, as, for example, in Tanzania, Mali, Djibouti or Ghana, where the constitution states that "every political party shall have a national character, and membership shall not be based on ethnic, religious, regional or other sectional divisions" (Art. 55), or in the proscription on religious parties, as for example in Kenya. Such constitutional regulation exists in many other new democracies on other continents as well. In Nepal, for example, political parties cannot be registered if they are based on religion, caste, tribe, language or sex or if the name, objectives, insignia or flags are of such a nature that they can be seen as religious or communal or tend to fragment the country.

Again typically for new democracies, constitutions often intervene in the internal structures and organization of political parties. This may include constitutional requirements relating to party membership. In Estonia, for example, only Estonian citizens can belong to a political party, which effectively excludes the approximately 15 per cent of the population who are stateless Russians. In Greece, the constitution restricts party membership to adult citizens; in Portugal, membership of more than one party is forbidden; and the Polish constitution prohibits parties with a secret membership structure. According to the Chilean constitution, the statutes of political parties should respect norms that ensure an effective internal democracy. Similarly, the 1997 constitution in Thailand requires that the internal organization, management and regulations of political parties be consistent with fundamental principles of democratic government (Art. 47). Some countries can be seen to micro-manage the activities of political parties. In Nigeria, the constitution prescribes the internal organization in minute detail, by requiring, for example, that the statutes of a party provide for the democratic, regular and periodic election (not exceeding a four-year interval) of the executive committee and that the membership of the executive committee reflect the federal structure of the country (incorporating at least two-thirds of the states).

Finally, in some countries the financial aspects of party activity and parties' access to the broadcasting media are regulated by the constitution. The constitution of Brazil in fact combines party access to these two public resources by stipulating that political parties have the right to public funds as well as free radio and television time. The Portuguese constitution states that political parties have the right to broadcasting time on publicly owned radio and television, and that this should be distributed in proportion to their representative strength. Similarly, the Maltese constitution stipulates that broadcasting facilities and time are to be fairly distributed between the different political parties. With regard to the financing of political parties, a frequent requirement relates to the transparency and public accountability of the party accounts. This provision entails that parties are constitutionally accountable for their expenditure, income, property, resources and/or assets, and that their accounts should be open to public inspection. In addition, there are countries where the principles of state funding of parties are actually enshrined in the constitution. In Argentina, for instance, the constitution stipulates that the state contributes to the financial support of the activities of political parties (Art. 38). In Greece, "[p]olitical parties are entitled to receive financial support by the State for their electoral and operating expenses, as specified by law" (Art. 29.2). These sorts of provisions, which in effect entail an entitlement to public resources by public law, are indicative of the interpretation of parties today as part of the public realm and their identification as public entities.

Conclusion

Although, clearly, not all the different modes of regulation can be considered equally relevant for all countries, the legal regulation of parties constitutes a key element of the party–state relationship in liberal democracies. The growing quantity of party legislation attests to a conception of democracy in which parties are seen as necessary and valuable institutions and reveals how the state is assuming an important role in securing the collective survival of parties and the management of their behaviour and activities as an essential public good. In empirical terms, although more systematic comparative research is needed, it appears that an increasingly strong and permanent linkage between the state and the parties is visible through a definition of their role and value in national constitutions and in public legislation more generally.

Indeed, the regulation of parties, and especially their constitutionalization, primarily seems to entail their identification as public entities rather than private associations, because it predominantly reveals a description (or prescription) of their functions and duties as public institutions, rather than their identification as voluntary associations belonging to the private sphere. Some differences appear to exist between the longer-established democracies, on the one hand, and the more recently established democracies (in particular those in Central and Eastern Europe), on the other, although these differences need to be teased out further by more systematic comparative research. In the newer democracies, some legacy of past totalitarian rule seems to persist, which is suggested by their constitutions insisting on maintaining a clear separation between parties and the state by underlining the private character of party organization and ideology, and often by associating parties with basic democratic citizen rights and freedoms (e.g. expression, assembly, association). This might follow from the way in which the constitutional design of the newer democracies has tended to position the state and society vis-à-vis one another in the wake of democratization: the corollary of the liberalization of formerly non-democratic polities was often the constitutional establishment of an explicitly private sphere of social life.[49] It is conceivable that the constitutional recognition of political parties in newer democratic polities should be understood in light of the desire to identify and strengthen spheres of life that are free from state intervention. However, the intensity of party constitutionalization and other party legislation in these newer democracies otherwise conforms, perhaps *a fortiori*, to the reconceptualization of parties as public utilities.

The broader relevance of party regulation as a contributor to the healthy functioning of democracy remains ambiguous. First of all, the institutional engineering and regulation of party activity is often not unequivocally successful, as evidenced by the fact that extreme right parties often continue to operate despite being banned or that, despite certain prohibitions, parties in Africa keep organizing on the basis of ethnicity. Moreover, although the state regulation of party finance has often been enacted with a view to curtailing corrupt practices and to enhancing public accountability, illicit party financing frequently persists in spite of relatively stringent legal frameworks. Secondly, and perhaps even more importantly, party regulation itself sometimes appears at odds with the objectives it seeks to achieve and the assumptions on which it is based, in particular in the context of the newer democracies.[50] Underlying the efforts of party regulation are – often implicit and possibly dated – assumptions about ideal-typical forms of party and representative democracy, in which parties are essentially understood as private associations. Paradoxically, however, the regulation of political party behaviour and activity implies embracing a notion of parties as public entities rather than private organizations. In liberal democracies, political parties were traditionally largely unregulated precisely because they were seen to belong to the private realm. In contemporary democracies, however, that state of affairs is probably neither possible nor desirable, principally because parties today, unlike their predecessors, have privileged access to so many public resources. Although this may justify their legal regulation, the implication is that the original notion of parties as private organizations is in fact associated with a different period of representative democracy; this particular understanding of political parties is of little relevance for party democracy in the twenty-first century.

Acknowledgements

I would like to thank Petr Kopecký for his valuable contribution and useful suggestions.

Notes

1. See, for example, Russell J. Dalton and Martin P. Wattenberg (eds), *Parties without Partisans: Political Change in Advanced Industrial Democracies* (Oxford: Oxford University Press, 2000); Peter Mair and Ingrid van Biezen, "Party Membership in Twenty European Democracies, 1980–2000", *Party Politics*, 7(1), 2001: 5–21; Susan Pharr and Robert Putnam (eds), *Disaffected Democracies: What's Troubling the Trilateral Democracies?* (Princeton, NJ: Princeton University Press, 2000).
2. Richard S. Katz and Peter Mair, "Changing Models of Party Organization and Party Democracy: The Emergence of the Cartel Party", *Party Politics*, 1(1), 1995: 5–28.
3. Petr Kopecký and Peter Mair, "Political Parties and Government", in Mohamed A. Salih (ed.), *Political Parties in Africa* (London: Pluto, 2003), pp. 275–292.
4. Richard S. Katz and Peter Mair, "The Ascendancy of the Party in Public Office: Party Organizational Change in Twentieth-Century Democracies", in Richard Gunther, José Ramón Montero and Juan J. Linz (eds), *Political Parties: Old Concepts and New Challenges* (Oxford: Oxford University Press, 2002), pp. 113–135.
5. Ingrid van Biezen, *Political Parties in New Democracies: Party Organization in Southern and East-Central Europe* (London: Palgrave Macmillan, 2003); Paul G. Lewis, "Party

Funding in Post-Communist East-Central Europe", in Peter Burnell and Alan Ware (eds), *Funding Democratization* (Manchester: Manchester University Press, 1998), pp. 137–157; Jon Pierre, Lars Svåsand and Anders Widfeldt, "State Subsidies to Political Parties: Confronting Rhetoric with Reality", *West European Politics*, 23(3), 2000: 1–24.

 6. Ingrid van Biezen and Petr Kopecký, "The State and the Parties: Public Funding, Public Regulation and Rent-seeking in Contemporary Democracies", *Party Politics*, 13(2), 2007: 235–254.

 7. Dan Avnon, "Parties Laws in Democratic Systems of Government", *Journal of Legislative Studies*, 1(2), 1995: 286.

 8. See Benjamin Reilly, "Political Engineering and Party Politics in Conflict-Prone Societies", *Democratization*, 13(5), 2006: 811–827; Kenneth Janda, "Measuring National Performance on Models of Party Regulation", paper prepared for delivery at the authors' meeting on Political Party Development in Conflict-Prone Societies, Clingendael Institute, The Hague, 26–27 October 2006.

 9. For a recent exception, see Lauri Karvonen, "Legislation on Political Parties: A Global Comparison", *Party Politics*, 13(4), 2007: 437–455.

10. Samuel Huntington, *The Third Wave: Democratization in the Late Twentieth Century* (Norman, OK: University of Oklahoma Press, 1991).

11. Van Biezen, *Political Parties in New Democracies*.

12. Mohamed A. Salih (ed.), *Political Parties in Africa* (London: Pluto, 2003).

13. See van Biezen and Kopecký, "The State and the Parties".

14. Richard S. Katz, "The Internal Life of Parties", in Kurt Richard Luther and Ferdinand Müller-Rommel (eds), *Political Challenges in the New Europe: Political and Analytical Challenges* (Oxford: Oxford University Press, 2002), p. 90.

15. Stefano Bartolini and Peter Mair, "Challenges to Contemporary Political Parties", in Larry Diamond and Richard Gunther (eds), *Political Parties and Democracy* (Baltimore, MD: Johns Hopkins University Press, 2001), p. 340.

16. Ingrid van Biezen, "Political Parties as Public Utilities", *Party Politics*, 10(6), 2004: 701–722.

17. Leon Epstein, *Political Parties in the American Mold* (Madison, WI: University of Wisconsin Press, 1986), p. 157.

18. See Giovanni Sartori, *Parties and Party Systems: A Framework for Analysis* (Cambridge: Cambridge University Press, 1976), especially Chapter 1.

19. Richard S. Katz, "Democracy and the Legal Regulation of Political Parties", paper prepared for the USAID conference on "Change in Political Parties", Washington DC, 1 October 2004, p. 3.

20. For a more detailed discussion, see, for example, Ian Shapiro, "Three Fallacies Concerning Majorities, Minorities and Democratic Politics", in *NOMOS XXXII: Majorities and Minorities* (1990).

21. Avnon, "Parties Laws in Democratic Systems of Government", p. 285.

22. Martin Shapiro and Alec Stone, "The New Constitutional Politics of Europe", *Comparative Political Studies*, 26(4), 1994: 397–420.

23. See, for example, Russell J. Dalton, "Political Support in Advanced Industrial Democracies", in Pippa Norris (ed.), *Critical Citizens* (Oxford: Oxford University Press, 1999), pp. 57–77; Russell J. Dalton, *Democratic Challenges, Democratic Choices: The Erosion of Political Support in Advanced Industrial Democracies* (Oxford: Oxford University Press, 2004); Michael Gallagher, Michael Laver and Peter Mair, *Representative Government in Modern Europe*, 4th edn (New York: McGraw Hill, 2005), pp. 288–296; Mair and van Biezen, "Party Membership in Twenty European Democracies, 1980–2000"; Dalton and Wattenberg, *Parties without Partisans*.

24. Kenneth Janda, "Adopting Party Law", working paper series on Political Parties and Democracy in Theoretical and Practical Perspectives, Washington DC, National Democratic Institute for International Affairs, 2005.
25. Ibid., p. 5.
26. Vernon Bogdanor, "The Constitution and the Party System in the Twentieth Century", *Parliamentary Affairs*, 57(4), 2004, p. 718.
27. Dimitris T. Tsatsos (ed.), *30 Jahre Parteiengesetz in Deutschland: Die Parteiinstitutionen im Internationalen Vergleich* (Baden-Baden: Nomos, 2002).
28. The fact that even at the European level parties have been given a privileged position, which also involves important financial benefits in the form of direct subsidies, is remarkable, because it is not obvious that they have a similar institutional necessity at the systemic level of the European Union as they do at the level of the nation-state; see Stephen Day and Jo Shaw, "The Evolution of Europe's Transnational Political Parties in the Era of European Citizenship", in Tanja A. Börzel and Rachel A. Cichowski (eds), *The State of the European Union, 6* (Oxford: Oxford University Press, 2006), p. 169.
29. Petr Kopecký, "Developing Party Organizations in East-Central Europe: What Type of Party Is Likely to Emerge?", *Party Politics*, 1(4), 1995, p. 516.
30. The database can be freely accessed from the National Democratic Institute's website at ⟨http://www.ndi.org/globalp/polparties/programspp/db.asp⟩ (accessed 27 March 2008). This database is not comprehensive or exhaustive, however, and does not contain all party laws for all countries. It includes both democratic and non-democratic regimes.
31. Katz, "Democracy and the Legal Regulation of Political Parties".
32. Details on candidate gender quotas can be found in the Global Database of Quotas for Women, a joint project of the International Institute for Democracy and Electoral Assistance (IDEA) and Stockholm University (see ⟨http://www.quotaproject.org/⟩, accessed 27 March 2008). For a conceptual and theoretical discussion, see Mona Lena Krook, "Candidate Gender Quotas: A Framework for Analysis", *European Journal of Political Research*, 46(3), 2007: 367–394.
33. Benjamin Reilly, *Democracy and Diversity: Political Engineering in the Asia-Pacific* (Oxford: Oxford University Press, 2006), p. 5. See also Jóhanna Kristín Birnir, "Stabilizing Party Systems and Excluding Segments of Society? The Effects of Formation Costs on New Party Foundation in Latin America", *Studies in Comparative International Development*, 39(3), 2004: 3–27; Matthijs Bogaards, "Electoral Choices for Divided Societies: Multi-Ethnic Parties and Constituency Pooling in Africa", *Commonwealth & Comparative Politics*, 41(3), 2003: 59–80.
34. Van Biezen and Kopecký, "The State and the Parties".
35. Petr Kopecký, "Political Parties and the State in Post-Communist Europe: The Nature of Symbiosis", *Journal of Communist Studies and Transition Politics*, 22(3), 2006.
36. Michael Pinto-Duschinsky, "Financing Politics: A Global View", *Journal of Democracy*, 13(4), 2002: 69–86.
37. Kevin Casas-Zamora, *Paying for Democracy: Political Finance and State Funding for Parties* (Colchester: ECPR Press, 2005).
38. Ingrid van Biezen and Peter Mair, "Political Parties", in Paul Heywood, Eric Jones, Martin Rhodes and Ulrich Sedelmeier (eds), *Developments in European Politics* (London: Palgrave Macmillan, 2006), pp. 97–116.
39. Van Biezen and Kopecký, "The State and the Parties".
40. Nathaniel Persily and Bruce E. Cain, "The Legal Status of Political Parties: A Reassessment of Competing Paradigms", *Columbia Law Review*, 100(3), 2000, p. 778.
41. James A. Gardner, "Can Party Politics Be Virtuous?", *Columbia Law Review*, 100(3), 2000, p. 667.

42. Samuel Issacharoff, "Introduction: The Structures of Democratic Politics", *Columbia Law Review*, 100(3), 2000, p. 597.
43. Van Biezen and Kopecký, "The State and the Parties".
44. Janda, "Adopting Party Law".
45. Kopecký, "Political Parties and the State in Post-Communist Europe".
46. Ibid.
47. The Bulgarian case demonstrates that constitutional provisions other than those explicitly referring to political parties might also be of direct relevance for parties. In 2000, for example, the Constitutional Court attempted to ban a small Macedonian party on the basis of Article 44.2 in the constitution, which contains a more general prohibition on organizations whose activity is "directed against the sovereignty, the territorial integrity of the country, and the unity of the nation". The ban on the Turkish-based Movement for Rights and Freedoms (MRF), on the other hand, was lifted in a ruling that placed the ban on ethnic parties in the context of other constitutional principles, prominently that of democratic pluralism, concluding that the MRF did not threaten the constitutional order.
48. See Matthijs Bogaards, "The Making of Party Systems: Crafting in the New Democracies of Africa, Latin America and Eastern Europe", unpublished PhD thesis, European University Institute, Florence, 2000.
49. Shapiro and Stone, "The New Constitutional Politics of Europe".
50. I owe this observation to Petr Kopecký.

3

Comparative strategies of political party regulation

Matthijs Bogaards

Introduction

In the literature on ethnic conflict management, most attention has been paid to electoral systems.[1] This chapter, in addition, examines the political regulation of parties in conflict-prone societies.[2] My aim is to explore how interventions in the development of political parties, whether through electoral law or through the direct regulation of parties, have been used and can be used to shape the political organization of ethnicity and to manage ethnic conflict.

The starting point for the analysis of electoral system design and the regulation of political parties for ethnic conflict management is the conceptualization of parties and the party system as intermediaries between society and politics. In a heterogeneous society, in which people differ from each other in language, religion, colour of skin or other socio-cultural attributes, parties can perform three functions. They can aggregate socio-cultural divisions, articulate ethnic differences or organize on other bases, thereby blocking the political organization of socio-cultural cleavages. In designing the electoral system and regulating political parties, policy makers should be clear about the desired role of political parties and the function of the party system. The choice is between interventions that promote the functions of aggregation, articulation or blocking. The choice of the appropriate electoral system and the examination of possible ways to regulate parties are technical matters that can be

Political parties in conflict-prone societies: Regulation, engineering and democratic development, Reilly and Nordlund (eds),
United Nations University Press, 2008, ISBN 978-92-808-1157-5

decided only after the principal question about the kind of parties the polity needs has been answered.

This chapter first discusses different types of parties and party systems, focusing on the three functions of aggregation, articulation and blocking. It then shows how these functions can be promoted through different electoral systems. Next, the chapter goes beyond the existing literature in demonstrating how party regulation has been used to the same effect, focusing on party bans and the conditions for party registration. The conclusion evaluates the effectiveness of the various measures to promote the emergence of multi-ethnic parties through electoral engineering and party regulations and puts forward some suggestions.

Political parties: Functions and types

In modern democracies, political parties are indispensable because they perform two sets of functions. First, parties have a representative function in that they represent societal interests within the political system. Secondly, parties perform a variety of "*institutional* functions, including the recruitment of political leaders and the organization of parliament and government".[3] This analysis focuses on the first, representative function of political parties. In Sartori's words, "parties are the central intermediate and intermediary structure between society and government".[4] Looking at the way parties link society and government, three functions can be distinguished. Parties can aggregate social cleavages, translate social cleavages into political cleavages or block the politicization of social cleavages.

These functions correspond to particular types of party, as can be illustrated with the typology of political parties developed by Gunther and Diamond.[5] This typology is based on three criteria: formal organization of the party, its programmatic content and its commitment to multi-party democracy. On the basis of these three criteria, the authors identify 15 types of party. For our purposes, the most important feature is a party's social base and especially the question of whether, first, a given party has a clearly identifiable social base and, if so, second, whether this base is narrow or broad. In conflict-prone societies, we can be even more specific since we are concerned with those social divisions that have a high conflict potential. For example, the emergence of a classic social democratic party catering to the interests of workers irrespective of ethnic background would be welcomed by most observers as a step away from communal politics, even though such a party would have a clearly identifiable and possibly quite narrow social base. What matters, therefore, is whether and how parties organize along the main cleavages dividing a conflict-prone society. In many cases, this cleavage will be ethnicity, broadly understood. The basic distinction is then between non-ethnic, mono-ethnic and multi-ethnic parties.[6]

Characteristic of the ethnic party is an electoral strategy "to harden and mobilize its ethnic base with exclusive, often polarizing appeals to ethnic group opportunity and threat, and unlike virtually all other political parties (including nationalistic parties), electoral mobilization is not intended to attract additional sectors of society to support it".[7] Gunther and Diamond have a very negative view of ethnic parties and point out the dangers of articulation: "The ethnic party's particularistic, exclusivist, and often polarizing political appeals make its overall contribution to society divisive and even disintegrative."[8] This view accords well with the much earlier assessment by Almond and Coleman of the limited aggregative potential of what they termed "particularistic parties".[9]

The contrast between particularistic articulation and aggregation helps to highlight the distinction between mono- and multi-ethnic parties. For Gunther and Diamond, a congress party is "a coalition, alliance, or federation of ethnic parties or political machines, although it may take the form of a single, unified party structure.... [T]he congress party allocates party posts and government offices, and distributes patronage and other benefits, with proportional or other quasi-consociational formulas. Its social base is broad and heterogeneous and the party's goal is to make it as inclusive as possible."[10] Because there is no empirical reason to assume that multi-ethnic parties by definition exhibit power-sharing features and there is an analytical need to keep multi-ethnic parties separate from what I have labelled elsewhere "consociational parties", this analysis focuses on the broader category of multi-ethnic parties rather than the much more specific case of congress parties, understood as a particular type of consociational party.[11]

In short, the polity needs to be clear about what type of parties it wants: non-ethnic parties, mono-ethnic parties or multi-ethnic parties. These party types correspond to the three functions that a party can play in the representation of societal interests: blocking, articulation or translation, and aggregation. The next step is then to connect objectives to means and to examine how electoral system design and the regulation of political parties can contribute to promoting the desired party type.

Choosing an electoral system

The first thing to clarify when designing or redesigning the representative institutions of a modern democracy, especially in a plural, conflict-prone society, should be how one sees the role of the party system as an intermediary between society and government. Should the party system block the politicization of ethnicity by restricting political competition to ideological and socio-economic issues? Should it aggregate socio-cultural divisions into broad-based multi-ethnic or explicitly non-ethnic parties? Or should it rather translate social cleavages into political fault-lines through particularistic parties? In the event that none of these pure functions is deemed desirable, should a mix of party system functions be pursued, and, if so, what should the balance be? Table 3.1 shows how the choice

Table 3.1 A brief menu of choice

Role of parties	Electoral system	Party regulation	Illustrative cases
Blocking	Only one party allowed	–	Many African countries in 1960s–1980s; Eritrea today
	–	Ban on ethnic parties	Bulgaria 1990– Albania 1992– Most contemporary African countries
Aggregation	Alternative vote	–	Fiji 1997– Papua New Guinea 2002–
	Single transferable vote	–	Northern Ireland 1998–
	Constituency pooling	(Only one party allowed)	Uganda 1970
	Electoral distribution requirement: *presidential* elections	– Spatial distribution requirement	Kenya 1992– Nigeria 1979– Indonesia 1999–
	Electoral distribution requirement: *parliamentary* elections	– Spatial distribution requirement	Comoros 1996 Nigeria 1998
	–	Spatial distribution requirement	Russia 2005–
Articulation	Reserved minority seats	–	Colombia Venezuela Kosovo 1999–
		Easier registration rules for minority parties	Romania 1990– Slovenia 1990–
	List proportional representation	–	South Africa 1994–

Source: compiled by the author.

of electoral system follows from the choice of party system function, focusing on some key cases. The strategies of blocking, aggregation and articulation are distinguished on the basis of intent and the nature of the measure (negative or positive), not on outcome, because this would pre-judge an analysis of the effectiveness of the respective choices.

Blocking

One of the avowed purposes of the one-party state in plural societies, es-pecially in Africa, was the prevention of open ethnic conflict. However, even when it did serve this purpose, the remedy normally proved worse than the illness. Blocking is a purely negative measure, which nonetheless may result in or be accompanied by aggregative outcomes, for example in the form of multi-ethnic ruling parties. Because any such aggregative ef-fect of blocking is indirect, it should be distinguished from positive and direct measures to promote aggregation discussed below.

In democratic regimes, plurality and majority elections typically achieve blocking in single-member districts in the case of a dispersed minority. Dispersed minorities will find it difficult to win seats under plu-rality elections in single-member districts. Little is known about how two-round majority elections perform in heterogeneous societies, although they would seem to disadvantage dispersed minorities, especially when they cannot agree to form electoral alliances with other parties.

Aggregation

Aggregation can be achieved through a range of electoral systems, most prominently preferential voting in the form of the alternative vote or the single transferable vote; vote distribution requirements; and constituency pooling. The alternative vote (AV), propagated by Horowitz, is a pref-erential majority voting system with strong incentives for vote pooling given the right circumstances.[12] Vote pooling occurs when political lead-ers seek support outside their own group to win elections and voters exchange votes across group boundaries. Reilly presents a favourable re-view of the pre-independence experience with AV in Papua New Guinea, especially when compared with the performance of the first-past-the-post system since independence.[13] Papua New Guinea and Fiji are two div-ided societies that at present use AV.

Constituency pooling is an alternative to AV.[14] Whereas AV works best when electoral districts are heterogeneous, constituency pooling also promotes vote pooling when districts are homogeneous. Constitu-ency pooling means that a candidate runs simultaneously in multiple con-stituencies that are geographically non-contiguous. These districts are selected in such a way that they correspond to societal cleavages. To decide the winner, the total number of votes for a candidate across all contested districts is calculated. The successful candidate thus has to pool votes from different parts of the country inhabited by different groups. Constituency pooling forces candidates to address issues important to voters across the country and in the long term should dilute the party political relevance of ethnic identity and promote the rise of national cleavages and issues, something many observers desire from an electoral system. Constituency pooling was invented by President Obote in 1970 in Uganda within the context of a one-party state. A coup prevented constituency pooling from being put into practice and this original electoral system has since been forgotten, despite its attractive features for multiparty elections.

Among proportional representation (PR) systems, only the single transferable vote (STV), practised in Northern Ireland, Malta and Australian senate elections, supports a measure of inter-ethnic vote pooling. STV is a proportional electoral system practised in small multi-member districts with typically between three and eight seats. Typical of STV is its preferential voting scheme and the transfer of votes. Under STV, a candidate needs a lower percentage of the vote to be elected than under AV. This reduces the need for candidates to reach out and broaden their appeal. STV is a proportional electoral system and provides only weak incentives for moderation. STV did not produce moderation in Northern Ireland in the 1970s but was more successful in the 1998 elections.[15] Because STV works with multi-member districts, it is somewhat easier to draw the necessary heterogeneous districts than with AV, preferably practised in single-member districts.

A less well-known electoral feature that promotes aggregation, practised in a growing number of countries, is the electoral distribution requirement. Electoral distribution requirements have been used for presidential and parliamentary elections. In Nigeria, Kenya and, more recently, Indonesia, the successful presidential candidate not only has to win an overall majority or plurality respectively, but also has to draw a minimum percentage of votes from a minimum number of regions.[16] Such a distribution requirement has also been proposed for presidential elections in Iraq.[17]

The Comoros and Nigeria have extended distribution requirements to parliamentary elections.[18] In the Comoros, a constitutional amendment restricted parliamentary representation to parties winning at least two deputies on each of the three islands that make up the republic in the legislative elections of December 1996. In the event that only one party satisfied the two-deputies-on-three-islands rule, as indeed happened, the runner-up would assume the role of opposition. The rule did not apply to independents. In Nigeria, General Abubakar reserved permanent registration to parties that garnered at least 10 per cent of the vote in 24 of 36 states in the December 1998 local government elections. After protest from newly registered parties that saw their future endangered, the electoral commission later relaxed the threshold to 5 per cent. In the end, only two parties qualified. A third, large but regional party was registered under a special clause. The extension of distribution requirements to parliamentary representation introduces a new threshold of representation, strongly encouraging aggregation. The electoral law of the Comoros was more effective than the solution of Abubakar in Nigeria because it pertained to national elections instead of local elections and was concerned with parliamentary representation rather than party registration.

Finally, the electoral law may require parties to field lists or candidates in all constituencies in order to take part in seat allocation. The effect of such a distribution requirement depends on the number of constituencies and the conditions for nomination in the form of financial deposits and signatures.

Articulation

The surest way to articulate ethnic differences is through a system of communal rolls, by which the electorate is divided along communal lines and whereby each communal group recognized as such by the electoral law elects its own representatives in separate elections. Communal rolls were typical of elections to native assemblies in pre-independence colonies. At the moment, Fiji still elects the majority of its deputies through communal rolls. This is one reason the adoption of the alternative vote there has not brought about the hoped-for effects of moderation.[19] More common today are reserved seats.[20] In Eastern Europe, several countries have reserved seats in their parliaments for minorities.[21] In Romania, the first electoral law of 1990 already stipulated the right of ethnic parties to one seat in the House of Deputies if they failed to obtain any MPs through the normal procedure.[22] Since 2000, no fewer than 18 minorities, all tiny, are guaranteed a seat in the Romanian parliament. Much more consequential for social peace was the inclusion of the party of the large Hungarian minority in the political system, which was accomplished without special provisions.[23]

In Kosovo, 10 of the 120 assembly seats were set aside for the Serb community and another 10 seats for other communities. "Great efforts were made to ensure that Kosovo's Assembly reflected the composition of society", and indeed "the effect of the electoral system is to facilitate the translation of ethnicity into representation, and, therefore, multipartism".[24] In Latin America, Colombia and Venezuela have reserved some seats for indigenous peoples.[25] The disadvantage, as with communal rolls, is that reserved seats rely on the predetermination of sociocultural groups and the identification of candidates and/or voters as belonging to designated groups. The same is true for compulsory inclusion of minorities on party lists, as in local elections in some regions in Peru and Nicaragua and in some state elections in Mexico.[26]

More commonly and less controversially, articulation is best served by list proportional representation, although it can also be achieved with plurality and majority elections in the case of geographically concentrated minorities. Still, evidence from for example Macedonia, which changed its electoral law from a double-ballot to a mixed electoral system, and then to pure PR, suggests that even concentrated minorities do better under PR.[27] PR facilitates the political organization of small dispersed social groups, which do not have to be geographically concentrated to have a chance of parliamentary representation.[28] The number of relevant parties can be reduced through the adoption of an electoral threshold. Lest the threshold inadvertently bar ethnic minority parties, they can be exempted from it, as is done for example in Poland and Serbia.

Some scholars maintain that PR combines the best of both worlds in allowing for both articulation and aggregation. For South Africa, the claim has been made that "PR can be effective in nation building efforts as it tends to encourage political parties to seek votes and membership across communities".[29] However, although South Africa's parties field multi-ethnic lists and their parliamentary caucuses are diverse, a content analysis of the electoral campaigns during the 1994 and 1999 elections revealed that those parties that appealed narrowly to their own sectors of society were more successful than those that campaigned on inclusive and consensual party platforms.[30] The two winners of the 1999 elections, the African National Congress and the Democratic Party, won because they positioned themselves as "the parties of black aspiration and protector of minority interests respectively".[31]

Regulating political parties

Until now, the regulation of political parties for ethnic conflict management has not received the same amount of attention as the design of electoral systems, although this neglect is starting to be remedied. Birnir observes that "the literature does not systematically consider the role that these institutions play in party formation and survival in new democracies".[32] As can be seen in Table 3.1, the most common means to regulate political parties is through party bans and conditions for registration.

Blocking

Most commonly, the main purpose of party regulation in conflict-prone societies is blocking. Bans on ethnic parties can be found worldwide, but are particularly common in Africa. At present, 40 sub-Saharan African countries have bans on particularistic parties.[33] Only six countries do not have the explicit capacity to ban a party because of its ethnic nature: Botswana, Comoros, Kenya, Mauritius, South Africa and Zimbabwe. If Western democracies prohibit parties, this measure is directed at extremist and undemocratic parties.[34] In Africa, there is a wide range of grounds on which parties are banned. These include, in alphabetical order: brotherhood, clan, community, ethnicity, faith/religion, gender, language, professional group, race, region, sect, section, social condition/ social or economic status, and tribe.[35] Even though this is not an exhaustive list, it serves to display the astonishingly wide range of grounds for party prohibition in Africa. The specificity of the concepts, such as sect and brotherhood, also indicates that countries do not simply adopt a blanket ban on ethnic parties but consciously address the particular forms of ethnicity that affect their societies.

Party bans can be found in a country's constitution, electoral law, law on political parties or law on voluntary associations. Often, a party ban is stated in general terms. For example, in the Democratic Republic of Congo, Article 22 of the constitution states: "The identification of a party or political group with a particular race, ethnic group, sex, religion, sect, language, or province, is prohibited." How such "identification" of a political party with one ethnic group, religion, language, etc. manifests itself and can be verified is left open.

Frequently, the ban addresses a specific aspect of party political organization. At least four "targets" of party bans can be identified: (1) party programme; (2) party symbols; (3) party organization; and (4) party membership. This list is not exclusive and more targets can be thought of, for example electoral campaigning. Party bans can be directed at any one of these aspects separately or in combination, as is evident when we look at some examples. The 1995 constitution of Tanzania, after affirming the freedom of expression and association, in Article 22(2) rules out the registration of any party and association that, "according to its constituency or policy", aims at "promoting or furthering the interests of any religious faith or group; any tribal group, place of origin, race or gender; only a particular area within any part of the United Republic". The Ghanaian constitution of 1996 (Article 55, clause 7(c)) stipulates that a party's "name, emblem, colour, motto or any other symbol has no ethnic, regional, religious or other sectional connotations or gives the appearance that its activities are confined only to a part of Ghana".

At the current count, 43 parties have been denied registration based on clauses against ethnic parties in Africa. In addition, 8 ethnic parties have been banned and 2 have been suspended. A closer look at the reasons for the denial of registration of ethnic parties produces the following picture: 5 parties were rejected as being Islamist in Kenya, Mauritania and Zambia; 1 party because it was judged to pursue regional secessionist goals (Tanzania); 2 parties for being ethnic (Burundi and Mauritania); and no fewer than 35 because they did not comply with the requirements for national presence and representation (Nigeria and Tanzania). Party bans were implemented against a regional secessionist party in Cameroon, two religious parties (Uganda and the Central African Republic) and five ethnic parties (Equatorial Guinea, Mauritania and Rwanda). Note that none of these countries is designated as "free" by Freedom House.[36]

In Rwanda, the Mouvement Démocratique Républicain (MDR), a Hutu-dominated political party, was banned in April 2003 on the basis of an alleged "divisionist" ideology. In light of Rwanda's experience with the politicization of ethnicity and the implication of the MDR's predecessor in the genocide against Tutsis and moderate Hutus, a ban on this party could be justified as emanating from the resolve to prevent history from repeating itself. This is what Peter Niesen, with reference to the post-war Italian ban on the reorganization of the Fascist party, calls "negative republicanism".[37] However, another reading is possible. It may not have been a coincidence that the party's leader, a moderate Hutu politician, was seen as the only viable opposition candidate to the incumbent president.[38]

In Eastern Europe, two countries – Bulgaria and Albania – have pursued blocking through ethnic party bans, and both desisted from enforcing them.[39] In Bulgaria, attempts to outlaw the Movement for Rights and Freedoms, a largely Turkish party, failed. Looking back, some commentators see the early contestation over communal matters as laying the foundation for a political culture of peace, competition and compromise.[40] The prohibition of the tiny Macedonian minority party Ilinden in 2000 had a different legal basis: the party was denied registration by the Constitutional Court on the grounds that it posed a threat to national integrity, not because it was ethnic in nature.[41] In Albania, the small Greek minority party Omonia transformed itself into the Unity for Human Rights Party in order to secure registration. In Albania and Bulgaria, the ban on ethnic parties can be interpreted as an attempt by the titular majority group to deny political representation to national minorities.

Aggregation

Most party bans specify only what is not desired and serve to block political organization on a particular basis. However, some party regulations go further and also include provisions that can be understood as incentives for aggregation. This is the case with distribution requirements. It was shown above that some countries have distribution requirements for presidential or legislative elections. Distribution requirements can be extended to party registration, in which case parties are compelled to have an organizational presence across the country. In this case, a party is requested to demonstrate "national presence" by operating branches across the country and having a nationwide membership, or, for first-time registration, to collect a minimum number of signatures from a given number of regions.

In Africa, 22 countries combine a ban on ethnic parties (blocking) with the requirement of national presence (aggregation). Many of these countries go on to specify spatial distribution requirements for party registration. These requirements pertain to party organization, party membership, or both. For example, in addition to a ban on religious, tribal, regional and racial parties, the Tanzanian constitution denies registration when a political association "advocates or intends to carry on its political activities in only one part of the United Republic" (Article 20(2)). The political party law of 1992 in Tanzania stipulates that, in order to be registered, a political party needs to have not fewer than 200 registered members in a minimum of 10 regions, covering both the mainland and the islands of Zanzibar and Pemba. Two parties have been denied registration for failing to demonstrate such a national presence.

In Nigeria, Article 223, clause 1(b), of the 1999 constitution requires a party constitution to "ensure that the members of the executive committee or other governing body of the political party reflect the federal character of Nigeria". To make sure the party follows its own rules, clause 2(b) adds that the members of the governing body of the party should "belong to different states not being less in number than two-thirds of all the states of the Federation and the Federal Capital Territory, Abuja". These regulations did not merely exist on paper. Between 1996 and 2000, no fewer than 32 parties were denied registration for failing to demonstrate a national presence. In the run-up to the December 2002 elections, however, several political formations successfully appealed against their denial of registration by the Independent Nigerian Electoral Commission (INEC) to the Supreme Court, arguing that some of the requirements in INEC's guidelines for registration were unconstitutional. Therefore, INEC can no longer verify the national character of a party, rendering the incentive for aggregative party organizations ineffective.[42]

Spatial distribution requirements for party registration can be imposed without a general ban on ethnic or sub-national parties. A good example is the changes to the law on political parties that were adopted in Russia in 2005. To contest regional and national elections, a party now needs to maintain regional offices and at least 500 members in no fewer than half of Russia's 89 regions.[43] In Thailand, new parties must establish a branch structure in each of four designated regions and must show they have at least 5,000 members drawn from each region within six months of being registered.[44] In Indonesia, "according to the new election law, a party should have branches in at least fourteen provinces and fourteen districts/special regions in order to qualify to contest in the election".[45] Before the 1999 election, the government established the Preparatory Committee for the Formation of the General Election Commission: "they had to travel to the provinces to check the accuracy of information provided by the political parties."[46] For the 2004 election, these rules were tightened further.[47] Although the distribution requirements for party registration in these countries in effect amount to a ban on parties with localized support (blocking), there is no formal ban on sub-national parties and the emphasis is on positive incentives for aggregation.

In Latin America, Ecuador, Mexico and Peru had restrictive spatial registration requirements at one time or another.[48] In one more country, Guatemala, there was a spatial registration requirement, but this was not restrictive enough to prevent the Mayan population, which is well represented across the territory, from forming its own parties. Such provisions in Latin America, which are different from spatial distribution requirements elsewhere, do not appear to be informed by a concern about ethnic conflict management or even a preoccupation with the politicization of ethnicity.[49] Another indication of this is the absence of a general ban on ethnic parties. Rather, as in Thailand, spatial distribution requirements seem primarily intended as a means to limit fragmentation of the party system. The effect may nonetheless be that segments of the population are excluded from direct political representation, as Birnir notes.[50] In contrast, in Indonesia and Nigeria the distribution requirement for party registration corresponded with distribution requirements in presidential elections, a good example of what Reynolds calls "institutional alignment" or institutions that work in concert.[51]

Articulation

Articulation is the default option in plural societies. Without intervention, the expectation is that communal parties will emerge. The advocates of articulation as the main function of parties and the party system are normally advocates of proportional representation. They may even recommend non-proportional methods to secure the representation of minority parties, such as communal rolls and reserved seats.[52] Party regulation can promote articulation by exempting minority parties from certain registration requirements or by providing them with more generous state subventions. In Slovenia and Romania, for example, minority parties need fewer signatures to register.[53]

Conclusion

Reilly has observed that, "despite the impressive body of scholarship on constitutional engineering that has appeared over the past decade, there has been surprisingly little attention given to the ways in which multi-ethnic parties can be developed and sustained".[54] This chapter has sought to provide a partial remedy by introducing a novel framework for analysing electoral engineering and by extending this framework to the classification and analysis of party regulations. This framework centres on the three functions of parties in heterogeneous societies: blocking, aggregation and articulation.

The first task of constitutional engineers in conflict-prone societies is to determine the preferred function of parties and the party system as an intermediary between society and politics. The choice is between – or a combination of – articulation, aggregation and blocking. For each function, a range of electoral systems is available whose effectiveness depends crucially on context.[55] However, more can be done than choosing an electoral system. The direct regulation of political parties can reinforce the working of the electoral system. The constitutionalization of political parties and the introduction of laws on political parties around the world indicate that policy makers are well aware of the importance of regulating political parties.[56] Ideally, electoral system design and party regulation reinforce each other but, as the empty cells in Table 3.1 indicate, such combinations are rare.

The argument for blocking and non-ethnic parties is based on the idea that particularistic parties threaten social peace, national integrity and political stability. The prevalence of bans on particularistic parties in Africa and their adoption in several new democracies in Eastern Europe indicate that such fears are widespread and not limited to a particular region. However, even in a country with a history of conflictual ethnic party politics, a ban on ethnic parties is not the only or even the best remedy. First, many countries with such bans ultimately desist from enforcing them. Secondly, party bans may be effective only in the short term. In Turkey, the banning in the 1990s of the Islamist Refah party as a threat to the secular character of the state could not prevent its successor party from becoming the majority party and forming the government.[57] Thirdly, the choice of blocking as a party system function is a negative one that will not by itself bring about the desired national integration.

Fourthly, there is evidence that ethnic party bans have been used selectively against national minorities and opposition forces. Finally, bans on particularistic parties limit freedom of expression and deny ethnicity a legitimate place in politics. In sum, ethnic party bans are of questionable democratic legitimacy and of unproven empirical efficacy.

The argument for aggregation and multi-ethnic parties is at the heart of what has been termed "centripetalism".[58] The idea is that moderation is fostered by cross-cutting cleavages and, if these do not exist or are limited in society, then electoral institutions have to foster them deliberately at the political level. Structural functionalism has already recognized that the party system is the political subsystem most suited to perform the aggregative function.[59] If the structure of conflict-prone or post-conflict societies privileges ethnicity as a cleavage for party formation, the challenge may be formulated as promoting multi-ethnic parties over parties that represent a single ethnic group. Most effectively, this is done through a combination of aggregative incentives in the electoral law and the regulation of political parties. This is especially clear in the case of spatial distribution requirements that promote aggregation. The Nigerian constitution of 1998, whatever its shortcomings, stands out as the most comprehensive package to promote aggregative parties. It combined geographical distribution requirements for presidential and parliamentary elections and for party registration. The electoral law and the regulation of parties mutually reinforced the aggregative character of the measures and the result was a three-party system in which the two main parties were truly national in appeal and support.

The argument for articulation and mono-ethnic parties has traditionally been made most forcefully by proponents of PR and consociationalism.[60] In the twenty-first century, PR is the favourite electoral system of scholars and policy makers. An expert survey of the preferences of electoral system scholars found that the top three electoral systems were varieties of proportionality.[61] At the same time, "party-list PR has become the de facto norm of UN parliamentary elections".[62] Nonetheless, there are reasons to question the desirability of PR for conflict-prone societies.

In Eastern Europe, a recent study found that "proportionality does not necessarily lead to higher levels of representation of minority ethnic parties.... [and] higher levels of representation in parliament do not automatically lead to a moderation of ethnic conflict".[63] Moreover, PR facilitates the electoral success of mono-ethnic parties. This is, indeed, a common complaint about the working of PR in Bosnia-Herzegovina,[64] hailed as an electoral law embodying "the most progressive international thinking in electoral design".[65] Claims about the aggregative incentives of list PR find only very weak empirical support. In some countries, PR is supplemented by reserved seats for designated minorities to strengthen the articulation function of the electoral system. Reserved minority seats seem to have a largely symbolic value. Sizeable minorities do not need them and the tiny minorities that profit from them are often politically insignificant anyway.

Most importantly, the experience in post-conflict societies seems to indicate that, in line with consociational theory, an ethnically representative party system needs to be accompanied by extensive power-sharing arrangements. Therefore, a choice of articulation often implies buying into the whole consociational package of a grand coalition, mutual veto and segmental autonomy.[66]

If the scholarship on electoral system design has shown one thing, it is that "plainly there is no 'one-size-fits-all' form of constitutional therapy. Particular circumstances and sound case-by-case judgments will always matter."[67] This lesson is well known to political leaders in new democracies or even outgoing dictators who were faced with the challenge of designing new political institutions.[68] The most innovative electoral designs have come from political practitioners, whereas political scientists have usually promoted existing formulas, adapting them to local circumstances. Exceptions are proposals for cross-voting, whereby members of one ethnic community vote for the representatives of the other, as in Cyprus,[69] and constituency pooling for Nigeria.[70] In the words of Dummett, scholars for the most part have behaved like supermarket customers rather than engineers.[71] Characteristically, the recent discovery by academics of the potential of party regulation or ethnic conflict management follows and documents rather than anticipates and guides the choices for policy makers in new democracies. This chapter on electoral system design and party regulation in conflict-prone societies has provided a framework that can aid in the analysis of comparative strategies of ethnic conflict management and help to clarify the goals and means available to political decision makers.

Notes

1. Donald Horowitz, *A Democratic South Africa? Constitutional Engineering in a Divided Society* (Berkeley, CA: University of California Press, 1991); Andrew Reynolds and Ben Reilly, *The International IDEA Handbook of Electoral System Design* (Stockholm: Institute for Democracy and Electoral Assistance, 1997); Ben Reilly and Andrew Reynolds, *Electoral Systems and Conflict in Divided Societies* (Washington DC: National Academy Press, 1999); Benjamin Reilly, *Democracy in Divided Societies: Electoral Engineering for Conflict Management* (Cambridge: Cambridge University Press, 2001);

Arend Lijphart, "Constitutional Design for Divided Societies", *Journal of Democracy*, 15(2), 2004: 96–109; Pippa Norris, *Electoral Engineering: Voting Rules and Political Behavior* (Cambridge: Cambridge University Press, 2004); Florian Bieber and Stefan Wolff, "Introduction: Elections in Divided Societies", *Ethnopolitics*, 4(4), 2005: 359–363; Renske Doorenspleet, "Electoral Systems and Good Governance in Divided Societies", *Ethnopolitics*, 4(4), 2005: 365–380.

2. This chapter has benefited greatly from the comments received at authors' meetings in The Hague, October 2006, and in Sydney, June 2007, and I wish to express sincere thanks to all participants.

3. Stefano Bartolini and Peter Mair, "Challenges to Contemporary Parties", in Larry Diamond and Richard Gunther (eds), *Political Parties and Democracy* (Baltimore, MD: Johns Hopkins University Press, 2001), p. 332, emphasis in original.

4. Giovanni Sartori, *Parties and Party Systems: A Framework for Analysis* (Cambridge: Cambridge University Press, 1976), p. ix.

5. Richard Gunther and Larry Diamond, "Types and Functions of Parties", in Larry Diamond and Richard Gunther (eds), *Political Parties and Democracy* (Baltimore, MD: Johns Hopkins University Press, 2001), pp. 3–39.

6. Here, the term "ethnic" is used in the broad sense of referring to any socio-cultural characteristic. See Robert Jackson, "Ethnicity", in Giovanni Sartori (ed.), *Social Science Concepts: A Systematic Analysis* (Beverly Hills, CA: Sage, 1984), pp. 205–233.

7. Gunther and Diamond, "Types and Functions of Parties", p. 23.

8. Ibid., p. 24.

9. Gabriel Almond and James Coleman, *The Politics of the Developing Areas* (Princeton, NJ: Princeton University Press, 1960), p. 44.

10. Gunther and Diamond, "Types and Functions of Parties", pp. 24–25.

11. The consociational party combines the internal representation of socio-cultural groups with the internal accommodation of these differences through the classic consociational features of a grand coalition, proportionality, segmental autonomy and a mutual veto. Matthijs Bogaards, "Power Sharing in South Africa: The African National Congress as a Consociational Party?", in Sid Noel (ed.), *From Power Sharing to Democracy: Post-Conflict Institutions in Ethnically Divided Societies* (Toronto: McGill-Queens University Press, 2005), pp. 164–184.

12. Horowitz, *A Democratic South Africa?*

13. Reilly, *Democracy in Divided Societies*, p. 94.

14. Matthijs Bogaards, "Electoral Choices for Divided Societies: Multi-Ethnic Parties and Constituency Pooling in Africa", *Commonwealth & Comparative Politics*, 41(3), 2003: 59–80.

15. Reilly, *Democracy in Divided Societies*.

16. Leo Suryadinata, *Elections and Politics in Indonesia* (Singapore: Institute of Southeast Asian Studies, 2002).

17. Andreas Wimmer, "Democracy and Ethno-Religious Conflict in Iraq", *Survival*, 45(4), 2003: 122.

18. Matthijs Bogaards, "Electoral Systems, Party Systems, and Ethnic Conflict Management in Africa", in Matthias Basedau, Gero Erdmann and Andreas Mehler (eds), *Votes, Money and Violence: Political Parties and Elections in Africa* (Uppsala: Nordiska Afrikainstitutet, 2007), pp. 168–193.

19. This feature is largely ignored in Fraenkel and Grofman's critical analysis of the failure of AV in Fiji. Jon Fraenkel and Bernard Grofman, "Does the Alternative Vote Foster Modernization in Ethnically Divided Societies?", *Comparative Political Studies*, 39(5), 2006: 623–651.

20. In several African states, including Zimbabwe and Kenya, additional non-elected members of parliament appointed by the president are supposed to represent specific interests.
21. See Chapter 5 by Florian Bieber in this volume.
22. Ciprian-Calin Alionescu, "Parliamentary Representation of Minorities in Romania", *Southeast European Politics*, 5(1), 2004: 60–75.
23. Mihaela Mihailescu, "Dampening the Powder Keg: Understanding Interethnic Cooperation in Post-Communist Romania (1990–96)", *Nationalism and Ethnic Politics*, 11, 2005: 25–59.
24. Andrew J. Taylor, "Electoral Systems and the Promotion of 'Consociationalism' in a Multi-Ethnic Society: The Kosovo Assembly Elections of November 2001", *Electoral Studies*, 24(3), 2005: 455–456.
25. Donna L. Van Cott, "Building Inclusive Democracies: Indigenous Peoples and Ethnic Minorities in Latin America", *Democratization*, 12(5), 2005: 820–837.
26. See Chapter 6 by Matthias Catón and Fernando Tuesta Soldevilla in this volume.
27. Eben Friedman, "Electoral System Design and Minority Representation in Slovakia and Macedonia", *Ethnopolitics*, 4(4), 2005: 381–396.
28. Moreover, PR offers far fewer possibilities for gerrymandering, which in the case of Macedonia seems to have benefited the ethnic majority. See Chapter 5 by Florian Bieber in this volume.
29. Denis Kadima, "Choosing an Electoral System: Alternatives for the Post-War Democratic Republic of Congo", *Journal of African Elections*, 2(1), 2003, p. 43.
30. Andrew Reynolds, "South Africa: Proportional Representation in the Puzzle to Stabilize Democracy", in Josep Colomer (ed.), *Handbook of Electoral System Choice* (Basingstoke: Palgrave Macmillan, 2004).
31. Gavin Davis, "Proportional Representation and Racial Campaigning in South Africa", *Nationalism and Ethnic Politics*, 10(2), 2004, p. 316.
32. Jóhanna K. Birnir, "Stabilizing Party Systems and Excluding Segments of Society? The Effects of Formation Costs on New Party Foundation in Latin America", *Studies in Comparative International Development*, 39(3), 2004, p. 4.
33. The African examples are drawn from a study on "Managing Ethnic Conflict through Institutional Engineering: Ethnic Party Bans in Africa". This project, financed by the Fritz Thyssen Foundation, is a collaboration between Matthias Basedau (GIGA Institute of African Affairs, Hamburg), Christoph Hartmann (University Essen-Duisburg), Peter Niesen (Technical University Darmstadt) and myself. I am indebted to Anika Becher for the collection of much of the data in this section.
34. Gregory H. Fox and Georg Nolte, "Intolerant Democracies", in Gregory H. Fox and Brad R. Roth (eds), *Democratic Governance and International Law* (Cambridge: Cambridge University Press, 2000), pp. 389–435.
35. Whether and how the constitutionalization of the Islamic character of the state in the new constitutions of Afghanistan and Iraq will affect party politics and amount to a ban on secular parties is unclear.
36. See ⟨http://www.freedomhouse.org/⟩ (accessed 27 March 2008).
37. Peter Niesen, "Anti-Extremism, Negative Republicanism, Civic Society: Three Paradigms for Banning Political Parties", in Shlomo Avineri and Zeev Sternhell (eds), *Europe's Century of Discontent: The Legacies of Fascism, Nazism and Communism* (Jerusalem: Hebrew University Press, 2003), pp. 249–286.
38. David E. Kiwuwa, "Democratization and Ethnic Politics: Rwanda's Electoral Legacy", *Ethnopolitics*, 4(4), 2005: 447–464.
39. Matthijs Bogaards, "Electoral Systems and the Management of Ethnic Conflict in the Balkans", in Alina Mungiu-Pippidi and Ivan Krastev (eds), *Nationalism after Communism: Lessons Learned* (Budapest: CEU Press, 2004), pp. 247–268.

40. M. S. Fish and Matthew Kroenig, "Diversity, Conflict and Democracy: Some Evidence from Eurasia and East Europe", *Democratization*, 13(5), 2006, p. 839.
41. Klaus Schrameyer, "Ilinden: Das Verbot der Partei der Makedonier in Bulgarien durch das Bulgarische Verfassungsgericht", *Südosteuropa*, 49(5–6), 2000: 283–290.
42. Bogaards, "Electoral Systems, Party Systems, and Ethnic Conflict Management in Africa".
43. Cameron Ross, "Federalism and Electoral Authoritarianism under Putin", *Demokratizatsiya*, 13(3), 2005: 361–362.
44. Benjamin Reilly, *Democracy and Diversity: Political Engineering in the Asia-Pacific* (Oxford: Oxford University Press, 2006).
45. Suryadinata, *Elections and Politics in Indonesia*, p. 91.
46. Ibid.
47. See Chapter 4 by Allen Hicken in this volume.
48. Birnir, "Stabilizing Party Systems and Excluding Segments of Society?".
49. Ibid., p. 21.
50. Ibid.
51. Andrew Reynolds, "Building Democracy after Conflict: Constitutional Medicine", *Journal of Democracy*, 16(1), 2005, p. 60.
52. Arend Lijphart, "Proportionality by Non-PR Methods: Ethnic Representation in Belgium, Cyprus, Lebanon, New Zealand, West Germany, and Zimbabwe", in Bernard Grofman and Arend Lijphart (eds), *Electoral Laws and Their Political Consequences* (New York: Agathon Press, 1986), pp. 113–123.
53. See Chapter 7 by Jóhanna Birnir in this volume. Both countries have reserved seats for designated minorities in parliament, so that party regulation and electoral system design are linked.
54. Benjamin Reilly, "Political Engineering and Party Politics in Conflict-Prone Societies", *Democratization*, 13(5), 2006: 811–812.
55. See the discussion of group size and geographical concentration in Chapter 7 in this volume.
56. See Chapter 2 by Ingrid van Biezen in this volume.
57. Dicle Kogacioglu, "Progress, Unity, and Democracy: Dissolving Political Parties in Turkey", *Law & Society Review*, 38(3), 2004: 433–461.
58. Reilly, *Democracy in Divided Societies*.
59. Almond and Coleman, *The Politics of the Developing Areas*, p. 40.
60. Arend Lijphart, *Democracy in Plural Societies: A Comparative Exploration* (New Haven, CT: Yale University Press, 1977).
61. Shaun Bowler and David M. Farrell, "We Know Which One We Prefer but We Don't Really Know Why: The Curious Case of Mixed Member Electoral Systems", *British Journal of Politics and International Relations*, 8(3), 2006, p. 446.
62. Benjamin Reilly, "Post-Conflict Elections: Constraints and Dangers", *International Peacekeeping*, 9(2), 2002, p. 130.
63. Sonia Alonso and Rubén Ruiz-Rufino, "Political Representation and Ethnic Conflict in New Democracies", *European Journal of Political Research*, 46, 2007, p. 238.
64. See, for example, Florian Bieber, "The Challenge of Democracy in Divided Societies: Lessons from Bosnia – Challenges for Kosovo", in Dzemal Sokolovic and Florian Bieber (eds), *Reconstructing Multiethnic Societies: The Case of Bosnia-Herzegovina* (Aldershot: Ashgate, 2001), pp. 109–121.
65. Carrie Manning and Miljenko Antic, "The Limits of Electoral Engineering", *Journal of Democracy*, 14(3), 2003, p. 51.
66. Bogaards, "Electoral Systems and the Management of Ethnic Conflict in the Balkans".
67. Reynolds, "Building Democracy after Conflict", p. 66.

68. Of course, these choices often are motivated more by self-interest than anything else, as was the case in Afghanistan. Andrew Reynolds, "The Curious Case of Afghanistan", *Journal of Democracy*, 17(2), 2006: 104–117.

69. Neophytos Loizides and Eser Keskiner, "The Aftermath of the Annan Plan Referendums: Cross-voting Moderation for Cyprus", *Southeast European Politics*, 5(2–3), 2004: 158–171.

70. Bogaards, "Electoral Choices for Divided Societies".

71. Michael Dummett, "Tailoring Democracy", *Transition*, 53, 1991: 143–146.

Part II

Regional experiences

4

Political engineering and party regulation in Southeast Asia

Allen Hicken

Introduction

Southeast Asia has been home to several dramatic transitions to democracy. In the Philippines, the EDSA (or "People Power") revolution of 1986 brought down the government of Ferdinand Marcos and restored democracy after 14 years of dictatorship. More than a decade before EDSA, a similar show of mass discontent with authoritarian government brought down Thailand's military regime. Although this particular democratic experiment was short-lived – military forces seized power again in 1976 – the events of October 1973 signalled the end of long-lived military governments in Thailand. Elections returned in 1979, beginning a more gradual transition to democracy over the next two-and-a-half decades.[1] In neighbouring Cambodia, that country's warring factions finally agreed to a UN-brokered cease-fire and peace plan in October 1991. Despite threats from the still powerful Khmer Rouge, 90 per cent of eligible voters turned out to cast their vote in UN-organized elections in 1993, handing a surprise victory to the royalist FUNCINPEC party and an electoral defeat to the Cambodian People's Party, which had been in power in Cambodia since the fall of the Khmer Rouge. Finally, after decades in power, Suharto was forced to step down as the President of Indonesia in 1998 in the wake of massive protests on the streets of Jakarta and demands from protestors, politicians and parties that he step aside and allow a democratic political framework to be put in place.

Political parties in conflict-prone societies: Regulation, engineering and democratic development, Reilly and Nordlund (eds),
United Nations University Press, 2008, ISBN 978-92-808-1157-5

These dramatic events demonstrated a domestic demand for democratic institutions and procedures that surprised some long-time observers of Thailand, Indonesia, Cambodia and the Philippines. And yet, although opinion polls consistently show that most citizens of these countries support the ideal of democracy, there is also a sense that democratic government has often fallen short of hopes and expectations. One consistent theme in criticisms of the way democracy operates in these countries is the perceived shortcomings of political parties and the party system. Ironically, in the eyes of many people, political parties – the hallmark of modern democratic government – have become the biggest obstacles to democratic consolidation and effective governance.[2]

My purpose in this chapter is to survey the party systems in Southeast Asia, focusing on the ways in which various engineering and regulation strategies have shaped (or failed to shape) the development and evolution of the party system in each country. If we were searching for a laboratory in which to study party regulation and party development we would be hard pressed to find a region as suitable as Southeast Asia. First, all of the states in Southeast Asia could comfortably be classified as divided societies with a history of conflict. In the Philippines and Thailand, conflict has taken the form of unrest and insurgency in these countries' southern regions, where ethnic, religious and language differences are a source of tension with the centre. Cambodia is still recovering from three decades of civil war. Indonesia and Malaysia are societies divided by ethnic, religious, language and regional cleavages that at times have given rise to violence. Even comparatively stable Singapore was home to ethnic riots and civil unrest in the not too distant past. Table 4.1 displays information on the ethnic and religious diversity for each of the seven Southeast Asian states discussed in this chapter.

The region also provides interesting variation in terms of its political institutions, party systems and the nature of regulation and reform efforts. At the macro level, we see presidential democracies (Indonesia and the Philippines), parliamentary systems (Thailand, Cambodia, Malaysia, Singapore) and hybrid regimes (East Timor). In terms of party systems, the region contains dominant-party semi-democracies (Singapore, Malaysia and Cambodia), multi-party democracies (the Philippines, Indonesia and, until recently, Thailand) and single-party states (Vietnam). We can also observe variation in the degree to which ethnic cleavages have given rise to ethnically based political parties. Such parties are uncommon in most of the region, but Malaysia has had ethnically based parties since before its independence. Finally, countries in the region have adopted a variety of reforms aimed at engineering certain outcomes in the party system, which have met with varying degrees of success.

Table 4.1 Ethnic and religious diversity

Ethnic diversity

	Majority	Largest minority	Second-largest minority	Other groups	Ethnic fractionalization[a]
Cambodia	Khmer 90.0%	Vietnamese 5.0%	Chinese 1.0%	n.a.	.186
East Timor	n.a.	n.a.	n.a.	n.a.	n.a.
Indonesia	Javanese 40.6%	Sundanese 15.0%	Madurese 3.3%	Chinese 3.0–4.0%	.766
Malaysia	Malay 50.4%	Chinese 23.7%	Indigenous 11.0%	Indian 7.1%	.596
Philippines	Tagalog 28.1%	Cebuano 13.1%	Bisaya 7.6%	Hiligaynon Ilonggo 7.5% Bikol 6.0% Waray 3.4%	.161
Singapore	Chinese 76.8%	Malay 13.9%	Indian 7.9%		.388
Thailand	Thai 75.0%	Chinese 14.0%	Malay 2.0%	Khmer 2.0%	.431

Religious diversity

	Majority	Largest minority	Second-largest minority	Other groups
Cambodia	Buddhist 95.0%	Muslim 4.0%	Protestant 1.0%	
East Timor	Roman Catholic 98.0%	Muslim 1.0%		
Indonesia	Muslim 86.1%	Christian 8.7%	Hindu 18.0%	Buddhist 1.0%
Malaysia	Muslim 60.4%	Buddhist 19.2%	Christian 9.1%	Hindu 6.3%
Philippines	Christian 92.6%	Muslim 5.1%		
Singapore	Buddhist 42.5%	Muslim 14.9%	Christian 14.6%	Taoist 8.5%
Thailand	Buddhist 94.6%	Muslim 4.6%	Christian 0.7%	Hindu 4.0%

Sources: CIA World Factbook at ⟨https://www.cia.gov/library/publications/the-world-factbook/⟩ (accessed 31 March 2008); Joel Selway, "Turning Malays into Thai-Men: Nationalism, Ethnicity and Economic Inequality in Thailand", *Southeast Research*, forthcoming.
Note:
[a] Ethnic fractionalization, as the name suggests, measures the degree of ethnic fractionalization in a given country on a scale of 0–1, with higher numbers representing greater fractionalization. The data come from J. D. Fearon, "Ethnic and Cultural Diversity by Country", *Journal of Economic Growth*, 8, 2003: 195–222.

Table 4.2 Democracy in Southeast Asia

	Polity II score 2003 (Scale: −10 to 10)	Freedom House 2005 (Scale: 7 to 1)	
Thailand	9	2	Free
Philippines	8	2	Free
Indonesia	6	3	Partly free
East Timor	6	3	Partly free
Malaysia	3	4	Partly free
Cambodia	2	6	Not free
Singapore	−2	5	Partly free
Brunei	n.a.	6	Not free
Laos	−7	7	Not free
Vietnam	−7	7	Not free
Burma	−7	7	Not free

Sources: Freedom House, *Freedom in the World*, 2005, ⟨http://www.freedomhouse.org/template.cfm?page=363&year=2006⟩ (accessed 31 March 2008); Keith Jaggers and Ted Robert Gurr, *POLITY IV: Regime Change and Political Authority, 1800–2003*, 2006, available at ⟨http://www.cidcm.umd.edu/inscr/polity/⟩.
Note: The Polity scale runs from −10 to 10, with higher scores representing higher levels of democracy. The Freedom House score runs from 1 to 7, with lower scores representing a higher degree of political rights.

I focus on political parties and the party system in 7 of Southeast Asia's 11 states. These include countries that have experienced relatively free and fair elections (the Philippines, East Timor, Indonesia since Suharto, and Thailand) as well as those countries where opposition parties are allowed to compete and win seats in regular elections but the electoral playing field is tilted heavily against the opposition (Singapore, Malaysia and Cambodia).[3] I do not include those polities where elections are not regularly held, or where autonomous opposition parties are banned outright (Vietnam, Burma, Brunei, Laos). Table 4.2 lists recent Polity and Freedom House scores for all 11 Southeast Asian states for comparative purposes.

The rest of the chapter proceeds as follows. I first review the role that parties and party systems play in modern democracies, highlighting the crucial part political parties play in conflict-prone developing democracies. I briefly discuss the two major institutional design approaches relative to managing conflict in divided societies – the articulation approach (which underlies the consociational model) and the aggregation approach (which is the foundation of the centripetal model). I argue that for the most part Southeast Asian states have favoured aggregative/centripetal institutions and political parties – with a few notable exceptions. In the third section, I discuss other dimensions of the party system that are germane to democratic stability in divided democracies but have been neglected in the debate between articulation and aggregation. Specifically, I focus on the degree to which the party system is "institutionalized". I define party system institutionalization, discuss the degree to which Southeast Asia's party systems are institutionalized and analyse the extent to which the goal of party system institutionalization is in harmony (or conflict) with the goals of the articulation and aggregation models. The fourth section of the chapter asks whether we can realistically expect parties in new democracies to develop gradually and organically from the ground up. Arguing that we cannot, I discuss ways in which institutional designers in Southeast Asia have attempted to "engineer" certain types of parties and party systems through manipulation of constitutions, electoral rules and party regulation. In the final section I briefly discuss examples of the unintended consequences of such engineering efforts.

Parties and party systems

Political parties play vital roles in modern democracies as aggregators, mediators and solutions to collective action problems. During elections, political parties provide a means of aggregating, organizing and coordinating voters, candidates and donors. Within the legislature, parties are vehicles for solving collective action problems and coordinating the behaviour of legislative and executive actors. Political parties also provide a means for balancing local concerns with national interests and long-term priorities with short-term political demands.

Political parties play an especially important role in the new and developing democracies. Indeed, the durability and success of democratic experiments often hinge on the health and strength of the democratic party system.[4] Within developing democracies, parties are often the most proximate and potent symbols of democracy to citizens and can either help build support for democratic norms and institutions or poison public attitudes towards the effectiveness and legitimacy of elected governments. Ultimately the distrust of political parties can undermine support for democracy. In addition, in the absence of strong parties and an effective party system there may be greater opportunities for intervention by military cliques or charismatic figures. Finally, political parties are crucial tools for managing the conflict and upheaval that are an unavoidable part of democratic transition and economic development. The need for an effective party system is especially acute in divided societies with a history of conflict.

What kinds of party and what kinds of party system produce the best chance of political stability, democratic consolidation and good governance, particularly in conflict-prone societies? Briefly, there are two contending schools of thought that resonate with the broader debate between advocates of proportional institutions and advocates of majoritarian institutions (see also Chapter 3 by Bogaards in this volume).[5] The first, which I call the articulation approach, argues that democracy works best when societal cleavages are acknowledged as fundamental to political life in a given polity. Institutions should be created that allow for the representation or articulation of all major interests in society. (This lies at the core of the model championed by Lijphart, dubbed the consociational or power-sharing approach.[6]) To maximize articulation, states should adopt a proportional representation electoral system and allow for (or encourage) the creation of ethnically based political parties. Cooperation and accommodation then take place between party elites within the government.[7]

A second approach contends that constructing a political system on a foundation of contentious societal cleavages is inherently unstable. Instead, the aggregative approach advocates moving the focus of politics away from societal cleavages by creating institutions that encourage moderation, cross-cleavage accommodation and cooperation. This is the foundation of the centripetal model.[8] Two pillars of this approach are an electoral system that gives candidates and voters incentives to look beyond the confines of their particular groups,[9] and a party system with broad-based parties or party coalitions that transcend cleavage boundaries.

The vast majority of Southeast Asian states have opted for institutions and regulations consistent with aggregative goals. The major exception is Malaysia between independence and 1969, which is cited by Lijphart as a model of consociational democracy.[10] Although the country's majoritarian electoral system regularly produced a legislative majority for the ethnically based United Malays National Organization (UMNO), UMNO did not govern alone. Instead, it entered into a tri-party alliance with parties representing Malaysia's two other largest ethnic groups, the Malayan Chinese Association (MCA) and the Malayan Indian Congress (MIC). The three members of the "Alliance" ran coordinated campaigns during elections and each took a share of cabinet seats in-between elections. At the same time, UMNO was clearly the first among equals in the Alliance. The consociational elements of Malaysia's political system were dealt a major blow when a sharp dip in the Alliance's vote share in the 1969 elections triggered clashes between Malays and Chinese throughout Malaysia. In the wake of the violence, a state of emergency was declared and parliamentary government was suspended. When elected government was finally restored in 1971, Barisan Nasional (BN) had replaced the Alliance. Although BN contained the same three core ethnic parties (UMNO, MCA, MIC) along with a number of smaller partiers, the veneer of power-sharing was largely gone. In this new alliance, UMNO was clearly dominant and has remained so ever since.

The pre-1969 Malaysia case is the closest we get to consociationalism in the region, though even this case is not without controversy.[11] However, other states in the region have used articulating institutions – namely, proportional representation (see Table 4.3). Cambodia, Indonesia and the new East Timor system each rely on pure proportional representation (PR) to elect their legislatures. A handful of other states combine proportional and majoritarian rules in so-called mixed-member systems (Thailand, the Philippines and the first East Timorese election).[12]

Yet, even in the states that use proportional electoral rules, there have been concerted efforts to limit the number of parties and reduce the partisan salience of social cleavages – consistent with an aggregative strategy. For example, Indonesia in effect bans regional or local parties not just from national elections but from regional and local elections as well (more about this below). Other recent changes to Indonesian electoral rules have made it more difficult for smaller parties to compete.[13] Similarly, the move from a "largest remainder" nationwide system to a "highest average" provincially based system in Cambodia harms the electoral chances of Cambodia's smaller parties.[14] The new East Timorese system also uses the "highest average" formula and includes an electoral threshold of 3 per cent specifically designed to "prevent an excessive party pulverization".[15]

The desire to reduce political fragmentation, promote government stability and reduce the salience of ethnic ties is also evident in the type of mixed-member systems Southeast Asian reformers have adopted.[16] Mixed-member systems consist of two tiers. The nominal tier is typically elected from single-member districts using the plurality rule, while the list tier is elected from national (or regional) party lists using proportional representation. The higher the percentage of seats devoted to the PR list tier, the more proportional the outcome – e.g. the better the correspondence between votes casts and seats won. At the same time, large list tiers will also tend to inflate the number of parties and increase the chances that no single party will capture a majority. By contrast, a smaller list tier will tend to reduce the number of parties winning seats but at the cost of greater disproportionality – i.e. larger parties will benefit at the expense of smaller parties.

Another thing to consider is whether the two tiers are linked. In mixed-member majoritarian systems, the distribution of seats in each tier occurs independently. In other words, the number of seats a party gets in each tier is not dependent on what happens in the other tier. Mixed-member majoritarian systems favour larger parties. Those parties that can mount an effective national campaign receive an electoral bonus, but this comes at the cost of greater disproportionality and fewer seats for smaller parties. In mixed-member proportional systems, a party's share of list tier votes is used to determine its total number of seats in the legislature. In effect, the list tier seats are used to correct for any disproportionality produced in the nominal tier elections. This has beneficial effects for representation but at the cost of greater political fragmentation. Faced with these trade-offs, Thailand and the Philippines opted for reducing political fragmentation by keeping the list tier relatively small and keeping the allocation of seats in each tier separate.[17] (East Timor also used a mixed-member majoritarian system for its first election, but reserved a large number of seats for the list tier.)

Table 4.3 displays summary information about the electoral and party systems for seven democracies and semi-democracies in Southeast Asia. As discussed above, most states in Southeast Asia have leaned toward aggregative principles of electoral design and party regulation. Looking first at electoral systems, only Cambodia, Indonesia and now East Timor use pure PR; the rest of the region employs either majoritarian systems or mixed-member majoritarian systems. This is reflected in a modest effective number of parties (ENP) in most countries, with most having two to three parties, and governments in which the largest party controls close to a majority of the seats.[18] The exceptions are 2007 East Timor, Indonesia (which combines multiple cleavages with a very permissive electoral system), and pre-2001 Thailand, where the incentives for national party formation were very weak.[19] In these three countries the ENP is quite high and the largest parties fail to secure even one-third of the legislative seats. On the other hand, disproportionality in Indonesia, 2007 East Timor and pre-reform Thailand is the lowest in the region.[20] The most disproportional system is Singapore's, which regularly turns electoral majorities into legislative supermajorities for the People's Action Party (PAP). Finally, note the sharp reduction in the number of parties and the increase in disproportionality and the number of seats for the largest party in the wake of the Thai reforms. This is consistent with Reilly's argument that, when states in Asia have attempted to engineer their party system, it has almost without exception been in the direction of less partisan fragmentation and larger parties.[21]

Party system institutionalization

While the debate about articulative versus aggregative institutions continues in one part of the literature, another set of scholars has focused on another issue germane to new democracies: the degree of party institutionalization. The recent focus on institutionalization by certain scholars comes out of observations about the differences between the party systems that characterized first- and second-wave democracies and those

Table 4.3 Aggregative tendencies in Southeast Asia

	No. of elections	Electoral system[a]	% of PR seats	Effective number of parties	Dispropor- tionality	% of seats for largest party (last election)
Cambodia 1993	1	Closed-list PR (LR)	100	2.8	5.4	48.3
Cambodia 1998–	2	Closed-list PR (HA)	100	3.2	7.3	59.3
East Timor (2001)	1	MMM	~85	2.8	8.3	73.3
East Timor (2007)	1	Closed-list PR (HA)	100	5.4	3.4	32.3
Indonesia 1999	1	Closed-list PR (LR)	100	5.1	1.9	32.9
Indonesia 2004	1	Open-list PR (LR)	100	8.3	1.5	23.3
Malaysia 1959–2004[b]	11	Plurality with SMD	0	2.6	15.8	90.4
Philippines 1946–1969	7	Plurality with SMD	0	2.3	9.0	80.0
Philippines 1992–1998	3	MMM	~20	3.6	10.4	50.5
Singapore 1976–2006	9	Party block vote/SMD[c]	0	1.2	20.8	97.6
Thailand 1986–1996	5	Block vote	0	7.2	2.7	31.8
Thailand 2001–2005	2	MMM	20	3.1	11.1	75.4

Sources: Author's calculations.
Notes:
[a] LR = largest remainder method; HA = highest average method; MMM = mixed-member majoritarian system; SMD = single-member districts.
[b] BN is counted as a single party.
[c] Until 1988 Singapore used only SMDs.

that have emerged during the third wave of democratization. Sartori was one of the first to draw this distinction, categorizing countries as having either "consolidated" party systems or no party "system" whatsoever.[22] Other authors have built on this work and proposed various definitions of party system institutionalization. I focus here on two key components of party system institutionalization, as formulated by Mainwaring and Scully.[23] These two components are common to many other authors' definition of institutionalization.[24]

1. *The pattern of party competition*: more institutionalized party systems exhibit stability in the patterns of party competition.

2. *Party–society links*: more institutionalized party systems have parties with strong roots in society and voters with strong attachments to parties. "Most voters identify with a party and vote for it most of the time, and some interest associations are closely linked to parties."[25]

Taken together, these two dimensions help us to assess where along the continuum of institutionalization a particular party system may fall. More specifically, fluid party systems exhibit instability in patterns of party competition. New political parties regularly enter the system, and existing parties exit. There is also a high degree of electoral volatility – the fortunes of individual parties will vary greatly from election to election. Fluid systems also contain political parties with weak roots in society. Voters have few lasting attachments to particular parties and there are no enduring links between parties and interest groups.

Before discussing the degree of institutionalization in Southeast Asia's party systems, it is useful to consider how institutionalization might affect democratic efficiency and effectiveness. The predominant view in the literature is that under-institutionalized party systems are a hindrance to democratic consolidation and good governance. To begin with, a lack of party system institutionalization can undermine the ability of the electorate to hold politicians individually and collectively accountable.[26] Weak institutionalization undermines accountability in two ways.

First, in order to hold politicians accountable, voters have to be able to identify who deserves blame (or credit) for particular outcomes.[27] It is not enough that parties be identified with distinct ideological or policy positions. Instead, the real question is whether political parties have distinct collective identities. When parties are short-lived electoral alliances, when "personalism" trumps party label, when party switching is rampant, it is difficult for voters to identify who to blame or credit for particular outcomes.

Weak institutionalization also undermines accountability by making it difficult to inflict electoral punishment in situations where blame *can* be assigned. The collective actor (the party) in weakly institutionalized party systems is ephemeral. If its electoral fortunes look bleak, it is likely to disappear and its constituent parts reconstituted in new or existing parties. Politicians and factions that are part of governments accused of corruption or incompetence are still able to return under a new party banner. Where incumbents develop local support networks tied to them as individuals rather than to the party, they may be shielded from collective punishment.

Another reason a lack of party system institutionalization may be a concern is that, where party institutionalization is low, the combination of disillusionment with the extant system and weak party loyalties may provide opportunities for anti-system/anti-party politicians to rise to power.[28] Specifically, a high degree of party turnover, low barriers to entry, weak links between voters and political parties, and high levels of voter dissatisfaction in weakly institutionalized systems open the door for maverick politicians and/or radical parties. The rise of such political mavericks is certainly a familiar phenomenon in Southeast Asia, whether it is Thaksin in Thailand, Susilo Bambang Yudhoyono in Indonesia, or Marcos in the Philippines. In some cases, these politicians have been reformers with agendas in harmony (or at least not in direct conflict) with democratic norms and institutions. This seems to be the case with Yudhoyono in Indonesia, for example. In other cases, however, charismatic anti-party/anti-establishment individuals have undermined democratic norms and institutions. Marcos and Thaksin in Southeast Asia along with Alberto Fujimori in Peru and Vladimir Putin in Russia are examples.

In short, where the party system is weakly institutionalized, the fluidity of the party system offers opportunities for individuals from outside the existing party system to win office and subsequently to centralize power. What is more, the underperformance of democratic government in weakly institutionalized party systems can generate a demand for "stronger" leadership.

Where do the party systems of Southeast Asian states fall in terms of institutionalization? I will focus here on the two criteria discussed above – the stability of inter-party competition and the extent to which parties are rooted in society. Stability and rootedness vary quite substantially across the region. I argue that Singapore and Malaysia appear to have the most institutionalized party systems, but both are at best semi-democracies, complicating the picture. The party systems of the "pure" democracies (the Philippines, Indonesia and Thailand, pre-2006 coup), all appear under-institutionalized, though there is some evidence that Indonesia is slightly more institutionalized than its two neighbours.

Stability of inter-party competition

The most commonly used indicator of the stability of the party system from election to election is the measure of electoral volatility. Electoral volatility refers to the degree to which there is variation in aggregate party vote shares from one election to another. Where there is a stable pattern of inter-party competition, we expect to see the same sets of parties receiving consistent levels of support from election to election, reflected in a low volatility score (e.g. the Democratic and Republican parties in the United States). High levels of electoral volatility, on the other hand, reflect both instability in voters' party preferences from election to election and elite-driven changes to the party system, such as the creation of new parties, the death of existing parties, party switching, party mergers and party splits.[29]

Electoral volatility is based on the net change in the vote shares of all parties from election to election. It is calculated by taking the sum of the net change in the percentage of votes gained or lost by each party from one election to the next, divided by two.[30] A score of 100 signifies that the set of parties winning votes is completely different from one election to the next. A score of 0 means the same parties receive exactly the same percentage of votes across two different elections. The higher the volatility score, the less stable the party system is.

The electoral volatility scores for Southeast Asian countries are listed alongside the volatility scores of several other democracies for comparative purposes in Table 4.4. Three things are particularly noteworthy. First, Malaysia and Singapore stand out as the two countries in the region with the most stable party systems – no surprise given that they are both dominated by one party. The vote shares of the PAP and BN change very little from election to election, reflecting both a high degree of stable support among voters for these parties and also the less-than-level electoral playing field that exists in both countries. Second, compared with much of the rest of democratizing Latin America and Asia, the party systems of Cambodia, Thailand, Indonesia, East Timor and the Philippines are just as fluid, if not more so.

A third noteworthy fact evident in Table 4.4 is Indonesia's volatility score relative to that of the Philippines and Thailand. It is interesting and somewhat ironic that Indonesia, one of the youngest democracies in the region and a country with very little experience with democratic elections, thus far has a less fluid party system than Thailand and the Philippines, each of which has a substantial history of relatively free and fair elections. Indonesia's electoral volatility score of 25.2 is 30 per cent lower than the volatility score in Thailand and 32 per cent lower than the Philippines' score.

Some scholars argue that the development of regular patterns of party competition is mainly a function of time. Voters' attachment to parties, information about the relative strength and position of various political parties, and knowledge about institutional incentives take time to develop.[31] Tavits, as well as Lupu and Stokes, finds that volatility declines and party identities strengthen the more time is spent under democ-

Table 4.4 Lower chamber electoral volatility

Country	Time span	Average volatility
United States	1944–2002	3.3
United Kingdom	1945–2001	6.8
Greece	1974–2000	10.4
Malaysia	**1974–2004**	**10.7**
Colombia	1958–2002	12.5
Singapore	**1968–2006**	**14.9**
Italy	1946–2001	15.1
France	1951–2002	15.3
Chile	1989–2001	16.7
Brazil	1986–2002	21.8
Mexico	1988–2000	22.7
South Korea	1988–2000	24.6
Cambodia	**1993–2003**	**25.1**
Indonesia	**1999–2004**	**25.2**
Argentina	1983–2001	25.1
India	1951–1999	25.5
Venezuela	1958–2001	31.4
Thailand	**1979–2005**	**36.1**
Philippines	**1992–1998**	**37.3**
Poland	1991–2001	46.6
East Timor	**2001–2007**	**49.0**

Sources: Author's calculations; Scott Mainwaring and Edurne Zoco, "Historical Sequences and the Stabilization of Interparty Competition: Electoral Volatility in Old and New Democracies", *Party Politics*, 13(2), 2007: 4.
Note: Southeast Asian countries are in bold.

racy.[32] Likewise, Roussias, Tavits and Annus find evidence for better strategic coordination by voters and candidates over time in new democracies.[33] By contrast, Mainwaring and Torcal, and Reich, find no evidence for a decline in volatility and the number of parties over time.[34]

Figure 4.1 compares changes in electoral volatility over time in six of the Southeast Asian cases. For countries that experienced a clear authoritarian interlude (the Philippines 1972–1986, Malaysia in 1969–1970 and Thailand in 1991–1992), I have broken the series into pre- and post-authoritarian elections. Southeast Asia offers only mixed support for the argument that party system stability increases with a country's democratic experience. In nearly every case there is a sharp drop in electoral volatility between the second and third elections – suggesting greater institutionalization of the party system. However, beyond the third election the story is more complex. In some cases volatility continues to fall (pre-martial law Philippines), in some it rises (early Malaysia), in some it seems to stabilize at a low level (Singapore and later Malaysia), and in others there is no discernible pattern (Thailand post-1991).

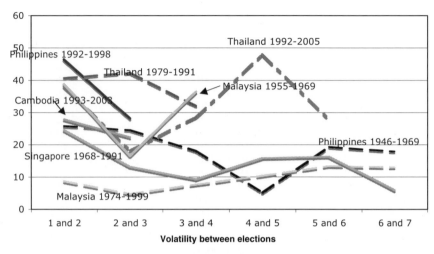

Figure 4.1 Change in volatility over time.
Source: Author's calculations.

Note too that longer authoritarian interludes, particularly those where the authoritarian regime tries to create a new party, seem more disruptive to the party system than shorter interventions. This is consistent with findings elsewhere in the party and transitions literature.[35] Under Marcos' 14-year rule, existing political parties were repressed and a new state-backed party created – the KBL. Since democratic elections returned to the Philippines in 1986, we have seen a much higher rate of electoral volatility than prior to martial law. By contrast, the shorter authoritarian interludes in Thailand and Malaysia caused less disruption to the existing party system. Thailand's volatility rises modestly in the wake of the military's year-long intervention, in part reflecting the rise and quick demise of the military-backed party – Samakkhi Tham. Malaysia's party system exhibits more stability after the two-year Emergency period. This reflects the fact that the core partners in Barisan Nasional were the same parties that came together to form the Alliance. It is also indicative of a political and electoral environment more heavily biased towards BN after the crisis.

Party–society links

The electoral volatility figures also communicate something about the degree to which political parties in these countries are "rooted" in society. Where parties have strong roots in society, there tends to be a degree of stability in electoral competition. As Mainwaring and Torcal state:

If most citizens support the same party from one election to the next, there are fewer floating voters, hence less likelihood of massive electoral shifts that are reflected in high volatility. Conversely, where parties have weak roots in society, more voters are likely to shift electoral allegiances from one election to the next, thus bringing about greater potential for high electoral volatility.[36]

On this basis, the Singapore and Malaysia party systems would seem to have the strongest roots in society – although once again the lack of a level playing field complicates the picture. On the other hand, the relatively high volatility scores for Thailand and the Philippines reflect the weak links between political parties and societal actors in both countries. Indonesia and Cambodia fall somewhere in between these two extremes.

Another way to assess the strength of voter–party links is to look at voter attitudes and behaviour toward parties. In Thailand, the Philippines and Indonesia, voters continue to exhibit weak ties to existing political parties. There are several indicators of this. In Indonesia, a poll prior to the 2004 House of Representatives election revealed that 58 per cent of respondents were unable or unwilling to commit to a particular party in the upcoming election.[37] Even worse, in the Philippines less than one-third of respondents reported being close to *any* political party, and in Thailand less than one-quarter of those polled felt close to a particular party.[38] In addition, many voters in all three countries support a different party each election, and, when given the opportunity, split their votes between different parties in the *same* election.[39]

Another indicator of party "rootedness" is the extent to which political parties are clearly associated with particular societal interests. Two questions are especially germane. To what extent do parties rely on different/distinct constituencies? Can we differentiate one party from another on the basis of its policy platform? By this score, Malaysia has the most rooted party system, with ethnically-based parties and a pan-ethnic ruling coalition that differs in important ways from opposition parties. Thailand and the Philippines lie at the other end of the spectrum (Singapore and Cambodia are somewhere in between). In both Thailand and the Philippines, the ties between parties and identifiable societal interests have traditionally been very weak. Parties tend to be shallow alliances of locally-based and locally-focused politicians, rather than cohesive national political parties with distinct policy visions. In fact, what distinguishes these party systems is the enduring lack of national policy or ideological orientation.[40] Party platforms are notable for their absence of distinctive ideological or national policy content. An extreme example occurred in the run-up to a recent election in the Philippines. Several different parties, including parties in both the government and the opposition, ended up hiring the same group of consultants to write their party platforms.

Because of the strong similarities across all of the platforms, the consultants adopted a simple rule to keep each distinct – use a different font for each.[41] As this anecdote illustrates, the major differences among parties are not differences in whom they represent or over the direction of national policy. Consequently, elections are not battles among different ideologies or party programmes but rather struggles among personalities for the control of government resources.

An interesting question is how to view the strength of party–society ties in Indonesia. There is some evidence that some Indonesian parties have stronger associations with particular regions and societal/religious interests than the typical Thai or Filipino party.[42] For other parties, however, the pattern of support is less obvious or the parties are still too young to enable us to make confident inferences. Dwight King has argued that the 1999 elections largely reproduced the religious, class and regional voting patterns that were observed in Indonesia's 1955 election.[43] However, Liddle and Mujani find voters' attachment to local and national party leaders plays a much bigger part in shaping their decision than sociological variables.[44] To the extent King is correct, Indonesia looks as though it may be further down the road of party "rootedness" than either Thailand or the Philippines (though perhaps not much further). If, on the other hand, Liddle and Mujani are correct, Indonesia does not look much different from Thailand and the Philippines on this dimension. In all three cases, loyalty is primarily to an individual candidate rather than to a particular party, region or social group.

Engineering party systems

Thus far I have discussed two dimensions along which to place parties and party systems in developing democracies: first, the way in which the system addresses social and ethnic divisions (articulation vs. aggregation), and, second, the degree of party system institutionalization. When we talk about the relative virtues of articulation or aggregation institutions, we are necessarily in the realm of institutional engineering. Can institutions play a similar role in facilitating, or hindering, party system institutionalization? Party systems in new democracies clearly vary in terms of the level and pace of institutionalization. But how do we explain this variation? How do strong parties and institutionalized party systems develop (or not) in new democracies?

These questions are behind an impressive amount of research about party formation, the development of party identity and party institutionalization in new democracies across the globe.[45] Among the reasons cited in the literature for why strong parties might develop more or less quickly in new democracies are the behaviour of the *ancien régime*,[46] the number of democratic (or partially democratic) elections a country has experienced,[47] the presence of ethnic divides[48] and the timing of elections vis-à-vis the expansion of suffrage and citizenship.[49] The bulk of these studies confirm that the development of strong political parties and stable, effective party systems is often a long, slow process, if it occurs at all. But what of political institutions and party regulation? Can they affect the speed or degree of institutionalization? Even if they play only a marginal role relative to other factors, the effects of institutional design on party system development are worth considering – especially given the fact that, as hard as institutional reform may be, it is inordinately easier than undoing history, changing social structures or speeding up the passage of time.

Institutional design necessarily involves trade-offs between competing goals. Proportional institutions will tend to advantage articulation and stronger ties between political parties and voters.[50] At the same time, there is a danger that articulation and rootedness might give way to recalcitrance and reification and that proportional institutions might produce hyperinflated party systems, higher volatility and government ineffectiveness. Aggregative or majoritarian institutions, on the other hand, may improve the chances for a small number of large, moderate and transcendent political parties, and by reducing fragmentation improve the chances for majority governments, but at the potential cost of poorer articulation and weaker links between parties and their constituents.

The countries in Southeast Asia have each dealt with these trade-offs in different ways, although most have attempted to engineer and regulate the development of certain types of parties and party systems. In this section I draw on the previous discussion of articulation, aggregation and institutionalization by breaking these engineering attempts into two categories: rootedness/articulation and accommodation/aggregation.

Rootedness and articulation

We see a variety of reforms across Southeast Asia aimed at increasing representation for marginalized groups, strengthening the link between parties and the society/citizens they are supposed to represent and increasing the value of party labels to voters and politicians. These include the adoption of mixed-member systems, restrictions on party-switching and the elimination of intra-party competition.

In 1997, Thai reformers adopted a two-tier electoral system to replace the block vote system Thailand had used for several decades. Reformers hoped that the addition of a 100-seat national party list tier, elected using proportional representation, would encourage parties to develop distinct policy platforms and invest in the creation and maintenance of a party label, and encourage voters to place party before person – all rarities in the pre-reform era. At the same time, Thailand's multi-member districts were replaced by 400 single-member districts, which eliminated the intra-party competition that had in the past undermined party cohesion and the value of party labels. The 1997 constitution also placed new restrictions on party-switching; specifically, it banned the candidates from switching parties in the few months prior to an election, a common practice in pre-reform Thailand. Again, the goal of these reforms was to encourage the creation of more cohesive parties and the development of party loyalty by voters and candidates, and to some extent they were successful at doing this.[51]

The first Asian democracy to adopt a mixed-member system was the Philippines, which added a party list tier to its plurality electoral system after the fall of Marcos. As in Thailand, 80 per cent of the seats are elected using single-member districts on a plurality basis, while the remaining 20 per cent are chosen from national lists. Among the motivations for including a party list tier in the Philippines was a desire to give marginalized interests/groups such as women, youth, labour, farmers and the poor a greater voice and a seat at the policy-making table.[52] However, the peculiarities associated with the Philippine mixed-member system (discussed in more detail below) have ultimately undermined its potential to facilitate greater representation and foster stronger links between political parties and marginalized citizens.

Indonesia, Cambodia and East Timor, the only Southeast Asian states that use pure proportional representation for their national legislative elections, have also attempted various reforms designed in part to better root political parties in the polity. In 2004, Indonesia reduced the geographical size of each district along with the number of seats elected from each district. This was part of an effort to bring parties closer to the masses.[53] The adoption of more single-seat districts in Cambodia prior to the 1998 elections was also in part a response to demands for stronger links between political parties and local electorates.[54] East Timor's new party law attempts to reduce party-switching between elections by requiring switchers to forfeit their seat in parliament (see Chapter 9 by Kadima in this volume for a discussion of party-switching regulations in Africa).

Accommodation and aggregation

The attempts to engineer better articulation and more rooted parties have not occurred in isolation. Instead, they have often been packaged with other reforms specifically designed to promote cross-group accommodation and coordination and to reduce the number of political parties in the political system. One popular regulatory tool is the requirement that political parties meet certain organizational hurdles to be eligible for elections. In Thailand, parties were required to have at least 5,000 members, distributed across all of the country's regions. The Philippines similarly requires new parties to establish regional offices in a majority of the country's regions and to gain support in more than half of the cities and provinces where their candidates run.[55]

Party list tiers in mixed-member systems have also been designed to encourage the formation of large national parties and discourage small parties. In Thailand, parties were required to submit a single national list, and the list tier seats were elected using a single nationwide district. The list tier seats were then awarded without reference to the number of seats already captured by the party in the district election. This arrangement significantly favoured large parties that are able to organize and compete nationwide. Both Thailand and the Philippines also bar parties that fall below a predetermined threshold (5 per cent in Thailand, 2 per cent in the Philippines) from winning seats in the list tier. (East Timor also employs a 3 per cent threshold for its parliamentary elections.)

The country making the most concerted effort at party system engineering is Indonesia. The diversity of Indonesia's population, the nature of Indonesia's geography and Indonesia's failed experiment with democracy in the 1950s all combined to instil in Indonesia's post-Suharto political reformers a keen desire to promote national parties over local, regional or separatist parties. Reformers tackled the challenge using a multi-faceted strategy. First, they established strict rules on party formation, requiring that parties set up branches in one-third of Indonesia's provinces and in more than half of the districts and municipalities or districts within those provinces. This dramatically reduced the number of parties eligible to stand for the 1999 election. These rules were then strengthened in advance of the 2004 elections. Parties are now required to establish branches in two-thirds of the provinces and in two-thirds of the municipalities within the provinces. In addition, each municipal party branch must have at least 1,000 members. Only 24 parties were able to meet this requirement for the 2004 election and, of those that were successful, most drew support from multiple regions – just as reformers had hoped.[56] Reformers have also established an electoral threshold: parties that fail to capture more than 2 per cent of the seats in the lower house of parliament, or 3 per cent in the regional assemblies, cannot compete in the next election unless they merge with other parties to reach this threshold. Finally, Indonesia's effective ban on regional parties applies not just to national elections but to regional and local contests as well. In other words, only national parties are allowed to compete in Indonesian elections – period. The net effect of these reforms is fewer, more national parties than we would otherwise expect given Indonesia's social diversity and very permissive electoral system.

Indonesia has also designed its system of electing its president in a way that privileges nationally oriented candidates with broad bases of support. To begin with, only parties that win at least 5 per cent of the vote or 3 per cent of parliamentary seats are permitted to nominate presidential candidates. The electoral system is a two-round, majority run-off system. In order to win the first round a candidate must gain over 50 per cent of the total votes and at least 20 per cent of the votes in half of Indonesia's provinces. If no candidate wins in the first round, a run-off is held between the two strongest candidates, this time without the explicit distributional requirements.

Finally, Singapore uses an interesting electoral system that combines a handful of single-member districts with Group Representation Constituencies (GRCs), each with three to six seats. GRCs can be contested only by teams of candidates from the same party (or allied independents) and at least one member of each team must be from the Malay, Indian or another minority community. Voters cast a single vote for a team, and the team with a plurality of the votes wins all the seats in that GRC. The stated purpose behind the use of GRCs is to ensure the representation of minority communities under the umbrella of broader, pan-ethnic parties. However, the move to GRCs came in the wake of minor inroads by small parties and individuals in single-member districts during the 1980s. Thus, the switch to GRCs is more properly interpreted as a strategy to undermine the capacity of the opposition and ensure continued victory for the PAP. The combination of winner-takes-all multi-seat districts with the minority candidate makes it extremely difficult for even very popular opponents to challenge the ruling PAP. Individual opposition politicians, even if they win the most votes in the GRC, cannot win a seat unless they are able to assemble an entire team strong enough to challenge the PAP. Formation of opposition party teams is made more difficult by the fact that opposition parties in Singapore are often ethnically based.

Conclusion: The unintended consequences of engineering

As useful a tool as institutional engineering and party regulation can be, institutional reforms and regulations do not take place in a vacuum. These reforms interact with each other and with societal and economic factors, often in unpredictable ways. As a result, institutional reforms always have some unintended and unexpected consequences. It is possible to make some predictions and to have strong expectations about the effects of reforms, but there are always things reformers cannot anticipate. The recent reform experiences of Thailand, the Philippines and Indonesia illustrate this principle.

Indonesia's efforts to promote national political parties and reduce political fragmentation may have had the unintended consequence of retarding the development of strong links between political parties and certain voters. Indonesia's effective ban on regional parties for all elections, even local elections, may mean that a significant portion of the electorate – those with strong local or regional identities – are less likely to feel close to any political party and less likely to participate in elections and perhaps ultimately will be less satisfied with Indonesia's developing democracy.[57]

Turning to the Philippines, the development of the party list elections has not proceeded in the way some advocates of marginalized interests had hoped. In setting up the party list tier, the drafters of the 1987 constitution made two decisions that have undermined the efficacy of the institution.[58] First, unlike most other mixed-member systems around the world, the major parties in the Philippines were barred from competing for seats in the party list tier. This in effect meant that the major parties were immune from the incentives generated by the addition of a list tier. Second, the number of seats each party list group could capture was capped at three – thus reducing incentives to develop parties with national reach. These reforms have, in the end, produced some perverse side-effects. Although the party list provision has probably resulted in more diverse interests being elected to Congress, it has also partially ghettoized those interests. Party list groups are too small to have a real voice in most policy debates, and mainstream political parties and politicians seem largely content to leave programmatic campaigning and the representation of marginalized interests to party list groups. The net effect of the party list in the Philippines is the further marginalization of the marginalized.

Finally, the drafters of the 1997 Thai constitution set out to correct some of the perceived weaknesses in the Thai party system. Specifically, they set out to reduce the number of parties and to promote party cohesion and the development of national, programmatic parties. The move to single-member districts, the introduction of a national party list and new incentives for cross-district coordination combined to drastically reduce the number of parties in the 2001 and 2005 elections.[59] The average effective number of parties in the pre-reform period was 7.2. This fell to 3.8 in 2001 and 2.6 in 2006. For only the second time in Thai electoral history, a single party (Thai Rak Thai) captured a majority of the legislative seats in 2001 and then repeated that feat in 2005. In addition, new restrictions on party-switching, an end to intra-party competition and new leverage for the prime minister over factions within his own party enabled the head of Thai Rak Thai, Thaksin Shinawatra, to keep his party together for the entire parliamentary term. In so doing he became the first and, thus far, only prime minister ever to serve a complete four-year term. The 1997 constitution also increased the incentives and rewards for party-centred campaigns and programmatic appeals via the introduction of the national party list. In short, electoral reforms meant that a national programmatic appeal was a much more viable strategy than it had been under previous constitutions. Thaksin and his party improved their electoral fortunes by recognizing and capitalizing on these new opportunities.[60]

In sum, the constitutional reforms played a part in the rise and success of Thaksin and Thai Rak Thai.[61] With a firm legislative majority and unprecedented leverage over his factional and party competitors, Thaksin moved quickly to centralize political authority and turn the government into an instrument of the ruling party – a sharp departure from past norms. There were costs and benefits to this change. On the one hand, the government was much more decisive than its predecessors and was able quickly to adopt a series of policies aimed at poor and rural voters. On the other hand, Thaksin's apparent use of government to enrich himself and his cronies undermined his support among some segments of the population, and his bid to centralize power eventually made enemies of the monarchy and the military. Eventually, Thaksin and his government were ousted in a military coup in September 2006. In the aftermath of the coup, the new junta immediately set about amending the constitution in an effort to re-engineer the party system once again. Although the details of the new constitution are still being debated, it is clear that Thailand's conservative forces are attempting to engineer out the excesses they perceived in the prior system. Specifically, they are trying to reduce the powers of the prime minister (e.g. by making it easier to switch parties and bring a no-confidence motion to vote, and replacing the elected Senate with a partially appointed body), discourage majority parties and encourage greater party fragmentation (e.g. by replacing the national party list with smaller regionally based party lists).

In summary, the experience of Southeast Asia's developing democracies suggests that party systems can indeed be engineered – whether the goal is producing democratic stability in the presence of societal divides or accelerating the pace of party system institutionalization. Institutional reforms throughout the region have enabled countries to reduce political fragmentation, promote the development of national parties and strengthen the links between political parties and the citizens they represent. But institutional engineering is no panacea. Whether conscious or not, reforms embody decisions about various institutional trade-offs and this means that all reforms come at a cost. Finally, the law of unintended consequences suggests that even the mildest of reforms should be undertaken with caution and due humility.

Acknowledgement

Parts of this chapter draw on Allen Hicken, "Stuck in the Mud: Parties and Party Systems in Democratic Southeast Asia", *Taiwan Journal of Democracy*, 2(2), 2006: 23–46.

Notes

1. This transition has been less than smooth, as the coups in 1991 and 2006 illustrate.
2. Allen Hicken, "Stuck in the Mud: Parties and Party Systems in Democratic Southeast Asia", *Taiwan Journal of Democracy*, 2(2), 2006: 23–46.
3. See William Case, *Politics in Southeast Asia: Democracy or Less* (London: Curzon Press, 2002).
4. Ironically, the durability of authoritarian and semi-authoritarian regimes also depends on building a strong, institutionalized party system. See Jason Brownlee, "Ruling Parties and Durable Authoritarianism", CDDRL Working Papers No. 23, Center on Democracy, Development, and the Rule of Law, Stanford Institute for International Studies, 2004; Barbara Geddes, "What Do We Know about Democratization after Twenty Years?", *Annual Review of Political Science*, 2, 1999: 115–144; Benjamin Smith, "Life of the Party: The Origins of Regime Breakdown and Persistence under Single-Party Rule", *World Politics*, 57(3), 2005: 421–451.
5. For a review of this debate, see Arend Lijphart, "Constitutional Design for Divided Societies", *Journal of Democracy*, 15(2), 2004: 96–109; Benjamin Reilly, "Electoral Systems for Divided Societies", *Journal of Democracy*, 12(2), 2002: 156–170. For a review of consociational versus majoritarian institutions in Asia, see Aurel Croissant, "Electoral Politics in Southeast and East Asia: A Comparative Perspective", in Aurel Croissant, G. Bruns and M. John (eds), *Electoral Politics in Southeast and East Asia* (Singapore: Friedrich Ebert Stiftung, 2002), pp. 321–362.
6. Arend Lijphart, *Democracies: Patterns of Majoritarian and Consensus Government in Twenty-One Countries* (New Haven, CT: Yale University Press, 1984).
7. The consociational model also emphasizes that each major group should get a share of power and the authority to block or veto policies that are of prime concern to that group's members. To do this one seeks to make ethnic/religious groups the building blocks of political parties and then ensure that each group is represented in a "grand coalition" government.
8. Donald Horowitz, *Ethnic Groups in Conflict* (Berkeley, CA: University of California Press, 1985); Donald Horowitz, *A Democratic South Africa? Constitutional Engineering in a Divided Society* (Berkeley, CA: University of California Press, 1991); Benjamin Reilly, *Democracy in Divided Societies: Electoral Engineering for Conflict Management* (Cambridge: Cambridge University Press, 2001).
9. A plurality electoral system is the simplest version, but most advocates of centripetalism advocate systems that allow for preference voting and vote-pooling, e.g. the alternative vote, the supplementary vote or the single transferable vote.
10. Arend Lijphart, *Democracy in Plural Societies: A Comparative Exploration* (New Haven, CT: Yale University Press, 1977). For a contrasting view, see Horowitz, *Ethnic Groups in Conflict*.
11. Horowitz, *Ethnic Groups in Conflict*.
12. Matthew Soberg Shugart and Martin P. Wattenberg (eds), *Mixed-Member Electoral Systems: The Best of Both Worlds?* (Oxford: Oxford University Press, 2000).

13. See Benjamin Reilly, *Democracy and Diversity: Political Engineering in the Asia-Pacific* (Oxford: Oxford University Press, 2006).

14. Ibid. Reilly notes that, although Cambodia uses a PR system, over one-third of its electoral districts are single-member districts. Elections in those districts are in effect plurality contests, which again favour large parties over small.

15. *Official Gazette: Democratic Republic of Timor-Leste*, "Law No. 6/2006: Law on the Election of the National Parliament", 2006, Introduction.

16. Reilly (*Democracy and Diversity*) argues this is part of a broader Asian model of institutional design.

17. Both systems will be discussed in more detail below.

18. The effective number of parties (ENP) is defined as 1 divided by the sum of the weighted values for each party. This measure weights parties according to their size – parties with large vote shares are weighted more than parties with small shares. The weighted values are calculated by squaring each party's vote share (v_j): $ENP = 1/(\sum v_j^2)$.

19. See Allen Hicken, *Building Party Systems* (New York: Cambridge University Press, forthcoming).

20. There are a variety of ways to measure disproportionality. I use the average seat–vote deviation of the two largest parties – consistent with Reilly (*Democracy and Diversity*). For other possibilities, see Arend Lijphart, *Electoral Systems and Party Systems: A Study of Twenty-Seven Democracies, 1945–1990* (Oxford: Oxford University Press, 1994).

21. Reilly, *Democracy and Diversity*.

22. Giovani Sartori, *Parties and Party Systems: A Framework for Analysis* (Cambridge: Cambridge University Press, 1976). For critiques of this dichotomy, see Scott Mainwaring and Mariano Torcal, "Party System Institutionalization and Party System Theory after the Third Wave of Democratization", in R. S. Katz and W. Crotty (eds), *Handbook of Political Parties* (London: Sage Publications, 2006), pp. 204–227.

23. Scott Mainwaring and Timothy Scully, "Introduction", in Scott Mainwaring and Timothy Scully (eds), *Building Democratic Institutions: Party Systems in Latin America* (Stanford, CA: Stanford University Press, 1995), pp. 1–11. The concept and operation are further refined in Scott Mainwaring, *Rethinking Party Systems in the Third Wave of Democratization: The Case of Brazil* (Stanford, CA: Stanford University Press, 1999), and Mainwaring and Torcal, "Party System Institutionalization". Mainwaring and Scully also include legitimacy and party organization as part of their definition.

24. Randall and Svasand refer to similar concepts using the terms "systemness" and "reification". They also include *decisional autonomy* and *value infusion* in their definition. Vicky Randall and Lars Svasand, "Party Institutionalization in New Democracies", *Party Politics*, 8(1), 2002: 5–29. For other work on party system institutionalization, see Angelo Panebianco, *Political Parties: Organization and Power* (Cambridge: Cambridge University Press, 1988); Mary B. Welfling, *Political Institutionalization: Comparative Analyses of African Party Systems* (Beverly Hills, CA: Sage Publications, 1973); Samuel P. Huntington, *Political Order in Changing Societies* (New Haven, CT: Yale University Press, 1968).

25. Mainwaring and Torcal, "Party System Institutionalization", p. 7.

26. Ibid.

27. G. Bingham Powell, *Elections as Instruments of Democracy* (New Haven, CT: Yale University Press, 2000).

28. Mainwaring and Torcal, "Party System Institutionalization".

29. Scott Mainwaring and Edurne Zoco, "Historical Sequences and the Stabilization of Interparty Competition: Electoral Volatility in Old and New Democracies", *Party Politics*, 13(2), 2007: 4.

30. That is, $(\sum |v_{it} - v_{it+1}|)/2$.
31. Philip E. Converse, "Of Time and Stability", *Comparative Political Studies*, 2(2), 1969: 139–171; Stefano Bartolini and Peter Mair, *Identity, Competition and Electoral Availability: The Stabilisation of European Electorates, 1885–1985* (Cambridge: Cambridge University Press, 1990).
32. Margit Tavits, "The Development of Stable Party Support: Electoral Dynamics in Post-Communist Europe", *American Journal of Political Science*, 49(2), 2005: 283–298; Noam Lupu and Susan Stokes, "Democracy Interrupted: Regime Change and Partisan Stability in Twentieth Century Argentina", unpublished manuscript, Yale University, 2007.
33. Nassos Roussias, "Electoral Coordination in New Democracies", unpublished manuscript, Yale University, 2007; Margit Tavits and Taavi Annus, "Learning to Make Votes Count: The Role of Democratic Experience", *Electoral Studies*, 25(1), 2006: 72–90. See also Russell J. Dalton, Ian McAllister and Martin Wattenberg, "The Consequences of Partisan Dealignment", in Russell J. Dalton and Martin Wattenberg (eds), *Parties without Partisans: Political Change in Advanced Industrial Democracies* (Oxford: Oxford University Press, 2000), pp. 37–63.
34. Mainwaring and Torcal, "Party System Institutionalization"; Gary Reich, "The Evolution of New Party Systems: Are Early Elections Exceptional?", *Electoral Studies*, 23(2), 2004: 232–250; Gary Reich, "Coordinating Party Choice in Founding Elections", *Comparative Political Studies*, 34(10), 2001: 1237–1263.
35. Barbara Geddes and Erica Frantz, "The Effect of Dictatorships on Party Systems in Latin America", unpublished manuscript, UCLA, 2007.
36. Mainwaring and Torcal, "Party System Institutionalization", p. 7.
37. Asia Foundation, *Democracy in Indonesia: A Survey of the Indonesian Electorate 2003* (Jakarta: Asia Foundation, 2003), p. 98.
38. "The Comparative Study of Electoral Systems: Modules 1 and 2", 2007, available at ⟨http://www.cses.org/⟩ (accessed 31 March 2008).
39. Paige Johnson Tan, "Party Rooting, Political Operators, and Instability in Indonesia: A Consideration of Party System Institutionalization in a Communally Charged Society", unpublished paper presented at the Southern Political Science Association, New Orleans, Louisiana, 10 January 2004; Hicken, *Building Party Systems*; Mahar Mangahas, "How the Voters Mix Their Candidates", *Social Climate*, Social Weather Stations, April 1998, available at ⟨http://www.sws.org.ph/index.htm⟩ (accessed 31 March 2008).
40. The only exceptions to this in the Philippines are parties on the left – which generally have performed poorly at the polls – and some new party list parties, each of which can capture a maximum of three seats in the House. In Thailand, the Democratic Party (with its roots in southern Thailand) and the newly-formed Thai Rak Thai looked to be partial exceptions. Unfortunately, the 2006 coup has deprived us of the chance to assess whether the ties between Thai Rak Thai and certain constituencies went beyond voter attachment/loyalty to the party leader, Thaksin Shinawatra.
41. Interview with consultant, July 2000; anonymity requested.
42. Tan, "Party Rooting, Political Operators, and Instability in Indonesia".
43. Dwight King, *Half-Hearted Reform: Electoral Institutions and the Struggle for Democracy in Indonesia* (Westport, CT: Praeger Publishers, 2003).
44. R. William Liddle and Saiful Mujani, "Indonesia's Approaching Elections: Politics, Islam, and Public Opinion", *Journal of Democracy*, 15(1), 2004: 109–123.
45. Staffan Lindberg, *Democracy and Elections in Africa* (Baltimore, MD: Johns Hopkins University Press, 2006); Anna Grzymala-Busse, *Redeeming the Communist Past: The Regeneration of Communist Parties in East Europe* (New York: Cambridge University Press, 2002); Geddes and Frantz, "The Effect of Dictatorships on Party Systems in Latin

America"; Joshua A. Tucker and Ted Brader, "The Emergence of Mass Partisanship in Russia, 1993–1996", *American Journal of Political Science*, 45(1): 69–83.

46. Geddes and Frantz, "The Effect of Dictatorships on Party Systems in Latin America"; Lupu and Stokes, "Democracy Interrupted".

47. Roussias, "Electoral Coordination in New Democracies"; Tavits, "The Development of Stable Party Support"; Lindberg, *Democracy and Elections in Africa*; Mainwaring and Zoco, "Historical Sequences and the Stabilization of Interparty Competition".

48. Jóhanna Kristín Birnir, *Ethnicity and Electoral Politics* (New York: Cambridge University Press, 2007).

49. Mainwaring and Zoco, "Historical Sequences and the Stabilization of Interparty Competition"; Josep M. Colomer, *Political Institutions: Democracy and Social Choice* (New York: Oxford University Press, 2001); Paul Hutchcroft and Joel Rocamora, "Strong Demands and Weak Institutions: The Origins and Evolution of the Democratic Deficit in the Philippines", *Journal of East Asian Studies*, 3(2), 2003: 259–292.

50. If we assume that a voter's propensity to develop an attachment to a particular party is some function of the distance between the voter's ideal point and what she perceives as a party's position, proportional rules should produce stronger voter–party links. This is because (a) PR tends to produce parties that have distinct policy positions and (b) the distance between voters and the nearest party is closer under PR compared with majoritarianism.

51. See Allen Hicken, "Party Fabrication: Constitutional Reform and the Rise of Thai Rak Thai", *Journal of East Asian Studies*, 6(3), 2006: 381–408.

52. The law putting the system into effect did not come into effect until the 1998 election.

53. These reforms also reduced political fragmentation (Reilly, *Democracy and Diversity*). See also Stephen Sherlock, "Consolidation and Change: The Indonesian Parliament after the 2004 Elections", Centre for Democratic Institutions, Canberra, 2004, available at ⟨http://www.cdi.anu.edu.au/research/1998-2004/research_publications/research_downloads/Sherlock_DPR_2004.pdf⟩ (accessed 31 March 2008).

54. Reilly, *Democracy and Diversity*. These reforms also reduced political fragmentation and helped the ruling party further sideline the opposition.

55. Reilly, *Democracy and Diversity*; C. Hartmann, G. Hassall and S. Santos, "Philippines", in D. Nohlen, F. Grotz and C. Hartmann (eds), *Elections in Asia and the Pacific: A Data Handbook* (Oxford: Oxford University Press, 2001), pp. 195–238.

56. Reilly, *Democracy and Diversity*; Tan, "Party Rooting, Political Operators, and Instability in Indonesia".

57. Jennifer Epley and Allen Hicken, "Region, Religion, and Representation: Electoral Behavior in Indonesia", unpublished manuscript, University of Michigan.

58. It is possible that this is exactly what some of the drafters intended.

59. Some of these reforms were adopted with goals other than a reduction in the number of parties in mind. See Hicken, "Party Fabrication", for more details.

60. Hicken, "Party Fabrication".

61. Although institutional reform was an important factor behind the rise of Thai Rak Thai, it was not the only factor. Thaksin's wealth, the weakness of existing parties and the fallout from the Asian economic crisis also played a role. Nevertheless, the new constitution presented Thaksin with power, opportunities and incentives that none of his elected predecessors had ever possessed. For a further discussion of the relative effect of institutional reform, see Hicken, "Party Fabrication"; Michael H. Nelson, "Institutional Incentives and Informal Local Political Groups (*phuak*) in Thailand: Comments on Allen Hicken and Paul Chambers", *Journal of East Asian Studies*, 7(1), 2007: 125–148; Allen Hicken, "Omitted Variables, Intent, and Counterfactuals: A Response to Michael Nelson", *Journal of East Asian Studies*, 7(1), 2007: 149–158.

5

Regulating minority parties in Central and South-Eastern Europe

Florian Bieber

This chapter will examine the experience of minority party regulation in Central and South-Eastern Europe. Here, the primary geographical focus will be on the countries that recently joined the European Union (EU) and the potential EU member states in the Western Balkans. In the early and mid-1990s, illiberal democracies (Slovakia, Romania, Croatia) across the region excluded and marginalized minority parties, whereas since the late 1990s there has been a transition to minority inclusion. As the chapter will argue, the legal regulation of political parties has remained largely unchanged since the early transition from communism to democracy. The change towards inclusion has been mostly the result of increased acceptance of minority parties by majority parties and society at large.

This chapter argues that, in addition to the electoral systems, historical legacies, in particular the communist legacy, have been a major contributor to the evolution of minority politics. Thus, the chapter will first examine the historical and demographic legacy of minority–majority relations, before turning to the impact of electoral systems on the structure of minority politics. Subsequently, it will discuss the impact of different electoral systems in Central and South-Eastern Europe. In terms of electoral systems, Flores Juberías has distinguished between mechanisms that (a) oppose minority participation; (b) are formally neutral; (c) support competition of minority parties; (d) secure representation; and (e) offer ethnic territorialization.[1] Similarly, in Chapter 3 of this volume, Matthijs Bogaards distinguishes three different functions of the electoral system: blocking, aggregating and articulating minority votes. Blocking, for

Political parties in conflict-prone societies: Regulation, engineering and democratic development, Reilly and Nordlund (eds),
United Nations University Press, 2008, ISBN 978-92-808-1157-5

example by banning ethnic parties, limits political participation through some criterion. Aggregation is generally represented by some type of majority/plurality electoral system, which can encourage vote-pooling across ethnic lines. Articulation is aimed at accurately reflecting voting preferences, which in most cases would mean proportional representation.

Based on these categories, this chapter will discuss (a) electoral mechanisms that aim at marginalizing and blocking minority political representation and (b) those that advance the representation of minority parties. The simplification of the above categories is based on the empirical reality in most of Central and South-Eastern Europe. Attempts at aggregating ethnically-based votes, such as alternative voting, which allows voters to rank candidates, have been few and short lived. Formally neutral measures are, as we shall see, in practice never neutral, so that it is more appropriate to examine the impact of electoral legislation on minority representation rather than just its formal intent. Further, different means of supporting minority inclusion blend into each other and belong to the same general category, and will thus be discussed together. Extremely ethnified systems, where ethnic representation dominates all forms of political competition, are rare (to be found primarily in Bosnia-Herzegovina and Kosovo) and fall into the category of complex power-sharing systems, which will not be discussed in great detail here.[2] Finally, the chapter will examine the experience of minority parties in government. Their inclusion in governments across the region has become a prominent feature since the mid-1990s, indicating and facilitating a shift in the legitimacy of minority parties and equally highlighting the limitations of minority representation without effective participation in decision-making processes.

The historical and demographic framework of minorities politics

For most Western observers, especially during the 1990s, Eastern Europe became associated with ethnic diversity and conflict. The nature of diversity, however, varies significantly across Eastern Europe, with some countries being largely homogeneous nation-states, whereas others have several significant minorities and no clear majority. As a result, it would be a mistake to look for one pattern of diversity across the region. Generally speaking, there are four types of minorities in Eastern Europe. The first are historical minorities living in geographically concentrated areas, often in proximity to their kin-state. These minorities include Hungarians in Romania, Slovakia and Serbia, or Serbs in Croatia and Bosnia-

Herzegovina. The second category encompasses minorities that have settled relatively recently (since World War II) in their current area of settlement. These groups moved within the three multinational federations – Czechoslovakia, the Soviet Union and Yugoslavia – that later dissolved, and became minorities in new states at independence. This category includes Croats and Serbs in Slovenia, Bosniaks in Croatia and, significantly, most Russians in the Baltic states. The third category comprises small historical minorities that lack a kin-state or whose kin-state is far removed. Such minorities include Slovaks in Serbia, Armenians in Romania and Vlachs in Macedonia and Albania. The last category is constituted by Roma (and other closely related groups such as Ashkali or Egyptians). Roma constitute an underestimated yet significant minority (an estimated 5–7 million in Eastern Europe)[3] characterized by a larger degree of social and economic marginalization than is experienced by other minorities. The conceptual distinction between these categories notwithstanding, some minorities might in fact belong to several categories, such as the Russian minority in Estonia, falling into a small group of a historical minority (group 1) and a larger community constituted through migration during Soviet times (group 2).

In the context of these different types of minorities, we can identify several groups of states in respect to their majority–minority relations (see Table 5.1). The first category incorporates the nation-states that have a majority of over 90 per cent of the titular nation and have no strong minority communities. Poland, the Czech Republic and Hungary fall into this category. Here, minority politics have been less contentious. The second group comprises most countries of the region. Here the majority coexists with one large territorially-concentrated minority, and Roma often constitute a geographically dispersed minority. Whereas in some cases, such as in Latvia, the titular nation might amount to only 58 per cent, elsewhere the majority might reach more than 90 per cent. Even in the latter case, as for example in Albania where the Albanian majority amounts to probably more than 90 per cent, the Greek community constitutes a coherent and well-organized minority. Finally, two countries fall into a third category of states without a dominant nation. In Bosnia-Herzegovina and in Montenegro, the largest group constitutes only a plurality, with several other large groups. These variations in the structure of the minorities are crucial in understanding the political engagement of minorities and their inclusion in the political system.

In addition to the structure of minority groups, the historical legacy of minority–majority relations has also shaped the post-communist development of minority political engagement. There is no unifying historical experience among minorities in Eastern Europe; conflict and integration, forced assimilation and coexistence all shape the history of inter-ethnic

Table 5.1 Majorities and minorities in Central and South-Eastern Europe

	Majority	Significant minorities (official census)[a]	Estimated Roma population
Albania (1989)	98.0% Albanians	1.8% Greeks	0.3–3.3% (10,000–120,000)
Bosnia-Herzegovina (1991)	43.5% Muslims/ Bosniaks	31.2% Serbs 17.4% Croats 5.6% Yugoslavs 0.2% Roma 0.1% Albanians 0.1% Macedonians	1.1–1.3% (40,000–50,000)
Bulgaria (2001)	83.9% Bulgarians	9.4% Turks 4.7% Roma	8.8–10.1% (700,000–800,000)
Croatia (2001)	89.6% Croats	4.54% Serbs 0.47% Bosniaks 0.44% Italians 0.37% Hungarians	0.7–0.9% (30,000–40,000)
Czech Republic (2001)	90.4% Czechs	3.7% Moravians 1.9% Slovaks 0.38% Germans 0.51% Poles 0.11% Roma	1.5–2.9% (150,000–300,000)
Estonia (2000)	67.9% Estonians	25.6% Russians 2.1% Ukrainians 1.3% Byelorussians	0.07–0.1% (1,000–1,500)
Hungary (2001)	93.5% Hungarians	0.5% Roma 0.3% Germans	5.0% (456,000)
Kosovo (est. 2000)	88.0% Albanians	7.0% Serbs 1.9% Bosniaks/Muslims 1.7% Roma 1.0% Turks	1.8–2.0% (36,000–40,000)
Latvia (2000)	57.6% Latvians	29.6% Russians 4.1% Byelorussians 2.68% Ukrainians 2.5% Poles 1.4% Lithuanians	0.08–0.14% (2,000–3,500)

Country (year)	Majority	Minorities	Roma estimate
Lithuania (2001)	83.5% Lithuanians	6.7% Poles 6.3% Russians 1.2% Byelorussians	0.09–0.11% (3,000–4,000)
Macedonia (2003)	64.2% Macedonians	25.2% Albanians 3.9% Turks 2.7% Roma 1.7% Serbs	5.4–12.7% (110,000–260,000)
Montenegro (2003)	43.2% Montenegrins	32.0% Serbs 7.8% Bosniaks 5.0% Albanians 4.0% Muslims 1.1% Croats 0.42% Roma	3.2% (20,000)
Poland (2002)	96.0% Poles	0.5% Silesians 0.4% Germans	0.04–0.13% (15,000–50,000)
Romania (2002)	89.5% Romanians	6.6% Hungarians 2.5% Roma 0.3% Germans	8.4–11.7% (1,800,000–2,500,000)
Serbia (2002)	82.9% Serbs	3.9% Hungarians 1.8% Bosniaks 1.4% Roma 0.9% Montenegrins 0.8% Albanians	6.0–6.7% (450,000–500,000)
Slovakia (2001)	85.8% Slovaks	9.7% Hungarians 1.7% Roma	9–10% (480,000–520,000)
Slovenia (2002)	90.0% Slovenes	2.2% Serbs 2.0% Croats 1.2% Bosniaks	0.36–0.51% (7,000–10,000)

Notes: Data from official census results from the respective national statistical offices. The data for Kosovo are based on OSCE estimates. For Bosnia and Herzegovina there have been no official population estimates or census since 1991. Owing to war and displacements, the current demographic balance is likely to differ. Data for Albania are from 1989, because the 2001 census did not ask about ethnicity. Because the 1989 census was conducted under communist rule, the results are unreliable. Generally, the number of Roma is likely to be significantly higher than indicated in census results. The estimates for the Roma population are based on United Nations Development Programme, *At Risk: Roma and the Displaced in Southeastern Europe* (Bratislava: UNDP, 2006), p. 12; and Jeremy Drucker, "Present but Unaccounted for", *Transitions*, 4(4), 1997, p. 23.
^aGroups over 1 per cent in size or otherwise politically significant minorities.

relations in the region. Nevertheless, certain historical trends played out in the post-communist period. First, states in Eastern Europe emulated the Western model of nation-state-building as they emerged in the nineteenth century. Although some states adopted the legal framework of a civic nation-state, based on the French model, all states were structured around one (or several) ethnically-conceived nations. Even the multinational states of the region – Yugoslavia, Czechoslovakia and the Soviet Union – adopted varying strategies of defining themselves in terms of one or several core nations. The aspiring nation-states, however, have been confronted since their emergence in the nineteenth and early twentieth centuries with large minorities, most of which became unwilling citizens of the new states through the border changes of the receding and collapsing empires in Eastern Europe (the Russian, Habsburg and Ottoman empires).

Although some states recognized minorities, the predominant state strategies toward them were either assimilation or expulsion. The tensions between the aspirations of the nation-states and some minorities' revisionist ambitions led to the establishment of the League of Nations minority treaty system, instituted after World War I. This system obliged most countries of Eastern Europe to protect minority rights. Most states saw these externally imposed obligations not only as limiting their sovereignty but also as an obstacle to nation-state ambitions. Coupled with the weak enforcement capacity of the League of Nations, the system rapidly collapsed, ushering in minority repression and border changes initiated across Eastern Europe by Nazi Germany and its allies during World War II. The war and the post-war period brought with them enormous changes to the population structure. The Holocaust and subsequent migration to Israel drastically reduced Jewish life in Eastern Europe. After the war, minorities identified with Nazi Germany were expelled in their millions. The diversity of the inter-war period was widely identified as the cause of the weakness of nation-states in the region. Consequently, under communism many countries more closely resembled nation-states than during the inter-war period.

As communist parties came to power across Eastern Europe between 1944 and 1947, minority organizations could exist only within the dominant ideological framework. In a number of communist parties, minorities were well represented, unsurprising considering that the communists opposed the predominant nation-state framework and at first promised a more integrative approach towards minorities. Modelled on the Stalinist approach to the national question,[4] minorities received full recognition and occasionally territorial autonomy within a tightly controlled totalitarian context. This policy, "national in form, socialist in content", suppressed what the party considered bourgeois nationalism but allowed the cultural and linguistic expression of minorities, often reduced to such "innocuous" activities as folk dancing.[5] From the 1960s onwards, the regimes in Eastern Europe pursued more autonomous paths towards socialism. Confronted with waning legitimacy and operating within a nation-state framework, a number of communist regimes adopted increasingly nationalist policies. Coated in the framework of unity and modernization, minorities became a target of assimilation and repression, in particular in Romania, Bulgaria and Albania. The alternative strategy, pursued by Yugoslavia, was to transform the façade of minority recognition into a genuine multinational federation with a high degree of minority rights protection. However, in Yugoslavia too, minority demands were repressed if they did not reflect the party line.

With the fall of communist regimes, minorities across the region largely lacked specific organizations, not to mention parties. Minority parties and associations emerged during the fall of communism, mostly from opposition movements. In only a few cases, such as Bulgaria, did minority associations already exist as underground movements under communism. Minority-specific parties emerged in three different types. In countries where minorities occupied a dominant position and risked falling into an underprivileged position through state dissolution, such as Serbs in Croatia and Bosnia and Russians in the Baltics, the minorities generally supported conservative, status-quo-oriented parties, placing them in conflict with the emerging pro-independence nationalist parties of the respective republican majorities. The parties favoured by these minorities were not necessarily minority-specific parties, but were often communist successor parties that embodied the status quo. The second type of minority organization, characteristic of the Czech and Slovak Republics, emerged together with broader opposition movements in the autumn of 1989 against incumbent communist regimes. Although part of larger mainstream groupings, minority parties and associations assumed a distinct identity from the beginning, in particular in the case of larger minority groups. The third type of minority party emerged neither in conflict nor in cooperation with opposition movements, but in parallel. In Albania and Macedonia, for example, the Greek and Albanian minority parties (respectively) established themselves independently of the emerging opposition parties of the ethnic majority. This trajectory was either a consequence of minority parties recruiting themselves in part from the communist nomenclature or from democratic transitions that lacked a broad opposition bloc.

Crucially, with all three typologies, the embryonic structure of postcommunist minority parties emerged *before* the institutional and legal groundwork for the democratic political system was set. The Hungarian Democratic Federation of Romania (UDMR) emerged just a few days after the violent overthrow of the Ceauşescu regime in late 1989, the predominantly Turkish Movement for Rights and Freedoms in Bulgaria had its roots in the dissident Turkish National Liberation Movement dating back to 1986, and the Greek party Omonia emerged in Albania as a human rights organization in early 1990, before the communist regime collapsed.[6] As a result of the early emergence of minority parties, electoral systems and institutional design in the immediate post-communist period were confronted with existing minority parties, which constrained the extent to which the political system could be shaped by the new institutions.

Minorities in electoral systems in post-communist Central and South-Eastern Europe

Minority–majority relations had different degrees of importance across post-communist Europe. In more homogeneous countries where inter-ethnic tensions had been low, institutional design was shaped by other cleavages and controversies. Inter-ethnic relations, however, were high on the agenda in a number of post-communist countries that had witnessed a rise in ethnic tensions in the last years of communism or immediately after its fall. Examples of such tensions range from Russian minority opposition to Latvian and Estonian independence, to the violent clashes between Romanian miners and Hungarian protesters in Târgu Mureş in March 1990, to the rising violence in Croatia in the summer of 1990. Because minorities were largely perceived either as a security threat (by majorities and states) or as a human rights issue (by international organizations), electoral systems and the political representation of minorities were not the primary focus of attention to minority issues.

Confronted with the multiple challenges of transition, from economic to social and political, the establishment of a new institutional framework – including revised electoral arrangements – took priority. All countries of Central and South-Eastern Europe held elections within a few months of the fall of communism. Thus, by late 1990, all countries (with the exception of Albania) had held their first multi-party elections.

Minority-specific measures in the party and electoral systems of these countries were shaped by three at times contradictory dynamics: (a) path dependency from the communist experience; (b) majority assertion over the state; and (c) emerging efforts at the accommodation of minorities.

The legacy of minority policies under communism is apparent when contrasting the post-Yugoslav space with other countries in South-Eastern Europe. All the countries of former Yugoslavia instituted formal or informal mechanisms facilitating minority representation in parliament. The recognition and inclusion of minorities and different ethnic groups was an integral principle of policy in communist Yugoslavia. Although the post-communist governments of former Yugoslavia often reduced minority rights, the formal recognition still exceeded that of neighbouring countries. As Dejan Jović noted, the primary fear of Yugoslavia's nations[7] was "becoming a minority", whereas in many neighbouring countries minorities were struggling to become a minority, i.e. to receive recognition.

These institutional traditions were supplemented by the self-conception of the dominant nation after communism and the often heightened fear of minorities. Strong majority nationalism, often coupled with the fear of potentially irredentist minorities, shaped policies towards minorities. Majorities often sought to emphasize the national role of the state. "Nationalizing nationalisms" found themselves in conflict with minorities who felt under pressure to assimilate or face political exclusion.[8] In particular, the newly emerging states from the Soviet Union and Yugoslavia were engaged in a policy of "constitutional nationalism", where new constitutions enshrined the dominance of the core ethnic nation and thus institutionalized the majority nationalism.[9] Mostly, this was reflected not in a ban on ethnic parties but rather in general neglect – for example, by not offering special measures for minority representation, or even in the preferential treatment of some minorities. Thus, the reserved seats introduced in Romania for smaller minorities sought to counterbalance the strong Hungarian minority.

Finally, the need to accommodate minorities shaped policies towards minority parties. This accommodation might be based on the recognition that minority inclusion is necessary for state stability, as was the case in Macedonia from 1990 when Albanian parties began participating in government.[10] Minority accommodation has also been a tool to pursue kin-state policies. Thus, Hungary's far-reaching cultural autonomy and inclusion of minorities at the local level are widely viewed as a policy to advance the demands of Hungarian minorities abroad. In addition, international pressure to seek accommodation and the implicit positive association between minority-friendly policies and EU integration constituted a further reason for inclusive minority policies.

In addition to minority-specific considerations, electoral systems have been shaped for a number of reasons that had little to do with minorities, but nonetheless had great potential impact on minority parties (Table 5.2). In designing their electoral systems, most countries opted for proportional representation (PR), either with their first multi-party elections or by later shifting from mixed or majoritarian systems to PR. Thus, by 2007, only 3 out of 17 countries in Central and South-Eastern Europe had a mixed electoral system; all other countries voted by PR. The

Table 5.2 Electoral systems in Central and Eastern Europe, 2007

	Electoral system	Special minority representation	Threshold (per cent)
Albania	Mixed-member proportional	n.a.	2.5
Bosnia-Herzegovina	List PR	House of Peoples (15) – reserved seats: 5 Bosniak, 5 Croat, 5 Serb	3.0
Federation	List PR	House of Representatives (98) – reserved seats: min. 4 Bosniak, 4 Croat, 4 Serb; House of Peoples (58) – reserved seats: 17 Croat, 17 Bosniak, 17 Serb, 7 Other	3.0
Republika Srpska	List PR	National Assembly (83) – reserved seats: min. 4 Croat, 4 Bosniak, 4 Serb; Council of Peoples (28) – reserved seats: 8 Croat, 8 Bosniak, 8 Serb, 4 Other	3.0
Bulgaria	List PR	n.a.	4.0
Croatia	List PR	8 reserved seats (out of 151): 1 Czech and Slovak, 1 Hungarian, 3 Serbian, 1 Italian, 1 Bosniak, Albanian, Montenegrin, Macedonian and Slovene, 1 Austrian, Bulgarian, German, Polish, Roma, Romanian, Rusyn, Russian, Turkish, Ukrainian, Vlah and Jewish minority	5.0
Czech Republic	List PR	n.a.	5.0
Estonia	List PR	n.a.	5.0
Hungary	Mixed-member proportional	n.a.	5.0
Kosovo	List PR	20 reserved seats (out of 120): 10 Serb, 4 Roma/Ashkali/ Egyptian, 3 Bosniak, 2 Turkish and 1 Gorani	–
Latvia	List PR	n.a.	5.0
Lithuania	Parallel	n.a.	5.0
Macedonia	List PR	n.a.	–
Montenegro	List PR	4 reserved seats from Albanian electoral unit (out of 80)	3.0
Poland	List PR	No threshold (total 460)	5.0

104

Country	System	Details	%
Romania	List PR	18 reserved seats (out of 332): 1 each Armenian, German, Turkish, Polish, Italian, Tartar, Ukrainian, Macedonian, Ruthenian, Greek, Serb, Lipovan Rusyn, Albanian, Slovak and Czech, Bulgarian, Roma, Croat, Jewish	5.0
Serbia	List PR	No threshold (total 250)	5.0
Slovakia	List PR	n.a.	5.0
Slovenia	List PR	2 reserved seats (out of 90): 1 Hungarian, 1 Italian	4.0

Source: Author's compilation

prevalence of PR has had other explanations than minority inclusion, but has had a significant impact on minority representation. Conventional wisdom in much of the academic discussion on minority representation suggests that proportional systems tend to be superior to majoritarian systems. In fact, a great variety of electoral systems can ensure minority representation.[11] The experience in Central and South-Eastern Europe suggests that PR, in combination with relatively high thresholds, might actually be a greater disadvantage to minorities than majoritarian systems when minorities are geographically concentrated. In Albania, for example, the Greek minority party has been able to enter parliament only owing to the mixed electoral system; similarly, Albanian and Roma minority parties entered the Macedonian Sobranie through the single-member constituencies used until 1998.[12] It appears that in the case of Macedonia the majoritarian electoral system in use from 1992 to 1998 in particular helped Roma representation owing to a high geographical concentration of Roma in the Skopje neighbourhood of Šuto Orizari (60.6 per cent in 2002).[13] This effect is difficult to replicate elsewhere, however, because Roma mostly lack such geographical concentration and electoral units to match it.

By contrast, most of the largest minorities in the region are geographically concentrated and have performed relatively well irrespective of the electoral system. In Serbia, for example, Hungarian, Albanian and Bosniak/Muslim parties regularly succeeded in entering parliament, while gaining less than 2 per cent of the vote during the 1990s. After the change to PR from a majoritarian system in 2000 in Serbia, minority parties failed to enter parliament in 2003 and returned to parliament only in 2007 once the threshold for minorities was lifted. With thresholds of 3–5 per cent in most countries, minorities with a smaller share of eligible voters than the formal threshold have no chance of entering parliament independently. However, thresholds were established not to prevent minority participation but rather to avoid excessive fragmentation of the parliament.[14]

Marginalizing and blocking minority representation

No single country in Central and South-Eastern Europe has completely prevented the representation of minorities in parliament since the introduction of multi-party systems in 1990. Nevertheless, reducing the representation of minorities in the political system has been an implicit and at times explicit policy of numerous governments in post-communist Europe. Reduced minority rights, such as limiting political activities in minority languages, can significantly diminish the ability of minorities to organize themselves. Here, I shall examine restrictions on the minority parties in the form of (a) the exclusion of minorities from the political system through restrictive citizenship laws; (b) bans and other restrictive measures directed against minorities; (c) gerrymandering; and (d) electoral thresholds.

The most radical form of excluding minorities from political life is denying minorities citizenship. Not only does this preclude the formation of minority parties, it also prevents minorities from voting for mainstream parties. This complete marginalization from political life has been a prominent feature for some minorities in Central and Eastern Europe. Of course, the primary motivation of denying citizenship might not be preventing political engagement, but nevertheless citizenship hurdles are often features of states reluctant to integrate (some) minorities. Restrictive citizenship laws are a feature of state dissolution: new states often craft new citizenship laws to exclude some groups. The most prominent examples across the region are the obstacles for Roma originally from Slovakia in the Czech Republic to receiving Czech citizenship and for Russian-speakers in Latvia and Estonia.[15]

When the Czech Republic split away from Slovakia in 1993, people originally from Slovakia had to apply for citizenship, which affected many if not most of the country's Roma.[16] The requirements included administrative obstacles that appeared to target particularly Roma and, until the revision of the law in 1996 and 1999 under pressure from the European Union and the Organization for Security and Co-operation in Europe (OSCE), at first excluded many Roma from political life.[17] The most significant and enduring form of political marginalization occurred in Latvia and Estonia. After independence in 1991/1992, the republics established laws that restricted citizenship to persons who had lived, or whose ancestors had lived, in the states prior to losing independence during World War II. As a consequence, most persons not belonging to either of the titular nations (between one-third and over 40 per cent of the population in Estonia and Latvia, respectively) had to apply for citizenship. The requirements, however, were so restrictive – including language tests and annual quotas in Latvia – that few non-citizens were eligible or able to obtain citizenship.

Since the mid-1990s, consistent EU pressure, combined with an OSCE presence in the form of the High Commissioner on National Minorities and local missions, has made the citizenship laws more permissive.[18] Still, political exclusion has remained a widespread phenomenon. According to the 2001 census, only 79.98 per cent of Estonia's inhabitants had Estonian citizenship; 12.43 per cent had no citizenship at all. In Latvia, the numbers are similar, with only 80.09 per cent of the population in 2006 holding Latvian citizenship. Both countries require citizenship for active and passive voting rights in national elections.[19] Language tests for candidates constitute another obstacle to the participation of parties representing Russian-speakers. Expanding voting rights to non-citizens has been resisted by mainstream political parties for fear that this would lead to a significant political shift and reduce the assimilatory project of nation-building.[20] Furthermore, lustration and restrictions on holding office for persons who were part of communist organizations after 1991 disproportionately affected Russian-speakers. Nevertheless, a number of parties continue to represent the interests of Russian-speakers. In Latvia, Russian-speakers are represented primarily by parties that emphasize human rights or have their roots on the political Left. Their share has risen from around 5–6 per cent in the early 1990s to approximately 20 per cent in 2006, reflecting the ongoing naturalization of Russians. In Estonia, parties primarily targeting Russians have fared considerably worse, suffering from low support and internal fragmentation and thus being represented in parliament only intermittently (1995–2003). In fact there has been a reversal, with parties targeting Russian-speaking voters in Estonia performing better in the early 1990s whereas in Latvia such parties were unable to make significant inroads at first.

Other state policies aimed more specifically at political parties by discouraging ethnic parties. This can be accomplished in several ways. First, laws on political parties or elections can reward multinational coalitions or parties, or require them outright. With the exception of a few timid experiments in Bosnia, such multi-ethnic parties and coalitions are not encouraged in Central and South-Eastern Europe.

Secondly, the law can indirectly promote such goals by requiring parties either to submit signatures across the country to register or to run candidates in any number of regions of the country in order to participate in elections, thus excluding geographically-concentrated minorities. Russia, Ukraine and Moldova have opted for some regional distribution requirements, which require signatures from a prescribed number of districts for a party to be registered, precluding regionally concentrated minorities from representation. What appears to be a Soviet legacy is also based on concrete experience with regional secessionist movements, similar to Georgia, which also bans ethnic parties. Whereas minority parties in Central Europe in the early 1990s were generally talking about but not pursuing a secessionist agenda, many regional movements in the ex-Soviet Union did pursue secession, so such restrictions have to be viewed in this light. Because the regionalist tendencies in Ukraine and Moldova were not following clear-cut ethnic lines, spatial requirements appeared more "appropriate" than an outright ban on ethnic parties.[21] In none of the countries of Central and Eastern Europe under study here are similar restrictions in place.[22]

The third approach is an outright ban on ethnic parties. Outright bans have also been the exception, enacted only in Albania, Bulgaria and Bosnia-Herzegovina. The briefest experiment was in Bosnia, where mono-ethnic parties were temporarily prohibited during the pre-election period in 1990. The Constitutional Court lifted the ban before the elections, thus having no impact on the outcome, which resulted in an overwhelming victory for the three nationalist parties.[23] In Albania and Bulgaria, experience with such bans has been longer, but not much more effective, as the main parties of Turks in Bulgaria and Greeks in Albania – the two key minorities in both countries – have not been prohibited. This has been for three reasons: first, the parties have avoided mono-ethnic labels, invoking human rights in their names instead and otherwise formally downplaying their minority appeal; secondly, international pressure on the authorities not to ban the key parties of the largest minorities has contributed to the lack of implementation;[24] finally, the legal framework banning ethnic parties was established in Albania and Bulgaria *after* minority parties had already emerged and would have thus required the banning of an existing party rather than just curtailing the emergence of such a party.

In Bulgaria, the effect of the constitutional ban on "political parties on ethnic, racial, or religious lines"[25] has been modest. It has been part of a larger restrictive policy towards (some) minority parties, which also obstructed minority party formation through non-recognition of minorities and the prevention of party registration on the grounds of supposed secessionist threats. Associations and parties of the Macedonian minority have been banned or denied registration over the years. These decisions have usually been based on other grounds than the ban on ethnic parties, such as incomplete registration details.[26] The Macedonian OMO Ilinden party was banned by the Bulgarian Constitutional Court in 1999, not for being an ethnic party but for threatening national security.[27] Some Roma parties have been able to circumvent the ban by either avoiding direct reference to ethnicity or benefiting from a permissive position by the authorities, but, in the early 1990s, the Roma Democratic Union was denied registration on the basis of the ban. The underrepresentation of Roma parties in Bulgaria is likely to have similar causes to those in other countries, rather than being the consequence of the ban.[28]

Although the ban itself did not prevent the emergence of minority parties, it might be argued that it helped the development of the Turkish-minority Movement for Rights and Freedoms in seeking a broader constituency basis.[29] More substantially, the ban reflects a restrictive approach towards minorities that denies recognition to some groups (e.g. Pomaks and Macedonians) and views minority groups with suspicion.[30]

The experience in Albania leads to similar conclusions. In Albania, the ban was established only for the second Albanian elections in July 1991. The Greek-minority organization Omonia participated in the first elections, but two laws that first banned the "formation of parties on religious, ethnic and regional basis", and then allowed only parties, coalitions and individuals, but not other organizations, to run in elections, resulted in the creation of the Unity for Human Rights Party, which circumvented the ban.[31] A new law on political parties in 2000, which replaced the 1992 law, lifted the earlier ban on ethnic parties.[32] The Human Rights Party has been represented in all parliaments since 1992 and joined the socialist-led government in 2001.

The Venice Commission, which advises member states of the Council of Europe on constitutional questions, has also examined party bans. It concludes that such bans are ineffective, unusual and incompatible with human rights standards.[33] Bans on ethnic parties have been clearly instituted to prevent what the state and the ethnic majority consider threatening, rather than as a tool for moderating or de-ethnicizing the political system. Only the short-lived ban on ethnic parties in Bosnia aimed at preventing the emergence of ethnically-based parties altogether, rather than only among minorities.

Most measures to hinder minority representation do not take the form of explicit bans, but rather express themselves through a number of obstacles, which sometimes inadvertently and at times intentionally seek to preclude or reduce minority representation. As the Venice Commission notes in its study of electoral systems and their impact on minorities, "[i]t is not always easy to identify which of these general rules promote and which hinder representation of minorities".[34]

A common tool has been ethnic gerrymandering, i.e. creating electoral units that reduce the representation of minorities in parliament. Because electoral commissions or other institutions charged with the establishment of electoral units have been dominated by majorities, districting has often disadvantaged minorities.[35] As voting in most countries under consideration here follows ethnic lines, electoral commissions secured electoral units that would prevent state majorities from becoming regional minorities and thus being outvoted. Furthermore, electoral districts can be drawn to reduce minority representation. One poignant example is electoral district 61 in Macedonia's 1998 elections. In the monitoring report of the OSCE Office for Democratic Institutions and Human Rights (ODIHR), the observers note that this snake-shaped district "curls around the mountains in the north west of the country, joining ethnic Macedonian villages together in a mainly ethnic Albanian area". As a consequence, electoral engineering secured additional seats for the majority and prevented the creation of a minority voting bloc.[36] In the case of Macedonia, gerrymandering was so widely recognized as disadvantaging Albanians that it was explicitly addressed in the demands of the Albanian National Liberation Army during the 2001 conflict.[37]

Similarly, the size of constituencies has been a tool to disadvantage minorities. A number of countries, such as Slovakia and Serbia, have held elections in one country-wide constituency, which can also disadvantage minorities.[38] Similarly, registration requirements constitute another potential obstacle for minority parties. A high number of required signatures for either registering a party or running in parliamentary elections can also disadvantage minorities.[39] In Bulgaria, for example, 5,000 signatures are required for the registration of a party. Considering that 5,071 citizens declared themselves to be Macedonian in the 2001 census, the high numerical requirement for party registration can be viewed as being directly linked to an effort to prevent the emergence of a Macedonian minority party. Poland and Serbia, which have abolished the threshold for minority parties, have also lowered the registration requirements of parties or for registering in elections accordingly. In Serbia, the abolition of the electoral threshold of 5 per cent for national minority parties effectively advanced their representation only after the electoral commission lowered the requirement to submit 10,000 signatures for national minority parties in order to participate in national elections to 3,000.[40]

The most frequent obstacle for minority parties across Central and South-Eastern Europe is the electoral threshold. Although the level generally varies between 3 and 5 per cent, all countries have an effective threshold.[41] In particular, because there has been a general trend towards proportional representation in the region since the 1990s, the importance of thresholds has increased. When considering the demographic map of Central and South-Eastern Europe, it is apparent that in most countries only the parties of the largest minority would be able to secure parliamentary representation, and then only if they were to run on a single ticket. Thresholds have thus stifled minority party formation among smaller minorities and at times resulted in consolidation of a single minority party. Coalitions among several smaller minority groups to overcome the threshold have been rare. The most significant attempt failed in 2003 in Serbia, when the "Coalition for Tolerance", composed of parties from the Hungarian and Bosniak minority and regional parties, failed to cross the 5 per cent threshold by winning only 4.2 per cent of the vote.[42]

Instead, thresholds contributed to minority parties or associations forming pre-election coalitions or securing seats on lists of majority and mainstream parties. In particular, parties of Roma and small minorities have been able to secure representation through such means only if no specific mechanisms favouring minority parties are in place. The regional experience with such representation through mainstream parties has been modest. If majority parties were willing to include minority candidates on electoral lists, such candidates were often placed at low positions on the ballot, resulting in only few seats gained by minorities. As Barany points out, in 2000 only seven self-declared Roma were represented in parliaments across Central and Eastern Europe, five of whom gained representation on majority party lists.[43]

Promoting minority party inclusion

Despite the prevalent challenge for minority parties arising from thresholds, only two countries in Central and South-Eastern Europe have opted to lift the threshold for minority parties. As will be discussed below, however, a number of countries have chosen more direct steps to include minority parties. Poland has allowed minorities to contest without a threshold since 1990. In practice, this has benefited only the small German minority, which has been able to secure between 2 and 7 seats in the Sejm, the lower chamber of the Polish parliament.[44] In Serbia, the abolition of the threshold was a direct response to the failure of any minority party to cross the 5 per cent threshold in the 2003 parliamentary elections. The impact in Serbia was immediate: five minority parties representing Hungarians, Bosniaks, Albanians and Roma were able to gain seats. In Poland, owing to the small number of minorities and the authorities' restrictive handling of the rules (for example, barring the Silesian minority from competing for seats without a threshold), the impact has been considerably lower than in Serbia.

In South-Eastern Europe, the most common and popular mechanism for promoting minority inclusion is to reserve minority seats in parliament (see Table 5.2). Slovenia, Croatia, Bosnia-Herzegovina, Montenegro, Kosovo and Romania have set aside seats on the basis of ethnic affiliation. The mechanisms for distributing such seats, however, vary greatly. Reserved seats primarily seek to secure representation of smaller minorities that would not be able to achieve representation without such special measures. Although a number of countries have upper houses of parliament, reserved seats are primarily located within the lower chambers. As the number of reserved seats is generally small, they have not been a major distortion of proportionality and equal representation.[45]

Slovenia provides representation for only two minorities – Italians (2,258 in 2002) and Hungarians (6,243 in 2002) – which are considered autochthonous. Their numbers are far lower than other minorities in the country, such as Bosniaks or Serbs, which lack parliamentary representation. The Hungarian and Italian MPs are elected in special minority electoral units and in parliament hold certain veto rights in areas of legislation pertaining exclusively to the minority.[46]

Another system of reserved seats has been in use in Montenegro since 1998 for the Albanian minority. Although Montenegro is treated as one electoral unit in parliamentary elections, a special electoral district was established with five reserved seats (four since 2002). What is unusual in the Montenegrin system is that the voters in the affected polling stations are not exclusively Albanian, nor are all Albanians included in these special polling stations. Furthermore, other minorities such as the much larger Muslim/Bosniak minority (14.6 per cent in 1991) have not benefited from similar treatment. The ODIHR has thus criticized this electoral mechanism for its legal uncertainties and for singling out one minority.[47] Because the system prescribes not who gets elected, but only how, not all of the reserved seats have been held by Albanian minority parties. Half of the seats have generally been won by the governing parties, which usually do not have Albanian minority candidates.[48]

The Romanian parliament has a large number of reserved seats, allowing new minorities to register with relative ease. Thus the number of minority seats rose from 11 in 1990 to 18 in 2004. A minority candidate is elected if he/she secures 5 per cent of the nationwide average number of votes needed for one seat, amounting to only 1,273 votes in 2000.[49] The system has secured the representation of even the smallest minorities (including some potentially invented minorities), but minority MPs have been largely passive.[50] For the Roma minority, however, it might be argued that guaranteed representation has facilitated Roma political organization.[51]

In Croatia, the key challenge since independence has been the representation of Serbs, and the 1990s saw several changes to the election law. Since 2000, minorities have the choice between voting for a general candidate list or for the specific minority list, amounting to a current total of 8 reserved seats. Confronted with the choice between voting for a minority list of candidates or the general list, a majority among all larger minorities opt for the general list; in the case of the Serb minority, less than a quarter voted for the minority list in 2003. Curiously, in Croatia, a number of minority MPs represent not only their own ethnic group but also other communities. The Croatian Constitutional Law on Minorities and the Election Law reserves one to three seats for minorities larger than 1.5 per cent, but in fact only Serbs qualify. Of the five seats reserved for smaller minorities, only Hungarians and Italians hold one seat each in parliament; the other minorities "share" the remaining three reserved seats. The candidates of the minorities assigned to the same seat thus compete with each other, with the candidate receiving the most votes winning the seat. Nazif Memedi, for example, elected to the

Croatian Sabor in 2007, represents not only his own Roma community but also the country's Austrians, Bulgarians, Germans, Poles, Romanians, Rusyns, Russians, Turks, Ukrainians, Vlahs and Jews.[52]

Unlike in Croatia, where minorities are forced to choose between voting for reserved seats or for the general lists, in Kosovo minorities have been able to receive representation through reserved seats since 2001, in addition to a share in the overall proportional voting for the assembly: 10 seats are reserved for the Serb community and an additional 10 seats represent other communities. As a result, in the 2001 elections minority parties gained an additional 15 seats in the parliament, increasing their share from 16.7 per cent (20 out of 120 seats) to 29 per cent (35 seats). In practice this has benefited only the larger Serb minority; other communities have little chance of entering the assembly owing to the threshold. Similar mechanisms are in use in the entities of Bosnia-Herzegovina, where a minimum number of seats are set aside for all communities whose candidates do not reach the threshold through the regular electoral procedure.[53]

In 8 of the 17 countries (including Kosovo) in Central and South-Eastern Europe, special mechanisms are in place to secure or facilitate the representation of minorities in parliament. In particular, all the countries of former Yugoslavia (with the exception of Macedonia) have some means of promoting the parliamentary representation of minorities. This trend is partly a reflection of the conflicts in the 1990s, but more a continuation of the elaborate institutionalization of ethnic representation that took place under communism. Because affirmative policies by definition favour minority parties that would be at risk of not being represented through the regular electoral system, the main beneficiaries tend to be smaller minorities that generally do not have great weight in parliament. The impact on policy-making of minority MPs has thus been generally weak, because the ability to constitute a key group in government formation has been limited. Only in Croatia, where the three Serb minority MPs have supported the conservative government of the Croatian Democratic Union since 2003, have minority parties been able to influence policy-making.

Minorities in government

Numerous minorities and their political parties have been represented in parliaments across Central and South-Eastern Europe (see Table 5.3). However, as noted above, minority representation in parliament does not automatically translate into the ability to influence policy-making. Minority representatives in parliament have often been marginal voices

Table 5.3 Minority participation in governments in Central and South-Eastern Europe

Country	Years	Minority	Party
Albania	2001–2005	Greek	Unity for Human Rights Party
Bulgaria	1992–1994, 2001–	Turkish	Movement for Rights and Freedoms
Croatia	2003–	Serb	Independent Democratic Serb Party
Macedonia	1990–	Albanian	Party for Democratic Prosperity, 1992–1998, 2007–; Democratic Party of Albanians, 1998–2002, 2006–; Democratic Union for Integration, 2002–2006
Romania	1996–	Hungarian	Democratic Union of Hungarians in Romania
Serbia	2000–2004	Hungarian Bosniak	Alliance of Vojvodina Hungarians Sandzak Democratic Party
Slovakia	1998–2006	Hungarian	Party of the Hungarian Coalition

Note: This list includes only minority parties that entered parliament independently (except Serbia, where minority parties were part of a broad democratic coalition) rather than as junior partners to majority party lists.

and window-dressing. Nevertheless, there has also been a trend towards minority inclusion in government. After the waning of ethno-nationalist mobilization across Eastern Europe in the mid-1990s, many minority parties have joined governments since the late 1990s and become key coalition partners. Broadly, we can distinguish between countries where minority inclusion in government is part of a power-sharing system either that requires the representation of all key groups (Bosnia-Herzegovina, Kosovo), or where such a government constellation has become a tradition (Macedonia), and countries where minority inclusion is neither required nor generally expected.

In all countries of the region with large minorities, with the exception of the Baltic states, the parties of these minorities have been included in government for at least one legislative period. Often, they entered government as part of broad opposition coalitions against semi-authoritarian and nationalist incumbents (Romania, Slovakia), but in a number of cases (Bulgaria, Romania) the minority parties have demonstrated their ability to form coalitions with parties across the political spectrum.

These coalitions emerged for three key reasons: EU conditionality, shifting values in the domestic political system, and the polarization of majority parties. In its conditionality for the accession of new member states, the European Union requires both democratic governance and respect of minority rights. However, EU conditionality in regard to minority rights has been weak and inconsistent, and the political representation of minorities, especially in government, does not form part of explicit membership requirements.[54] The regular EU progress reports, for example, did not systematically comment on the inclusion of minority parties in government.[55] Nevertheless, EU influence has been crucial in the formation of minority-inclusive governments. First, progress in the field of minority rights has often been linked to the inclusion of minority parties in government, such that fulfilment of the admittedly vague minority rights criteria for EU membership was de facto linked to minority participation. Secondly, minority parties' participation in government has been viewed domestically and by the European Union as an indicator of successful democratic governance and minority rights implementation. In the absence of a coherent EU minority rights policy, consensual politics between the majority and minorities have become a key measure of minority rights protection.[56]

Domestically, the inclusion of minority parties reflected a shift in the character of the political system. In countries with significant minorities, one of the main political cleavages in the early years of democratization was between ethnic groups.[57] The polarization along ethnic lines often contributed to the consolidation of semi-democratic regimes, such as those of Vladimír Mečiar in Slovakia, Ion Illescu in Romania and Franjo Tudjman in Croatia. Minority parties, although permitted by law, were denied legitimacy because they were described by the state and semi-democratic elites as being against the status quo.[58] A pattern in countries with substantial minorities has been the emergence of ethnic (semi-)democracies, wherein minorities are de jure or de facto not equal to the titular nation and suffer legal and political discrimination. This might go hand in hand with an otherwise democratic system of government, as in Latvia or Estonia, or emerge in combination with less democratic practices, as in Croatia or Slovakia.[59] As political cleavages shifted towards issues of economic and political reform and EU accession, the minority–majority division lost some of its significance. Consequently, minority parties became legitimate potential partners and, as noted above, even symbols of a country's desire to join the European Union.

Finally, the inclusion of minority parties in government has been a consequence of highly polarized political cleavages. In a number of post-communist countries, a deeply divided party system developed between either the left-leaning communist successor parties or a nationalist populist party[60] and a more conservative coalition or party. Amid such polarization, minority parties often became a crucial coalition partner. Thus, the predominantly Turkish Movement for Rights and Freedoms has been a key ally for majority parties in Bulgaria, even if it did not formally enter government until 2001. The relatively small size of minority parties also made them more attractive than larger mainstream parties, which would demand a larger share of government positions. It might also be argued that the minority focus of minority parties makes for less competition over government resources than occurs with mainstream parties, which lack such a particular and narrow interest.

Throughout Central and South-Eastern Europe, a common pattern of minority–majority coalitions has emerged. These coalitions fall short of qualifying as power-sharing because they have not – with the exception of Macedonia – acquired a tradition and continuity that would suggest they will remain a key feature of government formation. Furthermore, the clearly majority–minority relationship in the coalitions has meant that the impact of minority parties on government policies has been limited, with minority parties often controlling less important, non-sensitive ministries. In most cases, changes in the field of minority rights protection have been significant for minority parties coming to government, even if the policy agenda of minority parties generally faced serious resistance by majority parties. As a comparative study of minority party participation in governments in Romania, Macedonia and Slovakia suggests, the most significant shift has been the recognition of the legitimacy of minority parties and minority political demands.[61] Through government participation it became apparent to the state majority that minority parties no longer constitute a threat to the titular nation. As a result, minority party inclusion in government is both a consequence and a facilitator of a shift away from ethno-nationalist cleavages in post-communist societies.

Conclusion: The record of party regulation as a tool of conflict management

Institutional design and engineering have been a feature of either moderating minority–majority relations or securing majority dominance across Central and South-Eastern Europe since the fall of communism. However, the impact of both restrictive and promoting measures has been largely modest. Bans and other restrictive measures have been the exception in the region, and even where in place have had only limited success in preventing the formation of minority political parties. Smaller minorities have been largely unable to secure representation in parliaments across the region, except where special affirmative measures are in place, owing to high thresholds and at times high registration requirements for elections or party registration. Larger minorities have not been able to benefit from positive measures promoting minority representation, which

favoured smaller minorities. In fact, minority representation through reserved seats has sometimes been established to promote smaller minorities over larger minorities. Similarly, different electoral systems have
not significantly diminished or promoted the representation of larger minorities.

Political parties across Central and South-Eastern Europe have been
established and campaign with largely one ethnic group in mind, be it a
majority or a minority. This political cleavage emerged in most countries
even before the legislative framework for political parties or elections
was put in place during the transition phase. As such, the legal framework could not assume a *tabula rasa* but had to negotiate with existing
political realities, resulting in the acceptance of the Movement for Rights
and Freedoms in Bulgaria or the Unity for Human Rights Party in Albania.

More significant has been the impact of different electoral systems on
smaller minorities. On the one hand, restrictive measures had a greater
impact because titular nations could afford to ignore minority voices. On
the other hand, smaller minorities have been the primary beneficiaries of
reserved seats and other affirmative policies across the region. However,
parliamentary representation is often merely one aspect of a broader par-
cel of minority rights, involving representation at municipal and regional
levels and in some cases also some degree of cultural autonomy (e.g.
Slovenia, Croatia). Parliamentary representation, though symbolically
important, has often not been the most significant form of minority inclusion, because the impact of minority members in parliament has been
marginal. The most marginalized minority in the region, the Roma, have
been the least able to benefit from efforts to promote minority parties.
Struggling with a fragmented Roma party landscape in most countries,
suspicion towards mainstream politics and distrust of their own political
elites, the Roma have been consistently under-represented across the region.[62] In some cases, reserved seats or reduced thresholds have assured
Roma's inclusion in parliament; elsewhere, Roma either fail to be represented at all or have to rely on majority party support. The number of
Roma parties and members of parliament, however, still lags behind the
share of Roma in the population. Although many Roma vote for majority
parties, this voting pattern is hardly a reflection of the integration of
Roma into mainstream politics, but rather indicates the political and social marginalization of the community. The causes of and remedies for
the political under-representation of Roma thus lie beyond the field of
electoral systems.

Another key factor in the development of minority parties in post-
communist Central and South-Eastern Europe has been the European
Union. Although the European Union lacks a coherent minority rights

policy, it has strengthened the European legal framework, above all by insisting on the ratification of the Framework Convention for the Protection of National Minorities by accession states. However, in regard to the representation of minority parties in the political system, the European Union has not taken a clear position. Nevertheless, both the partial non-implementation of minority party bans in Albania and Bulgaria and the inclusion of minorities in parliament through lower thresholds and reserved seats, as well as in government, are to be explained in part by countries' desire to join the European Union. Rather than being the consequence of a particular EU policy, minority inclusion has been a feature of positive conditionality in the sphere of minority rights and a clear emphasis on linking minority representation with EU integration.[63] Although to a considerable degree the European Union's concern for minority rights has been security driven, minority politics have become less securitized since the early 1990s.

The widespread existence of minority parties in Central and South-Eastern Europe has meant that minority concerns are commonly aggregated through political parties rather than through other institutions such as extra-institutional movements or non-governmental organizations (NGOs). However, here one can observe considerable variation between minorities. Whereas larger minorities find their primary voice through minority parties, smaller minorities more frequently articulate their concerns relating to minority-specific interests through institutions for cultural autonomy, minority associations or local-level political activism. The most notable exception is Russian-speakers in Estonia, who despite their numerical strength have not been able to sustain a party that particularly represents their interests.[64] After some successes in the early 1990s, parties for Russian-speakers have since performed badly in national and municipal elections. This, however, is less the consequence of restrictive citizenship requirements, which are similar to those in Latvia (although there have been variations in the rate of naturalization). The ban on non-citizens joining parties in Estonia or the fragmentation of Russian-based parties are not sufficient to explain their poor performance at elections. More than in Latvia, mainstream parties have sought to court non-Estonian voters with campaign materials in Russian. The appeal by mainstream parties, such as the Centre Party, appears to have been successful, with non-Estonians supporting mixed majority–minority parties over minority-only parties, possibly in an attempt to avoid political marginalization. In addition, voting rights for non-citizens at the local level might have demobilized Russian-speakers in Estonia, whereas in Latvia the more complete exclusion of Russian-speakers might have facilitated their mobilization.[65] Like smaller minorities, Roma in most countries of the region have found their interests aggregated by NGOs, both those within the community itself and larger national and international organizations. Only in exceptional circumstances have mainstream parties, often small liberal or regional groupings, effectively represented minority-specific concerns.

Minority parties across Central and Eastern Europe are not carved out of a single block. The agendas of minority parties have changed over the more than 15 years of democratic transition and most parties encompass divergent political views. Having their origins in broad anti-communist coalitions, as in the case of Slovakia, or otherwise representing different political platforms, most minority parties are brought together not only by a common interest in representing a minority group but also by the need for cohesion to secure parliamentary representation. Multiple strong and competing minority parties, as in Macedonia, are exceptional and only possible among a numerically strong minority.

The internal diversity and differences between minority parties in the region are expressed in divergent views about how to secure minority interests and different positions along larger political cleavages. The first issue often juxtaposes views that seek greater inclusion in state institutions and minority rights with demands for political and territorial autonomy.[66] The second form of variation will express itself in terms of support for larger ideological concepts, such as conservatism or liberalism. Thus some minority parties, such as the larger Hungarian minority parties, tend to represent more conservative options, whereas others, such as the Movement for Rights and Freedoms in Bulgaria, cast themselves as liberal. However, these ideological variations are often not strongly developed because the political systems in general in most post-communist countries lack clear ideological differentiation.

Across Central and South-Eastern Europe, larger minorities' political parties have been a relatively stable fixture in highly volatile political party systems. Whereas there has overall been a degree of moderation in the demands of minority parties, linked to their inclusion in the mainstream political system through coalitions, such parties have not gone away, even in countries that do not promote or even discourage ethnically based parties. This consistency has been a reflection of the cleavages between majorities and minorities, especially in the early phase of the transition, as well as of the positive view taken by international organizations, in particular the European Union, of minority interest articulation through minority parties. Although minority parties have not been universally successful, the firm place that larger minorities have achieved in the political system (including the executive) has arguably improved the legitimacy of the state and political system for minorities and contributed to the institutionalization of minority grievances. This process has generally moderated majority–minority relations, as well as minority demands themselves, bringing about greater institutional stability. At the same time, however, minority parties have not generally been able to meet the needs of smaller communities and the Roma, who find their needs only inadequately addressed through state institutions, be they parliament or the executive.

Acknowledgements

I would like to thank Eben Friedman, Kalina Bozeva and Boris Tsilevich, as well as the various contributors to this volume, for their useful comments and suggestions.

Notes

1. Carlos Flores Juberías, "Post-Communist Electoral Systems and National Minorities: A Dilemma in Five Paradigms", in Johnathan P. Stein (ed.), *The Politics of National Minority Participation in Post-Communist Europe* (Armonk, NY: M. E. Sharpe, 2000), p. 33.
2. On these, see Florian Bieber, "Minorities and Electoral Systems in the Balkans", in Dusan Pavlović, Goran Petrov, Despina Syrri and David A. Stone (eds), *Democratisation in Southeast Europe: An Introduction to Election Issues* (Thessaloniki: SEERC, 2005), pp. 51–71.
3. According to World Bank estimates, Roma account for 8–12 per cent of the population in Macedonia, Romania, Bulgaria and Slovakia and for 4–8 per cent in Hungary, Serbia and the Czech Republic. Dena Ringold, *Roma and the Transition in Central and Eastern Europe: Trends and Challenges* (Washington, DC: World Bank, 2000), p. 1.
4. Joseph Stalin, *Marxism and the National Question, Selected Writings and Speeches* (New York: International Publishers, 1942).
5. Walker Connor, *The National Question in Marxist-Leninist Theory and Strategy* (Princeton, NJ: Princeton University Press, 1984).
6. Michael Shafir, "The Political Party as National Holding Company: The Hungarian Democratic Federation of Romania", in Stein, *The Politics of National Minority Participation in Post-Communist Europe*, p. 101; Maria Spirova, "Political Parties in Bulgaria. Organizational Trends in a Comparative Perspective", *Party Politics*, 11(5), 2005: 605; James Pettifer, "The Greek Minority in Albania: Ethnic Politics in a Pre-National State", in Stein, *The Politics of National Minority Participation in Post-Communist Europe*, p. 175.
7. In communist Yugoslavia, a three-tiered hierarchy distinguished between nations (groups that primarily lived in Yugoslavia and constituted a majority or plurality in one republic), nationalities (groups that had a nation-state outside Yugoslavia, such as Albanians or Hungarians) and ethnic groups (groups without a kin-state, such as Roma or Vlachs). Dejan Jović, "Fear of Becoming *Minority* as a Motivator of Conflict in the Former Yugoslavia", *Balkanologie*, 5(1 & 2), 2001: 21–36.
8. Rogers Brubaker, *Nationalism Reframed: Nationhood and the National Question in the New Europe* (Cambridge: Cambridge University Press, 1996), p. 5.

9. Robert Hayden, *Blueprints for a House Divided: The Constitutional Logic of the Yugoslav Conflicts* (Ann Arbor, MI: University of Michigan Press, 1999).
10. Macedonia's first post-communist government between 1990 and 1992 included three ethnic Albanians.
11. Venice Commission, "Electoral Law and National Minorities", Strasbourg, 25 January 2000.
12. Ibid.; Eben Friedman, "Electoral System Design and Minority Representation in Slovakia and Macedonia", *Ethnopolitics*, 4(4), 2005: 381–396.
13. Although Roma continued to be represented in parliament after the introduction of PR, Roma candidates entered parliament only through pre-election coalitions with majority parties. Friedman, "Electoral System Design and Minority Representation in Slovakia and Macedonia", p. 392.
14. Both Poland (1991) and Romania (1990) had no threshold in parliamentary elections. In Poland, 29 parties gained seats; in Romania, 16 parties (+11 minority representatives).
15. A different, yet related, problem has been the issue of the so-called "erased" in Slovenia. Here, the citizenship law was not restrictive but it offered a short period for applying for citizenship (less than one year, in 1991) and, in 1992, all those who had not applied for citizenship lost their resident status and all subsequent political rights. This measure, affecting some 18,000 people, targeted migrants from other Yugoslav republics in Slovenia who had settled in Yugoslav times. As most of those from other Yugoslav republics had opted for citizenship (approximately 170,000), the "erased" did not constitute a major obstacle to the political participation of this group. Matvez Krivic, "Post Scriptum", in Jasminka Dedić, Vlasta Jalušič and Jelka Zorn, *The Erased: Organized Innocence and the Politics of Exclusion* (Ljubljana: Peace Institute, 2003), pp. 158–159.
16. During communist rule, republican citizenship was irrelevant and most Roma in the Czech Republic had Slovak republican citizenship. As Slovakia imposed similarly restrictive citizenship requirements, Roma were in effect stranded between the two republics. See Eben Friedman, "Minority Rights in Europe: Roma in Slovakia and the Czech Republic", in Malte Brosig (ed.), *Minority Rights in Europe: A Fragmented Regime?* (Frankfurt/Main: Peter Lang Verlag, 2006), pp. 153–168.
17. Melanie H. Ram, "Democratization through European Integration: The Case of Minority Rights in the Czech Republic and Romania", *Studies in Comparative International Development*, 38(2), 2003: 40–41; "Roma in the Czech Republic. Foreigners in Their Own Land", *Human Rights Watch*, 8(11), 1996, available at ⟨http://hrw.org/reports/1996/Czech.htm⟩ (accessed 31 March 2008).
18. David Galbreath, "The Politics of European Integration and Minority Rights in Estonia and Latvia", *Perspectives on European Politics and Society*, 4(1), 2003: 35–53.
19. In Latvia, non-citizens can join parties and contribute funds, but citizens have to make up at least half of the membership of any party. In Estonia, non-citizens are barred from joining political parties, but on the other hand are able to vote in local elections, unlike in Latvia. OSCE Office for Democratic Institutions and Human Rights (ODIHR), "Republic of Latvia. Parliamentary Elections, 7 October 2006. OSCE/ODIHR Limited Election Observation Mission Final Report", Warsaw, 8 February 2007, p. 7. A number of other countries in Central and Eastern Europe (Albania, Bulgaria, Croatia, Czech Republic, Lithuania and Macedonia) do not allow non-citizens to join parties. In these countries, this has less of an impact on national minorities. Venice Commission, "Report on the Establishment, Organisation and Activities of Political Parties", Strasbourg, 16 February 2004, p. 10.
20. Peter Van Elsuwege, "Russian-Speaking Minorities in Estonia and Latvia: Problems of Integration at the Threshold of the European Union", European Centre for Minority

Issues, Working Paper No. 20, May 2004, pp. 32–34, available at: ⟨http://www.ecmi.de/rubrik/58/working+papers/⟩ (accessed 31 March 2008).

21. In Ukraine, a party requires 10,000 signatures from eligible voters in at least two-thirds of the districts of at least two-thirds of the administrative regions and in the cities of Kyiv and Sevastopol, and in at least two-thirds of the districts of the Autonomous Republic of the Crimea (Law of Ukraine on Political Parties, 2002, Article 10). Similarly, Moldova requires 5,000 active members residing in at least half of the second-level administrative territorial units, and no fewer than 600 in each of the administrative territorial units (Law of the Republic of Moldova on Parties and Other Socio-Political Organizations, 1991, Article 5.9), Flores Juberías, "Post-Communist Electoral Systems and National Minorities", pp. 38–39; see also Chapter 7 by Birnir in this volume.

22. Venice Commission, "Report on the Establishment, Organisation and Activities of Political Parties", p. 7. Proposals along similar lines have, however, been made in a number of Central and East European countries, such as Slovakia.

23. Suad Arnautović, *Izbori u Bosnia i Hercegovini '90* (Sarajevo: Promocult, 1996).

24. Matthijs Bogaards, "Electoral Systems and the Management of Ethnic Conflict in the Balkans", in Alina Mungiu-Pippidi and Ivan Krastev (eds), *Nationalism after Communism. Lessons Learned* (Budapest: CEU Press, 2004), pp. 257–259.

25. Constitution of the Republic of Bulgaria, 1991, Article 11.4.

26. International Helsinki Federation, "Bulgaria", *IHF Report 2007. Human Rights in the OSCE Region* (Vienna, 2007), p. 41.

27. Bulgarian Helsinki Committee, *Human Rights in Bulgaria in 2000* (Sofia, 2001); available at ⟨http://www.bghelsinki.org/annual/en/2000.html⟩ (accessed 31 March 2008).

28. Maria Spirova, "Electoral Rules and the Political Representation of Ethnic Minorities: Evidence from Bulgaria and Romania", paper presented at the Annual meeting of the Association for the Study of Nationalities, 15–17 April 2004, p. 16; available at ⟨http://www.policy.hu/spirova/ASN2004.pdf⟩ (accessed 31 March 2008).

29. Ibid., p. 26.

30. I would like to thank Kalina Bozeva for her helpful comments on the matter.

31. James Filippatos, "Ethnic Identity and Political Stability in Albania: The Human Rights Status of the Greek Minority", *Mediterranean Affairs*, 10(1), 1999: 146.

32. Advisory Committee on the Framework Convention for the Protection of National Minorities, "Opinion on Albania", ACFC/INF/OP/I(2003)004, 12 September 2002, pp. 12, 18.

33. Venice Commission, "Electoral Law and National Minorities".

34. Ibid.

35. Ibid.

36. ODIHR, "Parliamentary Elections in the Former Yugoslav Republic of Macedonia, 18 October and 1 November 1998", 1 December 1998.

37. Iso Rusi, "From Army to Party – the Politics of the NLA", in Conflict Studies Research Centre and Institute of War & Peace Reporting, *The 2001 Conflict in FYROM* (Wilts, UK: Advanced Research and Assessment Group, 2004), p. 3.

38. ODIHR, "The Slovak Republic Parliamentary Elections, 25 and 26 September 1998", 26 October 1998.

39. Most countries under consideration here have a minimum membership requirement. See Venice Commission, "Electoral Law and National Minorities", p. 7. In most cases, the numerical requirement is too low to constitute an obstacle for minorities (e.g. 100 in Croatia and Serbia).

40. Republička Izborna Komisija [Republic Electoral Commission], *Uputstvo Za Sprovodenje Zakona o Izboru Narodnih Poslanika*, 15 November 2006; available at ⟨http://www.rik.parlament.sr.gov.yu/latinica/propisi_frames.htm⟩ (accessed 31 March 2008).

41. In some cases coalitions had to clear a higher threshold. In 1998 in Slovakia, the law even required every party in the coalition to clear a 5 per cent threshold, rendering the establishment of pre-election coalitions superfluous. The measure was targeted against the coalition of the Hungarian minority parties and the main opposition coalition, both of which reregistered as a political party. Venice Commission, "Electoral Law and National Minorities", p. 6. Moldova too has had higher thresholds for coalitions.

42. B92 Vesti, "Konačni podaci RIK o broju mandate", 2003, available at ⟨http://www.b92.net/specijal/izbori2003/izborne_liste.php?nav_id=127234⟩ (accessed 31 March 2008).

43. Zoltan Barany, "Romani Electoral Politics and Behaviour", *Journal on Ethnopolitics and Minority Issues in Europe*, Autumn 2001: 8, available at ⟨http://ecmi.de/jemie/download/Focus11-2001Barany.pdf⟩ (accessed 31 March 2008). Considering that the number of Roma in the region is at least equal to the population of Slovakia or Croatia, the under-representation of Roma is considerable.

44. Michael Fleming, "The Limits of the German Minority Project in Post-Communist Poland: Scale, Space and Democratic Deliberation", *Nationalities Papers*, 31(4), 2003, p. 399.

45. In the case of Montenegro, however, reserved seats, as foreseen in the 2006 minority law, were declared unconstitutional by the Constitutional Court on these grounds. Biljana Pajak, "Novi zaplet na crnogorskoj političkoj sceni", *Politika*, 21 July 2006.

46. Ivan Kristan, "Die Rechtstellung der Minderheiten in Slovenien", in Georg Brunner and Boris Meissner (eds), *Das Recht der nationalen Minderheiten in Osteuropa* (Berlin: Berlin Verlag, 1999), pp. 167–168.

47. ODIHR, "Republic of Montenegro, Parliamentary Election, 10 September 2006", 28 December 2006, pp. 15–16.

48. Veselin Pavićević, *Izborni sistem. Distributivni činioci izbornog sistema na primeru izbora u Crnoj Gori 1990–2001* (Belgrade: CeSID, 2002), pp. 35–36.

49. Ciprian-Calin Alionescu, "Parliamentary Representation of Minorities in Romania", *Southeast European Politics*, 5(1), 2004, p. 64.

50. Ibid., pp. 69–70.

51. Spirova, "Electoral Rules and the Political Representation of Ethnic Minorities", pp. 22–23.

52. Antonija Petričušić, "Constitutional Law on the Rights of National Minorities in the Republic of Croatia", *European Yearbook of Minority Issues*, Vol. 2, 2002/3 (Leiden and Boston: Martinus Nijhoff Publishers, 2004), pp. 618–619.

53. Florian Bieber, *Post-War Bosnia: Ethnicity, Inequality and Public Sector Governance* (London: Palgrave, 2006), pp. 128–131. At the state level, reserved seats benefit the three dominant groups – Serbs, Bosniaks and Croats – to the disadvantage of minorities. Thus, in the second chamber of parliament – the House of Peoples – 5 seats each (out of 15) are reserved for the three dominant nations.

54. James Hughes and Gwendolyn Sasse, "Monitoring the Monitors: EU Enlargement Conditionality and Minority Protection in the CEECs", *Journal on Ethnopolitics and Minority Issues in Europe*, 1, 2003; available at ⟨http://ecmi.de/jemie/download/Focus1-2003_Hughes_Sasse.pdf⟩ (accessed 31 March 2008).

55. However, in 1997, the Commission noted that "[r]elations with the Hungarian minority have improved appreciably since the signing of a bilateral treaty with Hungary in September 1996 and the arrival in office of a government including two ministers from the UDMR". European Commission, "Agenda 2000 – Commission Opinion on Romania's Application for Membership of the European Union", DOC/97/18, Brussels, 15 July 1997, p. 17.

56. Martin Brusis, "The European Union and Interethnic Power-sharing Arrangements in Accession Countries", *Journal on Ethnopolitics and Minority Issues in Europe*, 1, 2003,

p. 13; available at http://ecmi.de/jemie/download/Focus1-2003_Brusis.pdf (accessed 31 March 2008).

57. Stephen Whitefield, "Political Cleavages and Post-Communist Politics", *Annual Review of Political Science*, 5, 2002: 181–200.

58. Most minority parties in Central and South-Eastern Europe did not promote a secessionist agenda. Secessionist movements usually did not recognize the legitimacy of the existing political system and thus boycotted elections and/or sought extra-institutional means of interest articulation, e.g. the Kosovo Albanian political parties during the 1990s in Serbia.

59. Sammy Smooha, "The Non-Emergence of a Viable Ethnic Democracy in Post-Communist Europe", in Sammy Smooha and Priit Järve (eds), *The Fate of Ethnic Democracy in Post-Communist Europe* (Budapest: LGI, 2005), pp. 241–258.

60. In Slovakia, for example, Mečiar's Movement for a Democratic Slovakia (HZDS) had its origins in the anti-communist opposition.

61. Monica Robotin, "A Comparative Approach to Minority Participation in Government", in Monica Robotin and Levent Salat (eds), *A New Balance: Democracy and Minorities in Post-Communist Europe* (Budapest: LGI, 2003), pp. 161–162.

62. Barany, "Romani Electoral Politics and Behaviour".

63. Frank Schimmelfennig, Stefan Engert and Heiko Knobel, "Costs, Commitment and Compliance: The Impact of EU Democratic Conditionality on Latvia, Slovakia and Turkey", *Journal of Common Market Studies*, 41(3), 2003: 495–518.

64. Even more than in other countries, many parties representing Russian-speakers in Estonia and Latvia are not exclusively minority parties but have a range of other ideological orientations. Whereas some might be oriented towards Russia, others have adopted a human rights or a social democratic platform.

65. Raimo Poom, "Notes from Tallinn: Where Have All Those Russian Parties Gone?", *Transitions Online*, 19 March 2003; available at ⟨http://www.tol.cz⟩ (accessed 31 March 2008); Maksim Golovko, "Russian Parties and Electoral Behavior: Cultural-Historical Background and Prejudice as Determinants of Electoral Behavior of Russian-Speaking Voters", Conference Paper, 13th NISPAcee Annual Conference, "Democratic Governance for the XXI Century: Challenges and Responses in CEE Countries", Moscow, 19–21 May 2005; available at: ⟨http://unpan1.un.org/intradoc/groups/public/documents/NISPAcee/UNPAN022175.pdf⟩ (accessed 31 March 2008); ODIHR, "Republic of Estonia, Parliamentary Elections, 4 March 2007", ODIHR.GAL/56/07, 28 June 2007, p. 26.

66. Bugajski distinguishes between minority parties on the basis of their primary political platform: 1. cultural revival; 2. political autonomy; 3. territorial autonomy; 4. separatism; and 5. irredentism. Generally speaking, most larger minority parties would fall into categories 2 and 3, whereas smaller minority groups often opt for category 1. There are few secessionist or irredentist minority parties, especially since the mid–late 1990s. Janusz Bugajski, *Political Parties in Eastern Europe. A Guide to Politics in the Post-Communist Era* (Armonk, NY: M. E. Sharpe, 2002), pp. li–lii.

6

Political parties in conflict-prone societies in Latin America

Matthias Catón and Fernando Tuesta Soldevilla

Introduction

Latin America is a vast region stretching from Mexico at the border with the United States to Chile in the south. Normally it is defined as including all Spanish- or Portuguese-speaking countries on the American continent. French-speaking Haiti is usually omitted, despite French being a Latin language. The common definition of Latin America thus comprises 19 countries that share a number of characteristics but differ considerably in others. Similar colonial history, language, religion and presidentialism are among their most important similarities. For analytical purposes it is important to group countries in a way that maximizes similarities. Therefore, it is appropriate to divide Latin America into three sub-regional groups: Central America and the Caribbean,[1] the Andean region,[2] and the Southern Cone (*cono sur*).[3] Owing to their size, Brazil and Mexico are difficult to put into any of these groups and they are usually treated individually.

Latin America is a democratic region today, as can be seen from the indices in Table 6.1. With the clear exception of Cuba, all countries are democratically governed. Venezuela under President Hugo Chávez is somewhere in between, in the grey zone of semi-authoritarian or hybrid regimes with increasing moves towards more authoritarian structures.

This predominance of democracy is by no means something that could be considered the norm in Latin America. For much of its history, authoritarianism prevailed. Most countries became independent from

Political parties in conflict-prone societies: Regulation, engineering and democratic development, Reilly and Nordlund (eds),
United Nations University Press, 2008, ISBN 978-92-808-1157-5

Table 6.1 Development and democracy indicators

	Polity IV[a]		Freedom House[b]		HDI[c]	Gini coefficient[d]	Indigenous population (%)[e]
	1980	2004	1980	2006			
Argentina	−9	8	6	2	0.863 (1)	52.8	1
Bolivia	−7	8	7	3	0.692 (16)	60.1	55
Brazil	−4	8	4	2	0.792 (7)	58.0	<1
Chile	−7	9	6	1	0.859 (2)	57.1	3
Colombia	8	7	2	3	0.790 (8)	58.6	1
Costa Rica	10	10	1	1	0.841 (4)	49.9	1
Dominican Republic	6	8	2	2	0.757 (12)	51.7	1
Ecuador	9	6	2	3	0.765 (11)	43.7	25
El Salvador	−2	7	5	2	0.729 (14)	52.4	1
Guatemala	−7	8	6	3	0.673 (18)	55.1	41
Honduras	1	7	4	3	0.683 (17)	53.8	7
Mexico	−3	8	3	2	0.821 (5)	49.5	30
Nicaragua	–	8	5	3	0.698 (15)	43.1	5
Panama	−6	9	4	1	0.809 (6)	56.4	6
Paraguay	−8	8	5	3	0.757 (12)	57.8	5
Peru	9	9	2	2	0.767 (10)	54.6	45
Uruguay	−7	10	5	1	0.851 (3)	44.9	0
Venezuela	9	6	1	4	0.784 (9)	44.1	2
Median	−2	8	4	2	*0.776*	*49.7*	*4*

Notes:
[a] Possible values run from −10 (highly autocratic) to 10 (highly democratic). Source: Polity IV Project.
[b] Freedom House Political Rights Index – possible values run from 1 (free) to 7 (not free). Source: Freedom House country reports, 2007.
[c] Human Development Index. Rank among Latin American countries in parentheses. Source: United Nations Development Programme, Human Development Report 2006.
[d] Income inequality – the higher the Gini coefficient, the greater the inequality. Source: UNDP, Human Development Report 2006, Table 15, pp. 335–338.
[e] Source: Central Intelligence Agency, The 2007 World Factbook.

Spain – or Portugal, in the case of Brazil – in the first part of the nine-teenth century, but during the entire century democracy was virtually un-known, and also during the twentieth century it was the exception rather than the norm.

Only since the third wave of democratization[4] that swept Latin Amer-ica in the 1980s has democracy become more stable in the region. In terms of democratic experience one can distinguish four groups of coun-tries: (1) those with a decade-long, uninterrupted democratic history; (2) those that have a long experience with democracy, interrupted by relatively brief authoritarian phases; (3) those that oscillated between democracy and authoritarianism more or less frequently; and (4) those that have democratized for the first time in the past two decades.

Only Costa Rica still belongs to the first group. It has had an uninter-rupted series of competitive elections since 1953. Until recently, Venezu-ela also belonged to this group, with democratic elections since 1958. However, as noted above, the democratic situation in Venezuela is cur-rently unstable. The second group consists of Chile and Uruguay, with only one democratic backlash each in the second half of the twentieth century. The third group comprises Argentina, Ecuador and Peru. The fourth group is by far the largest and consists of Brazil, Bolivia, Mexico, Paraguay and all Central American countries except for Costa Rica.

We shall first analyse the situation of Latin American parties and party systems. This is followed by an overview of presidentialism, the Latin American form of government. We then explain what political conflicts mean in Latin America, and give an overview of the types and the depth of party regulation. Finally, we provide two in-depth case studies. The first covers the Andean region and the second one deals with Peru.

The state of parties and party systems

There is a great deal of variation in terms of the structure of party sys-tems, the importance of political parties for the political process as a whole and the types of party that dominate in a country.[5] The variation ranges from a country such as Chile, where parties are well rooted in so-ciety and have played an important role in its political history, to Brazil, with a highly volatile, fragmented party system. The 2002 parliamentary elections in Brazil were contested by 30 parties, 19 of which gained seats. On the other hand, the strong institutionalization of the party system in a country such as Uruguay became obvious when the two parties that had dominated Uruguayan politics for much of its history reappeared in

1984 virtually unchanged after 11 years of military dictatorship. Even the leadership stayed the same in most cases. Despite recent changes in the party system, the institutionalization of parties remains high in Uruguay. In many Central American countries, in contrast, parties tend to be vehicles for individual politicians rather than stable institutions themselves.

In terms of fragmentation, there are a number of essentially two-party systems, such as Colombia, El Salvador, Honduras and Paraguay, and there are multi-party systems such as Bolivia, Brazil, Chile and Peru. It should be noted, though, that in Colombia the two traditional parties are highly factionalized, thus hiding a heavily splintered political landscape, and the Chilean multi-party system has been organized in two stable blocs since the return to democracy in 1990. Hence, looking only at the (effective) number of parties can be misleading.

The differences in the structure of party systems cannot be explained by the electoral system for parliamentary or presidential elections. Most countries in Latin America use a form of proportional representation (PR) for parliamentary elections, most commonly PR in multi-member constituencies (MMCs) (see Table 6.2). The role of presidential elections for the party systems will be explored in the next section.

The role of presidentialism

A party system is influenced by the structure of the political system as a whole. One of the most striking features in Latin America is the dominance of presidentialism. All Latin American countries use this form of government, and this has consequences for the way in which parties operate. The office of the president is the most important political position, so presidential elections are the centre of attention.

Latin American countries use three types of electoral system for their presidential elections today (see Table 6.2): plurality, absolute majority and qualified majority. Plurality is the easiest system in terms of design, because the candidate with the most votes wins outright. Majority systems require a candidate to win 50 per cent plus one vote. Qualified majority systems are a variation of absolute majority systems; they usually require a threshold that is somewhere below 50 per cent or a combination of two criteria, such as at least 40 per cent of the vote and/or a certain winning margin over the second-placed candidate. If no candidate passes the threshold of an absolute or a qualified majority, a second round is held. All Latin American countries that use absolute or qualified majority systems provide for a runoff between the two candidates with

Table 6.2 Overview of the political systems in Latin America

	Presidential electoral system	Parliamentary electoral system[a]	Average constituency magnitude (no. of seats)	Competitive elections since[b]
Argentina	Qualified majority	PR in MMCs	10.7	1983
Bolivia	Absolute majority[c]	Personalized PR	6.9	1982
Brazil	Absolute majority	PR in MMCs	19.0	1982
Chile	Absolute majority	Binomial	2.0	1990
Colombia	Absolute majority	PR in MMCs	4.8	1958
Costa Rica	Qualified majority	PR in MMCs	8.1	1953
Dominican Republic	Absolute majority	PR in MMCs	3.2	1978
Ecuador	Absolute majority	PR in MMCs	4.5	1978
El Salvador	Absolute majority	PR in MMCs	4.6	1989
Guatemala	Absolute majority	PR in MMCs	5.5	1985
Honduras	Plurality	PR in MMCs	7.1	1982
Mexico	Plurality	Segmented	1.7	1997
Nicaragua	Qualified majority	PR in MMCs	5.8	1990
Panama	Plurality	PR in MMCs	3.2	1989
Paraguay	Plurality	PR in MMCs	4.4	1992
Peru	Absolute majority	Pure PR	4.8	2001
Uruguay	Absolute majority	Pure PR	5.2	1985
Venezuela	Plurality	Personalized PR	6.3	1958
Average			*6.0*	

Source: Compiled by the authors.

Notes: Cuba is missing because it is not a democracy.

[a]PR = proportional representation; MMCs = multi-member constituencies.

[b]Uninterrupted to date. *Source:* Dieter Nohlen, ''Elections and Electoral Systems in the Americas: South America'', in Dieter Nohlen (ed.), *Elections in the Americas*, Vol. 2 (Oxford: Oxford University Press, 2005), pp. 1–58.

[c]No run-off, Congress chooses.

the most votes. The only exception is Bolivia, where parliament decides. Plurality systems are uncommon today: only 5 out of 19 countries in Latin America use them.

The type of electoral system is thought to have consequences for the party system as well. Lijphart found significantly lower numbers of effective parties in countries with presidential systems.[6] The incentive for political forces to agree on joint candidates is higher in plurality systems than in majoritarian ones. The qualified systems are somewhere in between. Absolute majority systems are often argued to be more democratic because the winner supposedly has a much broader base of support. However, the outcome of a runoff is largely determined by who makes it there in the first place. Several scholars point out that in Latin America the average share of the winning candidate in plurality systems is actually around or above 50 per cent,[7] therefore refuting the claim of a lack of legitimacy.

What are the conflicts in the Latin American case?

Ethnicity and inequality

The most common conflict is a socio-economic one that overlaps with ethnic dimensions. Latin America is the continent with the highest income inequalities in the world. The Gini coefficient, which measures income inequalities on a scale from 0 (totally equal) to 100 (totally unequal), is 49.7 on average for Latin America (see Table 6.1). As a comparison, the coefficient is around 25 for Scandinavia and Japan. Even in the United States, a society that has traditionally accepted much wider income gaps than most European countries, the coefficient is only 40.8.

In Latin America, economic status largely overlaps with ethnicity. The indigenous population is marginalized and the elites in most countries are dominated by whites or mestizos. The relevance of this ethnic cleavage depends, of course, on the proportion of indigenous population. For example, in Bolivia 55 per cent of the population are indigenous and only 12 per cent are white. In Uruguay, the proportion of indigenous population is below 1 per cent (see Table 6.1).

The middle class is weak in most parts of Latin America. Only a few countries, mainly Argentina, Chile and Uruguay, have a significant middle class at all. In most other countries, particularly in Central America, politics and the economy are dominated by a small oligarchic upper class. This constellation weakens political parties, because they are seen by the oligarchies only as vehicles to promote particular interests and have little incentive to create stable organizational structures. Moreover, the middle classes, historically, were crucial for expanding the franchise and democracy in the Southern Cone during the first three decades of the twentieth century, although Nohlen rightly points out that this very same middle class can easily turn to anti-democratic forces once they see their privileges threatened by the lower classes.[8]

Despite large economic problems, many countries in the region have recently performed better, with annual economic growth of 5 per cent on average from 2004 to 2007, low inflation and current account surpluses. This development has led to growing middle classes and less extreme poverty. It is too early, however, to assess the impact on political conflict and the stability of democracy. Even if the growth is sustainable, Latin America still has a long way to go until the entire population benefits from it.

Ideology

Another dimension of conflict is ideology. Mainly in the 1960s and 1970s the region was highly polarized and became a battlefield between right-wing military and leftist revolutionaries. Often these conflicts were violent and ended by military coups and strong repression. The military was a decisive actor in Latin American politics. During much of the twentieth century it saw its role as defending the country not only against external enemies but also against what it perceived to be internal enemies. This almost always meant fighting against the Left. The military was the ally of the conservative forces. An exception was Peru, which had a leftist military dictatorship under Juan Velasco Alvarado from 1968 to 1975. Ecuador's Guillermo Rodríguez Lara and Panama's Omar Torrijos also pursued social agendas that could be considered as leftist. The role of the military has changed since the end of the Cold War and, generally, the armed forces prefer to concentrate on defence issues today rather than directly interfere in politics.

Chile was, and is again, a country with strongly institutionalized parties. It had had competitive elections without interruption since 1932.[9] In 1970, Salvador Allende, the candidate of a Left coalition, became president and his government enacted a series of economic and social reforms. Although the measures were popular among wide sectors of society, they also generated strong resistance. The country became increasingly polarized and the political stage was dominated by ideological hard-liners on both sides. The tension culminated in a military coup led by General Augusto Pinochet, who then went on to govern the country for 17 years in a bloody dictatorship. For Chile, this meant the interruption of what had been a working democracy. For many other countries, the combination of polarization, violence and authoritarian repression was the norm during much of the twentieth century.

Civil wars

Several Central American countries experienced civil wars in the 1970s and 1980s. The introduction of democracy there was part of the peace-building process, and integrating the conflicting parties, mainly the former guerrillas, into the party system was crucial for a sustainable peace.

In Guatemala, a peace agreement was signed in 1996, ending 36 years of armed conflict between the military and leftist guerrillas. The peace agreement was made possible by a process of democratic transition that started with gradual liberalization at the beginning of the 1980s. When Jorge Serrano Elías took over the presidency in 1990, it was the first time in that century that the office was transferred from one civilian to another. Serrano started negotiations with the guerrilla movement URNG (Guatemalan National Revolutionary Unity), which eventually led to the peace agreement. The URNG transformed itself into a legal party and has since participated in elections. It has not been very successful, though, garnering only 4.2 per cent of the votes in the 2003 elections, or 2 seats out of 158 in the national parliament. In the presidential elections of 1999 and 2003 its candidates won 12.4 and 2.6 per cent of the votes, respectively. Neither of them made it into the runoff.

This weakness of former guerrilla parties is dangerous, because much of the overcoming of conflict depends on their successful integration into the democratic system. Still, it is rather unlikely that the URNG will take up arms again, mainly because it was already militarily beaten in the 1980s during the dictatorship of José Ríos Montt (1982–1983). The problem of violence has, nevertheless, not been solved. Human rights abuses are still frequently committed by the police and the armed forces.

The situation was different in El Salvador. The country also experienced a civil war, between the leftist FMLN (Farabundo Martí National Liberation Front) guerrillas and a right-wing civic military dictatorship in the 1980s. In contrast to the Guatemalan URNG, however, the FMLN negotiated peace with the government from a position of strength. Since the end of the civil war in 1992, the FMLN has established itself as one of the two dominant parties together with the right-wing ARENA (National Republican Alliance). ARENA has won all three presidential elections so far, but the FMLN won a plurality of seats in parliament in 2000 and 2003. ARENA came out as the strongest party in the recent 2006 elections, so the party currently holds both a plurality of seats in parliament and the presidency, but the FMLN is a serious contender and therefore well integrated in the political system.

Political parties and conflict today

Whenever we talk about potential political violence in Latin America, the question of the marginalized indigenous population and the problem of poverty and extreme inequality are usually related to it. The importance of ideology has diminished since the end of the Cold War, as in the rest of the world, but has recently resurfaced with the government of Hugo Chávez, who is actively trying to forge a leftist, anti-US alliance in the region with his "21st century socialism".

Currently, we can distinguish three main political currents in government.[10] First, there are centre–right governments closely allied with the United States, such as those of Mexico, Colombia and much of Central America. Second are centre–left governments with a focus on social equality, but based on market economies. These are the Southern Cone countries Argentina, Brazil, Chile and Uruguay and the Peruvian government of President Alan García. Third, there are leftist governments advocating a "Bolivarian" way or "21st century socialism". This last group is led by Venezuela's Hugo Chávez and also includes the governments of Evo Morales in Bolivia, Daniel Ortega in Nicaragua, and Rafael Correa in Ecuador.

These three types also represent the main competing political currents within the Latin American countries, with the Left overlapping with indigenous movements in some countries. The importance of indigenous movements depends on the percentage of the indigenous population and the ability of this group to organize politically.[11] This ability can vary considerably and does not just depend on the proportion of indigenous people in a country. Whereas the indigenous movement Movimiento al Socialismo (MAS) won the presidential elections in Bolivia in 2005, its Ecuadorian counterpart Pachakutik polled only 2.2 per cent of votes in the 2006 presidential elections, despite the fact that a quarter of the population is indigenous.

Not all political conflicts in Latin America deal with ideology or ethnicity, though. Especially in the past few years, issues of decentralization and regional autonomy have become more important. The reasons for demanding more responsibility for sub-national entities vary. Sometimes it is the feeling that remote areas are neglected by the central state or that lower levels of government are simply more efficient at providing services for citizens. In other cases, it is a fundamental disagreement over how the country should be run, such as in Bolivia between the lowlands in the eastern parts of the country and the Andean highlands.

Regulation of political parties

Political parties are affected by a number of regulations at different levels. We can distinguish between direct regulation that is explicitly targeted at political parties and indirect regulation that primarily concerns other aspects but still influences parties. The most important indirect regulation concerns elections. In addition to the distinction between direct and indirect regulation, there are also three different qualitative levels. The constitution is at the top, followed by ordinary laws; decrees and provisions that can be enacted by the executive come last.

As a general tendency, Latin American constitutions are much more detailed and exhaustive than, for example, those of Europe. Of the 19 Latin American countries, 11 regulate the role and functioning of political parties in their constitution: Argentina, Brazil, Chile, Colombia, Cuba, Ecuador, El Salvador, Mexico, Panama, Paraguay and Uruguay.[12]

Although all 19 countries have electoral laws, only half of them also have a party law. These countries are all Southern Cone countries except for Paraguay, the Andean region, Brazil and Guatemala.[13] Most of the party laws were enacted in the 1980s and 1990s after or during the third wave of democratization.[14]

One way to regulate political conflict is to specify certain legal requirements for political parties (see Table 6.3). Basically, there are three areas where legislation can affect parties and societal conflicts: (a) requirements to set up a party, (b) requirements on the internal structure and (c) the electoral system.

The first category encompasses aspects such as a minimum number of members or the requirement to have branches in different parts of a country (see Chapter 7 by Jóhanna Birnir in this volume). The latter requirement exists in 14 countries. Only Bolivia, Colombia, El Salvador and Uruguay do not regulate this. Closely related to preconditions for setting up a party are requirements to avoid dissolution. All countries but Argentina and Brazil require parties to win a minimum share of votes at parliamentary elections. The threshold ranges from 500 votes in Uruguay to 5 per cent of valid votes in Ecuador.

Criteria such as a minimum territorial representation or a minimum membership are intended to prevent small splinter parties from appearing. This is important in relation to conflict, because one of the central functions of political parties is precisely to aggregate different demands from society and accommodate them within the party, rather than bringing them to the political system unfiltered. It does not necessarily mean that all parties have to be catch-all parties and that there cannot be special-interest representation. Rather, it follows from the special position of parties as a link between society and the political system that

Table 6.3 Legal requirements for the recognition of parties

	Minimum number of votes at last elections	Percentage of party members	Previous assemblies held	Operation in territorial districts	Other requirements
Argentina	n.a.	Yes (4%)	Yes	Yes	(a) founding agreement; (b) adopted name and party office; (c) declaration of principles and programmes or the grounds for political action; (d) constituting charter; minutes of appointment of national and district authorities; (e) account books.
Bolivia	Yes (2%)	n.a.	Yes	N/R	Constituent assembly to define: (a) information regarding founders, as well as the name, symbols and colours to be adopted; (b) approval of the declaration of principles; (c) approval of the founding agreement; (d) government programme; (e) net worth statement; (f) election of their national leadership.
Brazil	Yes (0.5%), for elections of Congress representatives	n.a.	Yes	Yes	(a) minutes of the party's founding meeting, to be signed by no fewer than 101 founders, and an electoral office in at least one-third of the states where the party has representation; (b) authentic copy of the minutes of the party's founding assembly; (c) programme and statutes.

Country					
Chile	Yes (0.5%), for elections of Congress representatives	n.a.	N/R	Yes	Legal deed containing the following: (a) full list of participants at founding meeting; (b) declaration of the will to create a political party; (c) name of the party and, if appropriate, its abbreviation, slogan and exact description of its symbol; (d) declaration of principles; (e) statutes; (f) first and last names of the provisional members of the executive committee and the supreme tribunal.
Colombia	N/R	N/R[a]	Optional	n.a.	(a) request submitted by its executive boards; (b) copy of the statutes; (c) political platform, philosophy, principles, programmes and aspirations.
Costa Rica	n.a.	Fixed number of registered voters: 3,000	Yes	Yes	(a) certification issued by a notary verifying the party's foundation; (b) registration by a notary of the minutes of the corresponding assembly, be it at the district, county, province or national level, depending on the party's registration scale, containing the names of all the elected delegates in each case; (c) statutes; (d) list of the members of the superior executive committee.

Table 6.3 (cont.)

	Minimum number of votes at last elections	Percentage of party members	Previous assemblies held	Operation in territorial districts	Other requirements
Dominican Republic	Yes (2%)	n.a.	Yes	Yes	(a) principles, objectives and tendencies on which the party will be grounded; (b) list of provisional governing bodies; (c) name or slogan; (d) drawings contained in the symbol and emblem, or the shape and colours of the flag; (e) provisional governing bodies and functioning offices operating in each of the chief municipalities of the national provinces and the national district; (f) budget of revenues and expenses for the creation phase of the party and up to the next elections.
Ecuador	n.a.	Yes (1.5%)	N/R	Yes	(a) founding agreement of the political party; (b) declaration of ideological principles; (c) government programme; (d) statutes; (e) symbols, abbreviations, emblems and logos; (f) list of members of the executive committee.
El Salvador	Yes (3%)	n.a.	N/R	N/R	(a) Approval of supporters' signatures; (b) certificate of the minutes of the meeting of the highest body in which the declaration of principles and

Country					Registration requirements
Guatemala	n.a.	Yes (0.3%)	Yes	Yes	objectives, the statutes, name, colours and emblems were adopted and approved; (c) three copies of the statutes; (d) list of members of its highest body; (e) register of party members. Legal deed containing the following: (a) members of the provisional executive committee; (b) ratification of the declaration of principles; (c) affidavit certifying that the party has the number of members and the party organization required by law (0.3% of the total of citizens registered on the electoral roll), at least half of whom must be literate; (d) name, emblem, statutes; (e) members of the national executive committee; (f) location of the head office.
Honduras	Yes (2%)	n.a.	N/R	Yes	(a) testimony of the founding agreement; (b) declaration of principles; (c) emblem and name of the political party; (d) political action programme; (e) statutes; (f) certificate proving the organization of municipal and departmental authorities in more than half of the country's municipalities and departments.

Table 6.3 (cont.)

	Minimum number of votes at last elections	Percentage of party members	Previous assemblies held	Operation in territorial districts	Other requirements
Mexico	n.a.	Fixed number of registered voters: 3,000 members in at least 20 federal entities, or 300 members in at least 200 of the single-member districts. The total number of members may at no time amount to less than 0.26% of the registered voters on the federal electoral roll.	Yes	Yes	(a) declaration of principles, action programme and statutes; (b) a national constituent assembly and a certificate stating that the assemblies were held, that the declaration of principles, the action programme and statutes were approved, and that lists of members were drawn up.
Nicaragua	n.a.[b]	N/R	Yes	Yes	(a) legal deed whereby the political group is founded; (b) name and emblem of the party; (c) political principles, programmes and statutes; (d) net worth; (e) name of legal agent or representative, and his/her substitute; (f) national boards with no fewer than nine members; (g) departmental boards and boards of the autonomous regions with no fewer than seven members;

				Requirements
Panama	Yes (4%)	n.a.	Yes	Yes	(h) municipal boards with no fewer than five members in each municipality. Prior fulfilment of the requirements related to membership registration, the following procedures must be observed: (a) holding the party's constituent congress or convention where the definitive name, emblem, statutes, declaration of principles and programmes must be approved, and, if appropriate, the flag, other emblems and the anthem must be approved, and the first national directors and dignitaries must be appointed; (b) after the convention or congress has been held, a request must be made to the Electoral Court to declare the existence of the party legal.
Paraguay	Yes (0.5%), for Senate elections	n.a.	N/R	Yes	(a) legal deed of the founding agreement of the political party; (b) declaration of principles; (c) statutes; (d) names, abbreviations, slogans, colours, emblems and symbols; (e) names of the members of the executive committee; (f) evidence of the existence of organizations in the capital of the republic and in at least four departmental cities of the country.

Table 6.3 (cont.)

	Minimum number of votes at last elections	Percentage of party members	Previous assemblies held	Operation in territorial districts	Other requirements
Peru	Yes (1%)	n.a.	N/R	Yes	(a) founding agreement; (b) articles of association of party committees – the party must prove the existence of at least 65 committees from 17 different administrative departments of the country, composed of 50 members each; (c) party statutes; (d) appointment of regular and alternate legal agents accredited by the electoral body; (e) appointment of one or more legal representatives of the political party.
Uruguay	N/R^c	n.a.	Yes	N/R	By law, the court requires: (a) founding agreement of the political party; (b) signature (expression of will) and name of the attendees; (c) agreement on a mandate or power of representation for those who will pursue the electoral status of the party; (d) declaration or programme of principles; (e) party statutes;

		Yes	Yes
			(f) submission at the time of appearing before the Electoral Court of a sufficient number of members so as to be able to provisionally integrate all the bodies of the political party, until this can be done in a definitive manner.
Venezuela	n.a.	n.a.[d]	(a) articles of association: declaration of principles, political action programme and statutes; (b) certificate proving that the party has been duly constituted in at least 12 of all the regional entities; (c) description and drawing of the symbols and emblems of the party; (d) national governing bodies.

Source: This table is taken with kind permission from Daniel Zovatto, "Regulación jurídica de los partidos políticos en América Latina. Lectura regional comparada", in Daniel Zovatto (ed.), *Regulación jurídica de los partidos políticos en América Latina* (Mexico City: UNAM/International IDEA, 2006), pp. 3–187.

Notes: n.a. = not applicable; N/R = unregulated.

[a] In Colombia, 2% of the valid votes cast in the national territory are required for elections to the Chamber of Representatives or the Senate only when a party seeks to obtain legal status and, therefore, the benefits associated with it related to free access to state media and financing.

[b] Although the legislation requires 3% of the electoral roll used in the last national elections, this regulation does not apply by order of the Supreme Court of Justice.

[c] Although there is no express regulation, parties need to have at least as many members as are necessary to properly fill all party organs.

[d] The law does not expressly establish a minimum number of party members required at the national level. However, it requires an authentic certificate stating that the party has been founded in at least 12 regional entities. To register at the regional level, a list of party members is required amounting to no less than 0.5% of the population registered on the electoral register of the corresponding entity.

parties need to integrate positions.[15] This is especially important in conflict-prone societies, because these conflicts can destabilize a country if they are carried into the political system unmoderated.

The problem with some of these quantitative criteria is that they are difficult to control and to link to the desired outcome. For example, territorial operation requirements are easy to circumvent by setting up pro forma offices. Some countries also have qualitative criteria related to potential conflict. Bolivia and Panama both explicitly prohibit economic, sexual and religious discrimination, for example.

Equally important as requiring parties to stick to broad membership and democratic principles is the integration of all relevant groups into the party system. Several countries have started to take the problem of marginalized indigenous people more seriously. This is reflected in regulations regarding the political representation of indigenous populations, which, however, only six Latin American countries have so far (see Table 6.4). Interestingly, the Bolivian constitution of 2004 stipulates that political representation is undertaken not only by political parties but also by civic associations and "indigenous people".

We can distinguish two types of regulatory approach. The first gives indigenous people direct access to representation by creating special seats or constituencies. Colombia has a nationwide constituency for indigenous people with two Senate seats. In Venezuela, the indigenous elect three separate deputies and in Panama there is a minimum number of deputies for each indigenous territory. The second approach is to oblige parties to open up space on their lists for indigenous candidates. Nicaragua has done this for council elections in some regions with a high proportion of indigenous people. There, the top candidate on each list must be indigenous. Similar requirements exist in Peru for municipal elections, where 15 per cent of the candidates on each party list must be from an ethnic community that exists in that region. Some Mexican states also require parties to nominate indigenous candidates.[16]

Case studies

The Andean region

The Andean region is interesting because its party systems operate in an environment of sharp economic inequalities and extreme poverty, especially in Peru, Ecuador and Bolivia, which are also the countries that have witnessed notable ethnic and indigenous movements. The performance of democracy in these three countries has been weak. This is reflected in low levels of legitimacy for politics and political parties. Since

Table 6.4 Legal references to the participation of indigenous populations

Bolivia	Article 222 of the constitution states that popular representation is exercised through political parties, civil associations and indigenous peoples. Article 224 states that indigenous associations may nominate candidates directly for president, vice president, senators, deputy constituents, local council members, mayors and municipal agents on an equal legal basis and in compliance with the law.
Colombia	Article 171 of the constitution: The Senate of the Republic shall consist of 100 members, and will be duly elected at the national level. There shall be an additional number of two senators elected in a special national electoral district by indigenous communities. Article 176 of the constitution: The law may establish a special district to ensure the participation of ethnic groups, political minorities and Colombians residing abroad in the Chamber of Representatives. Up to five members may be elected through this district.
Nicaragua	Article 142 of the Electoral Law compels political parties to give special representation to ethnic minorities in certain jurisdictions of the Autonomous Regions on the Atlantic Coast.
Panama	Article 147 of the political constitution states that each administrative division (comarca) and the Darién Province may elect the number of deputies that they had at the time that the constitutional reform of 2004 came into force.
Peru	Article 10 of the Municipal Electoral Law provides that, on the lists of candidates for regional elections, there must be at least 15% who are representatives of the existing native and indigenous communities in each province.
Venezuela	Article 125 of the political constitution guarantees the right of political participation to indigenous peoples, and establishes that it is the responsibility of the state to ensure indigenous representation in the National Assembly and in the deliberative bodies of the federal entities. Article 186 of the constitution states that indigenous communities may elect three deputies in accordance with the Electoral Law, as well as in observance of their customs and traditions.

Source: This table is taken with kind permission from Daniel Zovatto, "Regulación jurídica de los partidos políticos en América Latina. Lectura regional comparada", in Daniel Zovatto (ed.), *Regulación jurídica de los partidos políticos en América Latina* (Mexico City: UNAM/International IDEA, 2006), pp. 3–187.

Table 6.5 Regulation of internal democracy

	Mechanisms to select candidates for public office			Mechanism for selecting authorities	Intervention of the electoral body	Public financing
	Constitution	Law	Internal elections held?			
Argentina	No	Yes	Yes, open	No	Yes	No
Bolivia	No	Yes	Yes[a]	Yes, electoral legislation	Yes	No
Brazil	No	No	Yes, closed/conventions[b]	No	No	No
Chile	No	Yes	Yes, closed. Plebiscite for the ratification of candidates	No	Yes	No
Colombia	No	Yes	Yes, open and/or conventions	Yes, electoral legislation	Yes[c]	Yes
Costa Rica	No	Yes	Yes, closed[d]/conventions	No	Yes	No
Dominican Republic	No	Yes	Yes, closed/primary, conventions	Yes, electoral legislation	Yes	No
Ecuador	No	No	–	No	Yes	No
El Salvador	No	No	–	No	Yes	No
Guatemala	No	Yes	Yes, closed/conventions	Yes, electoral legislation	Yes	No
Honduras	No	Yes	Yes, open	Yes, electoral legislation	Yes	Yes
Mexico	No	No	–	No	Yes[e]	Yes[f]
Nicaragua	No	No	–	No	Yes	No
Panama	No	Yes	Yes, closed	No	Yes	Yes
Paraguay	No	Yes	Yes, closed	Yes, electoral legislation	Yes	No
Peru	No	Yes	Yes, closed/open	Yes, electoral legislation	Yes	No
Uruguay	Yes	Yes	Yes, open	Yes, electoral legislation	Yes	No
Venezuela	Yes	Yes	Yes, closed	No	Yes	No

Source: This table is taken with kind permission from Daniel Zovatto, "Regulación jurídica de los partidos políticos en América Latina. Lectura regional comparada", in Daniel Zovatto (ed.), *Regulación jurídica de los partidos políticos en América Latina* (Mexico City: UNAM/International IDEA, 2006), pp. 3–187.

Notes:

[a] What the political party law defines the elective principle of internal democracy. Each party defines the selection mechanism.

[b] The law entrusts the definition of the framework of action related to internal democracy to political party statutes, but it does warn that the participation of party members must be accounted for.

[c] Optional.

[d] Even though internal elections are based on the national electoral roll, elections are considered "closed" because voters are asked to formally support the party at the moment of casting their vote.

[e] If there are irregularities in the internal procedures, and if the situation is not resolved after recourse to the internal procedures of the party, an appeal may be filed with the Electoral Tribunal of the Mexican Judiciary.

[f] The Superior Court of the Electoral Tribunal of the Mexican Judiciary decided that the election of political leaders, as well as the designation of their candidates, falls within the regular activities of political parties. This means that they may be financed with public funds as a means to support their permanent and regular activities.

2000, the presidents of five Andean countries have had their terms of office cut short;[17] and citizens show little support for governments and democracy.

Economic policies – based on the so-called Washington consensus – and institutional structures have been severely criticized by new political forces, which have proposed a *new order* in economics and politics. This involves moving away from neo-liberal policies and replacing the current democracy (dubbed "formal") with a better one, supposedly more participatory. Taking up positions on the left of the political spectrum, though with clearly populist overtones, these forces – several of them outsiders – proposed that new constitutions should be adopted.

This turn to the Left – a term open to dispute – of the Andean region kindled the so-called national re-foundational projects currently pursued by Presidents Hugo Chávez (Venezuela), Evo Morales (Bolivia) and Rafael Correa (Ecuador), as well as by Ollanta Humala (Peru), who lost in the 2006 presidential elections against Alan García. It should be noted, though, that not all governments in the region have turned to the Left. Colombia is governed by a conservative, pro-American president and Peru's new president, Alan García, is a moderate.

In short, dissatisfaction with democracy is accompanied by rejection of the most traditional and historically important political parties, which are associated with the few successes and many failures of governments in the region. Andean party systems are highly fragmented. On average, there were 19 parties in parliament in 2005 in each of the countries.[18] Fragmentation is accompanied by pronounced electoral volatility, both between parties and within them,[19] a notable presence of political outsiders and considerable cross-party movement. Three countries (Bolivia, Ecuador and Venezuela) are in the middle of a process of deep institutional restructuring through changes to their constitutions, and these changes are still difficult to evaluate since they have not yet been completed. What can be observed are the regulations concerning political parties.

As regards institutions dealing with political parties, the Andean countries generally rely on an independent electoral court.[20] All the countries have an entity of this kind, whose primary function is to ensure compliance with regulations concerning political parties, along with those connected with electoral activities. It has also been considered necessary to establish some kind of legal recourse to settle disputes among the parties, albeit with different powers from country to country. The legality of party regulations is guaranteed by a constitutional tribunal.

There is also concern in the region for the independence of political organizations when defining their internal organs in their respective statutes. The laws governing parties seek to guarantee some level of internal democracy within the party organization, either by establishing obligatory internal structures (such as an assembly) or by specifying intervals for the election of party officials. Regarding requirements for electoral registration, parties are required to present a minimum number of followers. In Ecuador, Peru and Venezuela, moreover, a national party presence is obligatory in a specified number of provinces. In this regard, it is noticeable that Andean countries attach great importance to the challenge of representation. Today those parties are favoured that are supported by a great number of citizens in several regions of a country.

In the matter of internal democracy, we can observe a transitional process from closed party structures to more open ways of decision-making, but internal elections – though regulated in all the countries – have had only marginal effect in practice so far. As noted before, the "challenge of representation" seems to collide with the challenge of control by the more traditional leadership, and this leads to internal elections that are not really competitive.

Regulation for public funding of political parties exists in all Andean countries except for Venezuela. In four countries, funding is limited by certain restrictions regarding donors, recipients and the amounts of money. There is an emphasis on administrative and financial penalties in the event of non-compliance with the rules. Generally, in the Andean region we can see that the emphasis is on having representative parties, leaving internal democracy and organizational structure in a position of secondary importance. Thus there are parties that, although clinging to an oligarchical internal structure, legitimize themselves through the number of signatures they submit to the registration authorities.

Despite this, the outlook in the Andean region cannot be considered as being negative. The appearance of leftist governments has not so far restricted political party development (as happened, for example, during the government of Alberto Fujimori in Peru). Anti-party rhetoric, although used by some leaders, has not yet affected the constitutional/legal framework, and this can be partly explained by the commitments to democratic government undertaken by Latin American political classes under the scrutiny of the international community.

Peru

Peru is a country that has oscillated between dictatorship and democracy throughout its history. At the same time, of all Latin American countries it has made the greatest effort to implement highly sophisticated judicial regulations for political parties.

The country has suffered from serious problems pertaining to party representation and fragmentation since the era of President Alberto

Table 6.6 Mechanisms for choosing candidates, authorities and minority representation in the electoral processes of Andean countries

	Posts filled by free elections			Mechanism for selecting authorities	Quota by sex			
	Constitution	Law	Internal elections		From	% of list	Placed	% of posts
Bolivia	No	No		Yes, electoral legislation	1997	30	Yes	30
Colombia	No	Yes	Yes, open	No	2000	30	No	
Ecuador	No	No		No	2000	40	Yes	
Peru	No	Yes	Yes, party chooses whether open or closed	Yes, electoral legislation	1997 & 2003	30	No	30
Venezuela	Yes	Yes	Yes, closed	No		30		

Source: Compiled by the authors.

Table 6.7 Choosing presidential candidates in the Andean region

	Open primaries	Closed primaries	Conventions	Executive board	Party leader
Bolivia			MNR, MIR, MAS, ADN		UCS
Colombia	PL	PC	PC, PL		
Ecuador		ID, DP	ID, DP, PSC	MUPP	PRE
Peru		PAP, AP	PAP, PP		
Venezuela	COPEI	AD, COPEI	AD, COPEI, MAS		MVR, PPT

Source: Compiled by the authors.
Notes: AD: Acción Democrática; ADN: Acción Democrática Nacionalista; AP: Acción Popular; COPEI: Comité de Organización Política Electoral Independiente; DP: Democracia Popular; ID: Izquierda Democrática; MAS: Movimiento al Socialismo; MIR: Movimiento de Izquierda Revolucionaria; MNR: Movimiento Nacionalista Revolucionario; MUPP: Movimiento de Unidad Plurinacional Pachakutik; MVR: Movimiento V República; PAP: Partido Aprista Peruano; PC: Partido Conservador; PL: Partido Liberal; PP: Perú Posible; PPT: Patria Para Todos; PRE: Partido Rodolsista Ecuatoriano; PSC: Partido Social Cristiano; UCS: Unión Cívica Solidaridad.

Fujimori in the 1990s.[21] After the fall of Fujimori in 2000, recuperating political parties coexisted with new organizations – many of them off-shoots of the former – and emerging political groups. The 2001 elections highlighted this panorama, in a context of democratic transition, but nevertheless offered conditions to seriously consider new rules of the game for political parties that would enable a solid representational system to be built. In this climate of democratic transition, public opinion demanded a new political party law. There had been several attempts since 1982, none of which had been successful. All-party talks with academics, electoral organizations and civil representatives – facilitated by International IDEA and its local partner, the non-governmental organization Asociación Civil Transparencia – reached a consensus in the Congressional Constitution Commission after nearly two years of discussion. On 1 November 2003, the first political party law (Ley de Partidos Políticos, LPP) in Peruvian history was passed. The fundamental purpose of this was to strengthen and consolidate the political party system on a national scale, to introduce mechanisms of internal democracy and to establish financial transparency.

The LPP consists of 41 sections grouped under six titles in three thematic areas: "Founding and Recognition of Political Parties",[22] "Intra-Party Democracy"[23] and "Political Party Financing".[24] The LPP had to deal with the rejection of political parties, as mediators and representatives, as well as problems such as party fragmentation, outsiders, cross-party movement, poor organization of the party apparatus, a decline in membership and scant economic resources. A study of the behaviour of politicians showed that they gave priority to initiatives with media impact and postponed or even blocked discussion and implementation of longer-lasting reforms that could combat poverty and that might affect interest groups.[25] This was seen as a considerable problem, although Peru is probably not the only country in the world featuring this kind of behaviour by politicians.

Although the LPP is a demanding norm, it was not applied as expected, showing that, without political will and without electoral entities dedicated to its proper application, party regulation can become ineffectual. Worse, when elections drew near, many parliamentarians realized they had approved a law that would make it difficult for them to take part (and perhaps be re-elected) in the 2006 elections. After becoming aware of this, not much effort was made to obtain agreements, since as time passed the parliamentarians were turning progressively into candidates and acting as such. Thus, institutional weakness revealed its most perverse effects.[26]

The challenges the law was supposed to overcome were not met, either because the norms were changed or because they were not effectively applied. This process can be observed in three areas in which it is possible to analyse the parties in the framework of application of the law.

The 36 political parties: Doubtful registration

Never was a law so demanding as regards requirements for the registration of political parties. The requirements were supposed to limit the number of parties, especially those with weak institutions. However, what happened was the opposite: the number of parties registered was the highest in history. Clearly, this fragmentation would not help to establish majorities, making it difficult to reach agreements or pacts and creating a threat to governance.

A starting point to explain this problem is the first temporary provision. It established that parties already registered at the time the law came into force did not have to submit the signatures of supporters (1 per cent of the voters – about 130,000 signatures), but that they did have to comply with the other five requirements.[27] This provision benefited 22 political groups. For unregistered parties, the requirement to submit the signatures of supporters and to set up party committees represented an enormous obstacle. The LPP demands that parties show proof that they have set up at least 65 provincial party committees with a minimum of 50 members each, distributed over two-thirds of the national territory (17 departments), which is to say 3,250 members. The objective of this rule was to restrict access for political parties that are not capable of having a permanent organizational structure and a broad base of support.

The main reason so many parties were eventually able to register is that the electoral authority in charge of the process, the National Jury of Elections (Jurado Nacional de Elecciones, JNE), did not rigorously verify if parties met all the requirements, particularly the one relating to party committees. Media reports later showed that in many provinces those committees did not exist or had been created by forging documentation and memberships. Also, signatures were not checked and many of them seem to have been falsified.

As the flaws of the registration process became obvious, Congress – pressured by public opinion – introduced a legal threshold of 4 per cent of valid votes at the national level for any party to obtain representation in parliament.[28] This was an attempt to prevent fragmentation, which the inadequate compliance with the regulation had actually encouraged. Nevertheless, in the end there were 23 presidential candidates and 25 parliamentary lists standing in the elections.[29]

Internal elections, yes; democratic ones, no

Low levels of internal participation, little say in party decisions and no part in the selection of the leadership and candidates were the subjects in the discussion on political parties. The LPP provided a legal framework and it was implemented in 2005, with the general elections in April 2006 in mind.[30] Here too, however, the implementation had obvious flaws. The LPP had established a logical sequence of deadlines connected with the electoral schedule. The registration of political parties and the setting-up of alliances should have been followed by internal candidate selections. The purpose was to institutionalize and strengthen parties by imposing a strict timeline that would ensure early awareness of candidacies and avoid the presence of outsiders.

However, Law No. 28581, passed on 27 June 2005, modified various articles of the LPP. Among other things it substantially changed the time periods established for the setting-up of alliances, internal elections and the registration of presidential and congressional candidate lists. The original law stipulated that the period for setting up alliances ended not less than 210 days before election day. The modifications shortened this to 120 days. The reduction of all the periods brought confusion and difficulty in clearly observing what stage the process was at. Given the fact that there were about 30 legally registered organizations participating, the scenario was not well suited for observing and supervising the candidate selection processes of the parties.

The selections had several problems, among them a lack of independence of the internal electoral entities and interference by the presidential candidates and prominent party leaders in drawing up the lists. Presidential tickets were not always approved by a competent internal body. Several parties actually rented themselves out, since they offered and accepted strangers as their presidential nominee. There were parties without candidates and candidates without parties, and mutual concessions were made in order to be able to compete, showing how precarious the level of institutionalization of parties was.

Lastly, in the case of internal elections to choose representatives for parliament, there was little competition and in many cases the result – if known – was not really binding. Besides, in many cases the decision of the presidential candidate had more weight than the wishes of the members of the parties. Reports from the electoral organizations – when they existed – were not taken into account, and almost none of the irregularities were taken into consideration by the JNE to prevent registration of a list or a candidate.

Party financing: Eyes on the voting booth

Until recently the financial operations of Peruvian parties were very opaque. The intention of the LPP was to regulate funding, both from public and from private sources. The law obliges parties to reveal their sources of financing and establishes that donations by an individual or a legal entity cannot exceed 60 taxation units (UIT) per year.[31] Candidates cannot receive direct donations of any kind, except with their party's knowledge and within the same limits that apply to the party itself. Incoming funds from whatever source are entered in the party's books and, unless proved otherwise, undeclared income is presumed to be from a prohibited source. Thanks to the LPP, this information was available for the first time, and was offered on the web page of the National Office of Electoral Processes (Oficina Nacional de Procesos Electorales, ONPE), one of the official bodies in charge of the elections. In many cases the requirements established by law were not complied with. Various irregularities were discovered, such as parties that claimed not to have any financial means despite being able to meet the registration requirements, which is a costly process.

There was a low level of organization of the parties and their financial behaviour was still informal and characterized by the intention of revealing as little information as possible. Nevertheless, the presentation of this information has been of vital importance in the attempt to regulate party activities. Simply having to comply with this obligation strengthens the parties, and citizens are able to know what is happening and also to play an active and supervisory role.

The Peruvian party law: Success or failure?

Lack of rigour in the application of the Peruvian party law weakened the potential of the law to reduce the number of competing parties. Although during the 2006 elections the large number of presidential tickets and parliamentary lists encouraged party fragmentation and created serious difficulties for political representation, the introduction of the threshold for representation was a measure that counteracted this danger. Nonetheless, the Peruvian party system remains fragmented and weakly institutionalized and a considerable number of citizens do not feel properly represented by the political system, a situation that generates the potential for conflict in the future.

Conclusion

The prospects for democracy in Latin America and the impact of conflict on the political system will depend to a great extent on the ability of the system to produce appropriate results. Large parts of the population in Latin America are still marginalized economically and politically, despite the fact that most countries have been democratic now for at least a decade. In the medium term, this dissatisfaction with the concrete results of government activity may very well translate into a decline in diffuse support for democracy as a form of government.

The region's great economic inequalities create a cleavage with huge potential for conflict. The decisive question will be the extent to which the political system will be able to integrate the large marginalized groups. If the party system is unable to take up their demands, upheavals such as the one in Venezuela are likely to re-occur and we will witness a rise of (neo-)populism in different flavours. This does not necessarily mean that conflicts will be violent, but virulent conflicts that arise outside the political system have generally paralysed the countries in Latin America and led to (further) instability.

Countries then risk entering a vicious circle where the inability of the political system to deliver results creates frustration among marginalized sectors of the population, who take their protest to the streets and, by paralysing the system, further aggravate the problems of the political system's performance. Recently, a number of Latin American countries have started new constitution-building processes in an attempt to "refound" their countries. It remains to be seen if these processes can actually fulfil expectations or if they will merely be a remake of the many futile institutional reforms of the past two decades.

Notes

1. Costa Rica, Cuba, the Dominican Republic, El Salvador, Guatemala, Honduras, Nicaragua and Panama.
2. Bolivia, Colombia, Ecuador, Peru and Venezuela.
3. Argentina, Chile, Uruguay and sometimes also Paraguay.
4. Samuel P. Huntington, *The Third Wave: Democratization in the Late Twentieth Century* (Norman, OK: University of Oklahoma Press, 1991).
5. Matthias Catón, "Wahlen und Demokratie in Lateinamerika: Stärkung der Output-Legitimation nötig", in Claudia Derichs and Thomas Heberer (eds), *Wahlsysteme und Wahltypen* (Wiesbaden: VS, 2006), pp. 302–316.
6. Arend Lijphart, *Electoral Systems and Party Systems: A Study of Twenty-Seven Democracies 1945–1990* (Oxford: Oxford University Press, 1994), pp. 130–134.
7. Dieter Nohlen, "Elections and Electoral Systems in the Americas: South America", in Dieter Nohlen (ed.), *Elections in the Americas*, Vol. 2 (Oxford: Oxford University Press, 2005), pp. 1–58; J. Marc Payne and Andrés Allamand Zavala, "Sistemas de elección presidencial y gobernabilidad democrática", in J. Marc Payne et al. (eds), *La política importa: Democracia y desarrollo en América Latina*, 2nd edn (Washington, DC: Interamerican Development Bank; International IDEA, 2006), pp. 19–39.
8. Dieter Nohlen, "Lateinamerika zwischen Diktatur und Demokratie", in Detlef Junker, Dieter Nohlen and Hartmut Sangmeister (eds), *Lateinamerika am Ende des 20. Jahrhunderts* (Munich: Beck, 1994), pp. 12–26.
9. Dieter Nohlen, "Chile", in Nohlen (ed.), *Elections in the Americas*, Vol. 2, pp. 253–293.
10. See Daniel Zovatto, "Balance electoral latinoamericano noviembre 2005 – diciembre 2006", working paper, International IDEA, Stockholm, 2007, who distinguishes four currents.
11. Raúl L. Madrid, "Indigenous Voters and Party System Fragmentation in Latin America", *Electoral Studies*, 24(4), 2005: 689–707.
12. Matthias Catón, Daniel Sabsay and Bernhard Thibaut, "La legislación electoral: Bases legales, estatus, mecanismos de reforma", in Dieter Nohlen, Daniel Zovatto, Jesús Orozco and José Thompson (eds), *Tratado de Derecho Electoral Comparado de América Latina* (Mexico City: Fondo de Cultura Económica, 2007), pp. 108–123.
13. Daniel Zovatto, "Regulación jurídica de los partidos políticos en América Latina: Lectura regional comparada", in Daniel Zovatto (ed.), *Regulación jurídica de los partidos políticos en América Latina* (Mexico City: UNSM/International IDEA, 2006), pp. 3–187.
14. For an overview, see Line Bareiro and Lilian Soto, "Los partidos políticos: Condiciones de inscripción y reconocimiento legal", in Dieter Nohlen, Daniel Zovatto, Jesús Orozco and José Thompson (eds), *Tratado de Derecho Electoral Comparado de América Latina* (Mexico City: Fondo de Cultura Económica, 2007), pp. 588–612.
15. Moisei Ostrogorski, *Democracy and the Organization of Political Parties II: The United States*, Seymour Martin Lipset (ed.) (Chicago: Anchor Books, 1964; first published 1902); Elmar Wiesendahl, *Parteien und Demokratie: Eine soziologische Analyse paradigmatischer Ansätze der Parteienforschung* (Opladen: Leske und Budrich, 1980); Klaus Von Beyme, "Theoretische Probleme der Parteienforschung", *Politische Vierteljahresschrift*, 24(3), 1983: 241–252.
16. Zovatto, "Regulación jurídica".
17. Gonzalo Sánchez de Lozada (2003) and Carlos Mesa (2005) in Bolivia; Jamil Mahuad (2000) and Lucio Gutiérrez (2005) in Ecuador; Alberto Fujimori (2000) in Peru. See Rafael Roncagliolo and Carlos Meléndez (eds), *La política por dentro. Cambios y continuidades en las organizaciones políticas de los países andinos* (Lima: International IDEA/Asociación Civil Transparencia, 2007).

18. Rafael Roncagliolo, "Los partidos políticos andinos: Entre la crisis y el cambio", in Rafael Roncagliolo and Carlos Meléndez (eds), *La política por dentro. Cambios y continuidades en las organizaciones políticas de los países andinos* (Lima: International IDEA/Asociación Civil Transparencia, 2007), p. 15.

19. Four out of five members of parliament were first-termers after the 2006 elections.

20. The names vary: court, tribunal, council, jury. In many Latin American countries there is a clear separation of functions. One entity plans and executes electoral processes and another one resolves electoral disputes.

21. Fernando Tuesta Soldevilla, *Representación Política: Las reglas también cuentan* (Lima: Fundación Friedrich Ebert/Pontificia Universidad Católica del Perú, 2005); Martín Tanaka, *Democracia sin partidos. Perú, 2000–2005* (Lima: IEP, 2005); Nicolás Lynch, *Una tragedia sin héroes: La derrota de los partidos y el origen de los independientes. Perú 1980–1992* (Lima: UNMSM, 1999).

22. Founding and registration, register of political organizations, requirements for the registration of political parties, founding charters, statement of supporting signatures, register of committee formation, party by-laws, reasons for rejecting a request to register a political party, effects of registration, opening of party offices, cancellation of registration, declaration of illegality of anti-democratic actions, party alliances and mergers of parties.

23. Electoral body of a party, participation of the National Office of Electoral Processes (ONPE), opportunity for elections, candidate lists, submitting and issuing programmes, mechanism for selecting candidates, mechanism for selecting party authorities, gender issues, election of delegates.

24. Direct public financing, private donations, prohibited sources, administration of funds, tax regimes, verification and control, publication of accounting records, sanctions, free allocation of airtime, paid political advertising.

25. Gustavo Guerra-García and Kristen Sample (eds), *La política y la pobreza en los países andinos* (Lima: International IDEA/Asociación Civil Transparencia, 2007), p. 341.

26. Fernando Tuesta Soldevilla, "Regulación jurídica de los partidos políticos en Perú", in Daniel Zovatto (ed.), *Regulación jurídica de los partidos políticos en América Latina* (Mexico City: UNAM/International IDEA, 2006), pp. 767–801.

27. Article 5 of the LPP states the requirements for registration of political parties: (1) a founding agreement; (2) proof of the creation of party committees; (3) a party statute; (4) the appointment of legal representatives, office holders and alternate officers and their accreditation with the electoral organizations; and (5) the appointment of one or more legal representatives of the political party, whose responsibilities have to be established in the party statute. The Registry Office of Political Organizations (Oficina de Registro de Organizaciones Políticas, OROP) of the National Jury of Elections (Jurado Nacional de Elecciones, JNE) is responsible for verifying compliance with the requirements. The supporters' signatures are verified by the National Office of Electoral Processes (Oficina Nacional de Procesos Electorales, ONPE).

28. The regulation sets the threshold at 5 per cent, but a temporary stipulation established it at 4 per cent for 2006; 7 of the 24 lists won seats in the end.

29. Some presidential lists withdrew. The number of parliamentary lists varies in each department because it is not obligatory for each party to present lists in all the electoral districts.

30. Article 23 of the law states that the posts subject to internal selection are those of candidates for president and vice-president, for seats in the national parliament and in the Andean parliament, for regional president and vice-president, for councillors and for mayors.

31. UIT (Unidad Impositiva Tributaria) is an artificial monetary unit established by the central bank. For 2007 it is 3.45 Peruvian soles (approximately US$1.10).

7

Party regulation in Central and Eastern Europe and Latin America: The effect on minority representation and the propensity for conflict

Jóhanna Kristín Birnir

Parties are at the centre of political life for voters in diverse democracies as the venues for the expression of group concerns in the legislative game.[1] According to some of the more influential political scientists, party system stability is essential to the proper functioning of a democracy.[2] High levels of party system fragmentation are also considered detrimental to the proper functioning of democratic regimes. Fragmentation complicates coalition-building in the legislature and inhibits compromise on policy issues.[3]

In general, the greater the social diversity, the greater the fragmentation of parties in the legislature, since parties will appeal to and represent distinct social cleavages.[4] Underlying ethnic cleavages interact with institutional barriers to partly determine the number of parties in the legislature. The barriers include allocation rules, particularly the number of seats in each district (district magnitude): the higher the district magnitude, the greater the number of parties in the system.[5] Interestingly, however, analysis of the effect of party regulation institutions, which affect electoral mobilization into separate political parties and the consequent potential for legislative fragmentation before allocation institutions ever come into play, is only beginning to emerge.[6]

Party formation requirements vary greatly between countries and it is important to define the term more precisely. Broadly speaking, party formation rules can apply to the initial registration of a party and/or regulate its continued survival and political participation. Requirements for registration of a political party and/or independent candidates are usually

Political parties in conflict-prone societies: Regulation, engineering and democratic development, Reilly and Nordlund (eds),
United Nations University Press, 2008, ISBN 978-92-808-1157-5

Table 7.1 Some common ballot access requirements

Pre- and/or post-election requirements	Examples of implementation
Popular support	(a) Collect a specified number of signatures. (b) Obtain a specified number of votes in a prior election at a lower level to qualify for a ballot. (c) Obtain a specified number of votes to retain registration after the election.
Spatially distributed popular support	(a) Signatures or votes obtained must be distributed in a specified manner in the country.
Financial viability	(a) Pay a specified amount to appear on a ballot. (b) Pay a specified amount in a fine if electoral showing does not reach a specified threshold.

Note: The table does not represent an exhaustive list. A ban on ethnic parties is, for instance, a restriction on party formation, but this rule is not common and therefore not included in the table.

contained in either electoral law or party law. The most common types of requirement, summarized in Table 7.1, are that a new party must register a certain number or a certain percentage of voters as supporters in order to qualify for the ballot the first time around. If the requirement is a part of electoral law, the party may have to register before every election. Alternatively, the party must have received a certain percentage of the vote in a lower-level election to qualify for the ballot in a higher-level election. When, however, the requirement is in the party law, parties may have to register only once, unless a separate clause in the electoral or party law rescinds their registration owing to, for instance, a lacklustre performance in elections.[7] Post-election requirements are not uncommon both in established democracies and in newer democracies in Latin America,[8] but they are rare in the Eastern bloc.[9] Occasionally, signature or vote requirements are accompanied by a spatial distribution requirement, in that signatures must be obtained from certain parts of the country or state. Sometimes, financial requirements are also a part of the ballot-access requirements, either as a pre-election deposit or as a post-election fine.

Little is written about the role of formation rules in party system development and to my knowledge only Birnir, Bogaards and Reilly explicitly make the connection between formation rules and hotly or even violently contested politics.[10] For example, the mechanism investigated by Reilly for the role of formation rules in mediating conflict is that they counteract natural tendencies of inter-group fracture and the consequent propensity for conflict by promoting consolidation of the party system.[11] In contrast, Birnir argues that ethnic politics are not inherently conflictual.[12] Rather, ethnic minority groups are likely to engage in protest and even violence when other electoral alternatives are exhausted.

Building on the emerging literature, this chapter ponders two related questions. First, which came first: the conflict or the institution? Does ethnic conflict prompt the adoption of institutions aimed at resolving ethnic strife or do institutional constraints contribute to conflict among ethnic groups? Second, once formation institutions are adopted in either conflictual or peaceful diverse societies, what is their effect.

The likely answer to the question of which came first, conflict or institution, is that it could be either. Where ethnic minority groups have mobilized and engaged in conflict prior to democratization for reasons exogenous to the electoral process, it is likely that ameliorating the conflict is a priority of democratic state builders. State builders may, for example, use formation institutions as one way to de-emphasize the existing divisions around which the conflict is taking place or to prevent the existing conflict from entering the electoral arena. For example, prior to democratization in Indonesia in 1998, several ethnic minorities used significant violence against the state. In addition to the East Timorese, these include the Acehnese, who have sought independence since 1976, and the Papuans, who were incorporated as the twenty-sixth province of Indonesia only in 1969.[13] As noted by Reilly, the explicit objectives of Indonesian state builders were to consolidate the party system and counter secessionism by, for instance, requiring that all parties have national support.[14]

In many cases, however, ethnic minority groups are not mobilized for political action and/or conflict prior to democratization.[15] In such cases it is unlikely that state builders consider ethnic conflict resolution an objective in state-building. Nonetheless, they may incorporate formation institutions into the construction of democratic institutions for reasons unrelated to ethnicity. For example, prior to democratization in 1979 in Ecuador, the indigenous were poorly mobilized and had only ever engaged in very low-level protests against the state. Consequently, it is unlikely that state builders in Ecuador had ethnicity in mind when fashioning party formation rules. Indeed, according to Mejia Acosta,[16] the spatial formation rules adopted in Ecuador were explicitly constructed to counter the extreme party fractionalization that was thought to draw on *regional divisions*, and there is no evidence to suggest that these rules were intended to exclude the indigenous population. Indeed, the Ecuadorian spatial registration requirements prevented representation of indigenous interests in the legislature only if the sole avenue for such representation was separate indigenous parties.[17]

As these examples illustrate, formation rules are instituted to consolidate party systems by preventing or reducing systemic fragmentation where parties draw on separate cleavages, but only in select cases are the pertinent social divisions ethnic. The answer to the second question, regarding the effect of these rules once instituted, is more complex. Let us first consider anecdotally the effect where formation rules were specifically instituted to handle ethnic conflict by eliminating ethnic and regional parties. In Indonesia, party fragmentation has decreased since democratization.[18] Conflict has not. According to the Minorities at Risk rebellion score,[19] there is no immediate evidence of a decrease in rebellion perpetrated by the Acehnese or the Papuans against the state. Indeed, Reilly points out that there may be a significant cost to retarding party fragmentation through the use of formation rules. These costs include favouring incumbents over challengers and upsetting the balance of politics to the point of encouraging a coup or other types of political crisis.[20] Similarly, Birnir and Van Cott suggest that the benefits of ethnic representation may outweigh the costs of increasing party fragmentation.[21] Therefore, although formation rules evidently reduce fragmentation, it is not clear that they have the effect of reducing ethnic conflict where intended to. However, many of the countries where formation rules were explicitly introduced to counter ethnic tension, manifesting through fragmented party systems, are new democracies and it is possible that the consolidation that is evident in these party systems is across ethnic cleavage lines or will eventually be across cleavage lines with beneficial effects on conflict. It is also possible that such consolidation has already improved ethnic relations, though this may not be evident in the available data. For example, in Indonesia the trajectory of the conflict might have been increasing but for the reform.[22] Alternatively, party system consolidation in these countries simply means that particular cleavages are excluded from representation. The probability of exclusion likely increases as polarization of ethnic groups in society increases, and in the long term may have detrimental effects on the development of ethnic conflict.[23]

The question that remains unanswered pertains to the effect of formation rules in diverse societies where these rules were probably not instituted to reduce conflict because there was little if any ethnic conflict prior to the institution of the rules. With the exception of conflictual states that were formerly a part of the Yugoslav republic, prior to democratization there was little if any sustained organized violence perpetrated by ethnic minority groups against the state in Central and Eastern Europe or in Latin America.[24] Furthermore, countries in Central and Eastern Europe and Latin America democratized more than a decade and a half ago, which allows for some better inferences about the effect of formation rules where they are temporally prior to sustained violent conflict. Consequently, the remainder of this chapter focuses on the effect of formation rules on political conflict in Latin America and Central and Eastern Europe, excluding the exceptionally violent politics of the former Yugoslav states.

In sum, the following discussion shows that formation rules are very effective at reducing overall party fragmentation. However, formation rules that by themselves exclude ethnic groups from political representation are problematic because there is circumstantial evidence to suggest that such rules provoke the ethnic minority group and contribute to conflict. Formation rules that pose restrictions that fall short of excluding a group are also associated with a reduction in the number of parties, but this reduction might have beneficial effects on the political consolidation of the ethnic group. Consequently, policy makers who want to maximize the benefit of party system consolidation and minimize the dangers of ethnic conflict might consider instituting system-consolidating formation rules, such as signature requirements, that pose barriers and may even encourage inter-ethnic cooperation but do not by themselves exclude a group, provided that the number of required signatures does not exceed the voting population of the ethnic minority.

The origin of formation rules

With the exception of the emerging literature on formation rules,[25] there is very little written on why formation rules were adopted in specific countries. The literature on the reasons for the adoption of electoral rules of allocation is, however, quite substantial. Since both types of institution shape party systems and political careers it is likely that the literature on the adoption of rules of allocation can inform us about why particular formation rules were adopted. A common belief in the electoral literature is that electoral rules in emerging democracies are adopted as a result of undemocratic pacts among select established actors.[26] Furthermore, politicians are thought to try to manipulate institutions or the choice of institutions to their own advantage,[27] to the extent possible under uncertainty[28] and with multiple and often contradictory incentives of the participating politicians.[29]

In Central and Eastern Europe, the initial rules governing elections were characteristically forged in roundtables focusing explicitly on procedural issues, and included incumbents and some members of the opposition.[30] Although Central and East European actors probably acted in self-interest in the selection of rules, as predicted by the literature, uncertainty in many cases prevented them from making choices that actually served their self-interest in the long run.[31] Generally speaking, the primary emphasis was on allocation rules, and formation rules were both simple and very minimal[32] or explicitly aimed at reducing party fragmentation.[33] In Poland, subsequent electoral reform to reduce party fragmentation also focused on allocation rules rather than party formation.[34] Changes to allocation rules and the institution of deposits for electoral participation have played a similarly important part in reducing party fragmentation in the Czech Republic. In addition, state funding of parties is an important instrument in reducing party system fragmentation and increasing party cohesion in the Czech legislature.[35] Whereas other law, for example in Albania and Bulgaria, has been used to restrict ethnic party formation[36] and political participation, I have found no evidence that in Central and Eastern Europe formation rules were initially instituted for this purpose. On the contrary, the institution of new rules in the late 1990s in Estonia and Latvia that require candidates to have advanced proficiency in the state language is thought by some to be aimed specifically at hampering the participation of Russian minority parties.[37]

In Latin American countries with large indigenous populations, formation rules were similarly instituted to reduce party fragmentation and/or solidify majority party control. In Ecuador, for example, the objective of formation rules was to reduce party fragmentation.[38] According to Balinski and Gonzales, a 1989 electoral reform in Mexico aimed at reinstituting the advantage of the PRI (the Institutional Revolutionary Party) after earlier reform had granted greater access to smaller parties.[39] In the aftermath of the Chiapas insurrection, a 1994 reform improved the 1989 law but did not update apportionment in line with new census data, with the result that the ethnically diverse region of Chiapas still has fewer seats than it should according to newer census data. Balinski and Gonzales do not, however, discuss any effects of formation rules.[40] This suggests that formation rules have not played a large part in restricting ethnic participation in Mexico and that these rules were probably not instituted with ethnic populations in mind but rather had the same purpose as other electoral rules.[41] This interpretation is consistent with Birnir, who argues that it is unlikely that spatial formation rules have had much effect to date on indigenous party formation in Mexico owing to the recent democratization and the continued violent state response to indigenous organization limiting the political opening.[42]

Similarly, I have found no evidence that formation rules in Peru were specifically intended to halt indigenous party formation.[43] Indeed, drawing on Van Cott, the slow progress of mobilization of indigenous communities in Peru makes it very unlikely that ethnic parties were considered a problem by state builders during re-democratization in the mid-1980s.[44] The first Peruvian indigenous party did not appear on the electoral scene until 1999, and then only in local elections.[45] A plausible explanation for this delay in indigenous party formation in Peru is that ethnicity continues to be very weakly politicized. According to a variety of specialists, from academics to party leaders, I interviewed during the electoral campaign in 2001, indigenous identity in Peru is not a salient political category. The reasons range from discrimination against indigenous groups, to alternative politicization and mobilization of indigenous constituencies on the basis of class, to the general political disarray of the 1990s, which deterred any new party formation. Furthermore, in concert with conventional wisdom about incumbents reforming the rules to their own advantage, some believe the revision of the 1993 election law that dropped the spatial formation requirement was intended to advantage President Fujimori's electoral vehicle and had nothing to do with considerations of ethnicity.[46] Similarly, Bolivia and Guatemala never employed registration requirements that were sufficiently restrictive to exclude indigenous party formation or evidently specifically targeted ethnic groups.[47] Colombia does not have a large indigenous population. However, Moreno has examined the effects of formation rules there and, gauging from her discussion, it is not apparent that changes of formation rules resulted from indigenous concerns but rather they aimed to "open up the political arena to marginalized and unrepresented interests" more generally.[48] In contrast, the elimination of restrictive formation rules in Ecuador probably did result from indigenous concerns.[49]

In sum, therefore, and as expected, it appears that, in ethnically diverse Central and East European and Latin American countries that had not experienced ethnic conflict prior to democratization, formation rules were not adopted with an eye to restricting ethnic representation. Rather these rules were instituted to prevent party system fragmentation and with the objective of furthering incumbent advantage when there was an articulated objective. When these rules were changed, indigenous and/or ethnic concerns or concerns about ethnic populations were not evidently the primary determinants of change, with the exception of liberalizing changes made in Ecuador and restricting ones in Estonia and Latvia.

The effect of formation rules on ethnic populations

The question then becomes: what is the effect of formation rules on ethnic populations where such rules were instituted for motives of party system consolidation rather than with the ethnic populations in mind? Put differently, do these formation rules have any unintended consequences for the ethnic populations in question? For example, Birnir argues that ethnic group propensity for rebellion against the state increases over time where electorally active ethnic groups are excluded from the executive.[50] Ethnic exclusion from the executive occurs where (a) ethnic parties are not institutionally viable; or (b) viable ethnic parties are unable to access government; and (c) non-ethnic parties that over time have access to government do not represent the ethnic issue in the executive. An implication of this argument is that, where ethnic groups are not represented by multi-ethnic parties, formation rules that prevent ethnic representation through ethnic parties are likely to increase the probability that an ethnic group engages in violence against the state.

Prior to examining the possible effects of formation rules on the domain of ethnic politics, it is imperative that we establish the conditionality of this hypothesized causal effect. This conditionality is determined by the interaction of the formation rules with (a) other institutions and (b) the demographics of the country and group in question. For example, changes in formation rules in Colombia show how the effects of formation rules may be offset by other institutions.[51] In 1991, party regulations were altered to allow movements to run in elections as opposed to only parties. One would expect this change to encourage the formation of new parties. In 1994, however, the requirement for votes or signatures was increased,[52] which may seem more likely to deter citizen-based organizations from functioning as parties. If, however, we take into consideration the added stipulation of party funding for any movement that clears the signature/vote/representation threshold, it seems likely that overall there should be a proliferation of parties.[53] In sum, the effect of the increased registration requirement pertaining to the party formation rules in Colombia was probably offset by allowing movements to run and by the new funding opportunities.

Assuming for a moment that we can hold the effect of such intervening institutions constant, below I discuss in some detail how attributes of ethnic minority groups, such as size, cohesion and geographical concentration, theoretically interact with formation rules to affect the group propensity for seeking representation by forming ethnic political parties and the consequent potential for conflict behaviour.

Differences in ethnic diversity and formation rules

A comparison between Tables 7.2 and 7.3 in this chapter and Table 5.1 in Florian Bieber's chapter shows that there are some very interesting differences in the ethnic composition of minorities between the two regions.[54] Generally speaking, ethnic minorities in Central and Eastern Europe are national minorities that often trace their roots to neighbouring countries. One notable exception to this is the Roma, who may constitute a racially distinct group.[55] In Latin America in contrast, notable minorities are racial (indigenous, black or mestizo) and linguistic (indigenous)

Table 7.2 Ethnic diversity in Central and East European countries that did not experience significant sustained ethnic conflict prior to the most recent democratization

Country	Ethnic fractionalization[a]	% Roma[b]
Albania	.22	2.94
Bulgaria	.40	3.70
Czech Republic	.32	0.30–2.90
Estonia	.51	0.06
Hungary	.15	1.30–7.78
Latvia	.59	0.58
Lithuania	.32	0.08
Macedonia	.50	2.30–10.30
Moldova	.55	4.65
Poland	.12	>0.10
Romania	.31	1.80–7.90
Slovakia	.25	1.50–6.60
Slovenia	.22	3.50

Notes:
[a] Calculated by A. Alesina et al., "Fractionalization", *Journal of Economic Growth*, 8, 2003: 155–194.
[b] Minority Rights Group, *World Directory of Minorities* (London: Minority Rights Group International, 1997); Pivi Hernesniemi and Lauri Hannikainen, *Roma Minorities in the Nordic and Baltic Countries. Are Their Rights Realized?* (Rovaniemi: Lapland's University Press, 2000; publication of the Northern Institute for Environmental and Minority Law). As reviewed by Peter Bakker, Institute for Linguistics, Aarhus University, at ⟨http://www.minelres.lv/minelres/archive/06032001-12:03:42-13702.html⟩ (accessed 3 April 2008).

minorities that, in the case of indigenous inhabitants, are native to the region. In a few cases (Brazil, Costa Rica and Peru), Chinese and Japanese also constitute a very small minority (1–3 per cent).

This variety in diversity leads to the expectation that the content and type of demographic interaction with party registration rules will differ between countries depending on the size, cohesion, geographical concentration and attributes specific to the group.[56] Attributes of the individual group interact with the specific types of party registration rules in ways that make them more or less of a barrier to electoral participation by the group and the resulting group potential for conflict behaviour. For example, a ban on ethnic parties affects only linguistically and/or culturally distinct groups such as indigenous peoples and national minorities, but not de facto racial groups. Consequently, where other avenues for the political representation of the group are prevented, one might expect a ban on ethnic parties to augment the conflict potential of linguistically and culturally distinct groups but not of racial groups.

Size of the group is another characteristic that is important to the impact that formation rules will have. Racial groups, for instance, tend to be

Table 7.3 Ethnic diversity in Latin American countries that did not experience significant sustained ethnic conflict prior to the most recent democratization

Country	Ethnic fractionalization[a]	% indigenous population[b]	% African-American[c]
Argentina	.26	1.40	No data
Bolivia	.74	62.05	0.04
Brazil	.54	0.16	45.00
Chile	.17	7.06	No data
Colombia	.60	2.70	26.00
Costa Rica	.24	0.75	2.00
Dominican Republic	.43	0.00	No data
Ecuador	.66	24.85	10.0
El Salvador	.20	1.69	No data
Guatemala	.51	63.00	No data
Honduras	.19	11.88	No data
Mexico	.54	9.47	No data
Nicaragua	.48	7.59	No data
Panama	.55	7.78	No data
Paraguay	.17	1.96	No data
Peru	.66	38.39	5.00
Uruguay	.25	0.00	4.00
Venezuela	.50	1.48	10.00

Notes:
[a] Calculated by A. Alesina et al., "Fractionalization", *Journal of Economic Growth*, 8, 2003: 155–194.
[b] Anne Deruyttere, *Indigenous Peoples and Sustainable Development. The Role of the Inter-American Development Bank* (Washington, DC: Inter-American Development Bank, 1997), except Bolivia (from 2000 census) and Colombia (from 1993 census).
[c] Inter-American Dialogue, "Afro-Descendants in Latin America: How Many?", *Race Report* (Washington, DC: Inter-American Dialogue, 2002).

larger than the average national ethnic minorities and may, therefore, demand greater input in a country's governance than small national minorities, whose primary objective is more likely to involve greater autonomy over their own affairs. When restrictive formation barriers successfully keep the larger groups from representation one might expect any subsequent political conflict to be more bitter and have as its objective a more radical change to national politics than the change a small national minority might seek. Which type of group, small or large, formation rules are likely to present the greatest barriers to is not, however, entirely clear. For example, larger more internally diverse groups are less likely to overcome the collective action problem required to mobilize successfully.[57] An example includes the indigenous peoples in Bolivia, who constitute a racially distinct group but are internally quite divided into divergent linguistic groups. Until recently this group was not unified in its political mobilization.[58] Any additional barriers presented by formation rules will likely further prevent successful collective action by such large groups. At the same time, small groups may experience difficulties in mobilizing enough of their members for political action. In the case of small groups, formation rules may therefore prevent the successful conclusion of an already difficult task. How small is too small for electoral mobilization is not evident. For example, in relatively homogeneous Poland the small German minority does run a separate party in national elections, and the same is true for Greeks in Albania, but a party representing the sizeable community of Ukrainians in Moldova has never gained legislative representation.

Pre-election signature requirements are among the specific rules that interact with the size of the group to alter its potential for mobilization and representation and consequent potential for conflict behaviour. Theoretically, pre-election signature requirements place a proportionally heavier burden on smaller groups and groups in the early stages of mobilization than on large and established ones. Indeed, where electoral institutions are very permissive, the registration requirements effectively substitute for the effects of more restrictive electoral institutions. Alternatively, because pre-election signature requirements work as an incentive for internal party consolidation, if the requirements are not sufficiently high, ethnic groups that might otherwise consolidate to run a unified political party fragment in their electoral competition to the detriment of ethnic group representation.[59]

For example, it is likely that Peru's delay in indigenous party formation until 1999, well after the spatial requirement was dropped in 1993, was influenced by the increase in the number of votes required for party registration, which occurred at the same time that the spatial portion of the requirement was eliminated.[60] Similarly, in Bolivia, the change in pre-election signature requirements, from no requirement to a requirement of 0.5 per cent of registered voters, is associated with a dramatic decline in the number of registered political organizations – from 72 before the 1985 election (of which 18 participated in the election) to 15 before the 1989 election (of which 10 participated in the election). However, only some of those parties were indigenous and none represented a substantial portion of the very large indigenous population. Had the requirement been more stringent, it might have helped consolidate the notoriously fragmented indigenous political picture in Bolivia sooner.

In Central and Eastern Europe, too, pre-election signature requirements present the greatest burden where the minorities that might seek to mobilize are relatively small. As shown in Table 7.4, signature requirements are used in all of the countries examined here except for Albania, Latvia, Estonia and one Moldovan election. Unless the group is very

Table 7.4 Some principal party formation rules in Central and Eastern Europe

Country	Election year	Requirement for		
		Signature	Deposit	Regional distribution
Albania	1991	No	No	No
Albania	1992	No	No	No
Albania	1996	No	No	No
Albania	1997	No	No	No
Albania	2001	No	No	No
Albania	2003	No	No	Large parties only
Bulgaria	1990	Yes	No	No
Bulgaria	1991	Yes	No	No
Bulgaria	1994	Yes	No	No
Bulgaria	1997	Yes	No	No
Bulgaria	2001	Yes	No	No
Czech Republic	1990	Yes	No	No
Czech Republic	1992	Yes	No	No
Czech Republic	1996	Yes	Yes but refundable	No
Czech Republic	1998	Yes	Yes but refundable	No
Czech Republic	2002	Yes	Yes	No
Estonia	1992	No	Yes	No
Estonia	1995	No	Yes	No
Estonia	1999	No	Yes	No
Estonia	2003	No	Yes	No
Hungary	1990	Yes	No	National lists only
Hungary	1994	Yes	No	National lists only
Hungary	1998	Yes	No	National lists only
Hungary	2002	Yes	No	National lists only
Latvia	1993	Yes	Yes	No
Latvia	1995	No	Yes but refundable	No
Latvia	1998	No	Yes but refundable	No
Latvia	2002	No	Yes but refundable	No
Lithuania	1992	Yes	Yes	No
Lithuania	1996	Yes	Yes	No
Lithuania	2000	Yes	Yes	No
Macedonia	1990	Yes	No	No
Macedonia	1994	Yes	No	No
Macedonia	1998	Yes	No	No
Macedonia	2002	Yes	No	No

Table 7.4 (cont.)

Country	Election year	Requirement for		
		Signature	Deposit	Regional distribution
Moldova	1994	No	No	No
Moldova	1998	Yes	No	Yes
Moldova	2001	Yes	Yes	Yes
Poland	1991	Yes	No	National lists only
Poland	1993	Yes	No	National lists only
Poland	1997	Yes	No	National lists only
Poland	2001	Yes	No	No
Romania	1990	Yes	No	No
Romania	1992	Yes	No	No
Romania	1996	Yes unless minority	No	Yes unless minority
Romania	2000	Yes unless minority	No	Yes unless minority
Slovakia	1990	Yes	No	Large parties only
Slovakia	1992	Yes	No	No
Slovakia	1994	Yes	No	No
Slovakia	1998	Yes	No	No
Slovakia	2002	Yes	No	No
Slovenia	1990	Unknown	Unknown	Unknown
Slovenia	1992	Unknown	Unknown	Unknown
Slovenia	1996	Yes unless minority	No	No
Slovenia	2000	Yes	No	No

Sources: International Foundation for Election Systems, *Election Law Compendium of Central and Eastern Europe* (Kiev: IFES, 1995). See also University of Essex, "Project on Political Transformation and the Electoral Process in Post-Communist Europe", at ⟨http://www.essex.ac.uk/elections/⟩ (accessed 3 April 2008), and Lexadin, *The World Law Guide*, at ⟨http://www.lexadin.nl/⟩ (accessed 3 April 2008).

small, however, pre-election signature requirements probably do not by themselves exclude groups from participating in electoral politics. For example, signature requirements in Bolivia did not prevent indigenous parties from registering. Similarly, in Ecuador the number of signatures required until 1995 was low (0.5 per cent of voters) given the size of the indigenous constituency. In 1995 the requirement was increased to 1.5 per cent of registered voters, but that is still a low number relative to

Table 7.5 Party formation requirements in Central and Eastern Europe and the Roma

Country	Most recent signature requirements	% Roma, 1997	Roma electorally active
Estonia	None	0.06	No
Lithuania	400 founding members for political parties	0.08	No
Poland	5,000 signatures for each constituency list	0.16	No
Latvia	None	0.58	No
Czech Republic	1,000 founding members for political parties	2.91	Yes
Albania	None	2.94	No (ethnic parties banned until 2001)
Slovenia	100 signatures accompanying every candidate list or 30 for minorities	3.50	No
Bulgaria	50 founding members for political parties	3.69	Ethnic parties banned – active only through non-ethnic parties
Moldova	5,000 founding members for political parties	4.65	Yes
Slovakia	10,000 declaration of number of members accompanying candidate list every election	6.60	Yes
Hungary	750 signatures for candidates in single-member constituencies every election	7.77	Yes
Romania	10,000 founding members for political parties, with the exception of minority organizations	7.93	Yes
Macedonia	500 founding members for parties	10.33	Yes

Sources: For population – Minority Rights Group, *World Directory of Minorities* (London: Minority Rights Group International, 1997), higher estimate in range; Pivi Hernesniemi and Lauri Hannikainen, *Roma Minorities in the Nordic and Baltic Countries. Are Their Rights Realized?* (Rovaniemi: Lapland's University Press, 2000; publication of the Northern Institute for Environmental and Minority Law); for law – see Table 7.4.

the size of the indigenous community. Likewise, it is unlikely that this requirement is responsible for the lacklustre political performance of the largest ethnic group in Central and Eastern Europe, the Roma.

Table 7.5 examines the relationship between the Roma population and the content of the latest signature law in some more detail. The table accounts for the most recent signature requirement, shows Roma as a percentage of the population by country according to one estimate,[61] and denotes whether the population has mobilized electorally. The first trend to emerge from the table is that electoral activity by the Roma population in a given country seems clearly tied to the size of that demographic. With the exception of the Czech Republic, the Roma are not electorally active where they constitute less than 3.5 per cent of the population. They are electorally active in Romania, Macedonia, Hungary, Moldova, Slovakia and the Czech Republic and through non-ethnic parties in Bulgaria. In all of these countries there is a signature requirement. Assessing the effect of the signature requirements on Roma mobilization, therefore, requires greater attention to the magnitude of the requirement.

Where the Roma are more numerous – in Slovenia, Bulgaria, Moldova, Slovakia, Hungary, Romania and Macedonia – they have accessed legislatures only in Romania and Macedonia. In Macedonia, the registration requirement is very low and required only once.[62] In Romania, minorities are exempt from the requirement.[63] In Hungary, the requirement is not much higher than in Macedonia. However, this requirement is associated with each election rather than a party's foundation.[64] Consequently, to sustain a political party over time, the organizational capacity of the Roma in Hungary must exceed that of the Roma in Macedonia. In Slovakia[65] and Slovenia,[66] too, the requirement is tied to elections. The Roma in Slovenia are not electorally active but do have some organization through the Union of Roma of Slovenia, which is quite dynamic on the cultural scene.[67] The most important difference in the effects of registration requirements on the Roma populations in Slovenia, Slovakia and Hungary compared with Macedonia is that the group is significantly smaller proportionally, making the collection of signatures potentially more difficult. In Moldova, there is no official registration requirement for elections but the registration obligation of "5,000 active members" for parties is not insignificant. More importantly, however, there is a stringent spatial component to the law in Moldova.[68] Finally, in Bulgaria ethnic parties are banned by the constitution. Whereas the Turkish minority has been able to circumvent this law to present a party that by and large is recognized as a Turkish minority party, the Roma have not.[69] In sum, therefore, registration requirements possibly hampered Roma mobilization in Slovenia but, with the exception of Moldova, the registration requirements clearly did not bar Roma parties from running in elections.

Furthermore, as demonstrated by the relative success of Roma parties in Romania, there is nothing inherently apolitical about the Roma but, for an ethnic minority in Central and Eastern Europe, they tend to be unusually poorly mobilized.[70] Consequently, the anecdotal evidence from

Slovakia, where Roma parties did register, suggests that the rule might have been of more use to Roma representation had it been more stringent. According to Barany, 13 "Romani parties registered prior to the 1998 Slovak national elections, but eventually no Gypsy party ran candidates for parliament on its own".[71] It is possible that the requirement of a declaration of 10,000 members attached to a candidate list in the election may have hampered the participation of these Roma parties.[72] It should be possible, however, for 13 Roma parties to have a voting age membership exceeding 10,000 because the population constitutes at least 350,000 individuals according to the Minority Rights Group and 400,000 according to Barany.[73] It is more likely, therefore, that the requirement was just high enough to make electoral follow-through difficult for the high number of would-be contestants, but not high enough to make them consolidate into a single or a few large parties that could have run successfully.

In Moldova, however, the spatial component of the registration rules prevents the electoral participation of the Roma and other ethnic minorities through ethnic parties.[74] The same is theoretically true for the party formation of geographically concentrated groups in other countries but not of regionally dispersed groups, unless the number of group members is very small in any one location.[75] Indigenous groups in Latin America and some national minorities in Central and Eastern Europe tend to be geographically concentrated, but geographical concentration is less common for racial non-indigenous minorities in Latin America. Existing spatial requirements in Central and Eastern Europe are, however, restricted to large parties in Albania and Slovakia or national lists in Hungary and Poland. Romania has spatial registration requirements for all parties, but the 1992 election law cancels this requirement out for minorities. Consequently, it is unlikely in Central and Eastern Europe that spatial registration requirements hamper ethnic political participation outside Moldova.

This class of requirements has presented some problems in Latin America. In Ecuador, spatial registration requirements prevented indigenous peoples from forming an indigenous party until this barrier was lifted in the mid-1990s, because the registration requirement exceeded the spatial location of indigenous groups in the country.[76] In Guatemala, the spatial registration requirement in the 1985 electoral code is not sufficiently restrictive to exclude indigenous party formation and at least one indigenous party has emerged.[77] The fact that this party did not emerge until 10 years after democratization is likely owing to the limitations on political openings created by continued state repression of indigenous communities until peace accords were signed in 1996 and to a lack of internal indigenous group cohesion.[78] Other countries with large indigenous populations and liberal electoral rules where spatial registration requirements might constitute a problem include Mexico and Peru. The rule has probably had little effect on ethnic representation in Mexico, but in Peru an indigenous party appeared only after spatial registration requirements were lifted, although continued organization is uncertain because indigenous identity remains weakly politicized.

Assessment and conclusion

The above anecdotal evidence provides ample support for the idea that formation rules have contributed to party system consolidation both in Latin America and in Central and Eastern Europe. Central and East European countries that instituted significant formation requirements experienced less fragmentation than those that did not, which have since had to adjust their electoral law to handle the fragmentation. Similarly, in Latin America there is evidence that an increase in formation requirements reduced party system fragmentation. Clearly, therefore, formation rules are very effective at reducing party system fragmentation.

Assessing the effect on conflict in the political system of formation rules that stop short of excluding minority groups from electoral participation is more difficult. The multitude of indigenous and Roma parties registering where signature requirements are low and the ethnic populations are large, but subsequently failing to present a viable electoral alternative, suggests that signature requirements may in those cases not have been sufficiently high to induce the necessary cohesion of the ethnic group for successful electoral participation. Increasing signature requirements is, however, a delicate balance, because high signature requirements, for example exceeding the size of the voting age population in a group, may prevent ethnic minority group political participation altogether. Ethnic politics in Bolivia, where signature requirements were increased, have become more hotly contested since democratization, but the indigenous vote was also consolidated enough for the first time in the last elections to take the presidency. Consequently, it is likely that indigenous grievances voiced over political exclusion resulted from causes other than registration rules. In Bulgaria, Hungary and Romania, data on Roma protest before and after democratization show that protest by this group against the state has increased. Among the countries examined here, the Roma have also protested in the Czech Republic and Macedonia. It is not clear, however, that formation rules played any role in this protest, although more stringent registration rules might help this minority consolidate sufficiently to achieve representation and address their grievances through the legislative process. Other smaller minorities, such as Greeks in Albania, Albanians in Macedonia and the indigenous in

Chile and Honduras, have increased their protest against the state during the current democratic period, but more information is needed to establish what effect, if any, formation rules play in this process.

Interpreting the causal effect of formation rules and conflict is similarly difficult because of the contingencies discussed above, but some tentative conclusions are nevertheless possible. There is evidence that rules that by themselves exclude minority populations from electoral participation pose problems for democracy by increasing the contentiousness of ethnic politics. Spatial registration requirements in Ecuador and Moldova are examples of such rules. Both Ecuador and Moldova experienced significant ethnic conflict after democratization.[79] Clearly these conflicts are not exclusively caused by the institution of formation rules, but the presence of such rules under conditions of ethnic polarization does not help in integrating rebellious populations into the mainstream party system. Other formation rules that in effect exclude particular populations, such as linguistic requirements in the Baltics, have also resulted in bitter protest by the affected groups. In none of these countries had the ethnic minorities initiated conflict prior to the institution of these rules, and in the case of Ecuador ethnic protest was reduced after the rules were changed to allow for indigenous participation through ethnic parties. Clearly, therefore, exclusionary formation rules have the potential to increase ethnic political conflict. At the same time, we know that reducing party fragmentation has beneficial effects for party system development. The potentially detrimental effects of ethnic conflict owing to the exclusionary effects of formation rules and the benefits of reducing party fragmentation may cancel each other out or have unforeseen consequences. It is therefore imperative that policy makers consider this trade-off explicitly in an effort to create an institutional framework that assists healthy party system consolidation while ensuring minority representation through single- or multi-ethnic parties.

Notes

1. Real parties and voters do not always live up to democratic ideals, but, at their best, party representatives present the interests of their constituency.
2. To name but a few, Maurice Duverger, *Political Parties, Their Organization and Activity in the Modern State* (London and New York: Wiley Methuen, 1954); S. M. Lipset and S. Rokkan (eds), *Party Systems and Voter Alignments: Cross National Perspectives* (New York: Free Press, 1967); Samuel P. Huntington, *Political Order in Changing Societies* (New Haven, CT: Yale University Press, 1968); Giovanni Sartori, *Parties and Party Systems: A Framework for Analysis* (Cambridge and New York: Cambridge University Press, 1976); and Stefano Bartolini and Peter Mair, *Identity, Competition, and Electoral Availability: The Stabilisation of European Electorates 1885–1985* (Cambridge: Cambridge University Press, 1990).

3. Markuu Laakso and Rein Taagepera, "Effective Number of Parties. A Measure with Application to Western Europe", *Comparative Political Studies*, 12(1), 1979: 3–27; Rein Taagepera and Matthew Soberg Shugart, *Seats and Votes: The Effects and Determinants of Electoral Systems* (New Haven, CT: Yale University Press, 1989); Gary W. Cox, *Making Votes Count: Strategic Coordination in the World's Electoral Systems* (Cambridge: Cambridge University Press, 1997).

4. Lipset and Rokkan, *Party Systems and Voter Alignments*; G. Bingham Powell, Jr., *Contemporary Democracies: Participation, Stability, and Violence* (Cambridge, MA: Harvard University Press, 1982); P. C. Ordeshook and O. Shvetsova, "Ethnic Heterogeneity, District Magnitude, and the Number of Parties", *American Journal of Political Science*, 38(1), 1994: 100–123; Octavio Amorim Neto and Gary W. Cox, "Electoral Institutions, Cleavage Structures, and the Number of Parties", *American Journal of Political Science*, 41(1), 1997: 149–174; Gary W. Cox, *Making Votes Count: Strategic Coordination in the World's Electoral Systems* (Cambridge and New York: Cambridge University Press, 1997); Michael Coppedge, "District Magnitude, Economic Performance, and Party-System Fragmentation in Five Latin American Countries", *Comparative Political Studies*, 30(2), 1997: 156–185; Shaheen Mozaffar, James R. Scaritt, and Glen Galaich, "Electoral Institutions, Ethnopolitical Cleavages, and Party Systems in Africa's Emerging Democracies", *American Political Science Review*, 97, 2003: 379–390; Jóhanna Kristín Birnir and Donna Lee Van Cott, "Disunity in Diversity: Party System Fragmentation and the Dynamic Effect of Ethnic Heterogeneity on Latin American Legislatures", *Latin American Research Review*, 42(1), 2007: 97–123.

5. Amorim Neto and Cox, "Electoral Institutions, Cleavage Structures, and the Number of Parties"; Cox, *Making Votes Count*; Ordeshook and Shvetsova, "Ethnic Heterogeneity, District Magnitude, and the Number of Parties; Mozaffar et al., "Electoral Institutions, Ethnopolitical Cleavages, and Party Systems in Africa's Emerging Democracies"; Taagepera and Shugart, *Seats and Votes*. For modifications of this argument, see Scott Mainwaring and Matthew S. Shugart (eds), *Presidentialism and Democracy in Latin America* (Cambridge: Cambridge University Press, 1997); for exceptions, see Marc R. Rosenblum and Michael Huelshoff, "Not Whether but When: Institutions, Structure, and Political Parties", unpublished manuscript, 2004.

6. Simon Hug, *Altering Party Systems: Strategic Behavior and the Emergence of New Political Parties in Western Democracies* (Michigan: Michigan University Press, 2001); Jóhanna K. Birnir, "Latent Stability of Electoral Preferences through Institutional Changes: Ecuador and Representation of Indigenous Communities", American Political Science Association Annual Conference, 1999; Jóhanna Kristín Birnir, "Stabilizing Party Systems and Excluding Segments of Society? The Effects of Formation Costs on New Parties in Latin America", *Studies in Comparative International Development*, 39(3), 2004: 3–28; Donna Lee Van Cott, "Institutional Change and Ethnic Parties in South America", *Latin American Politics and Society*, 45(2), 2003: 1–39; Benjamin Reilly, "Political Engineering and Party Politics in Papua New Guinea", *Party Politics*, 8(6), 2002: 701–718; Benjamin Reilly, "Political Parties and Political Engineering in the Asia Pacific Region", *Asia Pacific Issues* (East West Center), 71(1–8), 2003; Benjamin Reilly, "Political Engineering and Party Politics in Conflict-Prone Societies", *Democratization*, 13(5), 2006: 811–827; Erika Moreno, "Subnational Determinants of National Multipartism in Latin America", *Legislative Studies Quarterly*, 28(2), 2003: 179–201; Erika Moreno, "Whither the Colombian Two-Party System? An Assessment of Political Reforms and Their Limits", *Electoral Studies*, 24(3), 2005: 485–509.

7. In 2000, the Moldovan party law was amended to require "A registration fee equal to 10 minimum wages ... for the registration of the bylaws of the political party or socio-political organization, modifications and completions to it" (Article 15). International

Foundation for Election Systems, "Moldova", in *Election Law Compendium of Central and Eastern Europe* (Kiev: IFES, 1995). See also University of Essex, "Project on Political Transformation and the Electoral Process in Post-Communist Europe", ⟨http://www.essex.ac.uk/elections/⟩ (accessed 2 April 2008).

8. A. J. Bott, *Handbook of United States Election Laws and Practices* (Westport, CT, and London: Greenwood Press, 1990); Birnir, "Stabilizing Party Systems and Excluding Segments of Society?".

9. Jóhanna Kristín Birnir, "Formation Rules in Eastern Europe and Former Soviet Republics: The Roma", American Political Science Association, 2005.

10. Birnir, "Stabilizing Party Systems and Excluding Segments of Society?"; Matthijs Bogaards, "Electoral Systems and the Management of Ethnic Conflict in the Balkans", in Alina Mungiu-Pippidi and Ivan Krastev (eds), *Nationalism after Communism: Lessons Learned* (Budapest: CEU Press, 2004), pp. 247–268; Matthijs Bogaards, "Electoral Systems, Party Systems, and Ethnic Conflict Management in Africa", in Matthias Basedau, Gero Erdmann, and Andreas Mehler (eds), *Votes, Money and Violence: Political Parties and Elections in Africa* (Uppsala: Nordiska Afrikainstitutet, 2007), pp. 168–193; Reilly, "Political Engineering and Party Politics in Papua New Guinea", "Political Parties and Political Engineering in the Asia Pacific Region", "Political Engineering and Party Politics in Conflict-Prone Societies".

11. Reilly, "Political Engineering and Party Politics in Papua New Guinea", "Political Parties and Political Engineering in the Asia Pacific Region".

12. Jóhanna Kristín Birnir, *Ethnicity and Electoral Politics* (New York: Cambridge University Press, 2007).

13. Minorities at Risk Project, Center for International Development and Conflict Management, College Park, MD, users' manual and data, available at ⟨http://www.cidcm.umd.edu/inscr/mar/⟩ (accessed 2 April 2008).

14. Reilly, "Political Engineering and Party Politics in Conflict-Prone Societies".

15. Mobilization is a process that is notoriously difficult to define and means different things in different contexts. In this chapter, I define ethnic political mobilization as a public manifestation of collective action for a political purpose. For example, under democratic conditions ethnic groups, or at least significant parts of the group, are clearly politically mobilized when they register a party or support ethnic candidates in elections. Prior to democratization, ethnic groups may mobilize outside electoral politics. For instance, widespread protest by an ethnic group is an indicator that the group is collectively mobilized, at least for the purpose of protest.

16. Andrés Mejia Acosta, *Partidos Políticos. El Eslabón Perdido de la Representación*, Proyecto CORDES – Gobernabilidad (Quito, Ecuador: Corporación de Estudios para el Desarollo, 1998), pp. 53–54.

17. Birnir, "Stabilizing Party Systems and Excluding Segments of Society?".

18. Reilly, "Political Engineering and Party Politics in Conflict-Prone Societies".

19. Minorities at Risk Project.

20. Reilly, "Political Engineering and Party Politics in Conflict-Prone Societies", p. 824.

21. Birnir and Van Cott, "Disunity in Diversity".

22. I thank Allen Hicken for this insight.

23. Birnir, *Ethnicity and Electoral Politics*.

24. This includes indigenous groups in Latin America that may constitute demographic majorities in the aggregate but have historically been political minorities.

25. Hug, *Altering Party Systems*; Birnir, "Latent Stability of Electoral Preferences through Institutional Changes: Ecuador and Representation of Indigenous Communities"; Birnir, "Stabilizing Party Systems and Excluding Segments of Society?"; Van Cott, "Institutional Change and Ethnic Parties in South America"; Reilly, "Political Engineering

and Party Politics in Papua New Guinea", "Political Parties and Political Engineering in the Asia Pacific Region", "Political Engineering and Party Politics in Conflict-Prone Societies"; Moreno, "Subnational Determinants of National Multipartism in Latin America", "Whither the Colombian Two-Party System?".

26. Guillermo O'Donnell and Philippe C. Schmitter, "Convoking Elections (and Provoking Parties)", in Guillermo O'Donnell, Philippe C. Schmitter and Laurence Whitehead (eds), *Transitions from Authoritarian Rule: Prospects for Democracy* (Baltimore, MD: Johns Hopkins University Press, 1986).

27. William H. Riker, *The Art of Political Manipulation* (New Haven, CT: Yale University Press, 1986).

28. Adam Przeworski, *Democracy and the Market* (New York: Cambridge University Press, 1991); Barbara Geddes, "Initiation of New Democratic Institutions in Eastern Europe and Latin America", in A. Lijphart and C. H. Waisman (eds), *Institutional Design in New Democracies: Eastern Europe and Latin America* (Boulder, CO: Westview Press, 1996); A. Lijphart, "Democratization and Constitutional Choices in Czecho-Slovakia, Hungary and Poland, 1989–1991", *Journal of Theoretical Politics*, 4(2), 1992: 207–223.

29. Fabrice Edouard Lehoucq, "Institutional Change and Political Conflict: Evaluating Alternative Explanations of Electoral Reform in Costa Rica", *Electoral Studies*, 4(1), 1995: 23–45; Steven S. Smith and Thomas F. Remington, *The Politics of Institutional Choice: The Formation of the Russian State Duma* (Oxford and Princeton, NJ: Princeton University Press, 2001). For an excellent review article of the rationale behind the choice of electoral systems, see Kenneth Benoit, "Electoral Laws as Political Consequences: Explaining the Origins and Change of Electoral Institutions", *Annual Review of Political Science*, 10, 2007: 363–390.

30. Vernon Bogdanor, "Founding Elections and Regime Change", *Electoral Studies*, 9(4), 1990: 288–294.

31. Olga Shvetsova, "Endogenous Selection of Institutions and their Exogenous Effects", *Constitutional Political Economy*, 14, 2003: 191–212; Josephine T. Andrews and Robert W. Jackman, "Strategic Fools: Electoral Rule Choice Under Extreme Uncertainty", *Electoral Studies*, 24, 2005: 65–84.

32. Rein Taagepera, "The Baltic States", *Electoral Studies*, 9(4), 1990: 303–311; Zbigniew Pelczynski and Sergiusz Kowalski, "Poland.", *Electoral Studies*, 9(4), 1990: 346–354; Daniel N. Nelson, "Romania", *Electoral Studies*, 9(4), 1990: 355–366.

33. Stephen Ashley, "Bulgaria", *Electoral Studies*, 9(4), 1990: 312–318; András Körösényi, "Hungary", *Electoral Studies*, 9(4), 1990: 337–345.

34. Marek M. Kaminski and Monika A. Nalepa, "Poland: Learning to Manipulate Electoral Rules", in Josep M. Colomer (ed.), *Handbook of Electoral System Choice* (New York: Palgrave Macmillan, 2004). Compared with many other Central and East European countries, Poland is not very ethnically diverse. Nonetheless, the German minority, at least, has run parties in Polish elections.

35. Petr Kopecký, "The Czech Republic: Entrenching Proportional Representation", in Josep M. Colomer (ed.), *Handbook of Electoral System Choice* (New York: Palgrave Macmillan, 2004).

36. The ban on ethnic parties in Albania was lifted in 2001.

37. Edvald Mikkel and Vello Pettai, "The Baltics: Independence with Divergent Electoral Systems", in Josep M. Colomer (ed.), *Handbook of Electoral System Choice* (New York: Palgrave Macmillan, 2004).

38. Mejia Acosta, *Partidos Políticos*.

39. Michel Balinski and Victoriano R. Gonzalez, "A Case Study of Electoral Manipulation: The Mexican Laws of 1989 and 1994", *Electoral Studies*, 15(2), 1996: 203–217.

40. Ibid.
41. The spatial requirement demands at least "a number of affiliates that represents not less than 0.13% of the total amount of registered voters for the previous federal process, including at least 3,000 affiliates in 10 of the 32 states, or 300 in at least 100 of the 300 federal districts. An already registered national political party does not need to register for every national election." Mexico Electoral Law, Article 22-31, as cited by the ACE *Electoral Knowledge Network* at ⟨http://aceproject.org/epic-en/pc/Epic_view/MX⟩ (accessed 2 April 2008). Of the people who speak an indigenous language in Mexico, 90 per cent are concentrated in 10 states in the south and the centre of the country. Minority Rights Group, *World Directory of Minorities* (London: Minority Rights Group International, 1997).
42. Birnir, "Stabilizing Party Systems and Excluding Segments of Society?".
43. After 1979, Peruvian parties were required to present a list of at least 100,000 members in order to register. F. Tuesta Soldevilla, *Peru Politico en Cifras* (Lima, Peru: Fundación Friedrich Ebert, 1995). Each party also had to be registered as an organization in at least half of the country's 25 districts. The indigenous population is concentrated in only 11 of those districts. Instituto Nacional de Estadistica e Informatica, *Compendio de Estadisticas Sociales 1994–1995* (Lima, Peru: Instituto Nacional de Estadistica e Informatica, 1995).
44. Donna Lee Van Cott, *From Movements to Parties in Latin America: The Evolution of Ethnic Politics* (New York: Cambridge University Press, 2005).
45. Van Cott, "Institutional Change and Ethnic Parties in South America".
46. Charles D. Kenney, "The Death and Rebirth of a Party System, Peru 1978–2001", *Comparative Political Studies*, 36, 2003: 1210–1239.
47. Birnir, "Stabilizing Party Systems and Excluding Segments of Society?".
48. Moreno, "Whither the Colombian Two-Party System?", p. 492.
49. Birnir, "Stabilizing Party Systems and Excluding Segments of Society?".
50. Birnir, *Ethnicity and Electoral Politics*. Birnir further argues that voice in the legislature does not satisfy ethnic groups because voice is unlikely to translate into influence over policy unless the size of the group in the legislature is relatively large. Access to the executive does not guarantee policy influence either, but it does make it more likely.
51. Although the indigenous population in Colombia is quite small (under 3 per cent), the country is racially quite heterogeneous. Birnir and Van Cott, "Disunity in Diversity".
52. The requirement went from 10,000 to 50,000 signatures for an elected representative.
53. Moreno, "Whither the Colombian Two-Party System?".
54. In Bolivia and Guatemala the indigenous are a demographic majority but have, until recently, been a political minority. Thus, I include these groups in the discussion as minorities.
55. Angus Fraser, *The Gypsies* (Oxford: Blackwell, 1995); Zoltan Barany, *The East European Gypsies: Regime Change, Marginality, and Ethnopolitics* (Cambridge: Cambridge University Press, 2002).
56. In this chapter I do not attempt to address the additional complications arising from the fact that ethnic identity over time is fluid and context dependent – Daniel Posner, *Institutions and Ethnic Politics in Africa* (New York: Cambridge University Press, 2005); Kanchan Chandra, *Why Ethnic Parties Succeed: Patronage and Ethnic Headcounts in India* (New York: Cambridge University Press, 2004) – but point to some recent thought-provoking work by Chandra that considers how the idea of multi-faceted and fluid identities affects the analysis of institutions and ethnic political action. Kanchan Chandra, "A Constructivist Dataset on Ethnicity and Institutions (CDEI)", in Rawi Abdelal, Yoshiko Herrera, Alastair Ian Johnston and Rose McDermott (eds), *Identity as a Vari-*

able: A Guide for Social Scientists (New York: Cambridge University Press, forthcoming 2008); available at ⟨http://www.nyu.edu/gsas/dept/politics/faculty/chandra/chandra _home.html⟩ (accessed 2 April 2008).

57. Mancur Olson, Jr., *The Logic of Collective Action: Public Goods and the Theory of Groups* (Cambridge, MA: Harvard University Press, 1965).

58. Raúl Madrid, "Indigenous Voters and Party System Fragmentation in Latin America", *Electoral Studies*, 24(4), 2005: 689–707; Van Cott, *From Movements to Parties in Latin America*; Birnir and Van Cott, "Disunity in Diversity".

59. I thank Florian Bieber for this insight.

60. In 1993, the requirement was increased from 100,000 members, or approximately 1 per cent of the electorate, to 4 per cent of the electorate (Tuesta Soldevilla, *Peru Político en Cifras*).

61. According to Barany, estimates of this population are extremely varied and often notoriously unreliable. (Barany, *The East European Gypsies*).

62. Parties are obligated to submit a list of 500 founding members (previously 200 members). Article 33, Election Law 1994 amended 1999. (University of Essex, "Project on Political Transformation and the Electoral Process in Post-Communist Europe").

63. Political parties or other political groupings were in 1990 required to have 251 members for registration. In 1996 this registration requirement was changed to a list of 10,000 founding members in 15 counties and no fewer than 300 in each county. Article 17, Law No. 27 of 1996 on Political Parties; available at ⟨http://www.dsclex.ro/english/law/ law27_1996.htm⟩ (accessed 3 April 2008). However, according to the 1992 election law, "Organizations of citizens belonging to national minorities participating in the elections shall be, as far as electoral operations are concerned, juridically equivalent to political parties" (Article 4).

64. In Hungary, the election system is threefold: national list, territorial list and single-member constituencies. To be a candidate in a single-member constituency, 750 signatures are required. Only parties that have candidates in the territory are entitled to a territorial list. The party has to have 25 per cent of the vote and at least 2 candidates of the territory's eligible candidates. Only those parties that have at least seven territorial lists are entitled to a national list. Act No. XXXIV of 1989 on the Election of Members of Parliament, Hungary; available at ⟨http://www.legislationline.org/legislation.php?tid =57&lid=1669⟩ (accessed 3 April 2008).

65. A political party must submit a declaration that it has at least 10,000 members, or a lower number of members and additional signatures of voters who support the candidate list of the party, together totalling 10,000 voters. Article 17, Law on Election to the Slovak National Council (1990, amended 1992, 1994, 1995, 1998); available at ⟨http://www. legislationline.org/legislation.php?tid=57&lid=301⟩ (accessed 3 April 2008).

66. According to Article 37 of the Law on Elections to the Chamber of State, "A list of candidates in an individual constituency must be defined by at least a hundred voters who have residential status in the constituency." Only the Italian and Hungarian minorities have a lower requirement. (International Foundation for Election Systems, "Slovenia", *Election Law Compendium of Central and Eastern Europe*). Alternatively, according to Article 35, political parties can nominate candidates provided that "[t]he list of candidates must be supported by signatures of at least thirty voters, who have residential status in the constituency". Parties themselves, however, may be founded by no fewer than 200 adult citizens (Article 4). Consequently, the requirement is 100 signatures every election for independent candidates, or 200 initial members and 30 signatures thereafter.

67. Brian J. Požun, "News from Slovenia. Roma Anniversary", *Central Europe Review*, 3(5), 5 February 2001, p. 5.

68. The requirement mandates that members reside "in at least half of the second level administrative territorial units, but no less than 600 in each of the administrative territorial units mentioned above". (International Foundation for Election Systems, "Moldova").

69. In Albania, the 1991 law on political parties also outlawed the formation of parties on religious, ethnic or regional bases. According to Rufino, this law prevented Omonia, the association defending the interests of the Greek community in Albania, from contesting future elections after having secured 0.5 per cent of the vote and five seats in the 1991 election. See Rubén Ruiz Rufino, "Ethnic Parliamentary Incorporation in Central and Eastern Europe: Finding a Mechanical Explanation", paper presented at the 4th annual Graduate Student Retreat of the Society for Comparative Research, Budapest, 2005. The ban on ethnic parties in Albania was lifted in 2001.

70. Barany, *The East European Gypsies*.

71. Ibid., p. 231.

72. Since the requirement is associated with the list of candidates, it is not clear to me whether "registration" had to include the declaration of 10,000 members.

73. Barany, *The East European Gypsies*; Minority Rights Group, *World Directory of Minorities*.

74. In 1998 the Moldovan party law was amended to stipulate that "[p]arty or other socio-political organization statute shall be registered if: [it] includes at least 5000 members residing in at least half of second level administrative territorial units, but no less than 150 in each of the said administrative territorial units" (General Principles, Article 5.3). In 1999 the number was changed to "at least 5000 active members residing in at least half of the second level administrative territorial units, but no less than 600 in each of the administrative-territorial units mentioned above". Law of the Republic of Moldova on Parties and Other Socio-Political Organizations; available at ⟨http://www.parties.e-democracy.md/en/legislation/politicalparties/⟩ (accessed 3 April 2008).

75. Birnir, "Stabilizing Party Systems and Excluding Segments of Society?".

76. Ibid.

77. The requirement is that parties must at a minimum be organized in 12 departments and in 50 counties with at least one member for every 2,000 registered voters nationally, at least half of whom must be literate (Articles 19, 24 and 49). "Guatemala: Ley Electoral y de Partidos Políticos de 1985", *Political Database of the Americas*, Georgetown University; available at ⟨http://pdba.georgetown.edu/Electoral/Guate/guate.html⟩ (accessed 3 April 2008). However, Mayans, who are the only indigenous group in Guatemala, are represented in substantial numbers in all but approximately 5 of the 22 departments. Kay B. Warren, "Voting against Indigenous Rights in Guatemala: Lessons from the 1999 Referendum", in Kay B. Warren and Jean E. Jackson (eds), *Indigenous Movements, Self-Representation, and the State in Latin America* (Austin, TX: University of Texas Press, 2002). Consequently, the spatial requirement could not have delayed Mayan party formation in Guatemala.

78. Victor Montejo, "The Multiplicity of Mayan Voices: Mayan Leadership and the Politics of Self-representation", in Kay B. Warren and Jean E. Jackson (eds), *Indigenous Movements, Self-Representation, and the State in Latin America* (Austin TX: University of Texas Press, 2002).

79. Minorities at Risk Project.

8

Party regulation and political engineering in Papua New Guinea and the Pacific islands

Henry Okole

Introduction

Despite a generally successful record of democracy, the South Pacific receives little attention in most comparative discussions of political parties. The reason for this is not hard to find. The region is home to a dozen states and a similar number of related territories, all but one of which have a population of under 1 million, and several fewer than 20,000 inhabitants. With a few exceptions, despite having democratic political systems, the party systems of Pacific states are weak and underdeveloped, with some countries having no political parties at all.

As Reilly notes, on many comparative rankings of government performance, the South Pacific is amongst the most democratic regions in the post-colonial world. Despite this, Melanesia in particular has been plagued by violent internal conflict, precipitating an "Africanization" of politics in which democratically elected governments have been deposed through ethnic conflicts.[1] Papua New Guinea settled a decade-long war on its eastern island of Bougainville only in 2001, and faces localized armed conflicts in a number of regions, particularly the Southern Highlands. Fiji, one of the region's most developed states, experienced its fourth military coup in 2006, and in the Solomon Islands a regional peace enforcement mission led by Australia has been in place since 2003 following violence between rival ethnic militias that led to the collapse of central government.

Political parties in conflict-prone societies: Regulation, engineering and democratic development, Reilly and Nordlund (eds),
United Nations University Press, 2008, ISBN 978-92-808-1157-5

Perhaps because of this combination of ongoing electoral democracy with internal conflicts and poor governance, attempts to regulate parties and strengthen democracy in the South Pacific have relied upon unusual solutions to address problems of weak parties, fragmented parliaments and unstable governments. In recent years, the region has seen some of the world's most ambitious attempts to reshape party politics through regulation and engineering. These have been centred on the region's largest state, Papua New Guinea (PNG), which has a fast-growing population of 5.7 million people – larger than all the other Pacific islands combined.

In recent years, PNG has introduced a package of constitutional, electoral and party reforms that aim to stabilize executive government and build a coherent party system. These include, for the first time, explicit attempts to regulate the formation, organization and behaviour of political parties. These reforms, contained in an act of parliament that has the status of constitutional law, the Organic Law on the Integrity of Political Parties and Candidates (OLIPPAC), are designed to encourage the development of a more coherent party system, stabilize the formation of executive government and fundamentally change the conduct of the electoral process.

Attempts to regulate party behaviour have also been on the agenda in the other Melanesian states of Fiji (population 800,000), the Solomon Islands (520,000) and Vanuatu (200,000). Facing similar problems of party fragmentation and ill-discipline, both the Solomon Islands and Vanuatu are studying the Papua New Guinea experience closely. Fiji's suspended 1997 constitution contains detailed rules for government formation based on party numbers in parliament and attempts to regulate party membership and floor-crossing; whether these will change as a result of the 2006 military coup remains to be seen. In Polynesia, Samoa (population 170,000) also places restraints on party-hopping and has exhibited more stable government than the Melanesian countries – although this has come at the cost of also having a more limited form of democracy, with political office restricted to members of the traditional aristocracy.

Elements of communalism also continue in some of the region's political systems. In Fiji, two-thirds of all parliamentary seats are reserved for members of the country's three main ethnic communities (Fijians have 23 seats, Indo-Fijians have 19 seats, and there are 3 seats for "general electors" and 1 for the distant island of Rotuma). Fiji and Papua New Guinea have also introduced centripetal incentives to their political systems in recent years by adopting versions of the alternative vote, in an attempt to increase ethnic cooperation and ensure more broadly representative candidates.[2]

One of the few book-length studies of Pacific party systems argues that "a persuasive piece of evidence of the lack of party systems in the region is the growing consensus on the need to engineer them. Given the acute nature of the problem in Papua New Guinea, it is of little surprise that efforts to engineer a party system are most advanced in that country."[3] Accordingly, the remainder of this chapter will focus predominantly on the Papua New Guinea reforms, in particular the 2002 OLIPPAC and electoral system changes, which aim to fundamentally reshape the nature of party politics in that country.

Democracy in PNG

PNG has a history of uninterrupted democratic governance since the first national election was held in 1964. The most recent election, in 2007, was the country's tenth successive competitive national election, giving PNG one of the longest records of continuous democracy in the third world. Changes of government, both via elections and on the floor of parliament, have been frequent and peaceful.

With over 800 languages signifying the acute fragmentation of the country, PNG's modern history has been predominantly concerned with the daunting task of building a sense of nationalism sufficient to sustain a modern state in one of the most rugged topographies in the world. This has represented a serious challenge, given PNG's inherent diversity. The 10-year civil war (1989–1998) on Bougainville represented a serious threat to the state but did not ultimately threaten the unity of the country.

Despite its record of unbroken democracy, it has been evident to many observers of PNG that the quality of democratic governance has been eroding.[4] Poor governance correlated with declining economic and social indicators meant that throughout the 1990s some drastic economic reforms, including two structural adjustment programmes from the Bretton Woods institutions, had to be instituted to address various aspects of the political apparatus and public service. What was particularly worrying was the chronic instability that had circumvented the performance and effectiveness of the 109-seat National Parliament since the late 1980s and well into the following decade. Intricately woven into the causes of this instability was the role of political parties.

Despite its status as one of the continuing third world and third wave democracies, upon closer examination it is clear that many aspects of PNG's democracy have been procedural at best. Parties have remained weak and largely irrelevant to the electoral process. Individuals and groups would use and abide by laws only if it suited their ends. The repeated mid-term changes of government between 1977 and 2002 saw a succession of prime ministers deposed and new cabinets appointed as a result of shifting party loyalties on the floor of parliament, with little underlying rationale except the quest for political power. The end result was chronic instability in parliament, which then had reverberating effects down to the public service, engulfing the entire country.

State formation and the emerging party system

Despite there being no major colonial-related conflicts on the eve of PNG's independence in 1975, it was always naive to expect that the superimposition of a modern state structure on a fragmented traditional society was going to be unproblematic.[5] The adjustment was monumental. An ugly face of the adjustment was the seemingly unfamiliar role of political parties in society outside the parliamentary domain, where they performed more as competing factions than as properly articulated representatives of group interests.

The experience of Western colonialism had touched the average PNG citizen very lightly, if at all. Great Britain and Germany had claimed colonial authority over Papua and New Guinea respectively in the late 1800s. Australia subsequently assumed control of Papua from Britain in 1906 and New Guinea from Germany at the start of World War I. Nevertheless, colonial penetration was limited to accessible places along the coast and a few limited locations in the hinterland. By the 1960s, Australia was being pressured by the UN Trusteeship Council, among others, to start preparing Papua New Guinea for independence in the near future. The directive was surreal for those who knew PNG.

By the time Australia began seriously preparing PNG for independence in the 1960s, regional and ethnic divisions threatened to derail preparations for eventual statehood. All the while, the local economy was heavily in the hands of foreigners, propped up primarily by the mineral and cash crop sectors, and there was a very shallow reservoir of human capital. Such was the preparation of a modern state in a highly fragmented country, which lasted principally from the first national elections to the House of Assembly in 1964 until independence on 16 September 1975.

A nascent party system emerged in the 1960s in reaction to the introduction of universal suffrage. The fact that many parties were formed by settlers to protect their own interests explains why the parties were largely ephemeral and lacked local bases throughout the country. However, it was the independence issue – played out during and in-between the 1968 and 1972 national elections – that polarized the voting public. With independence in 1975, the one issue that had divided political parties effectively disappeared. It was as if the parties had outlived their original purposes and were now mere creatures of the National Parliament, which existed primarily for government formation. What had also vanished was these parties' public following, which had at one point been coerced by the independence issue.

The reality was that there was insufficient time for political parties to put down roots in society because the presence of government institutions in their midst conveniently assumed the focus of parties. As explained elsewhere, "with the transfer of power coming so soon after parties had developed, the incentive to mobilise disappeared. As the new political elite acquired a material interest in the continuation of the colonial institutions and economy, mobilization became, in its eyes, unnecessary."[6]

Despite PNG's exceptionally high levels of ethno-linguistic diversity, ethnicity has never featured prominently in the organization and activities of political parties at the national level. It is, however, a perennial issue at the constituency level, and especially so during elections. Perhaps it is prudent to employ Douglas Rae's typology in which he suggested we distinguish between two kinds of party systems:

> We are talking about two different party systems: (1) the *elective party system*, and (2) the *parliamentary (legislative) party system*. The former is a system of competitive relationships measured in votes, while the latter is a system of competitive relationships measured in parliamentary seats. The two are not unrelated, since the parliamentary system is formed from the elective system.[7]

Although the distinction might be far-fetched for many countries, especially those with strong and time-tested party systems, it fits the description of PNG well and is especially relevant where ethnic identities come into play. In PNG, ethnic affiliation is useful for aggregating electoral support. At this level, candidates' affiliation with political parties is hardly the deciding factor for electoral choice, with little in the way of tangible party factors that voters can use in making their choice. Instead, local village, clan, tribe and other identity connections are typically most salient.[8]

Compounding this, the winner-takes-all effects of the first-past-the-post (FPTP) electoral system used from 1977 to 2002 served to heighten ethnic identity, and consequently stimulated intense inter-ethnic competition, often with adverse results.[9] More and more candidates contested under the FPTP electoral system over time. Winning candidates therefore were backed by progressively smaller portions of the electorate. As winning margins dwindled under the plurality system, many groups felt unrepresented. To dramatize the point, the winner of the Lagaip Porgera seat in Enga province in the 1992 election claimed victory with only 5.9

per cent of the votes in a field of 32 candidates.[10] Such results reinforced the determination of losers and their supporters to do better next time around and thus provided an incentive for still more candidates to enter the contest.

As winning margins under the FPTP electoral system decreased, it became easier for social groups – be they naturally in existence or pragmatically created – to contest elections. Since political parties themselves had little appeal, candidates were often forced to align themselves initially with such core and secondary groups. If a majority or large plurality was required for victory, it was difficult for a single ethnic group or clan to provide the winning margin. But narrower bases of support become viable as the proportion needed for victory declined. Declining thresholds for victory also encouraged multiple candidates from the same social base. This was especially true with tribal groups. Such social groups are bigger than clans in size and may expand beyond a number of language groups, villages or topographically demarcated areas.[11]

The low thresholds required for victory under the FPTP electoral system also encouraged various sorts of threats to "voters and electoral officials, particularly through the use of weapons, murders, unauthorised road-blocks, snatching of ballot papers and ballot boxes".[12] Hence, not only was post-election violence evidence of anger and frustration, but it also demonstrated that candidates and their supporters were often unwilling to accept defeat.[13]

Political parties throughout this time were seen mainly in instrumental terms and, since parties were needed for coalition-building, winning candidates found the main utility of parties was manifested in parliament itself. In the post-independence period, the behaviour of political parties in parliament progressively affected the quality of governance in PNG. Parties and parliamentarians performed basically to undercut each other in their respective quests to gain control of government. Small parties were appearing and disappearing with such regularity that it was difficult to keep track of them. One observer labelled them "paper parties" because they were little more than printed names on a ballot paper, with little if any wider recognition or significance.[14]

Parties in parliament

Despite the centrality of political parties in parliament, the role of political parties was not viewed favourably in PNG before independence, partly for some of the very reasons that necessitated legislation more than two decades later. The most vocal criticisms, surprisingly, came from party members rather than independents. There were several elements to this critique.

First, party politics were not considered virtuous, given the way groups interacted with each other in an undignified manner as they competed for political supremacy. Second, parties were thought to be divisive for national unity. They appeared out of place at a time when national leaders were looking for ways to encourage nation-building, keeping in mind that nationalism was hardly in existence at this time. Third, party politics – and especially the bloc voting that is characteristic of disciplined parties in other countries – was thought to negate opportunities for negotiating settlements to pressing policy issues. Outcomes were thought to be predicated on party loyalty, rather than conscientious voting. And, in line with this reasoning, numerically stronger parties were not appropriate for reaching consensual settlements. Some members thought that party loyalty compromised their fundamental commitments to their local constituencies; hence, a case of serving two masters.

Finally, parties were not the only political organizations at this time. The existence of political and regional movements, especially in the critical years between 1970 and 1973, proved discomforting for some politicians, who were unsure of how to show their allegiance in public.[15] Such considerations caused some politicians to suggest that the party system be completely eradicated from parliamentary affairs.[16]

Other politicians had an alternative view – that all parties should form a "grand coalition". The notion of a grand coalition was not new, and had even been suggested by a senior administrator of the former territory of Papua and New Guinea.[17] The idea of a grand coalition was to surface sporadically again after independence, but by then it had little to do with the need for nation-building. Rather, it was an option suggested to curb the chronic instability of coalition governments.[18]

In reality, these aspirations for greater inter-party cooperation or grand coalition governments never materialized. Instead, political bickering in the legislature – driven by self-interest and opportunism – made parties little more than convenient vehicles for manoeuvring and shifting power for the benefit of Members of Parliament (MPs). After the 1987 elections, electoral and party politics became increasingly unstable as conniving political behaviour came to permeate the entire parliamentary system, the public service and national politics at large. Such was the case until the introduction of the OLIPPAC reforms in 2002 to regulate the behaviour and activities of parties.

Problems of parties in parliament

Prior to the recent political party reforms, PNG politicians were constantly changing parties in their quest to find niches that best served them and their constituencies. With little party loyalty, the manner in which PNG's Westminster system of government performed was almost predestined to be unstable. Members of Parliament reacted in calculated ways to the institutional design and rules of the unicameral legislature. Consider the general picture. From the 109 seats in the National Parliament, one MP is elected Speaker of the House by the other members. A simple majority of the remaining 108 MPs is 55. National governments in PNG have always comprised coalition alliances since no party has ever been able to muster the requisite 55-seat bare majority.

Keeping in mind that local constituencies generally expect their MP to be proactive in seeking development and other benefits, MPs know that they have a maximum of five years (the length of one parliamentary term) to show they can deliver such benefits or be thrown out at the next election. It thus becomes imperative for parties and individual MPs to place themselves in positions where they can access public resources. To that end, government ministries are the most prized allocations. With only 26 ministries to be allocated, it is understandable why negotiations and trade-offs between coalition partners are a protracted process.[19]

The Organic Law on the Integrity of Political Parties and Candidates was designed to bring some order into this process. Under the law, the most successful party following a national election has the first right to nominate the prime minister. This was not the case before the OLIPPAC, when the prime minister's post was subjected to wheeling and dealing amongst parties in the lead-up to the first sitting of parliament. This process was often repeated after a government's 18-month constitutional grace period from no-confidence votes had elapsed. Party loyalty and loyalty to a given prime minister were habitually fleeting, so that political instability and uncertainty affected all aspects of parliament.

It is necessary at this point to shed some light on the essence of government instability prior to the OLIPPAC. First, the limited number of ministries meant that there was constant jostling and manoeuvring by government backbenchers who had missed out on ministries and therefore would benefit from a change of leader. Threats of desertion from the government side were common. Second, the onus was on the prime minister to be vigilant at all times over the unity of his coalition government. Among the many strategies prime ministers employed was bribery of key coalition members.[20] Third, blocs in the parliament, including MPs from both sides of the House, were used to oust a prime minister because it was often the most legitimate way to change a government. To date, there have been three successful votes of no-confidence against incumbent governments, but mooted and attempted no-confidence motions have been far more numerous since the first attempt in the late 1970s. And, finally, there is an inherent gravitational pull from all sections of the parliament to the government side. This often comes at the expense of a weakened opposition in the House, where non-ministers are either government backbenchers or sit in the middle seats between the government and the opposition.[21]

Finally, one cannot discount the reality that MPs are driven by sheer opportunism too. Although this can be a natural inclination, it has been argued elsewhere that candidates crave status and recognition in order to measure up to traditional and cultural standards and expectations of leadership.[22] Generally, the manipulation of political power for personal gain and influence is a powerful coercive factor in this regard. The fact that the state institutions are not strong enough to prevent individuals from using the system to benefit themselves unfairly has only compounded the country's difficulties. The corruption that has affected the entire political structure and public service for so long is symptomatic of a weak state system.

OLIPPAC: Legislating for stability

The OLIPPAC came into effect in 2001 and was amended to include minor changes in 2003. There were different but related sides to the purpose of this piece of legislation. Certain provisions offered solutions to persistent problems that have been evident since the 1980s. The other side to the OLIPPAC was the perceived need to establish certain objectives and standards that parliamentarians and political parties were expected to honour. Thus, although the ultimate goal was to create stability in parliament, political parties were earmarked for special attention given their indispensability to the key actors in the political system.

Regulating political parties

In the absence of a positive culture and practices, parties cannot be expected to start behaving differently just because a law establishing limits on their activities has been promulgated. In other words, political parties have to be guided and regulated. This responsibility has to be centrally enforced and, under Section 16 of the OLIPPAC, this responsibility falls to the Office of the Registrar of Political Parties. The Registrar is subjected to codes of conduct outlined under PNG's Leadership Code. The Office of the Registrar of Political Parties is overseen by the Integrity of Political Parties and Candidates Commission (IPPCC). The Clerk of Parliament, the Electoral Commissioner, the Registrar and the Chairman of the National Fiscal and Economic Commission are *ex officio* members of the IPPCC. They are joined by a representative each for women and churches, who are appointed by the head of state. Members of the IPPCC are subjected to the Leadership Code too. It is essential that the independence of the IPPCC and Office of the Registrar of Political Parties is legally protected.

The next step then is to regulate political parties themselves. However, needless to say, meaningful regulation is very difficult when the parties are very fluid, lack an administrative structure, have no permanent membership and have only limited funding. In some cases, a party constitution or manifesto may have existed on paper, but these were hardly the determinants of how parties were to conduct themselves. For these reasons, the OLIPPAC has provisions designed to strengthen parties internally and to get them to espouse particular codes of conduct. Parties are required under Section 27 of the OLIPPAC to be registered with the Office of the Registrar of Political Parties. Grounds for registration include instances where a party intends to nominate at least one candidate for an election at either the national or local levels of government, or where a party member is already a Member of Parliament (MP). Also, under Section 25 of the OLIPPAC, a party should have permanent party officials: president, secretary and treasurer. These party officials are paid by the government through the Office of the Registrar of Political Parties and are considered ordinary public servants. They are prohibited from taking up other sources of employment.

Funding for political parties

The integrity of political parties is protected from external or foreign actors under the OLIPPAC, and this is especially so in the area of funding for parties. It has become apparent over the past two decades that many political parties have been funded by foreign business houses, which then expected special favours or kickbacks from the government. It was not unusual for these external actors to sponsor more than one party during national elections.

Sections 76–78 of the OLIPPAC provide for direct government funding to political parties through a Central Fund. Other sources of funding for parties are allowed too, even from foreign sources, but they have to be declared to the Office of the Registrar of Political Parties and assessed through relevant provisions of the OLIPPAC. Moreover, paid membership of parties is restricted to PNG citizens, and individuals are not allowed to be members of more than one party. A party may have a parliamentary leader chosen in a democratic process within the provisions of the party's constitution.

The OLIPPAC offers grounds for deregistration, dissolution and amalgamation of political parties, but only in specific circumstances and under the full gaze of the Office of the Registrar of Political Parties. The relevant provisions in this regard are designed to safeguard the political system from abuse. For example, it would be counterintuitive to the objective of the OLIPPAC if parties were registered and funded by the government but then disappeared when it suited party officials and members. PNG has a colourful history of political parties collapsing on the floor of parliament whenever their desired objectives were no longer tenable or attainable.

Encouraging party solidarity

The OLIPPAC encourages party members sitting in parliament to act in unison. The positions of MPs reflect the decisions taken by their respective political parties. However, to make sure that MPs do not act contrary to the stands taken by their parties over time, the OLIPPAC sets out four specific types of parliamentary vote that determine where MPs and their parties stand over the course of a parliamentary term.

First, political parties must abide by their allegiances when a parliamentary election takes place for a prime minister. This means that partisan MPs who voted for the prime minister cannot sponsor a vote of no-confidence against the head of the government during a parliamentary term. Likewise, independent MPs who have voted for the prime minister are prohibited from acting contrary to that position – unless the independent member joins a party and therefore is bound by the position of that party.

The second area concerns decisions taken during a vote of no-confidence against the prime minister. Again, MPs are expected to act in conformity with resolutions taken by their parties, most of which, if not all, are expected to be binding over the extent of a parliamentary term. In this vein, MPs from parties that voted in support of or against a prime minister are expected to honour that position throughout the entire term of parliament.

Voting on the National Budget and a Constitutional Law (i.e. to enact, amend or repeal) are the other two areas where political parties are expected to abide by their own resolutions.

Incentives for female candidacy

Political parties are not responsible for recruiting and grooming candidates in PNG. Parties would rather support candidates who are already favoured by voters. To that extent, female candidates have never fared well in PNG national elections since the 1960s. Very often voters look for candidates who show that they can deliver services. The fact that female candidates do not do well at the polls in spite of increased female candidacy over time indicates that it is still considered more worthwhile to support male candidates.

Rather than leaving matters to fate, the OLIPPAC therefore introduced a provision to encourage political parties to endorse more female candidates. Section 83 of the OLIPPAC says that if a political party incurs election campaign expenses for a female candidate, and where the candidate in question obtains at least 10 per cent of the votes, the political party can be reimbursed 75 per cent of their campaign expenses up to 10,000 kina (about US$3,000). Although the number of female candidates has progressively increased – reaching a high of 91 at the 2007 elections – only one woman, Lady Carol Kidu, won a parliamentary seat in the 2007 national elections, as was the case in 2002.

Implementation of the OLIPPAC

A number of positive developments have been apparent since the 2002 national elections in spite of ongoing debates about the OLIPPAC's merits.[23] First, the OLIPPAC – in accordance with its Section 76(1) – ensured that the National Alliance, the most successful party after both the 2002 and 2007 elections, was invited to form the government. This was a major change from past practice, when it was common for coalition governments to be formed using threats, bribery and brazen activities such as lock-ups in hotels and houses under armed guards. Under the new law, the public knew that Sir Michael Somare and his party would be in some position to at least form a post-election government.

Second, "party-hopping" (parliamentarians changing party membership) was effectively discouraged owing to the threat of sanctions under the Leadership Code. However, OLIPPAC has been unable to solve some of the deeper problems facing the parties. For example, there is no reason to believe that political parties are now always internally in harmony because of the OLIPPAC. Indeed, it was evident in parliament that some parties were split between the government and the opposition sides. One can only speculate what the situation would have been like in the absence of the OLIPPAC.

Third, there have been no votes of no-confidence since OLIPPAC's introduction. Although some parties in 2004 were preparing themselves for a showdown with the incumbent government, their attempts were curtailed by their own lack of agreement and cooperation and by the Somare government keeping a step ahead with pre-emptive actions such as the postponement of parliamentary sittings.[24] What took place goes to show that the insidious tactics of survival that governments used prior to the OLIPPAC were still being invoked when necessary. Apart from the postponement of sittings, Prime Minister Somare resorted to the effective measure of changing the ruling coalition's dynamics by firing individuals who posed a challenge to his leadership. Casualties in 2004 included his party's deputy, who was a minister in his cabinet.[25]

Other reforms to strengthen parties

It should be noted that the stability of politics in PNG goes beyond the implementation of the OLIPPAC. Although political parties are addressed through this piece of legislation, greater stability is likely to come from a need to carry out broader changes. To that end, the government needs to look closely at certain areas that are relevant to political parties, and consider further reform where needed.

Major policy reforms in PNG have been undertaken in many areas since the early 1980s. However, the execution of these much-needed exercises has not been wholly successful, either at the planning or at the implementation stages, for a number of reasons. Among them has been successive governments' lack of political will to carry out crucial reform exercises, and the late timing of reforms when the problems have got worse.[26] Nonetheless, a number of important political reforms beyond OLIPPAC have been introduced.

Independent candidacy

Despite the noticeable impact of the OLIPPAC since 2002, certain factors are still sources of concern. One of these is the role of independent candidates. Such candidacies are still coveted, especially if the candidate is successfully elected and can be used in the uncertain period just before the formation of a government, when changes in political allegiance can be crucial. Prior to the formation of the Somare government in 2002, for instance, one elected independent "appealed to all independents to remain outside of any political association as they might move together as a force in dictating the formation of a new government".[27] A similar call was made again by one successful independent candidate during the 2007 national elections.[28] These cases of independent candidacy beg an important question: why should independents be allowed the privilege to decide the balance and identity of a new government – and contribute towards greater uncertainty in the process – if they chose to remain aloof from party membership at the outset?

Moreover, the fact that independent candidates are still allowed by law to participate in the electoral process is likely to exacerbate another concern: the number of candidates. Political parties are allowed to endorse one candidate per seat under the OLIPPAC. One possible impact of this provision is that many candidates may choose to enter the race as independents. Some candidates prefer to avoid the constraints of party membership during the campaign period and therefore run as independents. Other independent candidates run as members of existing parties and switch later to their parties after success at the polls.

Parliamentary committee system

The National Parliament also needs institutional strengthening to assist the development of a stronger party system over time. Some studies have been conducted to identify areas that require changes to the procedures in parliament. Nonetheless, if existing rules were rigorously enforced then it is likely that more stability could be achieved in parliament. Perhaps the main area where change is needed in the PNG parliament at the moment is the parliamentary committee system. For a very long time the committee system has been moribund. A recent study expresses the reality of how the committees have been performing:

> The parliamentary committee system has not been very effective for many years because of a lack of resources. Despite this, members of the various committees continue to collect their allowances as these have been included in their normal salaries. What has transpired is that committees do not meet frequently, if at all, but Members continue to collect their allowances.[29]

By law and by virtue of Westminster traditions, parliamentary committees can help to strengthen political parties and stabilize politics on the floor of parliament in the course of carrying out their normal duties. The fact that such committees need to comprise MPs from both sides of the House as well as non-ministers offers these members an opportunity to remain active and bask in the same limelight as their ministerial colleagues. But, most importantly, the type of inter-party cooperation that may be forged can encourage accountability, transparency and trust among MPs on committees in the long run. This is crucial both for developing positive parliamentary practices and for enforcing other factors such as parliamentary identity.

Limited preferential voting (LPV) system

The electoral system has been one of the areas long overdue for change. In spite of claims in the 1980s that the first-past-the-post (FPTP) electoral system was producing unrepresentative results owing to a combination of the electoral formula itself (i.e. plurality rules) and the increasing number of candidates, governments were unwilling to make any change. One reason for this, it could be assumed, was that it would have been unwise from the MPs' point of view to change a system that got them elected in the first place, in spite of the increasingly clear need to do so.

During the 1990s, however, it became clear that a change of electoral system was the key reform needed to improve the functioning of the political system. The preferred reform was a "limited preferential voting" (LPV) system. The electoral formula of LPV requires the voter to indicate three choices. In the event that no candidate gains more than 50 per cent of the primary votes (i.e. votes marked number 1), the ballot papers of the lowest-scoring candidate are redistributed to the remaining candidates based on their second choices. This elimination process continues until a candidate reaches the 50 per cent +1 mark, or until only two remaining candidates are reached, when the candidate with the most ballots at that point is declared the winner.

After initially being used in 10 by-elections during the 2002–2007 parliamentary term with reasonable success, LPV was used in the 2007 national elections. This resulted in a marked difference from previous national elections, which were often rowdy and relatively violent. The 2007 contest was considerably more peaceful, in part owing to the dilution of the "winner-takes-all" incentives under the new system. In addition, for the first time ever, the number of candidates actually fell slightly at the 2007 elections, to 2,740 compared with 2,875 in 2002.[30]

Although the PNG voting public expressed certain reservations about LPV, there was a generally subdued atmosphere during the election period compared with recent elections under the FPTP electoral system. The key importance of LPV to the country is that it has the potential to encourage social groups (tribal, ethnic, regional, etc.) to vote across social divisions because the voter support needed to win a seat has to be acquired beyond a candidate's core support bases – assuming, that is, that a candidate does not achieve the unlikely scenario in PNG of securing more than 50 per cent of the votes from predetermined social divisions alone.[31]

Perhaps the ultimate success would be if political parties were anchored through both party membership and the appeals of candidates. If a candidate sponsored by a party is able to attract support across social divides, political parties could ideally reach out for wider appeal and support too. For now, it appears that the personality of candidates and party leaders is the core attribute that embodies the party – as has always been the case in PNG – rather than vice versa.

The drawbacks of the OLIPPAC

Despite meeting at least some of its intended purposes, the OLIPPAC could also prove to be a problem for parliamentary business itself. For years before the introduction of OLIPPAC, the independence of the legislature, for a number of reasons, had been compromised to the point where the executive was in effect usurping power in the National Parliament.[32] Then there is the fact that the OLIPPAC, for all its noble intentions, contains the most radical legal precepts to strengthen the executive, which has already acquired power through other unscrupulous means.

The most obvious casualty in this regard is the parliamentary opposition. For many years, it had been a mere hint of what it was meant to be in the classic Westminster tradition. There have never been proper shadow cabinets. Part of the reason was the ever-shifting party allegiances that gravitated towards the government side, while others MPs were hovering on the middle benches.

The early developments under the OLIPPAC indicate that the executive is still predominant in parliament. For example, the Somare government was formed in August 2007 on a count of 86 out of 108 MPs. Given this imbalance, something has to be done to protect and enhance the power of the opposition. If nothing is done, the OLIPPAC could itself introduce and strengthen an absurd outcome that would work against the precepts of good governance within parliament.

Concluding remarks

Describing how established parties became entrenched in Europe, Mainwaring reasons that they emerged "at a moment in world history that cannot be reproduced".[33] Logically, then, why should we expect parties in developing democracies to perform dynamically and parallel the established parties of developed democracies? The same can be said about legislative bodies and other government agencies.

Transplanting foreign political and administrative institutions into places where they do not have complementary cultures and practices is always going to be challenging. Although we may hold up a template of sorts to represent the ideal democratic apparatus, the historical context of many new democracies needs to be taken into account. The traditional political practices of Pacific island countries could not be any further removed from modern liberal democracy and models such as the Westminster system. How that gap can be bridged is what political engineering is all about.

It is in this light that the role of political parties in developing democracies needs to be understood. Heterogeneous or ethnically divided societies pose additional challenges when seeking the most appropriate institutions to facilitate a favourable atmosphere for good governance. Designing appropriate institutions with the hope of realizing desired outcomes may be the safest way to achieve results that might not be possible any other way. The case of Papua New Guinea discussed in this chapter is all about designing and guiding political parties so that their activities promote results that are at least comparatively predictable. Given the burden of problems in PNG, the counterfactual scenario – presupposing that there were no interventions such as the OLIPPAC – is now almost unthinkable. Suffice to say therefore that, if political parties and party systems in general are to be modified to attain a "greater good" in divided societies, the evidence to date suggests that positive outcomes can be achieved if sufficient effort is invested.

Notes

1. Benjamin Reilly, "The Africanisation of the South Pacific", *Australian Journal of International Affairs*, 54(3), 2000: 261–268.
2. For a discussion of these reforms, see Benjamin Reilly, *Democracy and Diversity: Political Engineering in the Asia-Pacific* (Oxford: Oxford University Press, 2006).
3. See Roland Rich, "Analysing and Categorising Political Parties in the South Pacific", in Roland Rich (ed.), *Political Parties in the Pacific Islands* (Canberra: Pandanus Press, 2006), pp. 20–21.
4. For example, see Bill Standish, "The Dynamics of Papua New Guinea's Democracy: An Essay", *Pacific Economic Bulletin*, 22(1), 2007: 135–157.
5. For an elaborate discussion on the formation of the state in PNG, see Lucy P. Mair, *Australia in New Guinea* (Melbourne: Melbourne University Press, 1970); Hank Nelson, *Papua New Guinea: Black Unity or Black Chaos?* (Middlesex: Penguin Books, 1974); D. Woolford, *Papua New Guinea: Initiation and Independence* (Brisbane: University of Queensland Press, 1976).
6. David Hegarty, "The Political Parties", in A. Amarshi, K. Good and R. Mortimer (eds), *Development and Dependency: The Political Economy of Papua New Guinea* (Melbourne: Oxford University Press, 1979), p. 190.
7. Douglas Rae, *The Political Consequences of Electoral Laws* (New Haven, CT: Yale University Press, 1967), p. 48, italics in the original.
8. See Yaw Saffu, "Survey Evidence on Electoral Behaviour in Papua New Guinea", in Michael Oliver (ed.), *Eleksin: The 1987 National Election in Papua New Guinea* (Port Moresby: University of Papua New Guinea Press, 1996).
9. For an explanation of these problems, see Benjamin Reilly, "The Effects of the Electoral System in Papua New Guinea", in Yaw Saffu (ed.), *The 1992 PNG Election: Change and Continuity in Electoral Politics* (Canberra: Department of Political and Social Change, Australian National University, 1996).
10. Papua New Guinea Electoral Commission, *1992 National Parliament Voting Statistics* (Port Moresby, 1992).
11. Bill Standish, "The Elections in Chimbu", in Peter King (ed.), *Pangu Returns to Power: The 1982 Elections in Papua New Guinea* (Canberra: Research School of Pacific Studies, Australian National University, 1989).
12. Ruben Kaiulo, *1997 General Election Report* (Port Moresby: PNG Electoral Commission, 1997), p. 5. Ruben Kaiulo was the PNG Electoral Commissioner during the 1997 national elections.
13. Sinclair Dinnen, "Violence, Security, and the 1992 Election", in Saffu (ed.), *The 1992 PNG Election*, p. 102.

14. See Saffu, "Survey Evidence on Electoral Behaviour in Papua New Guinea", p. 31 in Saffu (Ed.), The 1992 PNG Election. Parliamentarians engaged and disengaged themselves from parties so frequently that it was impossible to keep track of the affiliations of many of them. Some MPs were even members of more than one party at any one time.

15. A case in point was Paul Lapun, who was the patron of the micro-nationalist movement Napidakoe Navitu but also a cabinet minister. On the case of Paul Lapun, see Jim Griffin, "Napidakoe Navitu", in R. May (ed.), Micronationalist Movements in Papua New Guinea (Canberra: Australian National University Press, 1982).

16. Peter Loveday, "Voting Parties in the Third House 1972–1975", in Peter Loveday and Edward P. Wolfers (eds), Parties and Parliament in Papua New Guinea 1964–1975 (Port Moresby: Institute of Applied Social and Economic Research, 1976), pp. 81–83.

17. Woolford, Papua New Guinea, p. 126.

18. Sean Dorney, Papua New Guinea: People, Politics, and History (Sydney: Random House, 1990), pp. 75–76.

19. Interestingly, the issue of ministerial allocation surfaced during the formation of the Somare-led government after the 2007 national elections. With 86 out of 108 MPs re-electing Michael Somare as prime minister, it is clear that there are not enough ministries and other ministerial posts to be shared among all those who supported him. Perhaps it was not surprising that Prime Minister Somare was reportedly seeking an increase in the number of ministries at the start of his new term in August 2007 (Post Courier, 6 September 2007). The prime minister's explanation that eight new ministries were needed to account for the increased population and "the complexity of Melanesian ways of life" is hardly convincing to the public. It leads back to a point discussed below as to why the parliamentary committee system has not been fully activated to account for the MPs who are left at the fringes.

20. A high-profile case of alleged bribery was televised prime time in Australia showing the former prime minister, (the late) Sir William Skate, and close cohorts engaged in covert financial payments to some MPs to ensure victory during the stage of government formation after the 1997 national elections.

21. See Henry Okole, "Institutional Decay in a Melanesian Parliamentary Democracy: Papua New Guinea", Development Bulletin, 60, 2002: pp. 37–40.

22. Many studies have been conducted on the cultural aspects of leadership among many tribes and social groups in PNG. Perhaps the most cited work is Ben Finney, Big-Men and Business: Entrepreneurship and Economic Growth in the New Guinea Highlands (Honolulu: University of Hawaii Press, 1973). On national elections, see Bill Standish, "They Want to Be the Highest Always: The Elections in Simbu", in David Hegarty (ed.), Electoral Politics in Papua New Guinea: Studies on the 1977 National Elections (Port Moresby: University of Papua New Guinea Press, 1983). Also see Joe Ketan, The Name Must Not Go Down: Political Competition and State–Society Relations in Mount Hagen, Papua New Guinea (Suva: Institute of Pacific Studies, University of the South Pacific, 2004).

23. For example, see Alphonse Gelu, "The Failure of the Organic Law on the Integrity of Political Parties and Candidates", Pacific Economic Bulletin, 20(1), 2005: 85–97. Here Gelu talks about the "failure" of the OLIPPAC. However, given that, at the time of his writing, insufficient time had been given for the law to be fully tested, a better phrase for his title would have been the "weaknesses" or "loopholes" of the OLIPPAC.

24. See Louise Baker, "Political Integrity Laws in Papua New Guinea and the Search for Stability", Pacific Economic Bulletin, 20(1) 2005: 100–117.

25. This point needs clarification. Under Section 63 (7) of the OLIPPAC, voting for a prime minister is to be guided by Standing Orders of the Parliament if the most successful

party in an election fails to garner the necessary majority to enable its candidate for the prime ministership to acquire the post.

26. See David Kavanamur and Henry Okole, with Michael Manning and Theodore Levantis, "Understanding Reform in Papua New Guinea", *Pacific Economic Bulletin*, 20(1), 2005: 118–133.

27. The quote is from Tim Neville, the former governor of the Milne Bay province. It was first read out on PNG's National Broadcasting Commission on 10 July 2002. It later appeared in a feature article by Henry Okole entitled "Independents and Government Formation" in *The National*, 17 July 2002.

28. It was reported in *The National* on 31 July 2007 that the new governor of the National Capital District, Powes Parkop, had issued an open invitation to other successful candidates to join him and avoid being victims of the horse-trading that was taking place to form the new government.

29. Henry Okole, Bernard Narokobi and Quinton Clements, "Strengthening a Parliamentary Democracy for the 21st Century", Legislative Assessment Board, National Parliament of Papua New Guinea and UNDP Suva, 2003, pp. 58–59.

30. Personal communication, Ben Reilly, 13 September 2007.

31. Reilly, *Democracy and Diversity*, has explained the other key reasons why the LPV system was introduced: (1) the need to ensure that winning candidates are broadly supported because they may need to seek second and third votes from supporters of their rivals; (2) the likelihood of more peaceful campaigns if candidates are required to look beyond their core bloc votes to galvanize wider support and therefore more votes; and (3) the incentive for candidates and political parties to work together since LPV encourages reciprocity and dependence on one another's voting bases. See Benjamin Reilly, "Political Reform in Papua New Guinea: Testing the Evidence", *Pacific Economic Bulletin*, 21(1), 2006: 187–194.

32. Dame Carol Kidu remarked that there is a "parliamentary democracy with NEC dictatorship"; see Okole, Narokobi and Clements, "Strengthening a Parliamentary Democracy for the 21st Century", p. 21.

33. Scott Mainwaring, *Rethinking Party Systems in the Third Wave of Democratization: The Case of Brazil* (Stanford, CA: Stanford University Press, 1999), p. 221.

9

Party regulations, nation-building and party systems in southern and east Africa

Denis K. Kadima

Introduction

The argument of this chapter is twofold. First, although regulation of political parties in southern and east Africa have not put an end to the formation of ethnically based parties, these regulations have undoubtedly contributed to the containment of extremist ethno-regional politics and parties and allowed for a degree of inclusion of ethnic minorities in the political system, an essential process for nation-building in conflict-prone societies. Second, election alliances and party coalitions have also contributed to nation-building by bringing together parties from different ethno-regional backgrounds. However, inadequate, scanty or selective regulation of these alliances and coalitions or a lack of appropriate regulations, especially in the context of presidentialist systems, have led to governmental instability. This situation has also tended to affect the nature of the party system by favouring the emergence of dominant party systems through the strengthening of ruling parties and/or the fragmentation of opposition parties.

This study proposes that inclusive reform processes should be carried out, as needs arise, in order to correct the unintended negative consequences of party regulations. It also notes that the current laissez-faire approach to election alliances and party coalitions has made such groupings dysfunctional and resulted in undue advantage for the main parties.

Contemporary African political history starts with the Berlin Conference of 1884–1885, which resulted in the subdivision of the African continent

Political parties in conflict-prone societies: Regulation, engineering and democratic development, Reilly and Nordlund (eds),
United Nations University Press, 2008, ISBN 978-92-808-1157-5

into a multiplicity of states based on the economic and geopolitical interests of the participating powers of the time. This exercise resulted in the
creation of states composed of a diversity of ethnic groups, religions,
races and languages. The new states faced a daunting challenge of
achieving nation-building, having gone through the often divisive pre-
independence elections, which were essentially based on the "winner-
takes-all" system inherited from colonialism and therefore led to party
systems dominated by one party and excluded ethnic minorities. Pre-
independence political parties were, in essence, formed along ethnic
lines, a trend that has continued. In this context, an electoral defeat
meant a defeat not just of a political party but of the whole ethnic group.
Post-election resistance against state powers culminated in ethnic polarization and, in the worst of cases, civil wars and massacres, leaving deep
scars on the socio-political fabric of these plural societies.

In this context, states had to find ways of dealing with these centrifugal
trends in order to achieve some degree of national cohesion. Nation-
building became a fundamental objective for nearly all countries, given
that it was seen as the certain way of ensuring the peaceful coexistence
of the various societal groups. Since political parties were themselves
formed along ethnic, linguistic, regional and/or religious lines, several
types of political party regulation were attempted to address the excessive focus on ethnicity, which caused dangerous political polarization.

Nation-building can be defined as the process of constructing a nation
by using state power with the aim of unifying the various communal
groups within the state and ensuring political cohesion and stability, social harmony and a sense of common (desired) destiny. After a century
of "divide and rule" by colonialism, nation-building in Africa has often
entailed the construction of a national identity through the integration
of the various groups into a nation. Nation-building efforts have encom-
passed a range of initiatives, such as the careful choice of national an-
thems, flags, national days, national languages and national myths, the
use of military force, propaganda, the development of major infrastructure, massive investments, economic growth, and revenue redistribution,
as well as the engineering of particular political systems, electoral systems,
party systems and political institutions and the devolution of powers to
national and sub-national entities.

In relation to political parties, strategies included, but were not limited
to, the establishment of single-party systems (e.g. former Zaire, Togo,
Gabon, Cameroon, Malawi, Zambia, Kenya, Tanzania, Rwanda, Burundi, Congo-Brazzaville and Côte d'Ivoire); mergers of parties (e.g.
Zimbabwe); the imposition of two-party systems (as happened briefly in
Nigeria in the mid-1990s); electoral alliances, party coalitions and power-
sharing arrangements (e.g. Mauritius and South Africa); and the outright

banning of political parties (e.g. Swaziland and, until recently, Uganda). These regulations and their impact on nation-building are examined below.

The chapter studies five countries, namely, Kenya, Malawi, Mauritius, Mozambique and South Africa. The five countries were selected based on the need to combine parliamentary regimes (Mauritius and South Africa) and presidential regimes (Kenya, Malawi and Mozambique) as well as having a mixture of first-past-the-post (Kenya, Malawi and, in a way, Mauritius) and proportional representation electoral systems (Mozambique and South Africa). In addition, to be selected the country had to have gone through at least two consecutive general elections or referenda in order to allow for analysis of the party systems over time.

This chapter is divided into three main sections. The first section examines the regulation of parties in these plural societies and their intended and unintended effects on nation-building. The second section pays special attention to electoral systems and their effects on party systems. The third section analyses the effects of the regulation of inter-party relations (or lack thereof) on nation-building and on the entrenchment of dominant party systems.

Party regulation and nation-building

With the reintroduction of the multi-party democratic order in Africa in the post–Cold War period from the late 1980s, legal frameworks have been adjusted in most countries formally to end the one-party, military and apartheid systems. In some countries, the institutional and constitutional changes were preceded by wide consultations, which essentially took the form of national conferences, especially in francophone Africa (Benin, Congo-Brazzaville and former Zaire), political negotiations between the main parties (Mozambique and South Africa) and popular pressures (Zambia, Malawi and Kenya). In most cases, there was a combination of more than one of these approaches. Invariably, international pressures towards democratization were exerted on politicians discreetly or overtly.

In Mozambique, the political negotiations that culminated in the signing of the General Peace Agreement[1] were followed by constitutional and legal reforms providing space for citizens to be affiliated to any political party of their choice and to enjoy the freedom to form and to participate in political parties. The Mozambican constitution recognizes that parties are the expression of political pluralism, competing to form and express popular will, and are the fundamental instruments for the democratic participation of citizens in the government of the country. The critical role played by political parties in the democratic process is acknowledged by the Kenyan constitution, which states that Kenya shall be a multi-party democratic state. The Malawi constitution too guarantees fundamental freedoms, including freedom of association, which allows for the formation of political parties. In South Africa, the transformation of the party system in the post-apartheid period dates from the unbanning of the liberation movements in the early 1990s, including the African National Congress (ANC) and the Pan Africanist Congress (PAC). South Africa's transitional 1993 constitution and the 1996 constitution and its subsequent amendments broaden and guarantee the freedom of association to all citizens. In Mauritius, where political pluralism has been upheld since independence in 1968, with a short interruption between 1972 and 1975, the absence of any political party law is compensated for by the rules for ethnic balance provided in the constitution.[2]

Regulation of political parties in these countries seeks to achieve nation-building and stable party systems through one of the three functions of a given party system. In Chapter 3 of this volume, Matthijs Bogaards describes these functions as being the aggregation of social cleavages, the articulation of social cleavages into political cleavages or the blocking of the politicization of social cleavages. The aggregation function refers to mechanisms aimed at encouraging the emergence of parties across social cleavages; the articulation function ensures that the various social cleavages are represented in the representative institutions in proportion to their respective sizes; and the blocking function simply discourages or bans ethnic parties.

The legal frameworks in the five countries have used these three functions of party regulation to achieve nation-building (see Table 9.1). South Africa has clearly shown a preference for the representation of minorities by opting for proportional representation without imposing an electoral threshold. Tom Lodge and Ursula Scheidegger write that, "as a consequence of the very low threshold of support required for parliamentary representation, no significant parties exist outside parliament: this is a very inclusive system".[3] Indeed, "South Africa opted for maximum proportionality: one huge, nationwide district for the conversion of votes into seats, no electoral threshold at all and a very large assembly of 400 seats".[4] In addition, the minimal regulation of political party registration has made the formation of political parties, including explicitly declared ethnic parties, uncomplicated in South Africa. "The right to form political parties is protected by the entrenched Bill of Rights in the 1996 Constitution. Registration is comparatively easy: it requires a 'deed of foundation' signed by 50 registered voters and a payment to the IEC [Independent Electoral Commission] of R500 [equivalent to US$70]."[5] Aware of all the characteristics of a conflict-prone society that obtain in

South Africa – namely, ethnic, racial, religious and linguistic diversity, re-gionalism and socio-economic cleavages – South African leaders chose to have an inclusive system.

Like South Africa, Mozambique uses proportional representation, but with two main differences. First, there are 11 electoral constituencies matching the 11 provinces of the country, whereas in South Africa the state constitutes a single constituency for National Assembly elections. Second, Mozambique uses an electoral threshold of 5 per cent minimum for a party to enjoy representation in the National Assembly, whereas South Africa does not have such a threshold. Introduced ahead of the first democratic elections of 1994, the electoral threshold was aimed at blocking the entry of ethnic parties to parliament and ultimately achiev-ing nation-building through aggregation. In addition, Mozambique dis-courages ethnic, religious and regional political parties. According to the constitution, the formation and operation of political parties shall be na-tional in scope; uphold national interests; contribute to the formation of public opinion, especially on major national issues; and strengthen the patriotic spirit of citizens and the consolidation of the Mozambican na-tion.[6] Civil society and smaller parties have decried the electoral thresh-old because it has enforced a two-party system. They recently obtained the repeal of this provision, so that there will be no electoral threshold in the 2009 parliamentary elections.

The legal framework of political parties is underdeveloped in Kenya, thus creating uncertainties and doubts. In Kenya, there is no political party law or chapter in the country's constitution or laws that explicitly recognize and provide for the regulation and operation of political par-ties. Kenyan parties are legally required to register under the Society's Act, which regulates virtually all entities, including clubs, welfare groups, farms and shops. Not surprisingly, some party leaders tend to behave like entrepreneurs by establishing a party on their own, financing it from their private funds and subsequently recruiting members to join the newly formed party. It has been observed that most such party leaders and founders tend to consider the party as a private property in which they have invested funds, ideas and time, which entitles them to the payment of lifelong dividends. Such parties experience internal party democracy deficits that ultimately lead to their collapse. The absence of a political party law in Kenya and the fact that parties owe their legal existence to the Society's Act while invariably being regulated by the electoral law and a variety of other laws have caused uncertainties by confining party matters to the realm of "private matters".

However, while the absence of a coherent legal framework for parties has undermined their proper functioning, the use of a single-member electoral system has weakened the appeal of openly particularistic parties and compelled parties to enter into electoral alliances and party coalitions. This has been enhanced by the constitutional provision that "the candidate for President who ... receives a greater number of the valid votes cast ..., and who, in addition, receives a minimum of twenty-five per cent of the valid votes cast in at least five of the eight provinces shall be declared to be elected as President".[7] Since political parties in Kenya are essentially formed along ethnic and regional lines, the need to secure the constitutional requirement of 25 per cent makes it imperative for them to form coalitions based on their regional strength. The lessons of the three multi-party elections in Kenya are proof of this. President Moi and the Kenya African National Union (KANU) won the 1992 and 1997 general elections by building ethnic and regional alliances that enabled Moi to achieve 25 per cent in at least five provinces. In 2002, the affiliated parties of the National Rainbow Coalition (NARC) were able to mobilize votes in their various regional strongholds, which enabled Mwai Kibaki to win more than 25 per cent of the total vote in all eight provinces and become president.

In Mauritius, the first-(three)-past-the-post electoral system provides for the direct election of 60 Members of Parliament (MPs) in the 70-member National Assembly, each of the 20 constituencies returning three MPs. The island of Rodrigues returns two MPs and an extra eight seats are allocated to non-elected candidates based on their ethno-religious affiliation as a compensatory mechanism for underrepresented communal groups with the most votes in the elections. Indeed, the constitution requires that "every candidate for election at any general election of members of the Assembly shall declare in such manner as may be prescribed which community he belongs to and that community shall be stated in a published notice of his nomination".[8] It is also worth noting that the drawing of electoral boundaries has perpetuated a rural/urban divide based on ethnic agglomeration.

Known as the "best loser" system, this system is seen by some political observers as having resulted in the crude ethnicization of political parties. However, it may also be argued that this system has ensured a more or less balanced ethnic representation in parliament. Mauritius therefore has clearly opted for the articulation of communal groups.

In Malawi, too, it is easy to form and register a party.[9] The Malawi government has not tried to actively discourage the formation of ethnic parties. The country uses the single-member district electoral system, which, in theory, should stimulate party leaders to seek support outside their own group. However, Malawi's politics are dominated by regionalism, with the three regions – Northern Region, Central Region and Southern Region – competing for power through regionally based parties. These parties tend to seek and secure representation, in essence, in proportion to the size of the electorate in their region.

In summary, the regulation of political parties has led to the emergence of certain types of party system based on the contexts and needs of these different countries. South Africa and Mauritius have encouraged better representation of social groups through translation characterized by the use of proportional representation and the best-loser system and the absence of an electoral threshold. This has contributed to nation-building because all groups, including minorities, are accommodated in the representative chambers.

In Malawi, the combination of a first-past-the-post electoral system (which, in theory, should encourage aggregation), the existence of dominant regional parties (which should promote proportional representation) and the absence of mechanisms to block ethnic parties have all resulted in a neutral mechanism, leading to the articulation of votes more or less proportionally to the sizes of the respective social groups and parties. This observation on the Malawi party system is corroborated by Bogaards when he states that "Africa's geographically concentrated socio-cultural groups' translation can be achieved under any of the main types of electoral system: proportional representation as well as plurality and majority elections in single-member districts".[10]

The use of electoral thresholds in Mozambique and Kenya is aimed at preventing the perverse effects of explicit ethnic politics and compelling parties to aggregate or build electoral alliances and party coalitions across ethnic lines. In addition, first-past-the-post combined with the distribution requirement in Kenya has had the same results. Clearly, Mozambique and Kenya have created a system where there is limited space for ethnic minorities, a potentially dangerous path in the long run. The two countries have nonetheless made progress toward nation-building by compelling parties to focus more on matters of national interest for their own survival, through the aggregative function of alliance and coalition formation, as will be shown later in the chapter.

Engineering electoral systems and inter-party relations

In simple terms, an electoral system is a model by which the votes received by the contesting candidates, parties or groups of parties are translated into seats. In reality, electoral systems are more complex than just an application of a mathematical formula for the allocation of seats. Electoral systems can also be engineered to achieve direct and indirect political goals such as the restriction of the number of political parties, the

Table 9.1 Aspects of party formation regulations

Country	Kenya	Malawi	Mauritius	Mozambique	South Africa
Election threshold	Yes	No	No	Yes	No
Ban on ethnic parties	Yes	No	No	Yes	No
Distribution requirement	Yes	No	No	No	No
To be of national scope	No	No	No	Yes	No
Signatures	No	Yes	No	Yes	Yes
Monetary fee payment	Yes	No	No	No	Yes
Special seats	Yes	No	No	No	No
Compensatory seats	No	No	Yes	No	No

Source: Compiled by the author based on the constitutions of Kenya (1991 and 2001), Malawi (1995), Mauritius (1968), Mozambique (1990) and South Africa (1993 and 1996), and these countries' electoral, political party and various other laws.

discouragement of ethnically-based political parties, the inclusion of minority communal groups and the avoidance of single-party government, and vice versa. Therefore, different electoral systems have different effects not only on political representation but also on the shape of the party system itself.

Political parties are the primary channel through which the needs, expectations and even fears of the population as a whole are expressed and conveyed to state institutions, including parliament and government. As such, parties are central to representative democracy. However, for parties to play this central representative role effectively, the party system in a given country needs to be relatively stable. This means that there must be a more or less fixed number of stable political parties established over a relatively long period of time with clear ideologies and constituencies. A stable party system makes policy-making and alliance and coalition formation more predictable.

Generally speaking, in first-past-the-post systems such as those in use in Malawi and Kenya, where one can win with a mere simple majority, political parties choose to enter into pre-election alliances in order to avoid wasting their votes. By coming together, they increase their chances of winning the elections. In Kenya, the requirement that presidential candidates must obtain a minimum of 25 per cent in at least five of the country's eight provinces reinforces the need for parties to coalesce prior to the elections. Mauritius's top-three system, combined with the geographical concentration of the various communal groups in rural and urban areas, also requires pragmatism. Party leaders need to adopt a broad-based ethnic approach and enter into pre-electoral alliances in order to enhance their performance in electoral contests and their prospects of electoral victory.

In Mozambique, one of the political instruments used to discourage the proliferation of political parties has been the introduction of an electoral threshold of 5 per cent for a party to be represented in the National Assembly. The system has been decried not only because it sets a high barrier for entry into parliament but also because all the wasted votes are eventually shared between Frente de Libertação de Moçambique (FRELIMO) and the Resistência Nacional de Moçambique (RENAMO) in proportion to their shares of the vote, thus unduly increasing their parliamentary representation. This provision explains the entrenchment of a two-party system in Mozambique – although in the 2004 parliamentary elections RENAMO performed so badly that the country shifted toward a dominant-party system, with FRELIMO enjoying 62.03 per cent of the votes and RENAMO falling to 29.73 per cent. Since FRELIMO and RENAMO were the only ones to reach and exceed the 5 per cent electoral threshold, all the seats in the 250-member National Assembly were allocated to the two political formations. FRELIMO ended up increasing its share to 64 per cent (160 parliamentary seats) and RENAMO to 36 per cent (90 seats).[11]

This provision also explains the clustering of 10 small parties around RENAMO to form the RENAMO União Eleitoral (Electoral Union). This coalition has allowed these 10 small parties to enter parliament although they are essentially faceless because they are in parliament through RENAMO. Indeed, the RENAMO União Eleitoral is an atypical coalition of political parties: not only is it named after a dominant party in the coalition, RENAMO, but all of its members are in parliament by virtue of being on the RENAMO closed electoral party list. Should they decide to leave the coalition, they would lose their parliamentary seats to RENAMO.[12] It will be interesting to see the new configuration of Mozambique's party system following the 2009 parliamentary elections, at which the electoral threshold will no longer apply, and the impact this will have on national cohesion.

The effects of inter-party relations on nation-building and dominant party systems

This study argues that inter-party relations have had a positive effect on nation-building but also led to the entrenchment of dominant-party systems because of inadequate regulation of electoral alliances and party coalitions. Here, election alliance refers to a pre-election grouping of at least two political parties to contest the elections together; a party coalition represents the coming together of at least two parties with a view to working together in parliament; and a coalition government is a government consisting of a minimum of two parties to achieve the required majority and govern. In practice, however, there are provisions that make inter-party cooperation quite challenging, thus adversely affecting the whole party system. In the majority of the countries under study, regulations governing electoral alliances and party coalitions are either selective, or inadequate or just non-existent, reducing electoral alliances and party coalitions to mere gentlemen's agreements to the advantage of ruling parties. Ultimately, this situation has contributed to the consolidation of dominant-party systems in the countries concerned.

A few examples drawn from the five countries can illustrate this state of affairs. Election alliances in Malawi are not legally recognized. On the occasion of an election, alliances are not allowed to be formally registered or have their own symbols, nor can party candidates be nominated as the alliance's candidates. As a result, because electoral alliances are not unambiguously legally recognized in Malawi, when political parties do enter into an electoral alliance, the alliance's presidential candidate uses the symbols of his/her original party. Alliance partners will campaign for their alliance's presidential candidate using his party symbols, while at the same time campaigning for the parliamentary candidates of their particular party using its symbols. This situation not only confuses the electorate but also gives undue advantage to the main alliance partner, owing to the fact that its presidential candidate enjoys improved visibility at the expense of the parliamentary candidates of the other parties in the alliance.

A concrete example is the case of the 1999 presidential running mate, where strict interpretation of the law by the Malawi Electoral Commission (MEC) made it difficult for the Malawi Congress Party (MCP) and the Alliance for Democracy (AFORD) to enter into a pre-election alliance and contest the presidential election jointly. Although the MEC's refusal to recognize the MCP–AFORD alliance was subsequently reversed by the court, the MCP's symbols were used both for this party and for the alliance, resulting in undue advantage for that party in both the presidential and the parliamentary elections in terms of public visibility, at the expense of AFORD. Similarly, the Republican Party's symbols were used for the Mgwirizano electoral alliance at the expense of the other alliance partners.[13]

In Kenya, too, there is no law that unequivocally recognizes the legality of an electoral alliance. Aware of this inadequacy or omission, Kenyan opposition leaders formed an electoral alliance known as the National Rainbow Coalition (NARC), which they registered as a political party with the same legal standing as all its affiliated registered parties. The effect of the legal status of the NARC as a registered political party on the electoral alliance itself is that this political formation has an identity crisis. Although in practice NARC is an alliance of 15 political parties, legally this political formation is registered as a mere political party, facing all the challenges related to the inadequate legal status of political parties in Kenya, as explained above, while also being vulnerable to the lack of legal recognition of electoral alliances in the east African country.

The situation is fundamentally different in Mauritius, where any group of parties wishing to contest the elections together must register with the Office of the Electoral Commissioner. An alliance is also required to have its symbols registered with the Commission. For example, in the 2005 general elections, the Alliance Sociale, which comprised the Labour Party (LP) and five smaller parties, was registered as an alliance using the symbol of the LP and that of one of the smaller parties, the Parti Mauricien Xavier Duval (PMXD). The then ruling alliance was registered as the Mouvement Militant Mauricien (MMM)/Mouvement Socialiste Mauricien (MSM) alliance using the symbols of the MMM and the MSM. It is important to note, however, that registration with the Mauritian Electoral Commissioner is applicable only to election time, and at other times parties in an alliance are not legally bound. Bunwaree and Kasenally note that there are no specific rules for coalitions but there are various informal practices and unwritten rules by which parties have to abide.[14]

Electoral alliances, party coalitions and coalition governments have become a significant feature of African politics. The challenges facing electoral alliances also apply to party coalitions in parliament, where the lack of regulation of such groupings has at times come with a heavy cost in terms of governmental or even political stability. Kenya and Malawi have been largely ungovernable since their presidential and legislative elections of 2002 and 2004, respectively, owing to the dysfunctional nature of their coalitions. Electoral alliances and party coalitions are under-regulated. I do not advocate the over-regulation that arguably characterizes some Latin American countries,[15] but, at the same time, recognize the importance of coalitions in African plural societies. If some degree of regulation is not introduced, party coalitions will continue to be abused and to constitute a source of governmental instability and favour dominant-party systems.

The effects of election alliances and party coalitions on nation-building

Electoral alliances and party coalitions have contributed to nation-building in many countries by allowing political parties, especially those that are ethnically based, to reach out to parties from a different background and work toward common goals. In Malawi, these alliances and coalitions have focused on national matters, thus helping reduce the strong regionalism that characterizes the country. As for Mauritius, politicians often "sell" coalitions as the only means of accommodating ethnic diversity, building consensus and promoting social cohesion. The reality is, however, different, because coalition-building, and ultimately its breakdown, takes place along ethnic lines and these coalitions are essentially vehicles that allow politicians to access or maintain power. In other words, the *raison d'être* of a party coalition is ultimately to govern, and ethnic accommodation, though desirable and reassuring, has essentially been of peripheral importance. In order to guarantee electoral victory in 2000, the MMM entered into a coalition with a smaller party, the MSM, and agreed to share the post of prime minister, with the MSM taking the first three years and the MMM contenting itself with the remaining two years. This ethnic calculation was based on the recognition of the demographic weight of the Hindu majority, who constitute about half the population. Despite the true political motives of some alliance and coalition partners, there is nonetheless a strong perception that alliances and coalitions help reduce the communal divide, thus contributing to nation-building.

Inter-party cooperation has improved the image of some regionally based political parties, giving them some national relevance. Just such a case is the northern-based AFORD in Malawi, which had become a national role player through its intermittent alliances with the United Democratic Front (UDF) and the MCP, which is based in the Central Region. The same applies to the Inkatha Freedom Party (IFP) in South Africa, which, thanks to its participation in the ANC-led national government, changed its image from that of a provincial party concerned only with the interests of its Zulu constituents to that of a national player. The participation of its president, Mangosuthu Buthelezi, in government as minister of home affairs and his periodic appointment as acting president of the republic also enhanced his stature. Mauritius's third-largest party, the MSM, was able to maintain itself in power by taking advantage of the rivalry between the two main parties, the LP and the MMM. Anerood Jugnauth therefore managed to occupy the top job of prime minister for 13 consecutive years, a period that ended only when the LP and MMM agreed to join forces in 1995. However, thanks to a new coalition with the MMM, Jugnauth made a comeback in 2000 and led the country for a further three years as prime minister before he was elected by parliament as the (ceremonial) president of the republic, a position he still held in 2007. In Mozambique, some representatives of the 10 small parties allied with RENAMO have been able to enter parliament and enjoy better political visibility and financial security thanks to the alliance.[16]

In South Africa, the ANC has entered into alliances and cooperative arrangements with a variety of smaller and widely different political parties, including the IFP (its arch-rival in the KwaZulu-Natal province), the New National Party (NNP, the successor to the National Party), the United Democratic Movement (UDM, a party led by a former ANC member), the Minority Front, which strives for the interests of the Indian community, the Azanian People's Organisation (AZAPO, a black-consciousness party), the Freedom Front Plus (FF+, a right-wing party promoting the interests of the Afrikaners) and the Independent Democrats (ID, increasingly being presented as the party of the coloureds). The ANC's openness has enhanced the governing party's image as a moderate (dominant) party, and has contributed to the reduction of the country's ethnic and racial polarization and promoted nation-building. Beyond nation-building, inter-party cooperation has also contributed to the gradual move by parties from ethnic politics by embracing parties from different ethnic backgrounds. Indeed, in Mauritius and South Africa, it is the building of alliances, coalitions and other inter-party cooperative arrangements between the main parties that has, with time, contributed to some degree of ideological harmony.[17]

One important objective of immediate pre-independence and post-independence party coalitions in Mauritius in the second half of the 1960s and in South Africa in the early 1990s was to bring about national unity and nation-building. In Mauritius, after the pre-independence elections of 1967, the LP and its then arch-rival the Parti Mauricien Socialiste Démocrate (PMSD) formed a post-election coalition that lasted for 15 years, thus helping nation-building by reconciling the Hindu majority represented by the LP and what is known as the General Population, which consisted mainly of the Creole people and was represented by the PMSD. In South Africa, the 1994–1996 Government of National Unity, consisting of the ANC, the National Party (NP – before it became the NNP) and the IFP, contributed to nation-building in the racially and ethnically divided country. The transitional Government of National Unity brought together the architects of apartheid, the NP, and the party that led the liberation struggle against apartheid, the ANC. One of the most successful party coalitions in the post-apartheid era in South Africa has, surprisingly, been the successive post-election coalitions between the ANC and the IFP in KwaZulu-Natal and nationally. The ANC and IFP came together in an attempt to root out political violence in KwaZulu-Natal, and their coalition contributed to restoring peace in the volatile province after decades of hostility between supporters of the two parties.

Electoral alliances and party coalitions have had a positive effect on social harmony and nation-building more generally in those countries such as Mauritius and South Africa where communal diversity is acknowledged and accommodated. However, inter-party cooperation has not had the same effect where the electoral system and party system engineers have promoted the blocking or banning of ethnically based parties. In Kenya and Mozambique, in addition, inter-party relations have been hampered by the rigidity of the systems (i.e. if one leaves the coalition, one loses the parliamentary seat). This has resulted in the main party in the grouping often taking advantage of the alliance or coalition at the expense of the other parties. Malawi's failure to recognize electoral alliances unambiguously has led to political stand-offs within parliament and between the parliament and the president.

Inter-party relations and dominant-party systems

Although cooperation between different political parties has contributed tremendously to nation-building in African plural societies, it has, at the same time, affected party systems by contributing to the emergence or entrenchment of dominant-party systems and weakening the junior partners in the alliances and coalitions, often in favour of ruling parties. This situation has been caused either by inadequate regulations or by the absence of appropriate regulations. It is also the result of the limited institutionalization of African party systems.

Borrowing the definition of Giovanni Sartori, a dominant-party system can be defined as a system where one party has won a parliamentary majority (and, where applicable, the presidential elections) in three consecutive multi-party elections.[18] Party-switching has been one of the mechanisms through which dominant-party systems have been consolidated in some countries. Legislation in South Africa, Mauritius and Malawi provides for the crossing of the floor in parliament, with some procedural differences in each country. In South Africa, laws introduced in 2002 enable an elected representative in parliament, the provincial legislature or a local council to become a member of another party while retaining membership of the legislature. They also make it possible for an existing political party to merge with another party or to subdivide into more than one party, while allowing an MP affected by such changes to retain membership of the legislature. These laws have changed South Africa's party system and political representation because substantial realignments take place between elections, affecting the initial choice of the electorate.[19] The dominant-party system is strengthened directly by receiving opposition members by way of defection or indirectly through the fragmentation of the opposition.

It is worth noting that, in the South African context, for the floor-crossing legislation to apply, the number of members leaving the original party must represent not less than 10 per cent of the total number of seats held by the original party in that legislature. In addition, for the 10 per cent clause to apply, members must leave their parties at the same time. It has been argued that this provision is aimed at preventing solo, unprincipled departures. In reality, it in effect protects large parties at the expense of smaller ones, given that the smaller a party, the easier it is for those who wish to defect to achieve the required 10 per cent threshold. Undoubtedly the legislation has favoured the ANC, by allowing its expansion, and weakened the opposition and the whole party system through the fragmentation of opposition parties with the entrance of smaller parties in the national, provincial and local chambers between general elections. The Democratic Alliance (DA), South Africa's largest opposition party, was also a beneficiary of the floor-crossing legislation until September 2005, when it lost 10 per cent of its members in the National Assembly.

The floor-crossing legislation has led to a flurry of defections by elected representatives either to join other parties or to form new ones. This legal yet unprincipled practice has been decried for several reasons. Admittedly, floor-crossing gives effect to freedom of association, expression and conscience and reduces the party leadership's control over MPs. However, the disadvantages offset the advantages. The extent to which the legislation has affected the party system can be seen in the example of parties such as the NNP, which was deserted by a substantial number of its MPs and councillors, and the PAC, which lost one of its only three MPs; and in tensions in KwaZulu-Natal that threatened to undo the gains of peace consolidation when the IFP lost some of its elected representatives to the ANC. The UDM lost the majority of its parliamentarians to the ANC, which, as a result, and between elections, achieved and exceeded a two-thirds majority in the National Assembly. At times the floor-crossing practice had all the elements of a farce, as in 2003 when the sole national representative of the Afrikaner Eenheids Beweging, Cassie Aucamp, chose to quit and form a new party, National Action, probably to represent himself.[20]

The legislation undoubtedly undermines representative democracy by ignoring the choice of voters and weakening small parties because the 10 per cent clause protects only large political parties. In addition, floor-crossing creates the potential for political corruption with, for example, promises of jobs, money or other political or financial privileges, thus damaging the political integrity of the country. However, it has been argued that smaller parties such as the IFP, the UDM and the ID were personality driven, with internal democracy crises that culminated in their loss of members.[21]

Indeed, party leaders, the media and political analysts have raised serious concerns about the legitimacy of the floor-crossing legislation in

South Africa, which is seen as a threat to the young democracy. The IFP leader referred to floor-crossing as "crosstitution" and to those who cross the floor as "crosstitutes", an astute combination of "crossing" and (political) "prostitution". More explicit condemnations have come from the media, with a newspaper calling floor-crossing daylight robbery: the theft of party seats by politicians.[22]

It must be highlighted that the proponents of the floor-crossing legislation in South Africa have argued, for example, that the demise of the NNP and its subsequent integration into the ANC through floor-crossing was good for nation-building in a post-apartheid South Africa characterized by racial polarization.[23] Apart from floor-crossing, there are other mechanisms such as defections that have had the effect of fragmenting the party system. It has been observed in Mauritius and Malawi that politicians often leave opposition parties and form new ones as a strategy to make themselves more attractive to the ruling party as a coalition partner. This has contributed to the strengthening of the ruling parties at the expense of smaller parties. However, the Kenyan and Mozambican party systems have been less affected by fragmentation owing to the fact that both have an electoral threshold that encourages election alliances and party coalitions and discourages their disintegration – given that an MP who leaves a party coalition would lose his/her seat in the representative chamber.

A strong correlation exists between regime types and the effectiveness and survival of party coalitions. It has been observed, particularly in Mauritius and to a lesser extent in South Africa, which are both parliamentary regimes, that coalition partners have a say. The larger the number of seats controlled by the partner, the bigger the space this partner will enjoy in the coalition and government. In Mauritius, for example, the main party in the coalition will receive the post of prime minister and the leader of the second-largest party will be entitled to the post of deputy prime minister. Partners are accommodated in order to avoid their withdrawal from government and a subsequent vote of no-confidence, which might lead to the collapse of the coalition government and the formation of a new one or the calling of an early election. Consultation and consensus-building are the rules of the game in parliamentary regimes where coalition-building is needed to govern.

Party coalitions in parliamentary regimes tend to be more effective than those in presidential regimes. In presidential regimes, the presidential party may choose to ignore coalition agreements and give precedence to its constitutional prerogatives. Such situations can lead to divisions within the coalition, undermine the functioning and the effectiveness of government, and destabilize the party system.

In Malawi, the dominance of the executive over the legislature has made it possible for President Bingu Wa Mutharika to resign from the UDF, the very party that sponsored him to the presidency of the republic, and form his own party, the Democratic Progressive Party (DPP), without losing his post as the president of the republic. He was later joined by scores of MPs through floor-crossing. This development helped Mutharika to defuse the impeachment proceedings initiated against him by his UDF opponents. Although he did not control the majority of seats in parliament, Mutharika managed to continue to enjoy a great deal of influence and to rule the country using his presidential prerogatives, appointing opposition MPs to powerful and lucrative public posts, thus getting them to cross the floor and support him in crucial debates and policy issues.

Similarly, Kenya's presidentialism vests immense executive powers in the president of the republic. The president appoints the cabinet and can dissolve it at will, and has the power to dissolve and prorogue parliament.[24] In doing so, he or she is not obliged to seek advice from any authority, including his/her alliance partners, nor is he/she required to abide by the pre-election Memorandum of Understanding signed with the coalition partners. The executive authority vested in the president means that, once elected, he/she may choose not to be accountable to his/her coalition partners by virtue of his/her presidential prerogatives. This situation has been at the origin of the crisis within the NARC. The sustainability of party coalitions in a presidential system clearly depends, to a large extent, on the president's goodwill. This situation has affected the functioning of the NARC coalition and weakened the party system by exacerbating the divisions in the coalition and causing mistrust between party leaders.

Conclusion

Different African countries have developed different regulations for political parties with the common goal of preventing and/or containing the pervasive and polarizing effects of ethno-regional parties and politics and achieving nation-building in the post-independence and the post–Cold War eras. Although none has managed to put a stop to ethnic parties, many have managed to minimize the threat posed by extremist ethno-regional politics. However, those parliamentary regimes that have encouraged the translation of ethno-regional cleavages, such as Mauritius and South Africa, through the use of proportional representation without an electoral threshold or the use of a compensatory measure to correct the under-representation of ethnic groups, are well served in terms of political representation, ethnic accommodation and party system stability. Undoubtedly, these countries are governable, their party systems are more stable and nation-building is increasingly a reality. Mauritius has routinely experienced alternation in power and does not have one single dominant party, whereas South Africa has a democratically elected dominant party.

On the other hand, countries that have tended to promote the aggregation of social cleavages through the setting of high electoral thresholds (Mozambique and Kenya) and distribution requirements (Kenya) have equally managed to contain extremist ethno-regional politics and parties. However, it is unclear whether their minorities feel sufficiently included and accommodated in the political system. In addition, the presidentialist system in use in Malawi and Kenya has reduced the integrative function of election alliances and party coalitions. These groupings are not unequivocally legally recognized, and presidents have tended to use their constitutionally entrenched prerogatives against their coalition partners in parliament. This has led to parliamentary and governmental deadlocks.

I would therefore recommend that the unintended (negative) consequences of party regulations, such as the exclusion of minorities in some political systems, be addressed through inclusive reform processes. In addition, the laissez-faire approach, which entails the absence or the inadequacy of the rules governing election alliances and party coalitions, has led to the abuse of these partnerships and benefited the main party in the coalition. I therefore recommend that some regulation of alliances and coalitions be introduced for the sake of stable and balanced party systems, for the functionality of parliaments and governments, and for national cohesion.

Notes

1. Adriano Nuvunga (ed.), *Multiparty Democracy in Mozambique: Strengths, Weaknesses and Challenges*, EISA Research Report No. 14 (Johannesburg: EISA, 2005), p. xiv.
2. Denis Kadima and Roukaya Kasenally, "Formation, Collapse and Revival of Political Party Coalitions in Mauritius: Ethnic Logic and Calculation at Play", *Journal of African Elections*, 4(1): 133–164.
3. Tom Lodge and Ursula Scheidegger, *Political Parties and Democratic Governance in South Africa*, EISA Research Report No. 25 (Johannesburg: EISA, 2006), p. 3.
4. Arend Lijphart, "The South African Electoral System: Unusual Features and Prospects for Reform", available at ⟨http://www.fairvote.org/reports/1995/spot4/lijphart.html⟩ (accessed 28 April 2008).
5. Lodge and Scheidegger, *Political Parties and Democratic Governance in South Africa*, p. 7.

6. Article 32.2 of the Mozambican constitution.
7. *The Constitution of Kenya. Revised Edition (2001) (1998)*, Section 5(3)(f), available at ⟨http://www.bunge.go.ke/downloads/constitution.pdf⟩ (accessed 7 April 2008).
8. Republic of Mauritius, *The Constitution*, 1968, First Schedule, Section 3(1).
9. Nandini Patel, *Political Parties: Development and Change in Malawi*, EISA Research Report No. 21 (Johannesburg: EISA, 2005), p. 29.
10. Matthijs Bogaards, "Electoral Systems, Party Systems, and Ethnic Conflict Management in Africa", in Matthias Basedau, Gero Erdmann and Andreas Mehler (eds), *Votes, Money and Violence: Political Parties and Elections in Africa* (Uppsala: Nordiska Afrika-institutet, 2007), p. 188.
11. Constitutional Council, "Results of the Mozambique 2004 Parliamentary Election and Party Representation in Parliament", 2005.
12. Denis Kadima and Zefanias Matsimbe, "RENAMO União Eleitoral: Understanding the Longevity and Challenges of an Opposition Party Coalition in Mozambique", in Denis Kadima (ed.), *The Politics of Party Coalitions in Africa*, 2nd edn (Johannesburg: EISA & KAS, 2006), pp. 154 and 164.
13. Denis Kadima and Samson Lembani, "Making, Unmaking and Remaking Political Party Coalitions in Malawi: Explaining the Prevalence of Office-Seeking Behaviour", in Kadima (ed.), *The Politics of Party Coalitions in Africa*, pp. 130 and 131.
14. Sheila Bunwaree and Roukaya Kasenally, *Political Parties and Democracy in Mauritius*, EISA Research Report No. 19 (Johannesburg: EISA, 2005), p. 5.
15. Instituto Federal Electoral, *The Mexican Electoral System and the Federal Elections 2006* (Mexico City: IFE, 2006), pp. 56–57.
16. Denis Kadima, "African Party Alliances: Comparisons, Conclusions and Lessons", in Kadima (ed.), *The Politics of Political Party Coalitions in Africa*, p. 229.
17. Ibid., p. 233.
18. Giovanni Sartori, *Parties and Party Systems: A Framework for Analysis* (Cambridge: Cambridge University Press, 1976), p. ix.
19. The Constitution of the Republic of South Africa, Amendment Act 18 of 2002; the Constitution Second Amendment Act 21 of 2002; the Local Government Municipal Structures Amendment Act 20 of 2002; and the Loss or Retention of Membership of National and Provincial Legislatures Act 22 of 2002.
20. Denis Kadima, "Party Coalitions in Post-Apartheid South Africa and Their Impact on National Cohesion and Ideological Rapprochement", in Kadima (ed.), *The Politics of Political Party Coalitions in Africa*, p. 54.
21. *The Star*, 30 September 2005.
22. *City Press*, 4 September 2005.
23. Kadima, "Party Coalitions in Post-Apartheid South Africa and Their Impact on National Cohesion and Ideological Rapprochement", p. 39.
24. *The Constitution of Kenya*, Sections 58 and 59.

Part III

Thematic perspectives

10

Party regulation and democratization: Challenges for further research

Iain McMenamin

Introduction

The two great subjects of academic political engineers have been electoral systems and executive–legislative relations.[1] The main purpose of
engineering the electoral system has been to influence the party system.
The choice between presidential and parliamentary systems also has important consequences for parties. In the case of both electoral systems
and executive–legislative relations, the effect on parties is indirect. Incentives are provided for parties by prescribing the method of election to
office and the powers of elective offices. It is now clear that political practice has gone beyond merely providing indirect incentives to directly regulating the form political parties take.[2]

In this chapter, I concentrate on the most original subject matter cov-
ered in this book: how party regulation affects the nature of political parties. The incentives created by the electoral rules affect not just the party
system, in terms of number, size and stability of parties (the inter-
party dimension), but also the nature of the parties themselves (the
intra-party dimension).[3] In this chapter, the dependent variable is the
intra-party dimension and the independent variables are forms of party
regulation. As Shugart has pointed out, the intra-party dimension has
been neglected in the huge literature on electoral systems, and Reilly's
primary claim for the originality of this volume is the extent to which
the political practice of party regulation has outpaced its academic analysis. In terms of Reilly's taxonomy of attempts to engineer parties and

Political parties in conflict-prone societies: Regulation, engineering and democratic
development, Reilly and Nordlund (eds),
United Nations University Press, 2008, ISBN 978-92-808-1157-5

party systems outlined in Chapter 1, I confine myself to bottom-up (or extra-parliamentary) regulations. Thus, I exclude electoral rules, top-down (or parliamentary) regulations and international interventions.

The bottom-up regulation of parties seems to take four main forms. First, it can require that parties have a certain number and/or geographical distribution of members, branches or permanent offices. Second, it can proscribe certain bases of party mobilization, most notably ethnicity. Third, regulations can mandate that parties are internally democratic. Fourth, the source, size and reporting of party finances can be regulated. Whether these regulations are found in the constitution, ordinary statute law or a specialized electoral or party law,[4] they have in common that they do not merely provide a set of incentives for office-seeking or office-holding parties. Instead, they tend to set out in some detail the standards that parties are supposed to meet if they want to offer themselves for office.

Political engineering requires a reasonable basis on which to predict its consequences. Prediction in turn requires a very strong theoretical base. This chapter sets out the formidable theoretical challenges for the study of party regulation. These challenges can be understood in terms of the standard model of political parties and democratization, which should be especially familiar to students of electoral systems from their analysis of the interrelationship of electoral rules, political parties and social structure. Although this chapter is primarily situated in the academic literature, it does have policy implications. Firstly, the chapter contains some very strong arguments about the consequences of some types of regulation in some contexts. In effect, it represents the academic's response to the policymaker's question of "what works?". Secondly, to the extent that policymakers are operating without the analysis and data assumed by the standard model, they are lacking basic information. To the extent that they lack basic information, the consequences of engineering will be unpredictable and risky. Thirdly, in some limited respects, the analysis of this chapter presents theoretical arguments for concrete institutional solutions that have yet to be found amongst the current wave of experimentation overviewed elsewhere in this book.

The standard model of parties and democratization

Although it is rarely expressed as such, there exists a broad consensus on a standard model of parties and democratization. Indeed, it is assumed, or partially articulated, in virtually all of the other chapters of this book. Given the complexity of politics and political studies, these chapters, as well as the wider literature, generally focus on portions of the model.

Nonetheless, most studies of parties and democratization are involved in a collective endeavour to specify and test the model.

I will very briefly outline the structure of the model. The characteristics of political parties are hypothesized to affect democratization. Some types of parties are thought to be better for democratization than others. For example, the vast majority of scholars think institutionalized parties are better than uninstitutionalized parties. Many scholars think that ethnic parties are best avoided. The characteristics of parties are explained by a variety of institutional factors such as the electoral system and executive–legislative relations. These institutions cannot be considered one by one. They interact with each other. The effect of one institution varies according to overall institutional configuration. Party characteristics are also explained by social factors such as the divisions between classes, religions, regions and ethnic groups. Interactions of social and institutional factors are important. The effect of institutions will vary according to what type of society they are placed in. Finally, institutions are often endogenous to parties. In other words, not only do institutions influence parties; parties influence institutions. The model is summarized in Figure 10.1.

In the following, and principal, section of the chapter, I lay out the study of party regulation in terms of the standard model of parties and democratization. In doing so, I endeavour to provide a coherent synthesis of, and commentary on, the content of most of the chapters in this book. The chapter does not attempt an empirical summary. Moreover, it does not even claim to be a fully worked-out theoretical proposition. Instead, I merely hope that it will illuminate the theoretical challenges facing a

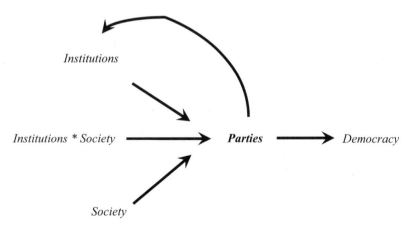

Figure 10.1 The standard model of parties and democratization.

research programme on party regulation. Given the newness and generality of the material, this last aspiration is not overly modest.

Party regulation

Parties

Two characteristics of parties are most frequently associated with prospects for democratization: their level of institutionalization and the degree to which they are "ethnic" parties. An ethnic party "derives its support overwhelmingly from an identifiable ethnic group ... and serves the interests of that group".[5] Note that this definition centres on "how the *party's* support is distributed, and not how the *ethnic* group's support is distributed".[6] I use ethnicization as a shorthand term for an ordinal ranking, with ethnic parties as the most ethnicized, multi-ethnic parties the second most ethnicized and non-ethnic parties as the least ethnicized.

Unfortunately, definitions of institutionalization are much more complex, vague and contested. In spite of this definitional morass, in practice observers tend to agree on whether a given party is institutionalized or not. Randall's conception[7] is a considered synthesis of a large literature.[8] In contrast to most other contributions, it is specifically designed to address the institutionalization of parties, as opposed to other organizations, and focuses on the intra-party dimension alone, as opposed to a mix of intra- and inter-party dimensions.[9] The first characteristic of the institutionalized party is "organizational systemness". It is a real organization, not a mere network, coterie or façade. Secondly, it exercises "embedded decisional autonomy". Although it has links to society, and may be influenced by other organizations, it has substantial control over its own decision-making. Thirdly, it exhibits "value infusion": its members do not treat it purely instrumentally. The continuity and success of the party are regarded, to some extent at least, as a good in itself. Finally, the institutionalized party has a "definite public image and presence" as well as a "relatively stable basis of support". This definition helps to convey both the complexity of institutionalization and the high standard that a party must achieve to be regarded as institutionalized. Although the rules under examination in this chapter tend to influence some of the four characteristics more than others, these differences are not essential for the following discussion. Neither are the differences between this and other definitions of institutionalization. Also, it is reassuring that these four dimensions of institutionalization do tend to co-vary.

In common with a wide consensus, I assume that, at least in the context of most of the societies under examination in this book, institutionalized parties are good for democracy. Nonetheless, it is worth noting that many people think that some Latin American parties, such as the traditional Colombian parties, have been over-institutionalized. Furthermore, the popular idea of the cartel party might be interpreted as a view that most West European parties are over-institutionalized.[10] In contrast, I am making no claim with regard to the connection between the ethnic status of parties and democratic outcomes, which is the subject of a vigorous debate between "centripetalists" and "consociationalists".[11] Competing schools of thought will care about the effect of institutions designed to remove ethnicity from party structures, even though they will, of course, have very different views as to the advisability of such attempts.

Institutions

In this section, I propose some hypotheses linking the four sets of party regulations with ethnicization and institutionalization. An internally democratic party is more institutionalized but is not necessarily more or less ethnic. It is more institutionalized because elections require a minimum level of organizational systemness. Democracy also promotes decisional autonomy. A genuinely democratic party cannot be the creature of another organization. Internal democracy also promotes value infusion. Members may identify with the party as a democracy. They will owe their loyalty to the party's democratic procedures rather than to personal connections with its leadership.

In contrast, whether internal democracy promotes ethnicization or not depends on the relative positions of leaders, members and voters.[12] Registration requirements are usually designed to discourage ethnicity by making it impossible or difficult for ethnic parties to register. Moreover, they necessarily require a relatively high level of institutionalization. In Indonesia, parties must establish an organizational network in two-thirds of the provinces across its archipelago and in two-thirds of the municipalities within those provinces. This represents quite a formidable level of institutional development. The proscription of bases of mobilization is again usually targeted at ethnic parties but does not affect institutionalization.

Finally, funding regulations affect institutionalization in that they require a more professional administration of resources. They have no relation to ethnicity. The relationship between these two characteristics of parties and the four main types of regulation are summarized in Table 10.1. A caveat to all of these hypotheses is that they hold only if the party regulations are enforced. The likelihood of enforcement can be best understood as a response to the incentives created by the institutions.

Table 10.1 Party regulations and party characteristics

	Affected dimension	
	Institutionalization	Ethnicization
Internal democracy	Yes	No
Registration requirements:		
Membership and branch distribution	Yes	Yes
Proscribed bases	No	Yes
Funding	Yes	No

Source: Author.

Incentives

There is a frustratingly wide range of definitions of institutions, most of which are useful in some context or other. For political engineers, the definition of institutions as incentive structures is a useful one. Thus, to understand any institution we must enumerate the rewards it offers and the punishments it threatens.[13] The incentive offered by electoral systems is clear: they help decide who does and does not exercise political power. However, the incentives presented by party regulation are less clear and less uniform. Here, I point out some of the challenges and opportunities in studying, evaluating and designing party regulations as effective incentive structures. I begin by considering whether the regulations rely on command and control or positive incentives to achieve their aims.[14] Then, I examine ways of monitoring and enforcing rules.

Command and control is not the only way for the state to modify behaviour. A good example is the continuing shift in environmental regulation from minimum standards to incentive schemes such as carbon emission trading. In spite of this fashion, virtually all cases of party regulation seem to rely on command and control: the regulations stipulate standards that parties must meet. If they do not meet these standards, they face two sorts of penalties. Parties that mobilize on proscribed bases or do not meet membership and branch requirements are refused registration or are de-registered. Command-and-control regulations may be so drastic, and so at variance with the structure of society, that they may be impossible to implement. Witness the failure of Turkey's ban on religious parties. Turkish courts disbanded the Welfare Party, but it has simply renamed itself as the Justice and Development Party, shuffled leaders and denied a religious identity, while clearly appealing to the more religious sectors of Turkish society. Less risky but still part of the command-and-control approach is the imposition of fines. Violations of financial regulations tend to be punished by fines but even in established democracies, with relatively undemanding regulations, enforcement tends to be patchy.[15]

The single exception to the command-and-control approach seems to be the Papua New Guinean incentive for parties to field female candidates. There is no quota of female candidates, the non-fulfilment of which attracts drastic, or not-so-drastic, consequences. Instead, parties that select female candidates receive a small but significant rebate on their election expenses. The aims of many of the command-and-control regulations could be pursued in a similar fashion. For example, parties' state funding could be partly a function of the distribution of their offices. In order to provide a further encouragement to real institutionalization, and to minimize the potential for straightforward corruption, non-cash incentives could be provided. Parties that exceed a threshold or geographical dispersion requirement could receive a subsidy to their phone or mail expenses or even receive a number of state-provided person-hours in administrative support. Despite the potential benefits and minimal risks of such an approach, there do not seem to be any cases of such incentives.

There is little analysis of how party regulations are monitored and enforced, other than to say that they are difficult to enforce and are frequently not enforced. A lot will depend on the design of the institutions charged with monitoring and enforcement. This responsibility is often given to the electoral commission, whose basic work has an obvious congruence with party regulation. However, there may be a tension between the administration of elections, which is best carried out with the cooperation of parties, and a seemingly partisan and aggressive process of selectively applying sanctions to parties. The other option is a dedicated "Party Regulator", which oversees party regulations separately from the conduct of elections. According to International IDEA, nine states have set up regulatory bodies exclusively to monitor and enforce political finance regulations.[16] A Party Regulator would be similar but with a wider remit. Such a body would be the analogue of the increasingly important institutions that regulate frequently oligopolistic and complex industries such as utilities and finance. There is a growing theoretical and empirical literature on this topic,[17] including that relating to central banks in developing countries.[18] The principal conclusion regarding central bank independence in developing countries has been that turnover on the governing body is the only reliable indicator of real independence. This is because nominal institutional autonomy is typically not respected in such contexts. Autonomy is achievable only if staff positions are insulated from political threats and blandishments. Therefore, it is reasonable to suggest that the key officers of any body charged with party regulation should have long or permanent terms of office and should be very difficult to dismiss.

Related to, but independent of, the design of the regulating institution is the monitoring strategy. "Police patrols" and "fire alarms" are two different ways of organizing oversight of rule compliance. A police patrol is "comparatively centralized, active and direct".[19] A state institution engages in police patrol on its own initiative and conducts investigations in order to uncover and discourage transgressions. A fire alarm "is less centralized and involves less active and direct intervention" than police patrols. Instead, procedures are established and information distributed that allow a wide range of actors to bring possible transgressions to the attention of the authorities. Under this approach, party regulations would be disseminated amongst civil society groups, the media and the bureaucracy. There could be toll-free numbers for those with information relating to party-regulation compliance. Rewards could be offered for information that eventually leads to a confirmed breach of regulations. Certain sorts of organizations could be given the legal standing to bring alleged transgressions to the courts if the regulator has not taken action. Legal standing might even be granted to individuals who can establish a reasonable suspicion of transgression that has not been punished. Fire alarms may be a useful alternative or supplement to police patrols. Fire alarms often do not have to be created by legislation. For example, there was an outcry in the media and public opinion over the failure of the Peruvian Jurado Nacional de Elecciones to verify that parties met the registration requirements. This public outcry led to a legislative response that attempted to reduce the number of parties that would be elected to the congress.[20]

If it is assumed that enforcement and monitoring are difficult, the all-or-nothing option of non- or de-registration should not be recommended. Weak institutions will not be able to implement the de-registration option and will instead default to a situation where nothing is done and regulations are openly flouted. Institutions that find it politically impossible to prevent parties from competing in elections may have the power to impose fines and to administer incentives that have a real effect on parties. It is worth noting that the all-or-nothing approach has a rhetorical advantage. It defines what is "democratic", including all democrats and treating them equally, while excluding all "undemocratic" actors. The calibrated approach of fines or positive incentives treats parties unequally on a basis other than popular support. Therefore, it could be construed as a violation of democratic principles.

Institutional interactions

Institutions do not exist in isolation. Instead of individual institutions we face a complex institutional environment, whose incentives are defined by the interaction of institutions. The effect of party regulations is likely to vary according to the configuration of other political institutions. This is far too complex a subject to be pursued systematically or comprehensively here. Instead, I provide an example of one of the many possible interactions between party regulations, showing that the effect of party regulations may vary according to electoral system. I also consider the interaction between the specific incentives and institutions for monitoring and enforcement considered above and a country's general institutional capacity for monitoring and enforcement.

Let us take the important case of a territorially concentrated minority. In its "home" region it is a large minority, say 20 per cent. In that region, it faces two national parties with about 40 per cent each. Very few members of the minority are found outside the home region. Since plurality electoral systems are virtually never recommended in divided societies, I will use the Bogaards typology in Chapter 3 in this volume to consider how a party regulation requiring supra-regional party structures such as branches and offices interacts with the difference between an alternative vote and a proportional representation (PR) electoral system. In the absence of such a party regulation, the PR system will translate the social structure into a regional party. If there is a party regulation, PR will incentivize aggregation in the form of the national parties having the opportunity to compete for the votes of the territorially concentrated minority. Now let us look at the alternative vote. Assume that the minority constitutes 20 per cent of the voters across a number of single-member districts. In the absence of a party regulation, the system will encourage aggregation in the form of national parties competing for the second preferences of the minority. In the presence of a party regulation, the system will give the national parties the opportunity to compete for the first preferences of the minority. Without the party regulation, the two electoral systems seem to produce different outcomes (translation and aggregation), whereas with the party regulation the two systems converge on aggregation.[21] The broad aggregative incentive of the preferential system is unaffected by the party regulation, but the PR system is shifted from translation to aggregation by the presence of the party regulation (see Table 10.2).

Many of the countries into which party regulations have been introduced have weak bureaucratic and judicial systems. A reliance on effective monitoring and enforcement of party regulations is especially problematic in states where effective monitoring and enforcement are lacking in other areas of state activity. The substitution of positive incentives for command and control does not remove the need for effective monitoring, but it may make enforcement easier. Similarly, in the context of a weak bureaucracy and judicial system, there is a particularly strong

Table 10.2 Interaction of electoral systems and party regulation

	Supra-regional party registration requirements	
	No	Yes
Non-preferential proportional representation	Translation	Aggregation
Preferential voting	Aggregation	Aggregation

Source: Author.
Note: The cells represent the effect on the relationship between regionally concentrated minority groups and political parties.

case for replacing, or supplementing, police-patrol procedures with fire alarms.

Society

Institutionalized parties generally exist only in systems where they are supported by, or in the past have been supported by, institutionalized social groups. Thus, both West European and East and Central European party systems exist in broadly post-industrial societies. The absence of a past social anchoring has made it difficult for structured party systems to emerge in East and Central Europe. This fundamental social characteristic may be such a powerful explanation for variations in the levels of party institutionalization that party regulations make almost no difference. Most of the cases where there have been attempts to engineer institutionalization are found in developing societies where institutionalized social groups hardly exist. Many of those that have developed economically, or have recently done so, have skipped the classic industrial stage, which tended to structure and institutionalize classes very strongly. Strong social structure in many recent democratizations is largely or entirely a reflection of ethnicity or another ascriptive category such as religion. Ethnicity could serve as a strong social anchor for institutionalized parties. For example, excluding parties that recently dominated authoritarian regimes, India's Bharatiya Janata Party, which mobilizes on the basis of the Hindu religion, has by far the highest membership rate of any of the parties listed in a review of party institutionalization in developing countries.[22] In this volume, Hicken's review in Chapter 4 of party system institutionalization in Southeast Asia concludes that Singapore and Malaysia are both the two most institutionalized and the two most ethnicized, although their status as semi-democracies makes the inference of a connection between ethnicization and institutionalization problematic.

A further issue for party regulation concerns the distinction between relatively structured and unstructured societies introduced above. A key question is how party regulations interact with societies that lack structure and institutionalization. In these societies, institutionalization, rather than de-ethnicization, is likely to be the aim of party regulations. Secondly, in the context of ethnically structured societies, I will examine how variations in the distance between groups can interact with party regulations. In these societies, de-ethnicization is likely to be a greater focus of party regulations than institutionalization.

Different societies tend to produce different types of link between parties and voters.[23] The material/individual link explains voting on the basis of links in a social hierarchy. This type of link is associated with societies that lack institutionalized social groups. The basis of support is a personal obligation and the "basis of the obligation is material". Internal democracy may undermine the hierarchy upon which this system is based. In the absence of institutionalized non-ethnic social groups to which an ideology can appeal, it is probably too optimistic to hope that internal democracy will promote a party based on a fairly coherent and stable ideological programme. It is a little more likely that it may promote a power-seeking party based on merit instead of a clientelistic network. Most likely of all is that the clientelistic nature of society will dominate internal party elections even more easily than it has done state elections. This seems to have been the result of recent reforms in Peru.[24]

Spatial registration requirements may be effective means of increasing average party institutionalization in relatively unstructured societies. Without social anchors, few parties are likely to achieve the requisite organization. Moreover, given the assumption of a lack of deep ethnic divides, such a reduction in parties should not come at the cost of effectively blocking the representation of well-defined social groups.

State party funding may well serve to entrench the material–individual link by increasing the power of elites to deliver benefits to their clients. Proscriptions on certain sources of funds, as well as transparency requirements, are likely to be largely ignored in such societies. Nonetheless, these rules may at least make the proscribed behaviour more expensive for the parties.

The effect of party regulations on de-ethnicizing parties in ethnically structured societies depends on several aspects of that ethnic structure. Chapter 5 by Bieber and Chapter 7 by Birnir in this volume have drawn attention to factors such as the fragmentation of groups, their geographical distribution and their internal cohesion. However, the contributions to this volume contain no systematic examination of the distance between

Table 10.3 Distance and party regulation

	Supra-regional party registration requirements	
	No	Yes
Moderate distance	Translation	Aggregation
Great social distance	Translation	Blocking

Source: Author.

Note: The cells represent the effect on the relationship between regionally concentrated minority groups and political parties. Assume a permissive proportional representation electoral system.

groups. Instead, they are treated as straightforwardly categorical. Notwithstanding their different names, groups are not all equally different. For example, although Czechs and Moravians may be separable, they are very similar. Levels of social interaction and political cooperation between the two groups are very high. In other words, there is little distance between Czechs and Moravians. In contrast, there is a great deal of distance between Czechs and the Roma. There is little social interaction and minimal political cooperation. Distance is different from fragmentation, which refers to the number and relative size of groups.[25] Distance is usually used in a strictly political sense, referring to competition and conflict between political parties.[26] Here, it is also used in a social sense, referring to empathy or antipathy between social groups.

As Table 10.3 shows, the distance between groups is a vital variable of interest when thinking about party regulations that are intended to aggregate ethnic groups. If the distance between groups is moderate, party regulations may bring about aggregation. If the distance is great, party regulations may fail to prevent the translation of social groups into political parties or, probably much worse, they may block the political representation of some social groups. For example, the Indonesian rules on party registration have sharply reduced the number of parties in the Indonesian legislature. Therefore, translation has not persisted in spite of the regulations. However, we do not know whether the social groups that supported the excluded parties have been aggregated into supraregional parties or have been blocked from political representation.

The effect of the proscription of particular bases of parties will also depend upon the distance between social groups. If the distance is close, groups may follow the intended aggregative incentives. If the distance is great, they may simply be blocked or repeatedly try to achieve translation by defying and/or evading the rules, as has been the case for both Islamists and Kurds in Turkey. Those who intend party regulations to aggregate ethnic groups need to make some assessment of distance before they can hope for aggregation instead of translation or blocking.

The measurement of distance is not straightforward. It is a latent variable that may be captured by a battery of questions. In some regions, survey data that ask relevant questions are available. In some other regions, a basic knowledge of the society might be all that is needed. For example, it is well known that the distance between Protestants and Catholics in Northern Ireland is wide: they are educated separately; they do not intermarry; they do not socialize together; and they do not go into business together. In yet other societies, the absence of such data may be a warning to policy makers that manipulation of party regulations in the absence of basic information is especially risky.

The distance between groups is no more primordial than their separate identities. Distance, like identity itself, is constructed by political and social institutions.[27] Indeed, the aggregative approach is predicated on the ability of political institutions to reduce the distance between groups. Nonetheless, such manipulation is usually slow, difficult and risky. The distance between groups is not likely to be reduced by political institutions that have been designed without any attempt to measure, however roughly, the distance itself.

Endogeneity

Endogeneity is the problematic situation in which at least one independent variable is explained by the dependent variable. From a practical point of view, the presence of endogeneity means that it will be difficult to assess the impact of institutions and that their independent effect may be minimal. In this section, I assess the extent to which endogeneity is likely to affect the relationship between our two party characteristics and four forms of party regulation and outline some research strategies for dealing with endogeneity.

Like the electoral system, party regulation affects the fundamental interests of political parties and is likely to be something they will do their best to control. Institutionalization per se does not affect the interests of parties differentially. In contrast, whether ethnicity is permitted, discouraged or banned privileges one type of party over another. Thus, I try to separate the two dimensions.

Let us begin with rules on internal democracy and finance, which affect the institutionalization dimension alone. Powerful institutions to establish internal democracy may have been introduced by powerful parties with internally democratic organizations. Weak institutions for internal democracy may reflect the interests of undemocratic party organizations in a façade of democracy. However, it may be that rules with institutionalizing effects such as internal democracy have a relatively neutral effect on a set of competitive but dominant parties. They are part of a package designed to disadvantage minor parties and new entrants. This is in effect the cartel party argument developed with Western Europe in mind. In such cases, there would be no endogeneity problem.

There are two obvious sources of party finance regulation. In one scenario, a legislative majority combines to disadvantage a minority that has greater access to business contributions. Parties that seek to regulate party finance are probably not necessarily more or less institutionalized than those that resist financial regulation. The second scenario is when political finance regulations are passed in reaction to corruption scandals. In this scenario, the source of the regulation comes from outside the dominant parties. Thus, there is little reason to worry about endogeneity.

Next, I turn to the proscription of ethnic parties. This is likely to suffer from endogeneity problems. Such laws will have been passed by non-ethnic parties. Some of the cases of party regulation represent a particular type of endogeneity. Several old regimes did allow some opposition parties or movements, but had themselves proscribed ethnically or religion-based parties or movements. Thus, the parties that were in a position to engineer the new democracy may have found it relatively easy to come to a consensus on regulations that discouraged ethnic parties. This is surely what has happened in Indonesia, where three putatively trans-ethnic parties were permitted under the authoritarian regime.

Finally, I look at rules on the distribution of members, branches and offices that affect both dimensions. The effect of branch and membership requirements on institutionalization is subject to endogeneity. Meeting these requirements necessitates quite a high level of institutionalization. It is possible that endogeneity on the ethnicity dimension may, by design, reduce endogeneity on the institutionalization dimension. In other words, non-ethnic parties, which easily have the institutional resources to meet the branch and membership requirements, may have intended to exclude ethnic parties without affecting their own competition. Thus, relatively uninstitutionalized parties that were too weak to prevent the introduction of anti-ethnic rules would be removed from party competition, while already dominant institutionalized parties become somewhat more dominant.

King, Keohane and Verba suggest five strategies for better research in the context of endogeneity.[28] Two of them, parsing the explanatory and dependent variables, do not seem practicable in the case of party regulations, institutionalization and ethnicization. The other three are difficult but possible to apply.

First, they suggest correcting biased inferences. If parties choose party regulations, this introduces a positive bias into assessments of the relationship between electoral systems and party systems. Therefore, estimates of the magnitude of the effect of party regulations should usually be revised downwards. In the absence of sufficient theory or data to implement either of the two following strategies, an endogeneity caveat should feature prominently in any evaluation of the effect of party regulations.

The second, and much better, strategy is that of controlling for an omitted variable that captures the source of endogeneity. In an application to our subject, the idea would be to control for the circumstances in which the party regulations were designed and implemented. This in turn requires a theory of institutional choice.[29] Bieber's careful taxonomy of East and Central European minority politics performs this function in Chapter 5 in this volume.

To simplify: in cases where minority politics were historically contentious, it is necessary to control for the majority's reaction to this contentiousness when trying to evaluate the effects of party regulations introduced by parties from the majority group. Ideally, therefore, we need to find similar institutions in societies with roughly similar histories of minority politics. This is, of course, rarely possible. Nonetheless, an approach such as Bieber's should allow us to make meaningful, if imprecise, assessments of the type and extent of endogeneity involved in the evaluation of party regulations. So, for example, the effect of Romania's reserved seats for minorities is largely endogenous to a history of hostility towards the largest minority – the Hungarians, who are territorially concentrated in the west of the country close to historically irredentist Hungary.

The third strategy is the selection of observations to avoid endogeneity. The most obvious way of doing this is to look for instances where parties did not choose the party regulations. In Bosnia, after the Dayton agreement, it seems that party regulations were created largely by international institutions rather than by the political parties themselves. These regulations constrained the espousal of certain positions, the recruitment of leaders and party finances.[30] One set of cases is where a constellation of parties inherits an electoral system originally chosen by a very different set of interests. Such relatively pure cases are rare. Another option is to seek out cases where the relative absence of interests and information underpinning institutional choice reduces endogeneity substantially. Many democratizations happen in the context of a fluid party system. Although parties may choose institutions that they calculate will serve their interests, those parties may be ephemeral whereas the institutions they create endure. Such a situation is likely when:

- there were no opposition parties or movements under the old regime – in effect, this means cases where the old regime was very close to the totalitarian regime type immediately before the transition to democracy;

- the mode of transition to democracy is a collapse of the old regime, as opposed to negotiation between the opposition and the authoritarian regime or a self-transformation of the old regime;
- the social structure is not characterized by a small number of institutionalized divisions, such as a small number of separate ethnic groups, religions or classes.

Some Central and East European cases partially fulfil some of these three conditions. For example, in Czechoslovakia there was a post-totalitarian regime that allowed only a token amount of organized dissidence or opposition. This regime collapsed suddenly and comprehensively. Although there were significant national and ethnic divides in Czechoslovakia, in the Czech half of the federation there was a relatively homogeneous population, whose social structure had been substantially flattened by four decades of communism. In such a situation of low endogeneity, we can place more trust in conclusions that are based on changes in the party system following the introduction of new regulations.

In summary, rigorous studies of the effects of party regulation will need to be aware of the sources of endogeneity identified here, such as the interest of non-ethnic parties in marginalizing ethnic parties. Convincing analyses will also need to design their research so as to use strategies for dealing with endogeneity such as controlling for the circumstances in which regulations were chosen.

Conclusions

The contemporary wave of party regulation is understandable in terms of the standard model of parties and democracy. This model is more of a guideline to future research than a predictive model. Nonetheless, it does have three sets of policy implications. Firstly, there are some relatively definite conclusions from the literature that apply to party regulation. The most important of these is the link between social structure and party institutionalization. Party institutionalization is extremely rare where it cannot anchor itself in the social structure or has had an opportunity to do so in the past. The current wave of party regulations is breaking over societies where the only potential social anchor is usually ethnicity. Thus, policy makers should be aware that they might not be able to achieve institutionalized non-ethnic parties. At best, they might be able to choose between encouraging institutionalization or promoting de-ethnicization.

Secondly, absences of data and theory explain the model's lack of predictive power. Where the model lacks data to make predictions, policy makers will be undertaking reforms without the relevant information. The "iron law of unintended consequences" is a function of uncertainty. In other words, the more information policy makers have, the less likely they are to suffer unintended consequences. One crucial example is party regulations that intend aggregation but do not measure the distance between ethnic groups.

In terms of theory, we need a better theory of how and why party regulations are chosen. If we cannot control for institutional choice, we will suffer from endogeneity problems. No reliable evaluation of existing party regulations and therefore no empirically based policy recommendations are possible without confronting the issue of endogeneity.

Thirdly, since the model situates party regulations in the massive literature on institutions, there is an opportunity to draw on both the theory and the experience of institutional design outside the specialized field of party regulation. This might enable academics to act "more like engineers than supermarket customers".[31] In particular, the literature on independent regulatory agencies and legislative oversight might offer some innovative, but theory- and evidence-based, solutions for the neglected issue of monitoring and enforcement. Overall, in the evaluation of party regulation, as in political engineering in general, genuine practicality requires rigorous theory and careful empirical testing.

Notes

1. Josep Colomer (ed.), *Handbook of Electoral System Choice* (Basingstoke: Palgrave Macmillan, 2004); Robert Elgie, "From Linz to Tsebelis: Three Waves of Presidential/ Parliamentary Studies?", *Democratization*, 12, 2005: 106–122; Michael Gallagher and Paul Mitchell (eds), *The Politics of Electoral Systems* (Oxford: Oxford University Press, 2005); Donald Horowitz, "Electoral Systems: A Primer for Decision-Makers", *Journal of Democracy*, 14, 2003: 115–127; Andrew Reynolds, Ben Reilly, and Andrew Ellis, *Electoral System Design: The New International IDEA Handbook* (Stockholm: International Institute for Democracy and Electoral Assistance, 2005); Giovanni Sartori, *Comparative Constitutional Engineering: An Inquiry into Structures, Incentives and Outcomes*, 2nd edn (Basingstoke: Macmillan, 1997).
2. Chapter 1 by Reilly in this volume.
3. Matthew Soberg Shugart, "Comparative Electoral Systems Research", in Michael Gallagher and Paul Mitchell (eds), *The Politics of Electoral Systems* (Oxford: Oxford University Press, 2005), pp. 25–55.
4. Chapter 2 by van Biezen in this volume.
5. Donald Horowitz, *Ethnic Groups in Conflict* (Berkeley: University of California Press, 1985), p. 291.
6. Ibid, p. 293.

7. Vicky Randall and Lars Svåsand, "Party Institutionalization in New Democracies", *Party Politics*, 8, 2002: 6–29; Vicky Randall, "Party Institutionalization and its Implications for Democracy", paper presented to the Congress of the International Political Science Association, Fukuoka, 9–13 July 2006, unpublished.

8. Samuel P. Huntington, *Political Order in Changing Societies* (New Haven, CT: Yale University Press, 1968); Kenneth Janda, *Political Parties: A Cross-National Survey* (London: Macmillan, 1980); Angelo Panebianco, *Political Parties: Organization and Power* (Cambridge: Cambridge University Press, 1988).

9. Scott Mainwaring and Timothy R. Scully (eds), *Building Democratic Institutions: Party Systems in Latin America* (Stanford, CA: Stanford University Press, 1995).

10. Richard S. Katz and Peter Mair, "Changing Models of Party Organization and Democracy: The Emergence of the Cartel Party", *Party Politics*, 1, 1995: 5–28.

11. Arend Lijphart, "Constitutional Design for Divided Societies", *Journal of Democracy*, 15, 2004: 96–109; Benjamin Reilly, *Democracy in Divided Societies: Electoral Engineering for Conflict Management* (Cambridge: Cambridge University Press, 2001).

12. The relative position of leaders, members and voters also influences in what sense internal democracy is democratic. Therefore, this chapter makes no claim or assumption that internal democracy is unproblematically democratic.

13. Sartori, *Comparative Constitutional Engineering*, p. ix.

14. Morris P. Fiorina, "Legislative Choice of Regulatory Forms: Legal Process or Administrative Process", *Public Choice*, 39, 1982: 33–66, at p. 36.

15. Graeme Orr, "Political Disclosure Regulation in Australia: Lackadaisical Law", *Election Law Journal*, 6(1), 2007: 72–88.

16. International IDEA, "Political Finance Database", at ⟨http://www.idea.int/parties/finance/db/⟩ (accessed 7 April 2008).

17. Robert Elgie and Iain McMenamin, "Credible Commitment, Political Uncertainty, or Policy Complexity? Explaining the Discretion Granted to Independent Administrative Authorities in France", *British Journal of Political Science*, 35, 2005: 531–548; Fabrizio Gilardi, "Policy Credibility and Delegation to Independent Regulatory Agencies: A Comparative Empirical Analysis", *Journal of European Public Policy*, 9, 2002: 873–893; Mark Thatcher, "Delegation to Independent Regulatory Agencies: Pressures, Functions and Contextual Mediation", *West European Politics*, 25, 2002: 125–147.

18. Alex S. Cukierman, *Central Bank Strategy, Credibility and Independence: Theory and Evidence* (Cambridge, MA: Massachusetts Institute of Technology Press, 1992).

19. Matthew D. McCubbins and Thomas Schwartz, "Congressional Oversight Overlooked: Police Patrols versus Fire Alarms", *American Journal of Political Science*, 28, 1984: 165–179, at p. 166.

20. Chapter 6 by Catón and Tuesta Soldevilla in this volume.

21. Of course, important differences remain, but the two systems now fall into the same category of the Bogaards typology.

22. Randall, "Party Institutionalization and Its Implications for Democracy".

23. Alan Ware, *Political Parties and Party Systems* (Oxford: Oxford University Press, 1996), pp. 200–201.

24. Chapter 6 by Catón and Tuesta Soldevilla in this volume.

25. Daniel Posner, "Measuring Ethnic Fractionalization in Africa", *American Journal of Political Science*, 48(4), 2004: 849–863; Benjamin Reilly, "Democracy, Ethnic Fragmentation, and Internal Conflict", *International Security*, 25(3), 2000: 162–185.

26. Horowitz, *Ethnic Groups in Conflict*, p. 359; Giovanni Sartori, *Parties and Party Systems* (Cambridge: Cambridge University Press, 1975), p. 126. Sartori's usage of "segmentation" seems close to the concept of social distance.

27. Benedict Anderson, *Imagined Communities: Reflections on the Origin and Spread of Nationalism*, revised edn (London: Verso, 1991).
28. Gary King, Robert Keohane and Sidney Verba, *Designing Social Inquiry: Scientific Inference in Qualitative Research* (Princeton, NJ: Princeton University Press, 1996), pp. 185–196.
29. Kenneth Benoit, "Models of Electoral System Change", *Electoral Studies*, 23, 2004: 363–389; Josep Colomer, "The Strategy and History of Electoral System Choice", in Josep Colomer (ed.), *Handbook of Electoral System Choice* (Basingstoke: Palgrave Macmillan, 2004), pp. 3–81; Josep Colomer, "It's Parties That Choose the Electoral Systems (or Duverger's Law Upside-Down)", *Political Studies*, 53, 2005: 1–21.
30. Chapter 12 by Kumar and de Zeeuw in this volume.
31. Michael Dummett, "Tailoring Democracy", *Transition*, 53, 1991: 143–146.

11

Party regulation in conflict-prone societies: More dangers than opportunities?

Vicky Randall

Introduction

The central concern of this book is the use of nationally prescribed rules or regulations to influence the character and behaviour of political parties in conflict-prone societies. The implication is either that unregulated parties could be helping to generate conflict, or at least that party regulation could be one way of reducing the risk of conflict. In this case, there is a risk involved in not introducing regulations.

At the same time it is acknowledged, for instance in Reilly's Introduction (Chapter 1), that the (attempted) regulation of parties could have other additional consequences to those apparently intended. Drawing in part on some of the preceding chapters and the cases they discuss, this chapter then asks: "In what circumstances could the regulation of parties help to diminish the likelihood of conflict and at what acceptable or unacceptable level of cost?"

When broaching a topic so far relatively unexplored and in which there is such a variety of relevant cases, the first precept has to be the need to avoid overgeneralization. Even so, this chapter is intended to strike a relatively sceptical note. It argues that party regulation is often unsuccessful in its ostensible aims, and specifically in terms of reducing the likelihood of conflict. Moreover, there appears to be a kind of paradox whereby the situations in which the case for such intervention is most urgent and morally compelling are also those where such intervention is least likely to be possible. In addition, party regulation can often have undesirable

Political parties in conflict-prone societies: Regulation, engineering and democratic development, Reilly and Nordlund (eds),
United Nations University Press, 2008, ISBN 978-92-808-1157-5

unintended, but also covertly intended, consequences – for instance for party institutionalization and for democracy more broadly. Consequently this chapter suggests that, although some minimal level of party regulation is probably advisable, ideally a "light touch" is preferable to more heavy-handed forms of intervention.

I shall begin by looking directly at the circumstances in which the use of regulations is likely to be "successful", both in the sense of being successfully implemented and in the more ambitious sense of actually helping to diminish conflict. After this I shall consider further how far or when this kind of regulation is actually necessary. Then I shall turn to the possible additional consequences – some intended, some unintended – of successfully implemented regulation. Finally, I will consider its implications more specifically for other aspects of party development – especially party institutionalization – and its broader contribution to democratic development.

Successful party regulation in conflict-prone societies

As earlier chapters have described, there has been growing interest in the possibility of using national regulations to influence the development of parties and party systems. In terms of academic enquiry, this can be seen as a logical extension of the application of currently fashionable (neo-)institutionalist perspectives to questions of state- and democracy-building, or "crafting". But it is simultaneously a response to a real observed trend in developing and post-communist countries. We now have a growing number of cases to reflect upon, although in many of these insufficient time has elapsed for us to have great confidence in our judgements. We also face the perennial problem of difficulties in disentangling the effects of regulations from those of other institutional elements such as electoral systems and from broader contextual influences.

The concept of a "conflict-prone" society has been discussed elsewhere in this book. It is obviously open to a range of constructions. Most societies are somewhat prone to conflict, and indeed for many political scientists that is what politics are about – without conflict there would be no need for politics. For present purposes, the assumption should be that we are talking about countries where conflict has meant or could threaten something serious: civil war, state collapse or serious threats to human security. In addition, the underlying tension may very often be related to polarized ethnic identities; and, although there is a tendency in some of the discussions in this book largely to focus on ethnically divided societies, there could be other kinds of cleavage, for instance ideological or regional, instead of or in addition to ethnicity (I return to these questions below).

The focus of this book relates to post-conflict democracies. This is clearly not the place to discuss the meaning of democracy in general. In the present context, however, it seems most realistic to include those countries in which democratizing measures, including the holding of multi-party elections, have been formally adopted although substantial progress may still be limited. This still pre-empts the question of whether democracy or these aspects of it are always appropriate for conflict-prone societies. In the "failed state" literature there is some disagreement on this matter. Marina Ottaway, for instance, citing the examples of Sudan in the mid-1980s and Angola in 1993, has argued that, although democratization is desirable in the long run, in the short run it may be extremely difficult to achieve voluntarily as well as being seriously disruptive.[1] On the other hand, there is the danger that, if democracy is organized out at an early stage, it will be much more difficult for it to develop later.

What at this point can we say about the application and "success" of party regulation in these contexts? First, of course, amongst such conflict-prone democracies there are societies where the likelihood and feasibility of these party regulations being introduced, let alone being implemented or achieving the desired effect, are extremely slim. Janda makes the important distinction between regulation of already established parties or party systems and the engineering of, in effect, new party systems.[2] In the former case, we may be talking about societies in which political parties, in the guise of militias or guerrilla movements, have been central to the conflict itself. As noted by Sisk, for instance, it would have been extremely difficult in the wake of civil war in either Cyprus or Lebanon to impose party regulations that seriously modified the existing party system in a way that encouraged party formation across existing cleavages and challenged the dominant party or parties' hold on power.[3]

To take another example, in Cambodia the Vietnamese-backed government that had ousted Pol Pot formed the Cambodian People's Party (CPP), under the leadership of Hun Sen, prior to the UN-sponsored elections of 1993. Although actually defeated electorally by FUNCINPEC, the party originally founded by Prince Sihanouk, CPP power was so entrenched that in effect it had to be allowed to continue to dominate. That pattern has continued. Even following the 2003 elections, McCargo commented: "It has such a tight grip that elections have become little more than a sideshow, helping to bolster the electoral-authoritarian regime that Hun Sen has built."[4]

Côte d'Ivoire is another country where an earlier intervention to prevent the formation of ethnically based political parties might have helped to prevent terrible conflict and suffering. Under Houphouët-Boigny, the ruling PDCI (Democratic Party of Côte d'Ivoire) was a multi-ethnic patronage party. Pressure from France led to the holding of multi-party elections in 1990, and in 1995, in the presidential contest following Houphouët-Boigny's death, his successor, Bédié, resorted to ethnic appeals, specifically promoting a concept of "Ivoirité", which excluded many northerners, including his main rival Ouattara. Because parties opposed to the PDCI boycotted this election, Bédié won with 96 per cent of the vote. According to Chiriot,[5] from this point ethnic polarization rapidly increased and any possibility of resolving these differences receded.

Second, however, in a number of conflict-prone societies, a range of relevant party regulations *have* been adopted or mooted – including outright bans, party registration requirements ruling out some criteria and insisting on others, such as thresholds in terms of votes or seats for parties to be allowed a legislative presence, and prohibitions on legislators switching parties. What can we say about their success? The initial question here is whether they have actually been implemented. There are cases where in practice regulations appear to have had little effect. This has sometimes been found where national regulations have prohibited the registration of parties based on ethnic identities. In Africa, such prohibitions have been introduced in a succession of countries, including Cameroon, Tanzania, Ghana and Nigeria. But, as Sithole has pointed out, it is not always necessary for party politicians explicitly to campaign on ethnic lines in order for ethnically identified voters to understand their ethnic allegiances and to vote on this basis.[6] Similarly Bieber, in Chapter 5 in this volume, suggests that an ethnic ban has had little effect in Albania or Bulgaria. Again, party registration requirements designed to ensure a "national" character have not always been seriously enforced. Catón and Tuesta Soldevilla in Chapter 6 in this volume describe the case of Peru's 2003 Political Party Law where the electoral authority failed to check parties' organizational claims.

Rules to prohibit party-hopping may also in some contexts be quite ineffectual. The Philippines is not a failing state but has been described as "flailing", and one of its major political handicaps is widely recognized to be its fragmentary, weakly institutionalized party system. When a new measure was being considered to ban party-hopping, which in the Philippine context is known as "turncoatism", Rogers was extremely doubtful that this would have the desired effect:

[I]n an environment where parties splinter with every political disagreement, where candidates routinely create parties of convenience, and where national leaders campaign as heads of ephemeral multiparty coalitions, a law against switching parties would have little impact. It would not, for instance, prevent whole parties switching from losing coalitions to winning ones.[7]

Incidentally, success in implementation in this limited sense may partly depend on the way in which the regulations were arrived at. As Per Nordlund remarks in Chapter 13 in this volume, the process of regulation may in some ways be as important as the content. Intuitively we would expect that regulations adopted as the result of a lengthy and inclusive process of consultation with key interested actors, including political parties themselves, would be more likely to be perceived as legitimate and to elicit voluntary compliance. (This would, however, suggest that conflict had already sufficiently diminished to make such a process of agreement possible.) By contrast, regulations adopted with minimal consultation – whether largely imposed and reflecting the interests of a nationally dominant group, simply unreflectively "borrowed" or imitated from practices elsewhere,[8] or, finally, externally imposed as in the cases of Iraq and Afghanistan – would enjoy less legitimacy. Depending on the government's ability to enforce the regulations, there would be either lack of compliance or more covert forms of resistance.

Thirdly, there are nonetheless, as recounted in several of this book's chapters, many instances of conflict-prone societies where party regulations, designed through their effects on parties and the party system to reduce or avert conflict or consolidate a recently achieved peace, have been both adopted and implemented. The further question remains whether in these cases, in addition to being successfully enforced, regulations have actually had the desired effect on the party system and lowered the overall risk of conflict. Indonesia is seen as a successful example of party regulation, where a combination of rules requiring parties to demonstrate their national character and of seat thresholds has greatly reduced the number of effective parties and enhanced their geographically aggregative capacity. Reilly, for instance, comments that "the Indonesian laws appear to have been relatively successful in their over-riding aim of preventing separatist parties", even if there continues to be a high degree of party fragmentation within the assembly.[9] In Papua New Guinea (see Chapter 8 by Okole in this book), party regulations that ban party-hopping and seek to prevent simultaneous membership of more than one party appear to have achieved some success in reducing the number of parties and enabling one party to form the government.

In these limited terms, Turkey in more recent times might also be regarded as a success story. Successive constitutions have insisted on the secularism of the state, and the 1983 Political Parties Law stipulates that parties cannot be based on class, religion, race or language. In 1998, the electorally successful Welfare Party (RP), which was widely perceived as an Islamic party, was closed down by the Constitutional Court for becoming a "focal point of antisecularist activities".[10] Consequently the party reformed, changing its name to the Virtue Party (FP) and winning over 100 seats in the 1999 general election, but it was again closed down by the Constitutional Court, in 2001. This brought to a head a developing split between a conservative wing under the leader of the FP and a more moderate wing led by Recep Erdogan. The moderate wing formed the Justice and Development Party (AKP), which went on to win 32 per cent of the vote in the 2002 general election and to form the government, whereas the conservative Saadet (Contentment) Party won only 2.5 per cent. Although assessments are divided, many perceive the AKP to be very different from its Islamic predecessors; according to Özbudun, "[t]he AKP represents the transformation of political Islam in to a moderate conservative democratic party, reconciled to the secular principles of the constitution".[11] Although the pressure of external regulations is by no means the only contributing factor – the other main consideration being the need to expand the party's electoral base – there seems little doubt that such pressures help to account for the formation of the AKP. Again to cite Özbudun, "[a]s a result of the closure of the RP and FP, a group of former Islamist politicians seems to have reached the conclusion that challenging the secular state in Turkey is a dead-end".

Nigeria, arguably, provides a vividly contrasting case to these relative successes. Beginning in 1979, rules, subsequently modified, for the formation of parties included the requirement that parties have a national headquarters in the capital, Abuja, and branches in at least two-thirds of the states. Ibrahim, investigating the four main parties under President Obasanjo, found that they were all essentially ethnic federations.[12] However, although possibly reducing inter-party conflict, this had the effect of shifting ethnic conflict to inside these parties, which all experienced paralysing factional disputes, including court cases.[13] In this context it is worth noting that even in Papua New Guinea one consequence of reducing the number of political parties appears to have been an increased tendency to party splits (see Chapter 8 by Okole). This prompts the question: is conflict within parties necessarily preferable to conflict, or competition, between parties?

In a different way, Thailand also provides an example of party regulation designed to encourage more aggregative parties ultimately contributing to increased conflict. As described in Chapter 4 by Hicken in this volume, the 1997 Thai constitution introduced measures, including new restrictions on party-switching, vote share thresholds for representation in parliament and requirements for membership levels and geographical distribution, designed to encourage the emergence of mass bureaucratic parties. Eligibility for state funding was also for a time partially linked to membership levels and the number of party branches.[14] Besides making life more difficult for smaller parties, these measures assisted the rise of "media mogul" Thaksin Shinawatra's Thai Rak Thai party, which indirectly led in turn to the military coup of September 2006.

Overall, then, this section has argued, first, that there are situations in which party systems are themselves both so entrenched and so implicated in divisive conflicts that party regulation to restructure them is pretty much a non-starter. In some other cases, party regulations may be adopted for a range of reasons but with little likelihood of their effective implementation. There remain, however, a growing number of cases where such regulations have been successfully implemented, in that they have helped to achieve a desired change in the character of parties, although again this has not necessarily or always had the broader desired effect of reducing the threat of conflict.

Is party regulation necessary?

In the second part of this discussion I want to ask whether this kind of party regulation really is needed. Of course, as Reilly points out, it is not necessarily the case that such regulation is imposed on post-conflict democracies. On the contrary, developing countries have themselves been "at the forefront of this movement" and its "most influential innovators".[15] But, even then, the motives of the party regulators or engineers may themselves be self-interested or at least complex and it is still worth raising this question.

First, it is perhaps relevant to distinguish between degrees of party regulation. For instance, it is a good idea to have some basic party registration requirements. It may be a good idea to have some minimal thresholds set for parties to gain parliamentary seats. Measures to curb excessive party-hopping seem generally advisable. What should really be the focus of discussion are more demanding party regulations, such as registration requirements, including various kinds of proscription, and higher thresholds. Measures to restrict party-hopping might seem the least problematic but, apart from doubts about their effectiveness in many contexts. they can also be used, as Chapter 9 by Kadima demonstrates in the case of South Africa, to strengthen the position of already dominant parties. "Light touch" regulations are not really at issue then, but more severe restrictions and requirements should be regarded with some suspicion.

Clearly, in focusing on party regulation in conflict-prone societies we are considering a range of possible situations. However, two kinds of situation in particular seem to feature most frequently in the present project. The first is where parties are aligned with ethnic cleavages; the second is where the party system is highly fragmented and centrifugal, with parties formed on a number of bases – not simply ethnicity, but also ideology, religion, regionalism or a charismatic and/or wealthy leader.

Ethnicity is, of course, a complex and varying phenomenon. Only some ethnic identities are politicized, and the consequences for political peace and stability of such politicization depend in part on what Scarritt refers to as the "morphology" of ethnicity,[16] that is, the underlying distribution – the numbers and proportions of ethnic groupings. Individual ethnically based parties, especially where they represent a minority group, are not necessarily a major problem and may even be desirable. As Birnir has shown, bans on ethnically based parties at an earlier stage in Latin America helped to silence the voice of the (highly disadvantaged) Amerindians.[17] Beyond this, Chandra, in particular, has advanced a broader defence of ethnically based parties.[18] With clear reference to India, she argues that, in the longer run at least, ethnically based parties need not be fatally disruptive. Part of Chandra's argument is that in general, but especially perhaps in India, people have multiple and cross-cutting identities and that more than one competing form of ethnicity has come to be institutionalized in the policy process. What is less acknowledged is that, in India, caste is often included as a form of ethnicity (going back to the point about the ambiguous content of the notion of ethnicity). Although there have been fierce caste wars and struggles between caste blocs over affirmative action, traditionally and more fundamentally caste has tended to function as a "horizontal" and stratifying, rather than vertical and divisive, basis of identity.

Chandra may thus underestimate the problems that ethnically based parties can pose. Still, the real danger in terms of conflict and instability mainly arises in bipolar or deeply divided societies, as opposed for instance to either homogeneous or multi-ethnic societies. But although this may be a situation in which regulations supplying new incentives to create parties transcending these cleavages would be most warranted, as in the case of Côte d'Ivoire in 1995, here we face the paradox that it is also one in which such regulations are least likely either to be mooted or to be seriously implemented. Parties that embody and may have violently promoted the conflict need to agree on or to such regulations, which is most unlikely. And, in post-conflict societies, external agencies' first priority may well precisely be to encourage former armed adversaries to convert into political parties.

We should in addition note the alternative "consociational" argument, associated in particular with Arend Lijphart.[19] This suggests that, if there are real polarizing conflicts in society, it may perhaps be better that they should be embodied in the party system, so that the party elites, to a degree able to speak for their respective communities, can come together and negotiate some formula for power-sharing. This is more likely to work if there is some degree of "balance" between rival groups. As already noted, where one group and party is overwhelmingly dominant, as in Cambodia or Côte d'Ivoire, there is little incentive to compromise. But where, for instance, rival army-parties have virtually fought themselves to a standstill, as in Mozambique or El Salvador, the best and politically the only acceptable way forward often seems to be for these forces to formalize as political parties.

The consociationalist position for a time went somewhat out of fashion, though it may currently be undergoing partial rehabilitation. One case used to discredit it is that of Lebanon, which operated on a consociational basis for several decades following independence in 1943. The argument has been that this system, in which different confessional communities shared power, failed to evolve, but this may not be entirely fair. According to el Khazen,[20] between 1970 and 1975 the Lebanese party system was developing: the number of parties and the range of issues and identities on which they were based were growing and closer links were emerging between parties and social agencies such as trade unions and student bodies. What thwarted these promising trends[21] was the growing presence of the Palestine Liberation Organization (PLO), from the beginning of the 1970s, in southern Lebanon. "The PLO's armed presence divided Lebanese parties and public into two camps: one opposed to the PLO's armed presence and to PLO-Israeli warfare in south Lebanon, the other giving it unconditional support."[22]

The consociationalist perspective has to some extent resurfaced in criticisms of decisions taken in regard to party formation in Afghanistan.[23] Political parties existed in Afghanistan from the 1940s, though often clandestinely. During the civil war in the 1980s many of the parties "functioned for all practical purposes as armed factions rather than parties".[24] Partly for this reason they have been regarded with extreme suspicion. Although the 2003 constitution, adopted under international occupation, legalizes parties, the Political Parties Law prohibits legalization of parties whose charters are "opposed to the principles of the holy religion Islam" or that incite violence on ethnic, religious, racial or sectarian grounds. The International Crisis Group is concerned that this vague wording is open to abuse. It fears that "restrictions on the legalisation of ethnic, sectarian and language-based parties would run contrary to the country's political realities. Indeed, most political parties, regardless of their formal manifestos and platforms, derive popular support along those lines. Narrowing legal channels within which to articulate ethnic, sectarian or regional priorities and grievances could promote sub-state tensions and discord."[25]

Making a similar point, Abramowitz, discussing party law in Iraq, warned that "an outright ban on religious parties may have the effect of adding to the groups' lustre as well as decreasing the legitimacy of the burgeoning democracy".[26] In the event, the list of requirements for party registration issued in 2004 prohibited links with militias or terrorist activity but otherwise did accept an ethnic or religious base for party formation.[27]

So, even in relation to societies polarized around ethnic divisions, the case for forms of party regulation that encourage cross-cutting aggregative parties is not always, or even often, compelling. In the other kind of situation, in which societies are extremely fragmented on a number of different fault-lines, we need first to consider the sense in which they are "conflict prone". What is the real danger posed by this situation? Is it devastating civil conflict or is it rather the risk of secessionism, as in Indonesia; or unstable, coalition-based government; or the inability of parties to provide an effective counterweight or check to executive power; or the risk that ineffectual parties will damage faith in democratic government and pave the way for military intervention? These are less drastic or definite kinds of danger than where a country faces the real possibility of again descending into civil war, and accordingly the justification for using party regulations in this "engineering" fashion may be weaker.

In some cases it could indeed be that creating large accommodating parties is not the answer. Sometimes – although this may go against the international community grain – secession may be a better option. Rather than trying artificially to construct large aggregative parties, it might be more productive to develop some form of federalism. India is the obvious example here, where federalism provides a framework within which local/regional or particularistic parties coexist and articulate with national parties and decision processes in a generally peaceful if sometimes cumbersome way.

One further aspect of this question about the necessity or otherwise of party regulation should be raised here, although no simple conclusion can be drawn. This is about timing: is it better to introduce regulations early on in the life of a party system or at a later stage of its evolution? Janda has persuasively argued that there is a real danger in imposing too many regulations early on and making life difficult for new parties.[28] As he points out, creating a party, especially in the context of emerging developing democracies, is "a risky business" both politically and in terms of economic resources. Assuming that we believe multi-party politics to be appropriate for a particular conflict-prone society, then parties have to be given some chance to form. On the other hand, the view could be expressed that it is important to create the right framework of rules at the outset in order to build a stable, centripetal party system;[29] otherwise, path-dependence theory suggests that the wrong kind of institutional momentum could be generated. The longer change is left, the higher become the transaction costs entailed and the more firmly entrenched the interests of those benefiting from the status quo. Again these arguments may be seen to relate primarily to somewhat different situations. Inchoate parties are more likely to be a feature of relatively new and fragmentary party systems, which I have suggested in any case are less of a problem. The path-dependence argument has most salience for party systems reflecting bipolar or deeply divided societies, but these are likely to have been extremely resistant to the introduction of centripetal kinds of party regulation earlier on.

This section has considered further the question of whether, or in what circumstances, party regulations to encourage centripetalism are really necessary. Taking first the case of party systems aligned with ethnic cleavages, it has suggested that, in many cases, ethnically based parties need not be viewed as a serious threat to peace and stability. They are most problematic in the context of bipolar or deeply divided societies. However, in this situation, parties reflecting such cleavages are least likely to agree to party regulations aimed at restructuring the party system. Moreover, in post-conflict situations, the priority may be precisely to induce armed forces to become political parties. Nor should the "consociational" argument – that the leaderships of parties based on contending communities offer the best chance of arriving at some kind of binding settlement – be dismissed too lightly. When it comes to party regulations in the context of fragmentary party systems, the case is still less compelling. The danger posed is less and there may be preferable alternative approaches. Finally, arguments that regulations are needed at a particular stage of party system development do not seem too convincing when the points raised earlier in this section are taken into account.

Unintended – and not so unintended – consequences

So far, I have considered the likelihood of party regulation or engineering succeeding in its immediate aims or in terms of reducing the likelihood of conflict, and whether such regulation is in fact necessary. But it is also relevant to consider the additional "unintended" consequences of party regulation, some of which may in fact be covertly intended.

Party regulation is one aspect of the broader enterprise of institutional design or engineering that currently is a subject of great academic and practical interest. However, as Bastian and Luckham have pointed out, the whole idea of designing political institutions is a kind of oxymoron –

institutions by definition grow.[30] True, the growth of institutions must inevitably involve decisions and choices. Going back to Janda's distinction,
one could say that, where one is dealing with already existing institutions
(such as parties), there might be grounds for intervention to correct for
earlier design faults. And, still more compellingly, where one is dealing
with a relatively blank sheet (where, for instance, political parties in
founding democratic elections need to be assembled or reassembled rapidly and almost from scratch), more deliberate reflection on and selection
of basic ground rules is unsurprising. At the same time, however, Bastian
and Luckham rightly warn against the unintended consequences of institutional design choices. In fact, they hold out the frightening prospect of
"an iron law of the perverse consequences of institutional design".[31]

This warning is particularly relevant in cases of external intervention in
a country's political institutions. The history of colonial intervention, the
self-interested intervention of the Cold War powers and most recently
the traumas of "regime change" in Afghanistan and especially Iraq have
all raised serious questions concerning not simply the legitimacy but the
appropriateness and effectiveness of such external interference. Such
questions have bedevilled the growing industry of external democracy assistance and more specifically of "party aid".[32] They are also relevant
to party regulation; for instance, unintended consequences may be compounded if national party regulators are overly influenced by Western
political science dogma or simply follow fashions in institutional design.
Again, party regulation could reflect the requirements of donor agencies
or occupying authorities, which might similarly have been based on a
misunderstanding of local political dynamics and the inappropriate transfer of outdated Western models. One of the recurrent features of this
kind of external intervention is a tendency to look for ready-made formulas that can be applied to a number of cases, rather than to recognize the
problems of this "one size fits all" approach and the need to devise policies closely tailored to each country's specific circumstances.

Even where party regulation is driven by purely domestic agendas, it
may in the longer run generate consequences other than those intended.
It is ironic, for instance, that the effective ban on left-wing, union-based
parties from the 1960s in Turkey may have contributed to the rise of
more ethnically or religiously based parties. According to Türsan, "with
the forced organising out of the class cleavage, the religious and ethnic
cleavages acquired salience, polarising politics between Kurds and Turks
and the secular and pan-Islamic population".[33]

There are also times, however, when it is more accurate to talk about
"unanticipated" consequences, meaning consequences not anticipated by
some of the sets of actors concerned but intended by others. That is to
say, institutional choices, including those concerning political parties, in

practice very often reflect the interests and political agenda of the dominant group. Even where the "regulators" adopt suggestions from the growing pool of international "experts", they may do so selectively. It is increasingly accepted that the choice of electoral system may reflect the perceived interests of key players.[34] But this can also be true of party regulations.

Most obviously this has been the case under authoritarian rule, such as in Indonesia under Suharto, in Nigeria under Babangida (1985–1993), who allowed only two parties to exist, or in Turkey, where, following the military coup of 1980, only three parties were allowed to form. Janda gives the example of Jordan, whose 1992 party law was, he argues, seeking to engineer a party system, where none existed, that would be favourable and acceptable to the regime.[35] In Zaire (later renamed Democratic Republic of Congo) in 1990, Mobutu, responding to external pressure to liberalize, allowed political parties but decreed there could be only three. He argued this was to avoid the dangers of the party system becoming the embodiment of multi-tribalism, but was clearly not believed, one paradoxical outcome being that later that same year an excessively liberal party regulation regime was introduced, leading to the registration, by 1997, of 440 parties.[36]

Even in more bona fide democratizing contexts, dominant parties may still be expected to further their own interests and make life difficult for minority parties through such devices as requiring parties to demonstrate a national character, imposing seat thresholds and even proscribing "party-hopping". This was clearly the case initially in a number of East European countries, though the prospect of joining the European Union was one influence tending to reduce this tendency. But it is also a criticism levelled at party regulations introduced in Indonesia. Thus Ufen maintains that "[t]he big political parties have designed the election and party laws to their advantage. They have banned individual or non-party candidatures and made it difficult for smaller parties to contest with their candidates. Regional parties are not admitted, with Aceh being the only exception."[37] As noted, Kadima suggests in Chapter 9 in this volume that the way party-hopping rules have been framed in South Africa advantaged the already dominant African National Congress.

To summarize this section, the enterprise of institutional design is in some ways a contradiction in terms, although there are situations in which it is unavoidable. Even then, one needs to be aware of the likelihood of unintended consequences, especially where Western-derived models of party regulation have been adopted with insufficient reflection on their appropriateness to the context in hand. Such unintended consequences can also result from more domestically framed party regulations, but here there is the additional danger of covert intended consequences reflecting the interest of dominant groups or major parties.

Consequences for party development

Party regulations, and their intended and unintended consequences, may in addition have specific implications for the development of parties individually and of party systems, and for their potential contribution to other desirable political goals (in addition, that is, to peace and stability). In particular, given that we are talking about conflict-prone "democracies", we may be concerned with the implications for the contribution of party regulations to democracy.

When discussing what kinds of parties and party systems are most conducive to democracy or democratization, there has been considerable agreement that a key criterion is the level of institutionalization, though less agreement or clarity about what this means. Mainwaring and Scully's criteria for party system institutionalization have been considered particularly helpful and quite widely applied.[38] And, clearly, party system institutionalization is closely associated with party institutionalization (two out of four of Mainwaring and Scully's criteria are really about the individual parties rather than the "system"), although one can also conceive of situations in which the (over-)institutionalization of a party may actually be harmful to party system institutionalization as a whole.

There is less clarity about (single) party institutionalization, but in broad terms it is referring to the process through which parties as organizations acquire a degree of both independent internal life and social recognition and embeddedness. Randall and Svåsand attempt to elaborate this concept systematically.[39] A more recent paper by Randall, which slightly modifies this earlier account, identifies a number of dimensions, some of which are internal and others external or outwards facing.[40] The first internal aspects are organizational, including scope (territorial and social reach), internal integration and rule-boundedness, and resources, notably membership and funds. Second are aspects to do with loyalty to the party or its value system, which can be a vital source of cohesion. External aspects include, first, the extent to which the party has "decisional autonomy", vis-à-vis for instance social movement organizations or the government. Second, they have to do with the extent of public recognition but also with social rootedness and support.

Again, the factors that contribute to or impede institutionalization are many and complex. Party origins and the circumstances in which parties emerge and develop will have an obvious bearing. But one thing is clear

– parties require time and a degree of independence if they are to develop into autonomous institutions. Heavy-handed regulation, especially early in party development but to some extent at any stage, could be counterproductive.

Although there are always limits to generalization, it is widely observed that, in practice, political parties in developing democracies tend to be weakly institutionalized, for a string of reasons. The kinds of party regulation considered in this book could have the effect of further weakening them. Thus, by putting pressure on existing smaller parties to combine in order to demonstrate "national" characteristics or to achieve legislative seat "thresholds", regulations could be helping to create parties that are in effect contingent alliances and highly factionalized. This would have implications for the different dimensions of party institutionalization that have been outlined above. So, for instance, such parties would tend to lack effective integrative internal procedures. They would also lack a tradition or symbolic status able to command their followers' transcending loyalty. Compliance with centripetal party regulations would further tend to weaken existing links with social constituencies or associations – that is, to diminish the party's "social rootedness". For instance, Ufen notes the weakening of links in Indonesia between the main political parties and the traditional "streams" (*aliran*) or movements in which political parties used to be embedded;[41] new party regulations may well have contributed to this trend, although a number of other factors are also at play. In Chapter 4 in this volume, Hicken also suggests a trade-off between centripetal party engineering and party rootedness, citing the case of Indonesia.

Ibrahim notes one related aspect of party regulation in Nigeria that may have wider application.[42] He suggests that to construct a party sufficiently national in character to satisfy the rules requires a great deal of money (not least for patronage purposes). This has tended in turn to necessitate extremely wealthy party leaders, who then treat the party in a high-handed way, almost as a personal fiefdom. To the extent that party regulations inadvertently reinforce a tendency to "personalistic" parties in this way, they again reduce the possibilities of party institutionalization: the leader will have little respect for internal party values or procedures.

Although there is widespread agreement on the centrality of political parties to democracy, the exact contribution that political parties make to democracy, and indeed to democratization, both in theory and in practice, has not been widely discussed.[43] One aspect of this contribution that must surely be vital, however, is representation. Party regulations ostensibly aimed at establishing national parties rather than particularistic ones could clearly have the effect of reducing parties' ability to perform this key democratic function. I have already noted the example of bans imposed on ethnically based parties which helped to silence the voice of Amerindians. Such bans have been used to proscribe religiously based parties, for instance in Egypt and also in Algeria, despite – or because of – the demonstrated popularity of the Islamic Salvation Front (FIS) in elections in 1990 and 1991. More generally, where party regulations designed to encourage the formation of large aggregative parties are successful (although there may be a certain amount of horse-trading between community leaders or representatives within such parties), the chances for particular, perhaps minority or disadvantaged, communities to make themselves heard must inevitably be reduced.

Political parties are also potentially agents of democratic socialization, helping to inculcate democratic attitudes and provide lessons in democratic behaviour, thereby contributing to democracy-building and consolidation. Admittedly it is extremely unusual in developing democracies (and by no means universal in established democracies) for parties to play such a role in practice. However, party regulations designed to encourage the formation of large, aggregative parties would be most unlikely to enhance such a propensity. They would, if successful, tend to reduce or limit the possibility of parties having a clear ideological character and thus of presenting electors with a meaningful choice. Given the cobbled-together character of such parties, they would tend to be elite dominated, with little scope or incentive for effective grassroots activism and participation. And the relative lack of internal party integration and cohesion would scarcely be conducive to processes of internal party democracy. In Turkey, Tepe notes that at the outset the AKP sought to differentiate itself from the standard hierarchical Turkish party model by adopting measures of internal democracy, including term limits for the highest party office holders.[44] Before long, however, many of these new rules were dropped, which effectively "handed the leader unrestrained powers". Although many factors are at play here, this must partially be owing to the weakening ties between the party leadership and its old core constituency as the party has become a broader coalition of diverse social forces, itself partly a consequence of responding to centripetal party regulations.

Conclusion

Party regulation aimed at counteracting centrifugal pressures is already going on, whether we are in favour of it or not. In addition, there are situations in which relatively new representative institutions are being put in place and there is an almost unavoidable need for a degree of "top-down" regulation, including regulations affecting the character of parties.

Needless to say, party regulations should as far as possible be agreed by the major political actors within a polity, not imposed by some external agency, and should take into account the particularities of the country and of the political conjuncture.

However, all such regulations should probably be applied with a light touch. It is often doubtful whether they can in fact be successfully implemented in terms of having the specific intended effect, let alone more broadly helping to reduce the risk of conflict. Moreover, the strongest moral or prudential arguments for imposing more demanding regulatory regimes apply to situations, notably in deeply polarized post-conflict societies, where the pattern of emerging parties threatens to prolong or revive the conflict, but in these circumstances they are likely to be least acceptable to the main contenders. And even here there may be grounds for accepting the consociationalist case that fundamental cleavages need to be embodied in parties rather than organized out if they are to be resolved. In more fragmentary newly democratizing contexts, such regulations may make life excessively difficult for new parties and by the same token tend to reflect the vested interests of established players.

In recommending or adopting party regulations, policy advisers or makers need also to bear in mind the likelihood of unintended consequences, and indeed of covert intended consequences. This must be of particular concern in relation to the prospects for democratic development. Political parties are generally seen as playing a crucial, even essential, role in such development. However, to do so they need to be relatively well institutionalized. Yet party regulations on the lines being discussed here could well work against this possibility. Similarly, they could significantly curtail parties' collective ability adequately to "represent" the voices and interests of the whole society and not just the privileged, as well as reducing the ability of parties to act as agents of democratic socialization.

In summary, it is difficult to envisage a situation in which, given the risks of associated unintended or covertly intended undesirable consequences, more radical regulatory regimes, and not just minimal requirements, could be simultaneously properly justified by the urgency of the situation and actually capable of successful adoption and implementation.

Notes

1. Marina Ottaway, "Democratization in Collapsed States", in William Zartman (ed.), *Collapsed States: The Disintegration and Restoration of Legitimate Authority* (Boulder, CO: Lynne Rienner, 1995).

2. Kenneth Janda, "Clarifying Concepts in Democracy Assistance: 'Engineering' v. 'Regulating'", unpublished paper, 2006.
3. This point was made by Timothy Sisk at the authors' meeting for this project in 2006 in The Hague.
4. Duncan McCargo, "Cambodia: Getting Away with Authoritarianism?", *Journal of Democracy*, 16(4), 2005, p. 98.
5. Daniel Chiriot, "The Debacle in Côte d'Ivoire", *Journal of Democracy*, 17(2), 2006: 63–77.
6. Masipula Sithole, "Ethnicity and Democratization in Zimbabwe: From Confrontation to Accommodation", in Harvey Glickman (ed.), *Ethnic Conflict and Democratization in Africa* (Atlanta: African Studies Association Press, 1995), pp. 121–160.
7. Steven Rogers, "Philippine Politics and the Rule of Law", *Journal of Democracy*, 15(4), 2004, p. 120.
8. At the authors' meeting in The Hague, Matthijs Bogaards pointed out that regulations were often adopted in this way, as part of a process of diffusion. He cited Francophone West Africa as an example.
9. Benjamin Reilly, "Political Engineering and Party Politics in Conflict-Prone Societies", *Democratization*, 13(5), 2006, p. 818.
10. See Hüri Türsan, *Democratisation in Turkey: The Role of Political Parties* (Brussels: PIE–Peter Lang, 2004).
11. Ergun Özbudun, "From Political Islam to Conservative Democracy: The Case of the Justice and Development Party in Turkey", *South European Society and Politics*, 11(3–4), 2006, p. 547.
12. Jibrin Ibrahim, *Nigeria – Country Report Based on Research and Dialogue with Political Parties* (Stockholm: International Institute for Democracy and Electoral Assistance, 2006).
13. The point about internal conflict was emphasized by Jibrin Ibrahim at an IDEA workshop in Stockholm in October 2005.
14. Duncan McCargo, "Thai Rak Thai: A New Form of Thai Party?", in Duncan McCargo and Ukrist Pathmanand, *The Thaksinisation of Thailand* (Copenhagen: Nordic Institute of Asian Studies, 2005).
15. Reilly, "Political Engineering and Party Politics in Conflict-Prone Societies", p. 825.
16. James R. Scarritt, "Ethnopolitics and Nationalism", in Peter Burnell and Vicky Randall (eds), *Politics in the Developing World*, 2nd edn (Oxford: Oxford University Press, 2007).
17. Johanna Kristin Birnir, "Stabilizing Party Systems and Excluding Segments of Society?: The Effects of Formation Costs on New Party Foundation in Latin America", *Studies in Comparative International Development*, 39(3), 2004: 3–27.
18. Kanchan Chandra, "Ethnic Parties and Democratic Stability", *Perspectives on Politics*, 3(2), 2005: 235–352.
19. The usual reference given is to Arend Lijphart, *Democracy in Plural Societies* (New Haven, CT: Yale University Press, 1977). Consociationalism as an approach is obviously concerned with a range of institutional arrangements, not simply the basis of political parties.
20. Farid el Khazen, "Political Parties in Postwar Lebanon: Parties in Search of Partisans", *Middle East Journal*, 57(4), 2003: 605–624.
21. This is more my conclusion than el Khazen's.
22. El Khazen, "Political Parties in Postwar Lebanon", pp. 609–610.
23. A point brought to my attention by Peter Burnell at the workshop in The Hague.
24. International Crisis Group, *Political Parties in Afghanistan*, Asia Briefing No. 39 (Kabul/Brussels: ICG, 2005).

25. Ibid., p. 4.
26. Morton Abramowitz, *Establishing a Stable Democratic Constitutional Structure in Iraq: Some Basic Considerations* (New York and Washington, DC: Century Foundation, 2003), p. 50; cited in Kenneth Janda, *Adopting Party Law* (Washington, DC: National Democratic Institute, 2005).
27. See the website of the Independent Electoral Commission of Iraq at ⟨http://www.ieciraq.org/English/Frameset_english.htm⟩ (accessed 8 April 2008).
28. Janda, *Adopting Party Law*, p. 19.
29. At the workshop in The Hague, Ivan Doherty suggested it might indeed be preferable to regulate more heavily to begin with and subsequently to relax the regulations. There was even talk of "sunset clauses", with however the fear expressed that the prospect of such a clause could itself stir up conflict.
30. Sunil Bastian and Robin Luckham, "Conclusion", in Sunil Bastian and Robin Luckham (eds), *Can Democracy Be Designed?* (London: Zed Press, 2003).
31. Ibid., p. 314.
32. Thomas Carothers, *Confronting the Weakest Link: Aiding Political Parties in New Democracies* (Washington, DC: Carnegie Endowment for International Peace, 2006).
33. Türsan, *Democratisation in Turkey*.
34. See, for instance, Kenneth Benoit, "Models of Electoral System Change", *Electoral Studies*, 23, 2004: 363–389.
35. Janda, "Clarifying Concepts in Democracy Assistance".
36. See H. Kabungulu Ngoy-Kangoy, *Parties and Political Transition in the Democratic Republic of Congo*, EISA Report No. 20 (Johannesburg: EISA, 2006).
37. Andreas Ufen, "Political Parties in Post-Suharto Indonesia: Between *politik aliran* and Philippinisation", German Institute of Global and Area Studies, December 2006, p. 19.
38. Scott Mainwaring and Timothy R Scully (eds), *Building Democratic Institutions: Party Systems in Latin America* (Palo Alto, CA: Stanford University Press, 1995).
39. Vicky Randall and Lars Svåsand, "Party Institutionalization in New Democracies", *Party Politics*, 8(1), 2002: 6–29.
40. Vicky Randall, "Party Institutionalization and Its Implications for Democracy", unpublished paper presented at the IPSA Congress, Fukuoka, 2006.
41. Ufen, "Political Parties in Post-Suharto Indonesia".
42. Ibrahim, *Nigeria – Country Report*.
43. For one initial attempt to think systematically about this, see Vicky Randall and Lars Svåsand, "Introduction: The Contribution of Parties to Democracy and Democratic Consolidation", *Democratization*, 9(3), 2002: 1–10.
44. Sultan Tepe, "Turkey's AKP: A Model 'Muslim-Democratic' Party?", *Journal of Democracy*, 16(3), 2005, p. 74.

12

International support for political party development in war-torn societies

Krishna Kumar and Jeroen de Zeeuw

Introduction

This chapter focuses on international support for political party development in a subset of conflict-prone societies, i.e. societies recovering from violent intra-state conflicts. In such "post-conflict" or war-torn countries, the established political order is seriously undermined by intensive and often prolonged violent conflicts. Examples of such situations include Angola, Bosnia, Burundi, Cambodia, East Timor, El Salvador, Guatemala, Liberia, Mozambique and Sierra Leone. Many of these societies were under authoritarian or semi-authoritarian rule during and prior to the conflict. Whatever little institutional infrastructure for democracy existed in these countries was undermined during the conflict. Personnel in state-level institutions, such as the judiciary, the legislature or the civil service, were killed and infrastructure destroyed. The few civil society and media organizations that existed were closed down or demolished. Opposition political parties that existed prior to the outbreak of conflict were usually banned or transformed into armed resistance movements.

In many of these countries, international actors were instrumental in brokering a peace agreement between the warring parties and supporting the country's post-conflict peace-building and recovery process. In the belief that, at least in the long run, a democratic political system is crucial to preventing future violent conflict, the "international community" promoted democracy in post-conflict societies.[1] In practically all recovering war-torn societies, free and fair elections were perceived as the first step

Political parties in conflict-prone societies: Regulation, engineering and democratic development, Reilly and Nordlund (eds),
United Nations University Press, 2008, ISBN 978-92-808-1157-5

towards establishing a multi-party democracy.[2] The international community generally supported post-conflict elections and provided assistance to conduct them. It gave technical and financial assistance to establish a legal framework for elections and build a functional electoral administration that can organize elections freely and fairly. It also helped the newly created or reformed electoral administration to frame rules and regulations for elections, to recruit and train the necessary staff to supervise polling, and to acquire the necessary equipment. More importantly, it facilitated the national and international monitoring of elections to prevent fraud and political manipulation. And the international community exerted political pressure on losing political parties to accept the election outcome.[3] Although its efforts did not always succeed in ensuring the integrity of elections, there is little doubt that, without international support and engagement, most post-conflict elections would not have been held or at least would not have gained credibility and acceptance.

It was in the context of holding post-conflict elections that the international community became aware of the need for assisting political parties. Recognizing the instrumental role that political parties could play in conflict management and democratic peace-building, it also realized that political parties lacked the capacity, and in some cases also the skills, to participate effectively in elections. They often needed assistance to draft party rules, recruit candidates, write election manifestoes and mount election campaigns. Moreover, opposition parties were at a serious disadvantage vis-à-vis incumbent parties in many cases, and therefore needed outside help. This was the case, for example, in Mozambique in the early 1990s.[4] Finally, it often found that a legal and regulatory architecture for a multi-party political system did not exist and a set of minimum rules and regulations had to be developed to facilitate political competition. As a result of this awareness, a wide variety of bilateral, multilateral and international non-governmental organizations started designing and implementing political party assistance programmes in various war-torn societies. In fact, many of the party assistance programmes in these countries during the 1990s were demand driven; international agencies engaged in assisting post-conflict elections responded to the demands from local political parties as well as their field staff. Once the elections were over, party assistance programmes often continued, albeit at a reduced scale and as part of more conventional party assistance and democracy promotion programmes.[5]

This chapter takes a closer look at international support for political party development in war-torn societies. It begins with a brief discussion of the state of political parties at the end of civil wars and then discusses the various forms of international assistance for party development. The chapter also draws a number of conclusions and provides several suggestions for future support to political party development in post-conflict societies.

Political parties at the end of conflict

The landscape for political parties differs from country to country in the aftermath of conflict. The relatively open party system in El Salvador, for example, was quite different from the more closed party system in Cambodia just after the peace agreements in both countries in the early 1990s. Conditions were quite different again in Rwanda, where the political party responsible for the genocide was militarily defeated by the Rwandan Patriotic Front, and its leaders and followers sought refuge in neighbouring countries. Factors such as the socio-cultural history of a country, its level of economic development, the presence of pluralistic and democratic institutions, ethnic cleavages, political and economic devastation wrought by civil wars, and the like also vary by country and affect the nature, growth and functioning of political parties. Therefore caution is necessary in making generalizations about the nature and functioning of political parties in recovering war-torn countries. With this caveat in mind, a few general conditions of political parties and the environment in which they operate can nevertheless be identified.

First, the political and governance situation in societies emerging from conflict is hardly conducive to the growth of political parties. Despite the end of war, the law and order situation is typically grim. Gangs composed of criminals, unemployed and uneducated youth and ex-combatants roam around the country, particularly in former war zones. The state has little or no presence in many parts of the country. Law enforcement agencies tend to be both ineffective and corrupt, further compounding the situation. A subculture of impunity can exist for many years in post-conflict societies, eroding the legitimacy of public and political institutions. The lack of security in remote and rural areas restricts the movement of political parties and further hinders their capacity to recruit and educate members or mount election campaigns. Worse, in many cases local parties become dependent on the mercy of criminal elements.

A second common condition of recovering war-torn societies is the severe economic problems they face. Wars tend to have devastating effects on the physical and institutional economic infrastructure of countries. Economic resources are diverted from productive to destructive use during the conflict. Whatever economic development programmes were launched prior to conflict are halted or disrupted. It is estimated that gross domestic product is typically reduced by 15 per cent in post-conflict societies as compared with non-conflict countries.[6] Recovering war-torn societies invariably face high inflation, widespread unemployment and budgetary deficits for many years to come. It takes time for the economy to recover. Under such conditions, corruption is rampant and public disillusionment remains high. But for the vast humanitarian and development assistance from the international community, many of these societies cannot survive. Poor economic conditions also adversely affect the prospects for the institutionalization of party organizations. Because of the scarcity of resources, many parties find it difficult to establish local offices or take part in expensive electoral campaigns. Some political parties become captured by powerful economic interests.

Third, many war-torn societies suffer from widespread social disorganization. The traditional bonds of family, kinship and community are adversely affected by prolonged war and bloodshed. Social and political trust across ethnic groups is eroded. The situation is undoubtedly worse in the countries that underwent ethnic conflict. In such societies, vast residues of hatred, resentment and anger exist among the people.[7] In addition, because of the neglect of education and limited employment opportunities, a sub-class of frustrated youth emerges, which has limited stakes in the existing socio-economic and political systems. Finally, the return of refugees and internally displaced persons puts an additional burden on community resources. The cumulative result is that the civic values of trust, mutual understanding and willingness to discuss differences, which are essential for the development of multi-party democracies, are often deficient in war-torn societies.

But, despite these adverse structural conditions, practically all war-torn societies have seen the emergence of multiple political parties. These parties can be divided into different categories, which is the fourth important point. During and prior to the conflict, countries such as Angola, Cambodia, Ethiopia, Mozambique and Uganda had authoritarian and semi-authoritarian regimes dominated by a single ruling party. In many of these "single-party states", there was no distinction between the ruling political party and the main state institutions. This dominance was undermined with the signing of peace accords, which invariably provided for the establishment of a multi-party political system. With the recognition of opposition parties and groupings, incumbent political parties often lost some of their authority and legitimacy in the immediate post-conflict period. The Popular Movement for the Liberation of Angola (MPLA), the Cambodian People's Party (CPP) and the Mozambican Liberation Front (FRELIMO) are all examples of long-serving ruling parties that saw their power and influence gradually waning prior to post-conflict elections. However, because of their control over the state machinery and access to economic resources, most of the incumbent parties have again consolidated their grasp on power and remain dominant in the post-conflict political arena.

In addition, in several war-torn societies there are politico-military or "rebel" groups that have waged wars against incumbents and are now expected to transform themselves into political parties. By signing peace accords, they agree to participate in the democratic process, giving up their violent struggle. However, in most cases where such a process of rebel-to-party transformation took place, it tended to be slow and painful and its success was not always assured. A politico-military group could renege on its commitment, as was the case with the Khmer Rouge in Cambodia. In other cases, such groups failed to transform themselves because of leadership and structural barriers. However, some did succeed; the Farabundo Martí National Liberation Front (FMLN) in El Salvador and the Mozambican National Resistance (RENAMO) are good examples of rebel groups that managed to change themselves into viable political parties.[8] In any case, the essential point here is that recovering war-torn countries often have new political parties composed of ex-militia and rebel forces.

In those countries where conflict was triggered or influenced by identity issues related to religion, race or linguistic or tribal affiliations, ethnic political parties emerged. Ethnic parties mobilize people on the basis of ethnicity rather than a cross-cutting ideology, and their goals often centre on the narrow interests of an ethnic group(s) rather than broader-based societal interests.[9] For example, when Yugoslavia disintegrated because of its failure to accommodate the aspirations of different ethnic groups, war and bloodshed did not undermine the ethnic loyalties of political parties; instead it consolidated them. Since the signing of the Dayton peace agreement in 1995, ethnic parties have continued to dominate the political scene in Bosnia-Herzegovina. This has been true in Kosovo as well.[10]

Finally, in many war-torn societies a host of smaller, new political parties emerges. Some of these are founded by special interest groups; others are established by (diaspora) intellectuals and democrats disillusioned by the existing state of affairs. Moreover, in some cases political entrepreneurs have formed parties with the aim of gaining short-term political and economic advantages. Many of these new post-conflict parties do not have strong roots in society, have limited political experience and draw their support mainly from urban areas. The Sam Rainsy Party in Cambodia and the Forum for Democratic Change in Uganda are cases in point.

To conclude, we find that different kinds of parties tend to populate the political landscape of recovering war-torn societies. Many of these parties are strongly influenced by the political, economic and social conditions of the civil war and its aftermath, and have organizational, ideological and behavioural characteristics that are often different from those of parties elsewhere.

International assistance for post-conflict party development

It is against the backdrop of these harsh realities that the international community has given assistance to strengthen political parties in post-conflict countries and to improve the legal and regulatory environment in which they operate.

The main international actors active in this field are the specialized democracy and party assistance organizations, including German and Swedish party foundations, the National Democratic Institute (NDI) and the International Republican Institute (IRI) in the United States, Britain's Westminster Foundation for Democracy (WFD), the Netherlands Institute for Multiparty Democracy (NIMD) and Australia's Centre for Democratic Institutions (CDI). It is important to emphasize that the majority of these party assistance organizations, although mostly funded by bilateral aid agencies and governments, are independent institutes that are relatively autonomous as regards how, with whom and where they execute their programmes. Some of the party assistance organizations work with only a few parties or even only one party, using ideological affinity as the main selection criterion. This so-called "fraternal method" of party aid is common to many European political party foundations that have a long history of providing assistance, in particular the Konrad Adenauer Stiftung (KAS) and the Friedrich Ebert Stiftung (FES). Other party assistance organizations offer their support to all the main political parties in the country, or at least to all parties represented in parliament. This "multi-party method" is being used by organizations such as NDI, IRI, NIMD and CDI. For all these organizations, the nature of their assistance consists predominantly of technical advice, dialogue and training.

More recently, support for political party development is also provided by multilateral organizations such as the United Nations Development Programme (UNDP), the Organization for Security and Co-operation in Europe (OSCE), the Organization of American States (OAS) and the International Institute for Democracy and Electoral Assistance (IDEA). Their assistance also consists of technical advice, dialogue and training, and sometimes includes more political-diplomatic activities, such as facilitation and direct negotiation with political parties and warring factions. And, finally, there is a group of organizations referred to as the "party internationals", including the Socialist International, the Liberal International, the Centrist Democrat International and the International Democrat Union. These organizations provide a network of contacts and a platform for the exchange of ideas between parties from the same ideological tradition, and have sometimes also played a role in post-conflict environments. The different methods of the various party aid organizations and the impact of their programmes have recently come under close scrutiny, albeit not with particular reference to post-conflict societies.[11]

The overall objective of international party assistance in post-conflict settings is to initiate and strengthen the nascent democratization process that often begins after the war is over. In the past, international actors have not followed a coherent and comprehensive strategy for party development in post-conflict societies. Instead, their approach has been rather ad hoc and opportunistic. Interested donor governments, multilateral agencies and non-governmental party assistance organizations have selected specific areas of assistance depending on the perceived local needs, available resources and their own specific mandates and interests. The international community has particularly focused on (a) constitutional and legal provisions for political party development, (b) organizational strengthening, as well as the functioning of political parties in elections, dialogue and parliament, and (c) the transformation of rebel movements into political parties.

International support for party regulation

Party laws refer to the constitutional and legal provisions concerning the legal status of political parties, including their organization and activities. They define what constitutes a political party, lay down the requirements for a party organization and explain what a political party can or cannot do. Kenneth Janda defines party law as "the body of state-based regulations that determines the legal status of political parties and that often specify what constitutes party membership, how parties must be organized, how they should campaign, how they must handle party funds, and so on".[12] Broadly speaking, party laws cover three aspects: party registration and organization, election and campaign laws, and regulations for political party financing.

Some post-conflict societies already had constitutional provisions permitting the formation and functioning of political parties before the outbreak of civil war. This was the case, for example, in El Salvador, Guatemala, Liberia and Nicaragua. In other cases, constitutions were revised prior to the signing of peace accords to permit the establishment of a multi-party political system. For example, Mozambique revised its constitution in 1990 to abolish the one-party political system that had previously existed in the country. In still other cases, the new constitutions made explicit reference to political parties to ensure that political parties are not banned by the incumbent political authority. The constitutions of Afghanistan, Cambodia, Ethiopia and Rwanda, for example, recognize citizens' right to form political parties.

In the early 1990s, in post-conflict countries such as Ethiopia, Cambodia and Mozambique, multilateral and bilateral agencies funded teams of legal and constitutional experts to advise interim or elected governments, usually at the specific request of the new governments. Such teams helped local experts in crafting new constitutions or amending existing ones. Some attention was given to party regulations, albeit on a very limited scale.

In the mid-1990s, in Bosnia-Herzegovina, the international community mandated the Office of the High Representative and the OSCE to oversee the implementation of the Dayton peace agreement, including the creation of a democratic multi-party system.[13] According to Carrie Manning, pressure from these institutions "produced restrictions on the means of party financing, on leadership recruitment and retention, and on the public espousal of political positions counter to the provisions or objectives of the Dayton agreement.... Rather than ban the nationalist parties outright, however, the High Representative used discretionary powers ... to remove elected officials and candidates from public office or from their party functions if they were judged to be obstructing the peace process."[14] Despite this interventionist approach, however, the international community has not been able to stem the popular appeal of the main "nationalist" political parties in Bosnia, mainly because they have handily adapted their electoral mobilization strategies to the new post-war context.

More recently, international actors played an important role in advising the government of Hamid Karzai in Afghanistan on the adoption of a new electoral and political party law in the run-up to the September 2005 elections for the Wolesi Jirga, the Afghan parliament. The United Nations Assistance Mission in Afghanistan, a key player in this regard, helped ensure that new political parties would be subject to a number of regulations (see Box 12.1).

However, the international community could not ensure the implementation of the enacted party laws during the 2005 elections. Despite the provision that banned parties and candidates associated with armed groups from participating in elections, several candidates with strong links to armed militias were elected to the Afghan parliament.[15] In addition, there are indications that the overall aim of the political party law – to create a stable party system that enables effective cooperation between the directly elected president and parliament by limiting fragmentation and factionalism – was actually undermined by the electoral

Box 12.1 Afghanistan's Political Parties Law (excerpt)

Chapter Two. Establishment and registration of political parties

Article 4

Afghan citizens of voting age can freely establish a political party, irrespective of their ethnicity, race, language, tribe, sex, religion, education, occupation, lineage, assets and place of residence.

Article 5

Political parties can function freely on the basis of the provisions of this law, and have equal rights and obligations before the law.

Article 6

Political parties shall not:
(1) pursue objectives that are opposed to the principles of the holy religion Islam;
(2) use force, or threaten with, or propagate, the use of force;
(3) incite to ethnic racial, religious or sectional violence;
(4) create a real danger to the rights and freedom of individuals or intentionally disrupt public order and security;
(5) have military organisations or affiliations with armed forces;
(6) receive funds from foreign sources.

Source: *Political Parties Law* of Afghanistan, available on the Chr. Michelsen Institute website at ⟨http://www.cmi.no/pdf/?file=/afghanistan/doc/ACF8C.pdf⟩ (accessed 9 April 2008).

law. The electoral law put in place the inappropriate single nontransferable vote (SNTV) electoral system, which limited the use of political party lists in the elections and allowed only the participation of "independent" candidates.[16] Despite contrary expert advice, many international actors did not fully realize the negative implications of this electoral system until it was too late. Others deliberately overlooked it, fearing that listing political parties could cause further fragmentation of the political landscape and a potential loss for President Karzai.[17]

Just as in many other conflict-prone societies highlighted in this volume, governments in recovering war-torn societies have themselves imposed strict restrictions on political parties in newly drafted constitutions and party laws in order to prevent the emergence of political parties that might ignite conflict by promoting ethnic and parochial interests. The

Afghan party law mentioned above is a good example. The Rwandan constitution adopted in 2003 lays down arguably the most stringent requirements for political parties. Article 54 of that constitution reads: "political organizations are prohibited from basing themselves on race, ethnic group, tribe, clan, region, sex, religion or any other division which may give rise to discrimination. Political organizations must constantly reflect the unity of the people of Rwanda."[18] Although the government has defended the restrictions on party formation with reference to the traumatizing events of the 1994 genocide, some have argued that the restrictions do not allow the emergence of real opposition parties and thereby hinder the development of a democratic multi-party system.[19] It is interesting to note that offers of technical assistance by the international community were rejected by the Rwandan Constitutional Commission. The civil society consultation process for the new constitution was financially supported by several international donor agencies, however.[20]

It is too early to ascertain the positive or negative effects of such restrictions in Afghanistan and Rwanda. Past experiences show that constitutional guarantees have not always prevented authoritarian governments or dominant parties from circumventing the growth and emergence of opposition parties. For example, in Cambodia and Ethiopia, ruling parties have circumvented legal and constitutional provisions in order to keep themselves in power. On a positive note, however, the government of Uganda had for a long time not allowed multi-party elections, but under public and international pressure its constitution was amended in 2005 to permit them.

In many war-torn countries, as in other transition nations, the international community has also supported the formulation of rules on the financing of political parties and electoral campaigns. Such regulations are usually designed to curb the influence of vested interests on public policies and to limit the opportunities for corruption and fraud. In post-conflict countries, political finance problems can have more serious consequences than in other transitional countries and are often related to electoral violence, unequal participation for minority parties and funding from undesirable sources (e.g. criminals and antisocial elements involved in organized crime, drugs or the unlawful depletion of natural resources).[21] The international community has given technical assistance to political parties and governments to discuss the different regulatory options and identify the most suitable reform package(s). The proposed legislative remedies include limits on donations to and expenditures by political parties and the mandatory disclosure of party finances, including private donations and public subsidies to political parties. In this context UNDP, for example, has provided technical assistance to finalize laws on the status of political parties and their financing in the Democratic Republic of Congo (DRC).[22] Similarly, the International Foundation for Electoral Systems (IFES) worked with the Liberian National Elections Commission on the drafting and implementation of campaign finance regulations.[23] International actors have also worked with local civil society organizations involved in educating the public (and politicians) about the new political finance regulations, particularly in order to improve their attitude towards political parties. International IDEA has been one of the many international organizations involved in this work.

Assistance for strengthening political parties

The international community has also designed and implemented modest aid programmes to strengthen the organizational base of political parties, to increase their capacity to conduct (post-conflict) election campaigns, to promote multi-party dialogue and to strengthen the functioning of parties in parliament.

Since most political parties in war-torn societies lack strong organizational structures and capacities, a major focus of international programmes has been on organizational development. The goal of such endeavours is to put forward a vision of a functional organizational structure that is well managed and has a democratic leadership. In some countries, international actors gave direct financial and material assistance to build party offices and strengthen party infrastructure. In East Timor, for example, UNDP helped to set up Political Resource Centres, which provided access to graphic designers, computers, internet connections and telephone lines.[24] A similar initiative has been undertaken in Bosnia, where the OSCE established Political Party Service Centres, aimed at providing all parties with free access to office equipment, a meeting space and relevant documentation. The international community has also funded numerous training seminars and workshops that focus on a wide variety of issues, including strategies to recruit members, the development of suitable messages, improving internal communication within political parties, strengthening relationships between national, regional and local units, and working with outside groups. Training programmes have also focused on practical mechanisms to raise funds, organize special events and conduct opinion polls and research. Some organizations such as NDI and IRI have developed training manuals to provide parties with general information about the role of political parties in a democratic system and to identify specific techniques and skills required to perform specific functions.[25]

The second area of party strengthening assistance has focused on election campaigns. The primary objective of assistance in this area is to enable newly established as well as older political parties to mount an effective election campaign following democratic norms and practices, particularly in a country's first post-conflict election. Assistance programmes focus on topics such as strategic planning, candidate identification and selection, message/platform development, voter outreach, media relations, campaign funding and budgeting, voter mobilization, opinion polls, debates among candidates, poll watching and vote counting. For example, during the October 2005 elections in Liberia, NDI and IRI organized a presidential debate in Monrovia and several senatorial debates throughout the country to acquaint the electorate with the views and positions of the main electoral candidates.[26] International organizations have also organized meetings and seminars to inform political leaders about the laws and regulations governing elections. In addition, some bilateral donors have funded the services of outside experts to strengthen selected opposition parties in an effort to create a more level playing field after the conflict.

The promotion of multi-party dialogue has also been a focus of international attention. The main motivation behind this area of assistance has been to try to bridge the large gap of trust that often exists in war-torn societies, not only between the formerly warring parties but also among the various opposition parties. In some countries, such assistance has been closely related to the ongoing peace negotiation process. For example, in the case of the DRC, NDI established a technical secretariat in 2001 that offered technical assistance to various (non-armed) political parties in order to engage them in the Inter-Congolese Dialogue and to facilitate consensus over the terms of the peace agreement.[27] Another internationally supported effort in this area has been the organization and facilitation of a multi-party dialogue in Guatemala by UNDP in collaboration with the NIMD. Key aims of this initiative were to initiate dialogue between the parties and to strengthen the country's highly fragmented party system. With international support, a large number of Guatemalan parties eventually elaborated a Shared National Agenda, identifying the country's main post-war socio-economic problems and formulating a vision to tackle them.[28] A similar type of dialogue process in Guatemala – the Forum of Political Parties – had been initiated by the OAS a few years earlier.

Finally, organizations such as the Inter-Parliamentary Union, Parliamentarians for Global Action, European Parliamentarians for Africa, UNDP and the United States Agency for International Development (USAID) have promoted a wide range of initiatives to improve the performance of political parties in parliaments. Such programmes help prepare legislators to play a more effective role in passing new legislation, to participate more effectively in parliamentary committees, to organize public hearings, to exercise oversight over the executive branch and to reach out to their constituencies. Some seminars and workshops also discuss more substantive issues such as the constitutional relationships between the executive and legislative branches and the rights and responsibilities of parliamentarians. The international community has organized foreign study tours, held meetings and seminars and even sponsored short-term training for legislators and their legislative staff.

Although some of these programmes have for a long time been rather generic, international actors have recently been making an effort to design programmes that cater more to the needs of parliamentarians in post-conflict settings. In such cases, parliaments not only suffer from severe personnel and administrative shortages, but also are confronted with problems related to their legitimacy, their limited experience in drafting legislation and/or keeping the executive in check, and their role in overseeing the difficult reconstruction and democratization process. Over the past few years, a number of special parliamentary capacity-building programmes for post-conflict countries have been initiated. In 2005, UNDP co-funded a parliamentary capacity-building project for the DRC with the Italian government and the Department for International Development of the United Kingdom, which aimed among others at training parliamentarians and administrative and technical staff and developing legislation covering the transition period.[29] Since February 2005, UNDP has also coordinated the Support to the Establishment of the Afghan Legislature (SEAL) project, a US$15.5 million two-year project financed by half a dozen bilateral donors. USAID has funded a similar US$10 million project by the State University of New York, NDI and IRI to strengthen Afghanistan's parliament.

Supporting the transformation of rebel movements into political parties

As mentioned earlier, a major challenge for some post-conflict societies is to ensure that former politico-military groups or "rebel movements" transform themselves into viable political parties. The experiences of former warlord militias in Afghanistan, the FMLN in El Salvador, RENAMO in Mozambique, the National Council for the Defence of Democracy – Forces for the Defence of Democracy (CNDD-FDD) in Burundi, the Revolutionary United Front (RUF) in Sierra Leone and the Sudan People's Liberation Movement/Army (SPLM/A) show that many factors shape the success or failure of so-called rebel-to-party transformations. These include the way the conflict ended, the terms of peace accords, if any, the organizational structure of the rebel group, its leadership, its political base and its previous experience in participating in political life. Engagement by the international community has been another factor, which assisted the transformation process in several countries.[30]

In addition to political pressure and influence, the international community has provided four kinds of direct and indirect assistance. First, it has given financial and technical assistance for disarming and demobilizing ex-combatants and their eventual reintegration in society in countries such as Mozambique, Cambodia, Sierra Leone and, more recently, the DRC and Burundi.[31] The United Nations, the World Bank, the European Commission and USAID have been among the largest donors for such disarmament, demobilization and reintegration (DDR) programmes. Although DDR programmes usually took more time than anticipated and the reintegration of ex-combatants was not always successful, such assistance proved vital to ensure peace in many post-conflict countries. In addition, these programmes helped the rebel-to-party transformation because they absolved leaders of rebel groups from the responsibility of providing for their militias. This helped them to concentrate on the new organization's political activities, particularly in the run-up to the first post-conflict elections.

Second, the international community has provided financial assistance to former rebel groups to convert themselves into political parties. The most conspicuous example of such financial assistance is the US$17 million "RENAMO Trust Fund" established in Mozambique.[32] The fund enabled RENAMO to launch a vigorous election campaign in addition to developing a political party apparatus.[33] Norway, Sweden and Spain provided similar assistance to the FMLN in El Salvador.[34] Many US organizations funded the Opposition National Union (UNO), which included rebel groups, in Nicaragua, and several Latin American and European countries helped the Sandinista National Liberation Front (FSLN).[35] In Afghanistan, Junbesh-i Milli Islami received some monetary support from Turkey, and Iran has reportedly provided some assistance to Hizb-i Wahdat.[36] However, most experts are against the provision of direct financial assistance to political parties for several reasons. It creates a bad precedent in which past misdeeds may be rewarded. Moreover, there is no guarantee that the funds would not be misused by party leaders for their personal gain. In addition, direct funding tends to help the established leaders to maintain their hold over the party because they use it to award patronage. And, finally, cash hand-outs to rebel leaders can contribute to the rebel groups' continued dependence on foreign assistance. This has been the case with RENAMO in Mozambique.

Third, in many cases, the international community has given logistical support to rebel groups. Such assistance enabled RENAMO to move from its headquarters in Gorongosa to the Mozambican capital, Maputo.[37] In El Salvador, such support enabled the FMLN to rent offices in the capital.[38] In addition, international organizations have given office equipment to rebel parties in El Salvador, Nicaragua and East Timor. For many donor organizations, commodity assistance is preferable to direct financial assistance, because the chances of misuse are more limited. Another reason this form of assistance is often popular with donor organizations is that it generally requires less effort and has a more visible impact than a training course.

Finally, the international community has sought the participation of all parties, including the newly formed political parties of former rebels, in its assistance programmes. For example, NDI, and to a lesser extent also FES and KAS, organized several workshops in Afghanistan for political parties that were also attended by the representatives of various parties controlled by warlords. CDI has done similar training workshops for East Timorese parties.[39] In Sudan, IRI has run a political party and candidate development programme, which also included a seminar to discuss the transformation of the SPLM/A from a military movement to a political party.[40] Mention should be made of the Burundi Leadership Training Programme, which focused on training for collaborative decision-making by a broad range of Burundian leaders, and also included a leadership workshop for former army and CNDD-FDD rebel commanders.[41] One advantage of such multi-party training workshops is that representatives of former rebel groups are able to interact with other parties, which might help them become more aware of the workings of multi-party politics.

General findings and conclusions

Because of the dearth of information on this topic and the problems of collecting reliable and accurate information in war-torn societies – particularly when it comes to assistance programmes that were carried out some time ago – it is difficult to come up with firm, general conclusions. Nevertheless, by complementing the limited literature available on this topic with information, project descriptions and personal views from country experts and practitioners, as well as one of the authors' own involvement in political party assistance, a few general conclusions can be mentioned here.

First, although the international community assisted many war-torn societies in amending existing constitutions or crafting new ones to permit the functioning of a multi-party democracy, it did not give much attention to specific party laws and regulations. The examples of strong international advice on party regulation in Bosnia and Afghanistan mentioned earlier have proven to be rather exceptional. This lack of attention from the international community stands in sharp contrast to the enthusiasm with which domestic political elites have crafted party laws, as is reported elsewhere in this volume. Two factors explain the scant attention given to party regulation in most international assistance programming. Prior to the first post-conflict elections, the international community has been primarily concerned with ensuring that people have the freedom to establish political parties, that they can vote in a secure and safe environment and that the ruling political party does not enjoy unfair advantages over opposition parties.[42] How parties originate or how they develop their organizational structures and political activities have generally received little attention. In addition, there is no unanimity among experts about the nature of party laws and regulations that are ideal for creating a multi-party democracy in war-torn societies. Even in consolidated democracies there is a marked variance in the existing provisions for party laws.

International experts advising post-conflict governments were concerned about the rise of parties that might reignite ethnic and regional conflicts, but they were equally concerned that new constitutional and legal restrictions on political parties could give unscrupulous governments an excuse to undermine opposition parties. Thus they faced a dilemma that could not be easily resolved. Although the international community in most cases did not have a coherent position on this issue, many experts sent by bilateral and multilateral agencies did voice their reservations about restrictions on political parties, for example with regard to the Rwandan and Afghan constitutions. However, as the above-described example of Afghanistan demonstrates, their concerns were largely ignored as other interests prevailed.

Even in cases where regulatory reforms have been implemented successfully, the aspect of the enforcement of these regulations has usually received little international attention. Much of the technical assistance provided in the field of party regulation seems to have focused on incorporating the status, organization, rights and responsibilities of parties into new or existing legislation, and less on creating mechanisms to ensure that such legislation will also be enforced. Particularly in post-conflict countries characterized by a weak rule of law, this lack of attention to enforcement has been rather problematic.[43]

Second, assistance to strengthen political parties as organizations, as electoral competitors and as key parliamentary actors has generally improved their technical capacities. Such assistance for organizational development has undoubtedly benefited many new and emerging political parties. Because many parties usually had no office space or access to communication technologies or to relevant documents, the provision of housing and logistical material, as well as the establishment of resource centres by international agencies, enabled them to organize themselves and establish party structures. The more specialized training workshops that focused on improving skills in message development, establishing relationships with civil society organizations and fund-raising were usually helpful. Assistance for improving parties' electoral preparations and election campaign skills has also been quite successful, in that large numbers of party activists have benefited from such training and the quality of parties' campaign techniques in many countries is said to have improved over time.[44] The emphasis on women's participation in political parties and the special workshops on the recruitment of women members also had a positive effect in some countries. This was the case, for example, in a tradition-bound society such as Afghanistan, where women successfully contested the 2005 parliamentary elections. At the same time, there have been some problems as well. For example, much of the organizational assistance provided has been short term, usually concentrated around the first post-conflict elections. In countries such as Ethiopia and Sierra Leone, this has not contributed to the long-term organizational capacity-building of political parties.[45]

Third, the overall impact of international assistance in rebel-to-party transformation has generally been limited. In Mozambique, timely and generous direct financial assistance combined with strong political pressure was a critical factor in persuading RENAMO's leadership to give up its armed struggle and move into mainstream politics. To a much lesser extent this was also the case with the FMLN in El Salvador. However, these positive examples of internationally supported rebel-to-party transformations seem to be exceptions rather than the rule. Past experiences highlight many problem areas. Often DDR programmes have not been effective in reintegrating ex-combatants in economic and social life. Moreover, conventional party assistance programmes, including workshops for political skills and leadership training, have not focused on the specific needs, requirements and problems faced by rebel groups in transforming themselves into viable political parties. The examples from Mozambique, El Salvador and Burundi indicate that international actors focus mainly on securing the engagement of former rebel leaders in the peace process and facilitating former rebel groups' participation in the first post-conflict elections. However, a successful conversion into a political party also requires that the former rebel group develops an accountable party organization and a viable political programme. These latter aspects have often been ignored by international actors.

Fourth, anecdotal evidence indicates that, in the political arena of post-conflict societies, regulatory reforms are necessary but not sufficient. In the absence of internal and external pressure, incumbent parties manage to manipulate the rules to their advantage. The problem is that the judiciary, civil society organizations, opposition parties and the media in these countries are not strong enough to monitor compliance, let alone take measures against non-compliance. These institutions are often dependent on the incumbent regimes and lack the resources to confront the dominant party. Moreover, in dominant authoritarian systems, many of these institutions are not allowed to operate freely. At the same time, with the passing of time and the formation of an elected government, the international community also loses its leverage and influence. The presence of international actors often declines within two to three years after the conflict has ended. Moreover, many foreign powers are not willing to spend their political capital on transgressions of laws and regulations designed to establish a democratic political party system. Often they are more concerned about political stability than about adherence to democratic norms by the ruling party.[46] One has only to look at the experiences in Cambodia, Ethiopia or Uganda to see that many bilateral actors ignored the violation of democratic norms by these countries' governments.

Fifth, a major problem that the international community has faced in practically all war-torn societies is that the majority of political parties have little or no incentive to introduce internal reforms and to aggregate the interests of diverse groups. Most of them lack a coherent ideology or clear political programme. Often they are led by charismatic leaders who monopolize power and do not tolerate dissent. Many are urban based and lack grassroots support in the more populated rural areas. In former single-party states, the ruling parties tended to be better organized because they often had a nationwide network of party offices, possessed a cadre of party officials and enjoyed access to power and resources to distribute patronage. But even they became weaker during and after the war and often lost much of their legitimacy, particularly if they were associated with human rights violations during the war. Most new parties emerging out of former rebel movements possess neither the organizational culture nor the experience to participate in a democratic system. Rebel movements are usually led by a single (military) leader or a coterie of leaders who favour secret decision-making, as in the case of RENAMO or the SPLM/A. Power within these organizations is concentrated in a few hands, while others are obliged to follow orders. In addition, their cadres are trained in military and guerrilla warfare rather than in democratic methods of discussion and compromise. Most mono-ethnic political parties are usually no better. Their leaders solidify their political base by referring to real or imaginary grievances of their sectional group and thrive by creating a sentiment of "us" versus "them" to mobilize their constituencies.[47] Against this background, international assistance has often had little impact. The leaders of political parties usually pay only lip-service to the reforms suggested by the international community. And, when faced by stronger external pressure, many parties embrace superficial reforms without undergoing real transformation.

Finally, international support for post-conflict party development has tended to suffer from the same limitations that have plagued many international democracy assistance programmes. These include a lack of coherent intervention strategy, limited donor coordination at the policy level, the short-term focus of donor agencies, bureaucratic delays and limited ownership of assistance programmes by the host societies. These have been examined in detail by various authors and do not require further elaboration here.[48] However, there are two remaining issues specifically related to party assistance that deserve closer scrutiny.

One problem that has plagued political party assistance more than any other form of democracy assistance has been an undue reliance on training seminars and workshops. For many of these events, it has proved difficult to recruit the senior representatives from political parties who are in a position to take decisive action on the findings and recommendations. Often the people who attend seminars lack the authority and prestige to push for change. In addition, many participants have often complained that the contents are too general and do not take into account the specific party context of war-torn societies. This is particularly problematic when workshops are given by trainers who are not familiar with the social and political conditions of the country, who do not speak the local language, or who present an idealized form of a political party (mass based, policy focused and ideologically distinctive) that is outdated or non-representative of parties even in established democracies. On this latter aspect, it is fair to say that international aid practice has improved over the past few years. There are now a number of party aid organizations that do make an effort to adapt their workshops to the local situation, take into account the varying nature of political parties and make more use of local or regional trainers and experts.[49]

A second problem concerns the impact of party assistance, and how to measure it. Party assistance organizations, like other aid organizations, regularly claim that their programmes have contributed to the creation of a stable party system and fostered the process of democratization by, for example, enabling multi-party dialogue or encouraging the formation of multi-ethnic parties.[50] However, such claims are difficult to verify in the absence of systematic and independent analyses. Despite numerous though modest party assistance programmes, there exists a dearth of evaluations. One reason for this is that party assistance programmes are generally part of electoral assistance and are not independent expenditure items in the budgets of bilateral and multilateral agencies. Therefore they are often overlooked by donor and implementing agencies. Secondly, because of political sensitivities, international donors and implementing agencies usually prefer to keep a low profile as far as political party assistance is concerned. In the fragile political environment of war-torn societies, party assistance easily arouses suspicion and misunderstanding because it can give the impression that a group of donors or an individual donor agency is directly or indirectly interfering in the political process. This has discouraged many donors and implementing agencies from launching evaluations. Third, in many cases, implementing agencies have conducted several internal evaluations, albeit usually not very detailed or systematically. Unfortunately, the majority of these internal evaluations are not available to the public. Fourth, a range of conceptual, methodological and practical issues plague evaluations of political party assistance programmes. It is, for example, extremely difficult to measure the political impact of an assistance programme and/or to attribute a certain change in the political system to a particular assistance programme by a specific party aid agency.[51] Whatever the reason, independent and rigorous evaluations of party assistance are needed both to improve the effectiveness of party assistance and to enhance our understanding of the strengths and limitations of foreign assistance in political party development.

Recommendations

Strengthen political party assistance

The first and undoubtedly most obvious recommendation is that the international community should revisit its political party assistance in the light of past experiences. Independent analysts, but also practitioners and policy makers themselves, have highlighted several areas where things should change to improve the effectiveness and impact of political party assistance. A few can be recapitulated here. First, international organizations should tailor their programmes to the specific security, political, economic and social challenges of post-conflict environments, taking into consideration the nature and working of existing political parties, the strength of their political base and economic resources, and the political leadership and their commitment to peace and a pluralistic political system. Second, local ownership of assistance programmes is extremely important. In addition to consulting with political parties and civil society organizations, international aid providers should try to engage more local and regional experts in designing and implementing their assistance programmes. Third, political party assistance should be more integrated with assistance programmes for civil society, independent media and conflict prevention, because healthy relationships between political parties, civil society organizations and media outlets are crucial for achieving a stable and democratic political system.

Focus on party laws from a conflict prevention perspective

In addition to exploring the design of electoral systems and power-sharing arrangements, the international community should advise war-torn countries about party laws that can reduce tensions or at least do not aggravate them. International and regional experts should help those countries to examine the existing or proposed party laws through the prism of conflict prevention. They should help identify those rules and regulations that might aggravate existing tensions and present alternative solutions for the consideration of the executive and legislative bodies. They should also explore the possibility of presenting rules and regulations that create positive incentives for political parties to build multi-party coalitions and to include women, ethnic minorities and members from remote and distant regions within their organization.

Work early on rebel-to-party transformation

The international community should start working much earlier on the issue of rebel-to-party transformation in war-torn societies. A first recommendation is to include the issue of rebel-to-party transformation in the peace negotiations and, if possible, in the final peace agreement. This not only ensures the recognition of a former rebel group as a legitimate political actor but also enables assistance to be set aside for its transformation into a political party, provided it receives sufficient popular support. Second, new assistance programmes will have to be developed that take into account the unique problems of former rebel groups. For example, there are currently no special training courses for higher-ranking soldiers who want to become politicians. Also, conventional party assistance training programmes are usually not accessible to groups that – directly or indirectly – still have access to weapons. And, finally, leaders of major (former) rebel groups have to be included in discussions about the post-war political future of their countries in order to enhance commitment to their new democratic responsibilities as party leaders. This is not solely a task of Western governments and aid agencies, but rests with domestic governments and regional organizations as well.

Address the unequal distribution of power in post-conflict party systems

One of the key political problems in war-torn societies is the existence of party systems that are dominated by one party. In dominant authoritarian systems, where opposition parties are either banned or can operate only under severe restrictions imposed by the ruling party, international actors are usually not allowed to work directly with opposition parties.

Apart from strong political pressure by key regional and international players on the dominant party to hold regular, free and competitive elections and to put in place a more permissive regulatory framework for political parties, international actors can only help by supporting key independent civil society, media and judicial organizations.

In dominant non-authoritarian systems, international actors usually have more room for manoeuvre. To ensure government accountability and genuine political competition, and to create the future potential for a peaceful alternation in government, international assistance will here have to focus specifically on strengthening the organizational capacities of opposition parties. In order to avoid being accused of partisanship, assistance providers will have to work with the governing party as well, however. The challenge here lies in finding the right balance between providing organizational support to opposition parties and strengthening the competitiveness of the party system for all parties.

Despite the good intentions and potential benefits of international assistance, the main impetus for change will have to come from within these countries, however. As long as the dominant position of certain parties is not challenged, either by internal splits within those parties or by a strong and concerted effort by opposition parties, it is unlikely that the party systems of many post-conflict societies will become more competitive.

Notes

1. Jeroen de Zeeuw and Krishna Kumar (eds), *Promoting Democracy in Post-conflict Societies* (Boulder, CO: Lynne Rienner Publishers, 2006).
2. Benjamin Reilly, "Elections in Post-conflict Societies", in Edward Newman and Roland Rich (eds), *The UN Role in Promoting Democracy: Between Ideals and Reality* (Tokyo: United Nations University Press, 2004), pp. 113–134; Terrence Lyons, "The Role of Post-Settlement Elections", in Stephen John Stedman, Donald Rothchild and Elizabeth M. Cousens (eds), *Ending Civil Wars: The Implementation of Peace Agreements* (Boulder, CO: Lynne Rienner Publishers, 2002), pp. 215–236.
3. Krishna Kumar (ed.), *Post-conflict Elections, Democratization and International Assistance* (Boulder, CO: Lynne Rienner Publishers, 1998).
4. Marc de Tollenaere, "Fostering Multiparty Politics in Mozambique", in de Zeeuw and Kumar (eds), *Promoting Democracy in Post-conflict Societies*, pp. 83–84.
5. For an overview and analysis of the broader democracy promotion agenda, see Peter Burnell (ed.), *Democracy Assistance: International Co-operation for Democratization* (London: Frank Cass, 2000); and Thomas Carothers, *Aiding Democracy Abroad: The Learning Curve* (Washington, DC: Carnegie Endowment for International Peace, 1999).
6. Paul Collier, "Post-Conflict Economic Recovery", a paper for the International Peace Academy, Oxford University, 2006, p. 2.

7. Donald Horowitz, *Ethnic Groups in Conflict*, 2nd edn (Berkeley: University of California Press, 2000).

8. Terrence Lyons, *Demilitarizing Politics: Elections on the Uncertain Road to Peace* (Boulder, CO: Lynne Rienner Publishers, 2005).

9. For more information on the main characteristics of mono-ethnic and ethnic congress parties, see Richard Gunther and Larry Diamond, "Types and Functions of Parties", in Larry Diamond and Richard Gunther (eds), *Political Parties and Democracy* (Baltimore, MD: Johns Hopkins University Press, 2001), pp. 22–25.

10. Carrie Manning, "Armed Opposition Groups into Political Parties: Comparing Bosnia, Kosovo, and Mozambique", *Studies in Comparative International Development*, 39(1), 2004: 54–77.

11. Thomas Carothers, *Confronting the Weakest Link: Aiding Political Parties in New Democracies* (Washington, DC: Carnegie Endowment for International Peace, 2006); see also Peter Burnell, "Political Parties, International Party Assistance and Globalization", in Peter Burnell (ed.), *Globalizing Democracy: Party Politics in Emerging Democracies* (London: Routledge, 2006).

12. Kenneth Janda, *Political Parties and Democracy in Theoretical and Practical Perspectives: Adopting Party Law* (Washington, DC: National Democratic Institute of International Affairs, 2005), pp. 3–4.

13. Elizabeth M. Cousens, "From Missed Opportunities to Overcompensation: Implementing the Dayton Agreement on Bosnia", in Stedman, Rothchild and Cousens (eds), *Ending Civil Wars*, pp. 539–541.

14. Manning, "Armed Opposition Groups into Political Parties", pp. 60–61.

15. Antonio Giustozzi, "Afghanistan: Political Parties or Militia Fronts?", in Jeroen de Zeeuw (ed.), *From Soldiers to Politicians: The Transformation of Rebel Movements after Civil War* (Boulder, CO: Lynne Rienner Publishers, 2008), pp. 179–204.

16. For an insightful account on how Afghanistan ended up with SNTV, see Andrew Reynolds, "The Curious Case of Afghanistan", *Journal of Democracy*, 17(2), 2006: 104–117.

17. Based on e-mail correspondence on 21 and 26 February 2007 between one of the authors and Thomas Ruttig, Afghanistan expert at the Stiftung Wissenschaft und Politik in Berlin and former Deputy EU Special Representative in Kabul.

18. *The Constitution of the Republic of Rwanda. Adopted on 26 May 2003*, available at ⟨www.chr.up.ac.za/hr_docs/constitutions/docs/RwandaC(rev).doc⟩ (accessed 9 April 2008).

19. See Filip Reyntjens, "Rwanda, Ten Years On: From Genocide to Dictatorship", *African Affairs*, 103(411), 2004: 177–210.

20. Priscilla Yachat Ankut, *The Role of Constitution-Building Processes in Democratization: Case Study Rwanda* (Stockholm: International IDEA, 2005), p. 25.

21. Jeff Fisher, Marcin Walecki and Jeffrey Carlson (eds), *Political Finance in Post-Conflict Societies* (Washington, DC: IFES, 2006).

22. UNDP, *UNDP's Engagement with Political Parties* (New York: UNDP, 2005), p. 9.

23. See the IFES Liberia Election Administration Program (LEAP) at ⟨http://www.ifes.org/liberia.html?page=project_119⟩ (accessed 9 April 2008).

24. UNDP, *UNDP's Engagement with Political Parties*, p. 15.

25. See, for example, NDI, *Political Party Development Program: Party Training Manuals 1 and 2* (Washington, DC: NDI, 2005).

26. See National Democratic Institute, "Central and West Africa: Liberia" at ⟨http://www.ndi.org/worldwide/cewa/liberia/liberia.asp⟩ (accessed 9 April 2008).

27. Shari Bryan, "Engaging Political Parties in Post-Conflict Parliaments", paper presented at the International Conference on Parliaments, Crisis Prevention and Recovery, Brussels, 19–21 April 2006, p. 6.

28. Based on e-mail correspondence on 18 January and 1 March 2007 between one of the authors and Heleen Schrooyen, policy officer Central and South America at NIMD. See also UNDP, *UNDP's Engagement with Political Parties*, p. 19.
29. Information from the UNDP DRC Country Office website at ⟨http://www.undp.org.cd. ws017.alentus.com/Home.aspx?lang=fr⟩ (accessed 9 April 2008).
30. For a more comprehensive analysis on rebel-to-party transformations and the role of international actors, see de Zeeuw (ed.), *From Soldiers to Politicians*. Other recent studies on this topic include Manning, "Armed Opposition Groups into Political Parties"; and Mimmi Söderberg-Kovacs, "From Rebellion to Politics. The Transformation of Rebel Groups to Political Parties in Civil War Peace Processes", PhD dissertation, Department of Peace and Conflict Research, Uppsala University, 2007.
31. Disarmament, demobilization and reintegration programmes in DRC and Burundi are part of the Multi-Country Demobilization and Reintegration Program (MDRP) that is currently taking place in seven countries of the greater Great Lakes region of Central Africa. See ⟨http://www.mdrp.org/⟩ (accessed 9 April 2008).
32. Lyons, *Demilitarizing Politics*, p. 126; de Tollenaere, "Fostering Multiparty Politics in Mozambique", p. 83.
33. Carrie Manning, "Mozambique: RENAMO's Electoral Success", in de Zeeuw (ed.), *From Soldiers to Politicians*, pp. 67–72.
34. Christine Wade, "El Salvador: The Success of the FMLN", in de Zeeuw (ed.), *From Soldiers to Politicians*, pp. 47–48.
35. Rafael López-Pintor, "Nicaragua's Measured Move to Democracy", in Kumar, *Post-conflict Elections, Democratization and International Assistance*, p. 44.
36. Giustozzi, "Afghanistan: Political Parties or Militia Fronts?".
37. Manning, "Mozambique: RENAMO's Electoral Success" .
38. Wade, "El Salvador: The Success of the FMLN".
39. See Centre for Democratic Institutions, "Timor-Leste", at ⟨http://www.cdi.anu.edu.au/timor_leste/timor_leste.htm⟩ (accessed 9 April 2008).
40. See International Republican Institute, "Sudan", at ⟨http://www.iri.org/africa/sudan.asp⟩ (accessed 9 April 2008).
41. Howard Wolpe and Steve McDonald, "Burundi's Transition: Training Leaders for Peace", *Journal of Democracy*, 17(1), 2006: 132–138.
42. See also de Tollenaere, "Fostering Multiparty Politics in Mozambique", who argues that early international political party support in Mozambique was mainly motivated by the desire to conclude the peace negotiations and organize the first post-conflict elections.
43. Fisher, Walecki and Carlson, *Political Finance in Post-Conflict Societies*, p. 7.
44. Carothers, *Confronting the Weakest Link*, p. 185.
45. Mohamed Gibril Sesay and Charlie Hughes, *Go Beyond First Aid: Democracy Assistance and the Challenges of Institution Building in Post-Conflict Sierra Leone*, CRU Working Paper 34 (The Hague: Clingendael Institute, 2005), p. 47; and Dessalegn Rahmato and Meheret Ayenew, *Democratic Assistance to Post-Conflict Ethiopia: Impact and Limitations*, Monograph No. 3 (Addis Ababa: Forum for Social Studies, 2004).
46. Partly based on telephone interview on 21 February 2007 between one of the authors and Renier Nijskens, former Belgian ambassador to the DRC and current regional representative for Southern and East Africa at NIMD.
47. Judith Large and Timothy D. Sisk, *Democracy, Conflict and Human Security: Pursuing Peace in the 21st Century* (Stockholm: International IDEA, 2006), p. 164.
48. See Burnell, *Democracy Assistance*; and Carothers, *Aiding Democracy Abroad*.
49. Krishna Kumar, "Reflections on International Political Party Assistance", *Democratization*, 12(4), 2005, p. 516; see also Carothers, *Confronting the Weakest Link*, pp. 120–217.

50. In order to establish the real *political* impact of assistance programmes it is necessary to include non-assistance variables, such as the nature of the party system and the power configuration between the main parties, the relevance of major (ethnic, linguistic, regional) divisions in society and the historical background of party politics. These factors may have a much more determining influence on party development than party assistance, and are largely outside the reach of international actors.

51. For a fuller discussion of some of the problems related to the evaluation of democracy and political party assistance, see Andrew T. Green and Richard Kohl, "Challenges of Evaluating Democracy Assistance: Perspectives from the Donor Side", *Democratization*, 14(1), 2007: 151–165.

13

Conclusion

Per Nordlund

Since the start of the third wave of democratization in 1974, various forms of multi-party system have been introduced in new, restored and emerging democracies around the world. Today we therefore live in times where more countries than ever before decide on their leaders through multi-party elections, and where more people than ever before are governed by rulers of their choice. Multi-party politics, however, are no guarantee for development. They may empower vulnerable groups, increase transparency, mediate conflict and achieve redistribution of income to the poor, but multi-party politics may also give more influence to already powerful elites, marginalize the poor and minorities and be used to mobilize ethnic, regional and religious groups against each other. Multi-party politics have therefore been at the centre of studies and promotion of democracy and development since 1974, and even more so with the demise of the Cold War after 1989. Since political parties are the central component of multi-party politics, it is therefore surprising that comparatively little attention previously has been given to the regulation of parties and party systems. This volume on *Political Parties in Conflict-Prone Societies: Regulation, Engineering and Democratic Development* makes a substantial contribution towards alleviating this shortcoming.

Whereas the impact of electoral systems on politics in conflict-prone societies has been widely researched and analysed,[1] the regulation of political parties and party systems is much less studied. Yet there can be no democracy without political parties. The number of competitive

Political parties in conflict-prone societies: Regulation, engineering and democratic development, Reilly and Nordlund (eds),
United Nations University Press, 2008, ISBN 978-92-808-1157-5

democracies has increased threefold since the start of the third wave of democratization in 1974, and the number of political parties now contesting elections worldwide has increased many times more over the past 30 years. The examples of regulation of political parties are therefore manifold and growing. Ben Reilly rightly observes in his introductory chapter to this volume that highly ambitious and far-reaching attempts at engineering and regulation of political parties are a worldwide trend. Furthermore, most of the initiatives and innovations emanate from new democracies rather than old ones, and the impetus for crafting parties is often nationally or regionally driven – rather than dictated or inspired by Western examples.

Party system design therefore raises similar questions to those regarding elections: How to design parties and party systems so that democracy is promoted and not circumscribed? How can the design of party regulations assist in mediating conflict rather than increase the risks of social tension? How can vulnerable groups and minorities in society be ensured a voice instead of exclusion? What is the right balance between the regulation of parties and allowing the free formation and mobilization of parties? Should parties be regulated through constitutions or laws – allowing for different levels of flexibility, adjustments and change? Do party regulations harmonize with international and regional human rights norms and standards? Before attempting to draw some conclusions from the rich theoretical and empirical findings in this volume, let us briefly reflect on a couple of the latest important contributions to knowledge about political parties and party systems.

The existing literature on party systems and party regulations in new, restored and emerging democracies provides some, but still limited, guidance. In a recent article, Joseph LaPalombara reflects on political parties and political development over the past 40 years: "The general conclusion ... is that the political party is everywhere in decline. Party identification is weakened. Party legitimacy is problematical. The professionals have replaced old-line party leaders, and the once-critical party activists or cadres have largely disappeared. Electoral participation is also generally lower than in the past."[2] Accurate as this observation is, there are surprisingly few references to the importance of the regulation of political parties and party systems in new, restored and emerging democracies in this analysis from the 2007 special issue of *Party Politics*. It also clearly shows that the regulation of parties and party systems was not high on the agenda some 40 years ago, most probably because comparatively few regulations actually were in place at that time – a significant change from the situation today, as has been shown in this volume.

When approaching political party development more from the angle of democracy promotion, a similar conclusion emerges. In his recent book

Confronting the Weakest Link: Aiding Political Parties in New Democracies, Thomas Carothers provides an excellent analysis and overview of past and current work on development cooperation and political parties. Whereas aspects of internal party matters have received considerable attention, Carothers illustrates how party regulation at the national level has received little attention beyond discussions about electoral systems, the funding of political parties and women in politics.[3] He goes on to argue that, in new democracies, supporting reform of the regulatory framework of parties and party systems may sometimes be as, or more, effective for supporting political parties as work on capacity-building and the internal democracy of parties – especially in more dominant party systems.[4] In this book, we have aimed at providing new knowledge about how this might be achieved in new and emerging democracies.

New parties – old theories: Implications for theory and practice

This volume proves how some important conclusions drawn from the literature building primarily on Western experiences do not apply to the discussion on new and emerging democracies. International assistance to strengthen parties and party systems could gain broader acceptance by local communities and become more successful if these differences were recognized. At least four arguments can be made as to why theories of political parties based on Western experiences have limited validity for political party development in restored and emerging democracies.

The first argument comes from the failure even in Western democracies to explain current political party development based on existing theories. The mass party model no longer applies and the explanatory power of other theories is not sufficient for understanding present developments.[5] Today's parties in Europe show declining levels of membership, increased voter mobility between parties and erosion of earlier bonds between parties and social environments. In new democracies, however, most political parties do not emerge as mass-based movements with strong aggregation and articulation functions. Instead, they are often the result of elite initiatives with a focus not on aggregation and articulation, but rather on the representative function of parties, i.e. providing candidates for elected and government positions. Our analysis of political parties in new democracies shows that parties are becoming increasingly dependent on the state and less dependent on their constituencies – to which they often relate primarily through media channels and election campaigns. Yet much party assistance work by international actors concentrates on replicating a mass party model that does not even apply in their own political systems.

The second argument relates to how the institutionalization of parties varies owing to the very different historical trajectories of political parties in established, Western democracies and of political parties in new, restored and emerging multi-party systems and democracies. This is well illustrated by Robert Dahl's classification of political regimes along the dimensions of political competition and inclusiveness, which demonstrates the process of moving from non-democratic forms of government to more democratic regimes.[6] In many new and emerging democracies, the trajectory towards democratization has not been one of gradual development along the dimensions first of competition and then of inclusiveness. Instead, the political systems have moved from little or no competition or inclusion to full competition and inclusiveness owing to rapid processes of decolonization or democratization. Naturally, this affects political parties in very specific ways and limits their capacity to develop a mass base and to ensure internally democratic structures and the prospect of developing more institutionalized parties.[7]

The third difference between "old and new" multi-party systems and democracies is that the regulation of parties emerged gradually and rather late (if at all) in the established democracies in the West, whereas regulations on political parties in many new democracies have been present from the onset of multi-party politics.[8] Whether party regulations were introduced in order to promote political competition or to protect ruling parties' positions in government, party regulations are today much more of a factor in processes of democratization than was the case for political parties in emerging Western democracies. Another difference is that party regulation in new democracies often comes in the form of constitutional provisions, which – again – is different from the Western experience. Our look at regulations confirms Janda's claim that regulations are more frequent today than when parties emerged in Western countries some 100 years ago.[9] Even now, political parties in the West are less regulated than parties in new and emerging democracies. This is also confirmed by International IDEA's research on the external regulation of political parties,[10] and by Bogaards, who observes that party bans in Africa are most frequently found in national constitutions.[11]

The fourth argument for understanding the differences between party system development in old and new democracies concerns the relationship between political parties and the state. In Chapter 2 in this volume, Ingrid van Biezen articulates one strong driving force behind the upsurge in the regulation of parties when identifying the shifting relationship of parties away from their constituencies and towards much closer relations with – and dependence on – the state. With state funding of political parties, the character of parties is changing from that of private, voluntary associations to constituent parts of the (democratic) state, performing essential public functions and filling government positions. With this change, she argues, parties are in many instances increasingly becoming bearers of public utility. Using state resources for supporting political parties is a growing trend in new democracies and we may therefore need to rethink our conception of political parties, allowing for a perspective more open to the legitimacy of regulating parties, given their mutual relationship with the state.

Whereas elitist parties with a narrow focus on the representative function of winning elections tend to be the reality on the ground, more grounded political parties that fulfil aggregation and articulation functions are most often the ideal type assumed in international democracy assistance. This changing character of political party and state relations therefore poses a serious challenge to policy formulation and international assistance. Do researchers, practitioners and parties themselves base their actions on different conceptions of the role and character of political parties than is the reality in the field? What is the consequence for policy recommendations and international assistance if parties are seen as state-dependent institutions that do not grow from below – the reverse of what most parties and democracy promoters may want to recognize?

Political parties and regulations

What should be the balance between protecting rights and freedoms and imposing regulations for establishing functioning democracies in conflict-prone societies? The starting point for any discussion of political parties should be the international, regional and nationally recognized standards, conventions and laws that stipulate that free, fair and equitable competition between political parties is central to democratization. These declarations and standards are increasingly having an impact on party systems around the world, in particular for minority rights and parties. The Universal Declaration of Human Rights, Article 21, stipulates:

(1) Everyone has the right to take part in the government of his country, directly or through freely chosen representatives.

(2) Everyone has the right of equal access to public service in his country.

(3) The will of the people shall be the basis of the authority of government; this will shall be expressed in periodic and genuine elections which shall be by universal and equal suffrage and shall be held by secret vote or by equivalent free voting procedures.

The International Covenant on Civil and Political Rights, Article 25, states that:

Every citizen shall have the right and the opportunity, without any of the distinctions mentioned in article 2 and without unreasonable restrictions:

(a) To take part in the conduct of public affairs, directly or through freely chosen representatives;

(b) To vote and to be elected at genuine periodic elections which shall be by universal and equal suffrage and shall be held by secret ballot, guaranteeing the free expression of the will of the electors;

(c) To have access, on general terms of equality, to public service in his country.

We therefore need to keep in mind that a democratic election – contested by political parties – is both an aim in itself and a means towards democracy, human dignity and development. The protection of multi-party politics, and thereby also political parties, in these human rights instruments signed by most countries around the world makes it legitimate for the international community to intervene and work together with parties and governments towards the fulfilment of these rights. How are these rights upheld in practice?

If political parties are constrained by less than democratically motivated means, this has a negative impact on their capacity to aggregate preferences, articulate demands, compete for elected office and hold rulers accountable, and on citizens' rights to enjoy these freedoms. In principle, the law should therefore treat parties equally rather than restricting or discriminating for or against specific interests that political parties might reflect. Political parties should have the right to decide on their own organization and management, and they should enjoy freedom of expression, opinion and assembly.[12] More often, as documented in this volume, parties are closely regulated and the regulation of parties is far-reaching, globally present and increasing, and often infringes basic, constitutional freedoms in most of the countries studied. At the same time, we have shown that the regulation of parties and party systems often is necessary for promoting functioning democracies. It is therefore important to keep in mind that there always is a trade-off between regulations and political rights and freedoms – and that every institutional reform comes at a price.[13]

The tools available for engineering and regulating parties and party systems that we discuss in this volume conform closely to Richard Katz's definition of party law as being state law that:

- determines what constitutes a political party, who benefits from public resources, who participates in the government and how;
- regulates the types of activities that parties may engage in: raising and spending of funds, campaign activities, party manifestos, and more;
- ensures specific forms of party organization and behaviour. This form of regulation can interfere with the internal functioning of political parties and impose certain electoral processes for candidate selection and election, and minority protection.[14]

Apart from specific party law, the most common form of party regulation is through electoral laws, campaign laws and political finance laws. In addition, a number of other regulations exist in the form of court decisions, administrative procedures and, very importantly (as shown in this volume), constitutions.

Democratic – and effective – regulation?

Two dimensions are central to the debate on how much regulation of political parties there should be. Which limitations on the free formation of political parties should be introduced? And do these limitations result in forms of political competition that are better for democracy than would have been the case without regulations? One example that illustrates why these dimensions may be useful in evaluating regulations is the case of quotas for women in parliaments. Whether voluntary or legislated, quotas – as with any question on affirmative action – raise the issue of whether such measures are compatible with democratic principles. Although this is a valid discussion for any regulation of parties or party systems, it is also widely recognized that more equal participation and representation by women are indeed good for democracy, and that quotas can often achieve more inclusive forms of political competition than would otherwise have been the case.[15]

Many other forms of regulation – such as regulations preventing parties from mobilizing along ethnic, religious, regional or linguistic lines – should also be discussed in relation to democratic principles such as freedom of association and speech. Most often, countries' own constitutions include protection for the freedoms of association, assembly and speech, which arguably could be infringed by specific party regulations –

often enshrined in the same constitutions. The second dimension of the consequences of regulations for political competition and democracy is important but also very delicate to analyse. In many cases, not enough time has passed since the introduction of regulations for us to pass judgement on the success of the engineering of laws for democratic purposes. As Bogaards points out in Chapter 3, party bans may be effective only in the short run. Birnir raises a similar point in Chapter 7 that is relevant for party system consolidation. Blocking, to use Bogaards' terminology, of ethnic party formation may initially reduce fragmentation. However, the effect of denying that particular interest group the possibilities of articulation and representation may in a longer perspective have negative effects on consolidation by creating protest outside the channels of the political system.

Ultimately, regulations that are less than democratic and do not achieve their stated aims should be identified and avoided. The same applies to cases where democratic regulations do not achieve their aims, because such regulations may even have harmful (although sometimes quite unintended) consequences for democratization and party system consolidation. Democratic regulations that achieve their aims are less problematic, and of perhaps most interest are cases where the regulations can be questioned on the democratic freedom dimension but achieve longer-term, positive outcomes for democratization and democratic consolidation – as in the case of quotas for women's representation.

Finding the right balance?

As soon as we move away from direct democracy, a trade-off is introduced between democratic freedoms and the implementation of representative democracy. For nation-states, the processes of aggregation, articulation and representative functions that follow from indirect representation through political parties all contribute towards – necessary – restrictions. Institutional trade-offs and reforms always come at a cost.[16]

What needs to be clear to legislatures and constitutional engineers is therefore that every choice has consequences and that electoral and party system regulations can work together or cause conflicting outcomes. The same legislatures and engineers must also remember that regulations and their effects are highly context specific and that importing solutions from other countries may result in very different outcomes than those intended. Blocking, or banning, of ethnic parties in much of West Africa is an example of such regulatory diffusion. For this reason, Bogaards rightly argues in Chapter 3 that every choice with a regulatory impact should be the result of a conscious decision-making process, and that the choices made have either articulation, aggregation or blocking functions. Depending on whether the aim is blocking (banning of parties, frequently ethnic parties) or articulation (lack of intervention to allow for diversity and communal parties) or aggregation (achieving moderation of politics by legislating for or encouraging national, cross-cutting parties), certain options are available. Articulation may be more easily achieved in a proportional electoral system; and aggregation is more often associated with majoritarian electoral systems. Electoral system choice and direct engineering and regulation of parties and party systems should reinforce each other – something that all too often is not the case.

Conscious, strategic planning as proposed by Bogaards is desirable in order to achieve synergies between electoral and party system regulations. However, regulations through such engineering often become entrenched in constitutions rather than ordinary law, thus leaving too little flexibility for change over time. When also considering that the outcomes of engineering often are difficult to predict (and this volume provides many examples of this), a good case can be made for a more incremental approach to engineering and regulation that allows for greater flexibility over time. This argument is developed in more detail below.

From the vast empirical material analysed in this volume, we find many good and bad consequences following sometimes rather comprehensive restrictions on political party competition. Finding the right balance of restrictions on parties and party systems is therefore not easy. It is, as emphasized throughout this volume, also a highly contextual process: regulations that work well in one country may lead to a very different outcome in another. In some cases there may be reason to introduce rather far-reaching limitations on parties and party systems, not least in war-torn societies.[17] The same may be true for deeply divided societies such as Côte d'Ivoire, where regulation against ethnically based political parties could possibly have mediated some of the atrocities and sufferings caused by the ethnic violence that occurred, as argued by Randall in Chapter 11 in this volume. But conflicts can be of very different magnitude and scope.

There is a tendency to apply a "better safe than sorry" approach when adopting limitations on political parties, not least in regard to ethnic political mobilization, because of the worst-case scenarios that we have seen in Bosnia, Côte d'Ivoire and Rwanda. At the same time, most of the ethnic divisions in West Africa are not of the character of the Côte d'Ivoire, and yet most countries in the region have introduced limitations on the establishment of ethnic parties. Bogaards shows in Chapter 3 how bans on ethnic parties are in place in the vast majority of African states, concluding that ethnic party bans are problematic not only with regard to democratic legitimacy but also from a human rights perspective, and that the empirical findings lend very weak support to the efficacy of ethnic party bans. Interestingly enough, South Africa, with its ethnic, religious, race and regional cleavages, still manages democratic politics without similar restrictions imposed on political parties.

Political competition that becomes void of many of the cleavages in society that matter to people, such as regional issues, religion and ethnicity, may either reduce interest in politics, move the same conflict issues to within national parties and threaten the stability of parties and the party system in that way, or lead to strategies of violence outside established political institutions. Nigeria provides critical lessons about the dangers associated with the creation of aggregate, national parties, where the consequence is that many of the genuine political issues in a country – in the case of Nigeria, regionalism, ethnicity and religion – to a large extent are moved from the inter-party to the intra-party arena. This has very concrete and negative impacts on the chances for the institutionalization of political parties and party system consolidation over time. The alternative, to allow political mobilization along ethnic, religious and regional lines, may at the same time have even more negative consequences for political competition and democracy. This illustrates the complexity and contextual importance involved in predicting outcomes of party regulations.

Political party competition must therefore be seen as relevant for, and capable of, attracting citizens to engage with the political system, instead of against or outside the system. This is crucial for confidence in political institutions, the institutionalization of political parties and the consolidation of democracy. It is also far from the reality today. In the regions studied in this volume, we see two trends that are diverging further apart from each other and that need to be addressed. Whereas support for democracy and interest in politics remain relatively high across regions, trust in and support for political parties are low and decreasing.[18] These two trends cannot continue to move away from each other. Trust in political parties and party systems needs to be restored – or established where it was never present in the first place – or interest in politics will start to deteriorate, with serious consequences for further democratization. The impact of party regulations on public trust in parties and the political system therefore needs to be analysed in much more detail.

A balanced approach

If we for a moment leave aside cases of war-torn societies that remain deeply traumatized and violently divided, how can we arrive at a more balanced process of party system development? Keeping in mind the context-specific character of party system development, some, such as

Randall (Chapter 11) and Birnir (Chapter 7), argue for more limited and incremental engineering and regulation, avoiding too much engineering too soon. At the same time, the cases studied in this volume indicate that party engineering often works well and should be present and that there are some things that seem to work across countries and regions. Important tools for avoiding excessive party formation and fragmentation include: some threshold requirement to legislative representation, some basic party registration criteria (a party constitution and competition for party positions), basic rules for the transparency of political party funding, and possibly also basic criteria recognizing party coalition-building and measures to prevent excessive party-switching in the legislature. A strong argument for the application of quotas or effective incentives for female candidates for party and legislative assemblies is also advocated here.

These tools for engineering and regulation can be applied to various degrees and still fall within a strategy of articulation – allowing for the relatively free formation of political parties. It is when moving towards a more aggregative party system and legislation for national parties that trade-offs between freedoms and regulations become critical. In conflict-prone societies, should legislators seek to craft national, aggregative parties that cut across ethnic or other social cleavages and establish a stable two-party system that moderates differences in the electorate, or should they allow for ethnic or other cleavages in society to shape political competition and party systems? Finding a balanced position on how much engineering and regulation can be imposed on the free formation of parties in the name of more effective party system development and strengthened democracy is at the heart of this discussion. Are ethnicity and multi-party politics inherently conflictual, should issues of ethnic politics be addressed through strategies of aggregation or blocking, or do the benefits of ethnic politics outweigh the cost of potentially increased party fragmentation and increased inter-party competition?

Taking a more cautious approach to engineering that limits the formation of parties, Birnir observes in Chapter 7 that excluding sections of the population on the basis of ethnicity, linguistic group or region has led to conflict in both Latin America and Eastern Europe where there previously was none. Ecuador and Moldova are examples where spatial requirements have had this effect, and the exclusion of linguistic groups in the Baltic states displays similar effects. Birnir goes on to argue that ethnic violence increases over time if electorally active groups fail to reach executive influence and representation.

Reilly, while presenting a more positive interpretation of aggregative party systems, also observes in Chapter 1 that engineering comes at a cost. Strategies of aggregation and blocking often work in favour of in-cumbents over challengers and therefore risk upsetting the balance of power in countries to the point of crises or coups. Thailand is an example from Asia, and Bogaards observes that extensive banning of ethnic par-ties in Africa has had very limited positive effect on conflict management in Africa. Another possible consequence of aggregative party systems is that establishing parties with the required level of organization and na-tional presence leaves the field open for those with considerable amounts of money to gain control over the parties – which increasingly is the real-ity in Nigeria.[19]

One final observation on how to find the right balance between regula-tions and freedoms is associated with the institutionalization of political parties. Randall observes in Chapter 11 that political parties in new and emerging democracies tend to be weakly institutionalized and that the promotion of aggregative, national parties and the blocking of parties on ethnic and other grounds could make institutionalization very hard to achieve. Aggregation and blocking could make it more difficult for par-ties to integrate various constituencies, creating problems for achieving identification with common traditions and symbols, weakening links with social constituencies, and resulting in parties less rooted in societies. This trade-off between aggregative party regulations and parties firmly rooted in their societies is confirmed in Hicken's research in Southeast Asia (see Chapter 4 in this volume). McMenamin comes to the conclusion in Chap-ter 10 that party institutionalization very seldom can be established un-less parties are allowed to root themselves firmly in society, or had the opportunity to do so previously.

Although the institutionalization of parties is crucial for the consolida-tion of democracy, it is also a long-term process. It may therefore be pre-mature to determine the impact of aggregative and blocking regulations, but it is one aspect of party development that needs to be closely ana-lysed and followed over time.

Regardless of the arguments for and against aggregative national par-ties, sometimes in combination with the outright banning of parties on ethnic or other grounds, the empirical trend towards more aggregation and blocking is clear across the regions analysed in this volume. With this trend also follows the need to address minority representation and rights. In Latin America, where aggregation is commonplace, Catón and Tuesta Soldevilla (Chapter 6 in this volume) observe that only six coun-tries have some regulations in place to promote the representation of marginalized, indigenous groups. The two forms of regulation used to promote the inclusion of indigenous populations are, first, to provide di-rect access to representation through creating special parliamentary seats or constituencies, as in the cases of Colombia, Venezuela and Panama. The other approach to inclusion is to demand that parties open up space for indigenous candidates on their party lists, as in Nicaragua. At the local level, this is also the case in Peru and some Mexican states. The impact of these regulations has, however, been limited.

In Central and South-Eastern Europe, the inclusion of minorities has been more successful. Florian Bieber shows in Chapter 5 how there has been a trend towards minority inclusion in government in Central and South-Eastern Europe. In countries with large minorities (with the exception of the Baltic countries), the parties of these minorities have been in government for at least one legislative term. These parties have gained access largely by joining broad coalitions. An important factor driving this development, together with shifting values in the domestic political system and the polarization of majority parties, has been EU conditionality for the accession of new member states, which requires democratic governance as well as respect for and protection of minority rights. Ratification of the European Union's Framework Convention for the Protection of National Minorities has been crucial for accession states and is a clear indication of the positive effect for minority representation that can be achieved by international organizations working for the implementation of human rights instruments. Reilly shows how the documents of the Organization for Security and Co-operation in Europe (OSCE) – the Copenhagen Document of the Conference on the Human Dimension (1990) and the Helsinki Document (1992) – demonstrate the legal protection and encouragement of ethnic minority parties in Europe.[20]

We therefore see a clear divide between Europe and other regions on how to deal with minority rights and political parties. Minority parties in Asia, Latin America and Africa often face elaborate spatial requirements that make registration and recognition difficult. In other cases, parties face outright bans on ethnic grounds. It is therefore not unlikely that in the future we may see a trend in regions outside Europe for ethnic and other minority parties to seek legal recognition through international and regional human rights instruments as one of several strategies to protect their place in the political system.

Scope for adjustment

Any approach to engineering must have the capacity to adjust regulations over time if the outcome of regulations becomes less than what was anticipated or desirable. Flexibility is therefore required and this is not always promoted if party regulations are enshrined in constitutions.

An interesting illustration of this argument is provided by Kenneth Janda in a recent study of anti-defection laws in national parliaments:

> It [Janda's paper] reveals that anti-defection laws are rare in established democracies but common in developing democracies. There, anti-defection laws are often defended as temporary measures to consolidate a chaotic party system. However, most nations enshrine anti-defection provisions in their constitutions, which are not depositories for temporary legislation.[21]

This observation on anti-defection laws applies also to many other forms of regulation of parties and party systems, as observed throughout this volume. Ingrid van Biezen shows in Chapter 2 how political party identity, activities and behaviour in various ways are engineered through constitutional means. This holds true across Latin America, Africa and Eastern Europe for nearly all recently established democracies and is, as mentioned earlier, very different from the regulation of parties in established, Western democracies.

We must therefore carefully consider what measures need constitutional protection and where laws, decrees and voluntary engineering and regulation are more suitable institutional arrangements. The conclusion here seems to be that constitutional regulations are used excessively and that this limits the space for gradual reforms and adjustments of party regulations over time.

In this volume, we also find examples of limited engineering followed by further regulation at a later stage. Birnir discuss in Chapter 7 how several East European countries with few formation rules had to adjust electoral laws to prevent fragmentation. This is not necessarily an example of failed engineering; it can also be seen as a good example of limited engineering and then adjustment through regulations. Seen this way, it can also be regarded as a commentary on the strategic thinking advocated by Bogaards in Chapter 3: sometimes an incremental approach starting with limited formation rules may be preferred over carefully crafted strategic engineered approaches, especially if the incremental approach starts with limited constitutional provision and instead applies regulation by law to allow for flexibility. It should also be observed that the incremental approach may create uncertainty about the rules of the game over time, which may lead to difficulties for party institutionalization and possibly also have a negative impact on party system consolidation.

It is imperative to consider strategies of engineering and regulation beyond aggregation and bans on party formation. Applying voluntary and other incentive-creating structures has proven successful for promoting quotas for women in politics but also for creating more transparent funding of parties,[22] and the lessons learned here should be explored in relation to other areas of party regulation.

Regulations and enforcement

Once regulations are in place, they must be enforced. Enforcement can be the responsibility of different authorities, but electoral management bodies (EMBs) often play a central role in the process. EMBs are the custodians of the electoral system and administration, but they also play an increasingly frequent and important role in the oversight of party system regulations. Mechanisms for the enforcement of regulations vary, but from International IDEA's research on political parties it is clear that relations between EMBs and political parties are frequent.[23] This holds true across regions and for both formal representation of parties in EMBs and informal, consultative forms of engagement.

We know from other research that political parties are among the least trusted institutions in all parts of the world,[24] and that opposition parties and electoral observation missions often question the independence of EMBs on good grounds. Hence, two of the central institutions of democracy, EMBs and political parties, are increasingly interlinked and often characterized by low levels of mutual confidence and trust. At the same time, political party and EMB relations are of central importance for conflict management and democracy, because democratic consolidation can be established only through citizens' trust in the institutions that represent them.

The regulation of political parties affects politics whether the regulations are enforced or not. The non-enforcement of regulations may serve as a political weapon for ruling parties because the choice of timing for imposing the enforcement can be a powerful political threat against opposition parties. EMBs are often also influenced – or directly controlled – by ruling elites to produce the desired outcomes, with Zimbabwe as an unfortunate example of this practice. There are also important examples of good relations prevailing between political parties and EMBs, as in Ghana and India, and we need to learn more from these positive experiences.

There are few studies of the enforcement of party regulations, and the observations that do exist tend to indicate that actual enforcement is selective and infrequent, rather than systematic and commonplace. Bogaards finds that, despite numerous bans on parties in Africa, bans that are protected by the constitution itself, there are few examples of parties that have actually been banned in practice, although bans have been enforced in Nigeria and Tanzania for parties that have not been able to es-

tablish a "national presence". Catón and Tuesta Soldevilla's elaboration
on the Peruvian party law in Chapter 6 illustrates how regulations can be
undermined by the lack of enforcement.

Drawing on the lessons learned from quotas for women in politics, it is
clear that one way of ensuring enforcement can be through EMBs, because in most cases they can choose not to register parties for elections
if they are in breach of the regulations. By contrast, Okole shows in
Chapter 8 how in Papua New Guinea a separate body, the Office of the
Registrar of Political Parties, was established outside the EMB to administer the new party law – an institutional arrangement that so far has had
a positive impact on party law enforcement.

Kumar and de Zeeuw emphasize in Chapter 12 the importance of creating mechanisms for ensuring that critical regulation is also enforced in
post-conflict states, where the rule of law often is weak – which is often
overlooked by national and international actors alike. McMenamin's observation in Chapter 10 that effective engineering of parties and the party
system is dependent on legitimate and authoritative institutions for enforcement therefore underscores why more knowledge and best practices, not least the enforcement of quotas for women in politics, must be
generated. Academics, legislators, development practitioners and political parties themselves would therefore do well to spend more time on understanding how the relationship between parties and EMBs – or other
oversight institutions – can be improved.

Conclusion

What has emerged with the new knowledge produced in this volume is an
approach to thinking constructively about electoral and party system regulation that allows for democratic competition in conflict-prone societies
while at the same time allowing for as free as possible formation of political parties and competition between them, including respect for minority
rights and freedoms. It is therefore not an ideal-type for party regulation
across regions and countries that we are advocating, because the highly
context-specific character of party engineering and regulation prevents
the construction of such models. The right balance of regulations in one
country may simply be the wrong balance in another.

Starting with how to conceptualize political parties, it can be argued
that the international policy and development cooperation community
takes a rather narrow perspective on political parties and democracy promotion, often based on the view that parties grow organically from below
and in so doing perform important aggregation and articulation roles. Important and desirable as these functions may be, we have shown that

parties in new democracies seldom grow from below – as was the case in Western Europe – nor do they necessarily see aggregation or articulation as their primary tasks. With their strong dependence on the state – not least through public funding arrangements and management by the state through extensive regulations – parties often concentrate more on representative tasks and relations with the state than on mobilizing and giving voice to the electorate. This shift to thinking of parties less as private, voluntary associations and more as public service agencies is an important conceptual shift that needs to be recognized by national and international actors. More attention to party and party system engineering and regulation and how this impacts on the role and function of political parties would provide for more informed democracy assistance, and needs to emerge from a deeper understanding of differences in party formation and their character in new and old democracies.

This leads to our second important lesson learned. Because of the different historical trajectories of the emergence of parties in new and old democracies, and given the highly context-specific nature of party regulations, parties and party systems must be developed from a thorough understanding of the deep structures of economic, cultural, gender and power relations in individual countries. There are therefore no shortcuts for achieving success in the engineering and regulation of parties and party systems. From this it also follows that reform may be a longer-term process as engineering and regulations aim to mediate and change patterns of conflict that arise from structural social divisions and legacies. A thorough analysis of traditions, structures and relations of power in each society is essential to any work on party system design and support, and needs to be consciously constructed while also taking into account the impact of the electoral system and other relevant institutional factors.

A clear trend can be found towards greater reliance on strategies of aggregation for building parties with a national character that cut across the conflict that arises from diversity in societies. It is also clear that the blocking or banning of parties, often on ethnic grounds, is frequent and increasing. The authors in this volume present many arguments for and against the aggregation of parties and party systems. Regardless of one's position in this debate, attention must be given to minority rights and representation. We see that international and regional human rights instruments can make a difference for minorities, and although this so far has been limited to countries in Central and South-Eastern Europe it holds potential for the advancement of minority rights in other regions as well.

A problematic fact arising from the new knowledge produced in this volume is the extent to which engineering and regulation are enshrined in constitutions rather than laws. Such constitutional entrenchment limits flexibility and the capacity for adjustment over time and favours incumbents with greater influence than other political actors over constitutional formation and reform. Legislative assemblies and international development cooperation would do well to think hard about alternative ways in which party regulation could be given legal protection.

The institutionalization of political parties is considered crucial for democratization and much of the international assistance to parties is therefore focused on capacity-building efforts to achieve this.[25] The use of aggregation and blocking aimed at establishing parties with a national character may at the same time have directly contradictory effects on parties and party systems. This is an important lesson to keep in mind not only for national legislators but certainly also for the international assistance community, which invests major resources in party development without paying sufficient attention to how this is affected by regulations for aggregative parties in many of the countries where they work.

Once regulations are in place, through constitutions, party laws or other means, they need to be enforced. Without enforcement, regulations will become tools for incumbents to invoke arbitrarily and for selfish political gains. Electoral management bodies are already tasked with some of these powers of enforcement, but EMBs – or other implementing agencies – must be independent and resourceful to fulfil this role properly. More knowledge about the enforcement of regulations is a key priority for the future.

Regardless of electoral and party system design, every citizen must be ensured participation, representation and non-discrimination. This can be achieved only through a combination of the collective process of democracy and states' protection and fulfilment of individual citizens' human rights. In conflict-prone societies – where political processes often are less than fully representative and states are not sufficiently capable of ensuring human rights and security for everyone – political decision makers and the international community need to make use of both political and human rights strategies for ensuring the consolidation of democracy and development.

Notes

1. Arend Lijphart, "Constitutional Design for Divided Societies", *Journal of Democracy*, 15(2), 2004: 96–109; Pippa Norris, *Electoral Engineering: Voting Rules and Political Behavior* (Cambridge: Cambridge University Press, 2004); Andrew Reynolds and Ben Reilly, *The International IDEA Handbook of Electoral System Design* (Stockholm: Institute for Democracy and Electoral Assistance, 1997); Benjamin Reilly, *Democracy in Divided Societies: Electoral Engineering for Conflict Management* (Cambridge: Cambridge University Press, 2001).

2. Joseph LaPalombara, "Reflections on *Political Parties and Political Development*, Four Decades Later", *Party Politics*, 13(2), 2007, p. 149.
3. Thomas Carothers, *Confronting the Weakest Link: Aiding Political Parties in New Democracies* (Washington, DC: Carnegie Endowment for International Peace, 2006), p. 190ff.
4. Ibid., pp. 71–72, 220, 226.
5. Peter Mair, "Democracy beyond Parties", paper for the workshop on "Political Parties and Democracy" at the ECPR Joint Sessions, Granada, April 2005, p. 11; see also Ingrid van Biezen and Richard Katz, "Democracy and Political Parties", paper for the workshop on "Political Parties and Democracy" at the ECPR Joint Sessions, Granada, April 2005, and Chapter 2 by Ingrid van Biezen in this volume.
6. Robert A. Dahl, *Polyarchy: Participation and Opposition* (New Haven, CT: Yale University Press, 1971), p. 4.
7. See Ingrid van Biezen, "Building Party Organization and the Relevance of Past Models: The Communist and Socialist Parties in Spain and Portugal", *West European Politics*, 21(2), 1998: 32–62, for an elaboration of how this shaped the communist and socialist parties in Spain and Portugal.
8. Kenneth Janda, *Political Parties and Democracy in Theoretical and Practical Perspectives: Adopting Party Law* (Washington, DC: National Democratic Institute for International Affairs, 2005), p. 23; Chapter 2 by Ingrid van Biezen in this volume.
9. See Janda, *Adopting Party Law*, pp. 5–6, for a more detailed discussion. On political finance law, see also Reginald Austin and Maja Tjernström (eds), *Funding of Political Parties and Election Campaigns* (Stockholm: International IDEA, 2003).
10. Per Nordlund and Mohamed Salih, *Political Parties in Africa: Challenges for Sustained Multiparty Democracy* (Stockholm: International IDEA, 2007).
11. See ⟨http://www.idea.int⟩ and ⟨http://www.political-parties.org⟩ (accessed 9 April 2008); also see Chapter 3 by Bogaards in this volume.
12. See Pippa Norris, *Building Political Parties: Reforming Legal Regulations and Internal Rules*, internal report for International IDEA, 2005, for a more detailed discussion. Also United Nations Development Programme, *A Handbook on Working with Political Parties* (New York: United Nations Development Programme, 2005).
13. See, for example, Allen Hicken's discussion of Southeast Asia in Chapter 4 in this volume.
14. Richard S. Katz, "Democracy and the Legal Regulation of Political Parties," paper prepared for a USAID conference on "Changes in Political Parties: United States Agency for International Development", Washington, DC, 1 October 2004, p. 2.
15. Visit ⟨http://www.idea.int/publications/browse/participation.cfm⟩ (accessed 9 April 2008) for free downloads of several IDEA publications on quotas and women in politics that support this argument. For example, *Women in Parliament: Beyond Numbers. A Revised Edition* (2005) and the regional series *The Implementation of Quotas* (Latin America, Africa and Asia). See also Drude Dahlerup (ed.), *Women, Quotas and Politics* (New York: Routledge, 2006).
16. See Chapter 4 by Hicken in this volume.
17. See Chapter 12 by Kumar and de Zeeuw in this volume.
18. See ⟨http://www.globalbarometer.org⟩ (accessed 9 April 2008).
19. See Jibrin Ibrahim, *Nigeria: Country Report Based on Research and Dialogue with Political Parties* (Stockholm: International IDEA, 2005), available at ⟨http://www.idea.int/parties/upload/Nigeria_report_14June06.pdf⟩ (accessed 9 April 2008).
20. See also Benjamin Reilly, *Democracy and Diversity: Political Engineering in the Asia-Pacific* (Oxford: Oxford University Press, 2006), p. 179.

21. Kenneth Janda, "Assessing Laws That Ban Party Switching, Defecting or Floor-Crossing in National Parliaments", paper prepared for the UNDP Workshop "Right to Recall: A Right of the Party or of the Electorate?", Suriname, 11 August 2007, p. 1.

22. See IDEA work on quotas for women, but also Austin and Tjernström (eds), *Funding of Political Parties and Election Campaigns*.

23. For an authoritative account of EMBs, see *Electoral Management Design: The International IDEA Handbook* (Stockholm: International IDEA, 2006).

24. See ⟨http://www.globalbarometer.org⟩ (accessed 9 April 2008).

25. Carothers, in *Confronting the Weakest Link*, provides the most-informed analysis of the efforts to support the establishment of internally democratic and institutionalized parties.

Index